Thoreau's Reading

Thoreau's Reading

A Study in Intellectual History

WITH BIBLIOGRAPHICAL CATALOGUE

Robert Sattelmeyer

PRINCETON UNIVERSITY PRESS

PRINCETON, NEW JERSEY

Copyright © 1988
by Princeton University Press
Published by Princeton University Press,
41 William Street, Princeton, New Jersey 08540
In the United Kingdom:
Princeton University Press, Guildford, Surrey

Library of Congress Cataloging in Publication Data

Sattelmeyer, Robert.
Thoreau's reading.

Bibliography: p.
Includes index.
1. Thoreau, Henry David, 1817–1862—Books and reading.
2. Thoreau, Henry David, 1817–1862—Knowledge and learning.
3. Thoreau, Henry David, 1817–1862—Library—Catalogs.   I. Title.
PS3057.B64S27   1988   818'.309   88–2491

ISBN 0–691–06745–7

This book has been composed in Linotron Sabon

Clothbound editions of Princeton University Press
books are printed on acid-free paper,
and binding materials are chosen for strength and durability.
Paperbacks, although satisfactory for personal collections,
are not usually suitable for library rebinding

Printed in the United States of America
by Princeton University Press
Princeton, New Jersey

For Sue

Contents

Preface

THIS VOLUME consists of an analytical overview of the principal developments in Thoreau's reading during the course of his career from 1833, when he matriculated at Harvard, to his death in 1862, and a bibliographical catalogue of his reading during the same years. The catalogue is organized conventionally by author and title, and contains standard bibliographical data as well as information about Thoreau's source for particular items, when known, and citations of the references to each work in his writings. It is followed by an index of short titles. I have included not only works quoted or referred to in Thoreau's writings for publication and in his Journal, but also works cited in his unpublished notebooks and commonplace books and in his correspondence, his library charging records, his required texts at Harvard, and of course the catalogue of his personal library. At the same time that I have tried to be comprehensive, however, I have also been fairly restrictive in defining what constitutes "reading." I have excluded works alluded to without sufficient particularity to indicate direct acquaintance, and works proposed by scholars as "possible sources" for passages in his writings—unless, again, there is corroborating evidence of his having actually read them. Similarly, titles Thoreau listed for future reference or study are not included.[1] Books, articles in periodicals or collections, pamphlets, and, wherever traceable, articles in newspapers and other ephemeral publications are all included.

Both sections of this book are intended to serve as primary tools for the study of Thoreau's thought and art, but the expository section is

1. The most extensive of these lists of works he planned to consult may be found in the endpapers of the various Indian books (see abbreviations for Bibliographical Catalogue, pp. 114–115); see also Kenneth Walter Cameron, "Ungathered Thoreau Reading Lists," in *The Transcendentalists and Minerva*, 3 vols. (Hartford: Transcendental Books, 1958), 2.359–388.

less neutral an instrument than the catalogue. Obviously, principles of selection came into play, and the essay as a whole reflects my judgment about major developments and shifts in Thoreau's interests during his life. I was especially concerned to trace the course of his reading in disciplines—history and natural history, for example—that were of increasing importance to him as he grew older but that have received relatively scant attention from scholars previously. Concomitantly, I felt that I could afford to devote less attention proportionately to other of his interests that have already received extensive treatment: Oriental scriptures and philosophy, the subject of Arthur Christy's *The Orient in American Transcendentalism* (1932) and a host of subsequent studies; travel literature, treated by John Aldridge Christie's *Thoreau as World Traveler* (1965); and his classical studies, the topic of Ethel Seybold's *Thoreau: The Quest and the Classics* (1951). None of these works pretended to have treated its subject exhaustively and much remains to be done in all three areas, but I have written my introduction to Thoreau's reading on the assumption that the reader will be familiar with or will want to consult these standard works.

Otherwise, I have tried in the introductory essay to assemble the bits of evidence furnished by his reading of particular texts as though they were the pieces to a puzzle in intellectual history, the putting together of which would provide a picture not only of Thoreau's shifting interests over the years but also of his participation in the life of his times, of his engagement with some of the most pressing and controversial issues of mid-nineteenth-century American literature and culture: the tension between conventional, classical literary culture and the new views of literary nationalists and Transcendentalists; the nature and destiny of America itself (in the context of a period of unbridled expansionism); the rights and responsibilities of government, society, and individuals, and the points at which they collided with one another, especially over the issue of slavery and governmental authority; the history, nature, and destiny of native Americans (in the cultural context of dispossession and genocide); and the escalating scientific controversies of the age that pitted apologists for special creation and design against the gathering forces of materialist and positivist interpretations of nature. Despite his reputation as an iconoclast who withdrew from or was harshly critical of his age (a pose reinforced by his modern reputation as a detached and meticulous craftsman), Thoreau was a writer who participated fully if idiosyncratically in his age, and there is less a contradiction here than may at first appear. It took someone widely familiar with newspapers and the level of current events described in them to compose the marvelous critique of the popular press in *Walden*, and the same holds true for many of his other targets, from the railroads to politics to the gold rush. The satirist and social critic is of necessity profoundly affected by and implicated in his age, whatever his rhetorical stance toward it may be. And if we look past the monumental preeminence of *Walden*, it is apparent that Thoreau was a man of letters whose writing treats a wide variety of subjects, each more or less reflecting major preoccupations of his times: politics, reform, government, literature, travel, the Indian, wilderness, history, natural history, even sexuality.

Even more fundamental to my purpose, however, is the fact that Thoreau was a writer, and as such the primary tools of his trade were the works of other writers. As a thoroughgoing Transcendentalist, he could echo Emerson's scorn for the book when it was held up as a sacred object and the truly sacred inspiring force behind the book— the act of creation itself—was lost sight of. And he was careful, likewise, to avoid disclosure of many of his own most important sources, in order to preserve the bloom of originality in his works. But in other moods, especially in the privacy of his Journal, he could express an almost Jamesian sense of the enormous richness of accumulated history and tradition out of which the serious writer works. After going through the shelves of the Harvard Library in 1852 in search of the essential books on the early exploration of Canada, he mused: "Those old books suggested a certain fertility, an Ohio soil, as if they were making a humus for new literature to spring in. I heard the bellowing of bullfrogs and the hum of mosquitoes reverberating through the thick embossed covers when I had closed the book. Decayed literature makes the richest of all soils" (JL 3.353).

Of an innately scholarly cast of mind, Thoreau read widely, deeply, and eclectically; and as he grew older he kept more and more extensive notes on his reading, although he had begun the practice of systematic note taking in college. As any careful reader of *Walden* knows, his writings reflect this bookish side no less than his love of outdoor life. One of the principal obstacles for students reading the book today, in fact, is what appears to be a bewildering thicket of allusions to everything from relatively obscure classical mythology to contemporary pseudo-science (the "Symmes Hole" of the conclusion). Virtually all the Transcendentalists were energetic readers, in spite of their proclamations of disdain for convention and tradition, and Thoreau, if he lacked the deep knowledge of the German literature and philosophy that was so seminal to the movement—the kind of familiarity that Margaret Fuller or Theodore Parker possessed, for example—was more deeply read in other subjects (notably classical and early English literature, American history, and natural science) than any of his circle. He drew upon this reading in all the obvious and not-so-obvious ways that reading affects writing, and in the introductory essay I have speculated both upon the influence of particular works on his own writing and upon his basic orientation to the various contemporary disciplines according to which his interests may be classified. I have attempted to place him, as much as possible, in his times and to assess his studies in the contexts provided by the disciplines as they then existed rather than by what we now know about them or by current theory or methodology.[2]

Ralph Cudworth, whose *True Intellectual System of the Universe* was one of the eclectic philosophical works Thoreau read with Emerson in the early 1840s, expressed a sentiment in his preface that I can only repeat in mine: "Though, I confess, I have seldom taken any great pleasure in reading other men's apologies, yet must I at this time make some myself." First and foremost, I am sensible that this work is by its nature as well as my own shortcomings incomplete. I have been unable to identify some references, and I have doubtless missed many others. Anyone who has attempted to annotate or identify all the works quoted by a writer as widely read and allusive as Thoreau can testify to the impossibility of achieving completeness. New sources and new evidence of his reading will doubtless continue to come to light, especially as the definitive edition of his writings currently in progress at Princeton University Press and the University of California–Santa Barbara moves toward completion, and I have already benefited greatly by the work completed by its staff. But a project such as this is necessarily a draft of a draft, and as I have so obviously built upon the labors of others I trust that it will at least prove useful and serve those who will build upon and improve it. I should be grateful to learn of omissions and errors, particularly regarding specific editions of works that Thoreau used. I have not been able to examine all the relevant editions of every work he quotes from, and as the headnote to the catalogue indicates, I have frequently cited the most recent contemporary edition when his source for a given work (e.g., Emerson's library) was not evident. I have, of course, wherever possible cited the editions he used.

It may also be well to call attention to the obvious and state that if a work is listed in the catalogue Thoreau read it—or at least owned it—but if it is not listed the reverse does not hold. Even if I were confident that I had been able to trace to its source and proper edition every reference and quotation in all of Thoreau's writing, there would doubtless be hundreds of works missing from the catalogue. As is the

---

2. I also follow, for the sake of consistency and clarity, contemporary usage in referring to native Americans as "Indians," despite the cultural biases historically associated with the term.

case for virtually any reader, Thoreau did not leave a record of everything he read: He did not always read with pen in hand, especially during his earlier years; many notes that he did take were surely lost or discarded when their purpose was served; some of his own books have probably disappeared and left no trace (despite the fact that he kept a catalogue of his own library); and many works that he read simply did not register in such a way as to cause him to quote or refer to them in his writings, despite the fact that they may have exerted a considerable influence. We are not always eager to reveal to the world the forces that have most shaped us, and Thoreau, whose trade had more secrets than most, as he said, was especially guarded. He was understandably touchy about the insinuations of his contemporaries that he was merely an imitator of Emerson, and the nature of Transcendental aesthetic theory would tend to inhibit the acknowledgment of profound debt. One did not study religion or philosophy or history to learn systems or to distinguish and discriminate so much as to detect likeness and the uniformity of truth in all ages. Hence, one did not go to school to earlier writers so much as search them for evidence of likemindedness, and the nature and extent of influence, always a difficult issue to do justice to, is especially nebulous given such an orientation. In any event, this study and its accompanying catalogue can only be a starting point for anyone interested in exploring the myriad sources for and influences upon Thoreau's writing, and I trust that none will stretch the seams when putting on the coat, for it may be of service to those who use it judiciously.

Apologies aside, it is a far pleasanter task to thank the many people and institutions that have helped me over the decade during which this book has been in preparation. I am most grateful to the National Endowment for the Humanities for a Summer Research Stipend, the Henry E. Huntington Library for a Research Fellowship, and the Graduate School and Office of Research of the University of Missouri–Columbia for a Summer Research Fellowship—each of which was of great help to me at a different stage of writing the introductory monograph and assembling the bibliography.

I also wish to thank the staff members of the following libraries, without whose cooperation my task would simply have been impossible: the Abernethy Library of Middlebury College, the American Antiquarian Society, the Boston Athenaeum, the Boston Public Library, Brown University Library, the Concord Free Public Library (with special thanks to Marcia Moss), the Houghton Library of Harvard University, the Henry E. Huntington Library, the New York Public Library, the Pierpont Morgan Library, Princeton University Library, and the University of Virginia Library. I also appreciate the faithful efforts of Jeanice Brewer of the Ellis Library of the University of Missouri–Columbia to fill my never-ending requests for interlibrary loan materials.

I have had the benefit of kind and critical readings of earlier versions of my study by Robert A. Gross, Walter Harding, Joseph J. Moldenhauer, Tom Quirk, Robert D. Richardson, Jr., William J. Rossi, Robert F. Sayre, and Elizabeth Hall Witherell. Each had loftier structures of his or her own to raise, but took the time to make corrections and offer suggestions, for which I am very grateful. Although my references will make clear the extent of my debt to him, I wish to acknowledge the invaluable and pioneering work in the collection and publication of primary documents relating to my subject by Kenneth Walter Cameron.

Rebecca Arnold, Rick Boland, Paul Taylor, and Heather Thomas ably assisted with various phases of the research for the book, and Sandy Camargo gave it the benefit of her editorial skills. Paul Taylor performed magical and I fear all too time-consuming feats of computer programming that helped me prepare the bibliography. His contributions have been invaluable. I also wish to thank Julie Apple, Marilynn Keil, Laurinda Jett, and Kathie McCoy of the English Department of the University of Missouri–Columbia for their assistance in typing the manuscript.

Over the years my colleagues and fellow editors at the Thoreau Edition have played a special part in this project, sharing with me their own research into the sources of Thoreau's reading and making available their files and hand lists. I wish to thank especially Carolyn Kappes, Linck C. Johnson, William L. Howarth, Mark Patterson, Steve Quevedo, Nancy Simmons, Kevin Van Anglen, and Elizabeth Hall Witherell.

Special thanks are due Joel Myerson for his support and encouragement of the project in its early stages, and to Henry and Beverly Shames and Lorna and John Mack for putting me up and putting up with me while I was working far from home. Finally, and most importantly, I thank my wife, Sue, to whom this is dedicated, and my children, Sarah and Daniel, without whose expressions of interest this probably would have been done in far less time but far less happily.

Abbreviations

*of Thoreau's Writings Used in Parenthetical
Documentation*

CC *Cape Cod,*
ed. Joseph J. Moldenhauer
(Princeton: Princeton University Press, 1988)

COR *The Correspondence of Henry David Thoreau,*
ed. Walter Harding and Carl Bode
(New York: New York University Press, 1958)

EEM *Early Essays and Miscellanies,*
ed. Joseph J. Moldenhauer and Edwin Moser,
with Alexander Kern
(Princeton: Princeton University Press, 1975)

JL *The Journal of Henry David Thoreau,*
ed. Bradford Torrey and Francis H. Allen, 14 vols.
(Boston: Houghton Mifflin, 1906)

MW *The Maine Woods,*
ed. Joseph J. Moldenhauer
(Princeton: Princeton University Press, 1972)

PJ *Journal,*
John C. Broderick, general editor,
in *The Writings of Henry D. Thoreau*
(Princeton: Princeton University Press, 1981–);
2 vols. to date:
Journal 1: 1837–1844,
ed. Elizabeth H. Witherell et al. (1981)
and *Journal 2: 1842–1848,* ed. Robert Sattelmeyer (1984)

RP *Reform Papers,*
ed. Wendell Glick
(Princeton: Princeton University Press, 1973)

WA *Walden,*
ed. J. Lyndon Shanley
(Princeton: Princeton University Press, 1971)

WE *A Week on the Concord and Merrimack Rivers,*
ed. Carl Hovde et al.
(Princeton: Princeton University Press, 1980)

Thoreau's Reading

I

Harvard College, 1833–1837

HENRY THOREAU "was fitted, or rather made unfit," as he later said, for college at Concord Academy under the tutelage of Phineas Allen. The academy, which Thoreau himself would later conduct with his brother John, had been founded as a college preparatory school in 1822, and its curriculum was explicitly designed to prepare its students for the Harvard entrance examinations. There were the "English Branches," where the scholars might study, depending upon the term and year, mathematics, composition and declamation, geography, history, and philosophy; but the primary emphasis was on languages: Latin, Greek, and French.[1] The entrance exams themselves, according to the Harvard catalogue for 1833, the year Thoreau matriculated, covered the "whole of Virgil, Cicero's Select Orations, and Sallust; Jacob's Greek Reader, and the four Gospels of the Greek Testament," in addition to Greek and Latin grammar, arithmetic and algebra, and geography.[2] Students were also expected to have some preparation in modern foreign languages. Thoreau's schoolmates at the academy remembered him as a quiet, somewhat standoffish boy who was both physically active and "very fond of reading," but he was an indifferent scholar at this age. In fact, he passed the entrance exams by the barest of margins and was "conditioned" (the rough equivalent of probationary status) in Greek, Latin, and mathematics, the three principal subjects. President Quincy told him bluntly, "You have barely got in" (EEM, 114).

Thoreau's parents, his mother especially, were eager for one of their sons to attend Harvard, and the family sacrificed to help put Henry

1. See Hubert H. Hoeltje, "Thoreau and the Concord Academy," *New England Quarterly* 21 (March 1948): 103–106; and Kenneth Walter Cameron, *Young Thoreau and the Classics* (Hartford: Transcendental Books, 1975).

2. Christian P. Gruber, "The Education of Henry Thoreau, Harvard 1833–1837," Ph.D. diss., Princeton University, 1953, pp. 17–18.

through, but he apparently did not feel any corresponding pressure or burning ambition to excel. Compared with the educational regimen a decade earlier of the Emerson boys, who were required from the age of three to recite to their parents before breakfast,[3] the pedagogical atmosphere in the Thoreau household was relaxed. Nor did Thoreau possess the sort of single-minded doggedness of application that enabled his Concord Academy friend and Harvard roommate Charles Stearns Wheeler to rank second in the class of 1837. Nevertheless, after his somewhat unpropitious start, he ranked sixth in a class of about fifty by his sophomore year. Thereafter he slipped somewhat from this relative eminence. Illness caused him to miss a term during his junior year, and as an upperclassman Thoreau apparently shared the skepticism of many of his fellows about Harvard's system of evaluation and ranking. President Quincy, in a letter to Ralph Waldo Emerson about some exhibition money Thoreau had won, ascribed Thoreau's failure to rank higher in his class to his having "imbibed some notions concerning emulation & College rank which had a natural tendency to diminish his zeal, if not his exertions."[4]

Such notions would be difficult not to imbibe, given the system then in place. Class meetings, as well as class rank, were almost wholly based on recitation, which required mainly rote memorization and repetition of assignments. Class rank was determined by the accumulation of points assigned for everything from written themes to chapel attendance. The curriculum itself had remained essentially unchanged since the time of the Revolutionary War. During Thoreau's freshman year, members of all four classes petitioned to have the rank and recitation system changed, protesting with considerable justification that it "encouraged superficial scholarship," but as is usual in such cases the administration declined to consider their complaints.[5] A few months later a more serious incident occurred: A student refused to translate in a Greek recitation class. When he withdrew from school rather than apologize to his tutor, the pent-up anger of his classmates erupted in the "Dunkin Rebellion," in which students destroyed the recitation room, attacked watchmen with rocks, and disrupted mandatory chapel services with "scraping, whistling, groaning and other disgraceful noises" such as anyone who has ever been in the company

3. Gay Wilson Allen, *Waldo Emerson: A Biography* (New York: Viking Press, 1981), p. 10.

4. Quoted in Walter Harding, *The Days of Henry Thoreau* (New York: Alfred A. Knopf, 1965), p. 47.

5. Ibid. p. 33.

of adolescent boys can imagine.[6] Several students were expelled, and the entire sophomore class was suspended for a term.

Nevertheless, despite this disorder and the narrowness of the system, Thoreau finished in the upper half of his class and won a place in commencement exercises. His generally good record suggests that he found Harvard to offer an unsophisticated New England village boy considerable impetus to intellectual growth. It had its share of inspiring teachers, the stimulation of gifted classmates, and a tradition of literary and debating societies that fostered independent learning in areas outside the formal curriculum. Most important of all its opportunities, perhaps, was the library, which, although small by modern standards (about forty thousand volumes), was at that time the best in the country. The library's stacks were open, too, so students could explore the collection as well as charge books required for class use. Nor was the preparation required for recitations so time consuming as to discourage independent reading. The published charging records of Thoreau and some of his classmates show that they all used the library extensively,[7] and it may be presumed that Thoreau read a great deal more, informally and casually, than his charging record indicates. Additionally, the Institute of 1770, a literary and debating society to which he belonged, maintained its own library of some fourteen hundred volumes that Thoreau also patronized regularly. Since its members generated acquisitions, the institute's library tended to supplement the college library with better holdings in contemporary literature and periodicals. It was through this library, for example, that, during his senior year, Thoreau first became acquainted with the seminal work of American Transcendentalism, Emerson's *Nature*.[8]

The overall record of Thoreau's reading at Harvard suggests that his intellectual development during these years proceeded on two paths that were not always parallel but that were eventually convergent. On the one hand, the reading required by his formal program of studies gave him a foundation in subjects and modes of inquiry and discourse that would serve him all his life. On the other hand, the "more valuable education," as he was to term it in *Walden*, that he got by "associating with the most cultivated of his contemporaries" (WA, 50) included reading that would lead him away from the careful Unitarian ortho-

6. Ibid. p. 42.

7. See Kenneth Walter Cameron, "Books Thoreau Borrowed from Harvard College Library," in *Emerson the Essayist*, 2 vols. (Raleigh, N.C.: The Thistle Press, 1945), 2.191–208, and "Reading of Thoreau's College Friends," in *Emerson and Thoreau as Readers*, new ed. (Hartford: Transcendental Books, 1972), pp. 90–129.

8. Kenneth Walter Cameron, "Thoreau Discovers Emerson: A College Reading Record," *Bulletin of the New York Public Library* 57, no. 7 (June 1953): 319–334.

doxy of Harvard and prepare the way intellectually for his conversion—or development, really—to Transcendentalism, a process that
was well advanced by the time he graduated. Other areas of his mature
interest, however, most notably early American history and natural
history, were relatively undeveloped in his Harvard years, and more
than a decade would pass before he would return to the Harvard library and the library of the Boston Society of Natural History to begin
to train himself systematically in these subjects.

Thoreau's formal studies at Harvard may be divided, according to
the branches of the curriculum itself, into classical and modern languages, mathematics and science, rhetoric and oratory, and philosophy and religion. Literary studies, which in practice loomed large in
the curriculum, were subsumed in the programs in languages and rhetoric. Likewise, history was not a major component of the curriculum
(Thoreau studied history formally only in his freshman year), although
a good deal of ancient and European history was included in the study
of classical and modern languages.

Among these divisions, the study of languages was preeminent; classical languages prevailed, of course, but modern languages were offered as electives and Thoreau enrolled in them regularly. During his
first three years, Thoreau took Greek and Latin every term, and usually
one and sometimes two modern languages as well. During his senior
year he continued his study of modern languages, so that by the time
he graduated he had completed—in addition to the standard Greek
and Latin curriculum—five terms of Italian, four of French, three of
German, and two of Spanish.[9] Of these, he was most fluent in French,
which he had begun to study at the Concord Academy. Although he
had the occasion to speak the language only briefly, on his visit to
Montreal and Quebec in 1850, he read it fairly often and fairly easily,
from French translations of Oriental scriptures to the accounts of early
explorers and missionaries in North America.

Despite this extensive acquaintance with modern languages, Thoreau seems not to have developed a correspondingly strong interest in
European literature. His courses did not include a great deal of reading
of important contemporary literary works, and he supplemented his
reading with only a few library withdrawals that were probably outside assignments for class work: Tasso, a volume of Chateaubriand,
dramas by Racine and Metastasio. The one exception to this pattern
was German. He studied German with Orestes Brownson while teaching school in Canton, Massachusetts, in 1836; and during the last term

9. Kenneth Walter Cameron, "Chronology of Thoreau's Harvard Years," *Emerson
Society Quarterly* no. 15 (2 Qtr. 1959): 13–18.

of his senior year, prompted in all likelihood by the lectures of the newly installed Smith Professor of Modern Languages, Henry Wadsworth Longfellow, he read Carlyle's translation of Goethe's *Wilhelm Meister's Apprenticeship*.[10] This last work was *de rigueur* reading for literary-minded youths of Thoreau's generation, and both Goethe and Carlyle were to exert considerable influence on Thoreau during the early years of his career. Back in Concord the year after his graduation, reading Goethe in German was an interest he shared with Emerson and a marker of the growth of their friendship. In general, however, Thoreau's interest in languages would later tend to express itself chiefly in what might be termed philological concerns—especially etymology, plays on words and conventional expressions, and the origins of language. This interest, in turn, would manifest itself in the basic traits of his style rather than in any particular or longstanding preoccupation with foreign languages and literatures.

Classical languages and literature, on the other hand, were both the central core of the Harvard curriculum and, as Ethel Seybold has shown,[11] an integral part of Thoreau's literary imagination throughout his career. From a decidedly mediocre entering student he made himself into an able classicist—perhaps the best among the Transcendentalists, excepting Jones Very—who would count among his first literary ventures an essay on the Roman satirist Persius and translations of Aeschylus and Pindar. Freshman Latin and Greek classes began with Horace's *Odes* and selections from Livy, and Xenophon's *Anabasis* and the orations of Demosthenes and Aeschines. Each class studied grammar and composition as well, of course, and also the "antiquities" of Greece and Rome—that is, the culture, geography, and civilization of the classical world. Included in Thoreau's reading either in required texts or library withdrawals his first year, for example, are Cleveland's *Epitome of Grecian Antiquities*, Harwood's *Grecian Antiquities*, Adam's *Roman Antiquities*, and Rollin's *Ancient History*.[12] The long deserts of translation recital must have been at least occasionally interrupted by lectures, discussion, or allusion to contextual works such as these.

Sophomore Greek concentrated on the tragedies of Sophocles— *Oedipus Tyrannus, Oedipus Coloneus,* and *Antigone* and Euripides' *Alcestis*. Latin covered Cicero's *De Officiis*, Horace's *Satires* and *Epis-*

10. See Cameron, "Thoreau Discovers Emerson" and "Books Thoreau Borrowed from Harvard College Library."

11. *Thoreau: The Quest and the Classics* (New Haven: Yale University Press, 1951).

12. Cameron, "Chronology of Thoreau's Harvard Years," pp. 13–14.

tles, and the *Medea* of Seneca. In his junior year Thoreau studied Juvenal in Latin (perhaps as a balance to the Horatian satires of the previous year) and the *Iliad* in Greek.¹³ Thoreau showed his enthusiastic response to Homer in a letter to a classmate (COR, 9), and the Greek epic made a powerful impression on him as an expression of the heroic potential in life. Ten years later, at Walden Pond, he would keep a copy of the *Iliad* on his desk to remind him of that potential, and he would take time from hoeing beans to translate from it in his Journal and read passages to Alek Therien, the woodchopper (WA, 144; PJ 2.160, 172–173). Reading Greek became the intellectual analogue of the physical struggles described in the *Iliad*: "The student may read Homer or Aeschylus in the Greek without danger of dissipation or luxuriousness," he said, "for it implies that he in some measure emulate their heroes, and consecrate morning hours to their pages" (WA, 100). As a student himself, Thoreau devoted time to the classics beyond required hours, for in his senior year when he was no longer enrolled in Latin and Greek he wrote reviews, probably for the Institute of 1770, of H. N. Coleridge's *Introductions to the Study of the Greek Classic Poets* and Adam Ferguson's *History of the Progress and Termination of the Roman Republic* (EEM, 50–58, 63–66).

According to Christian Gruber's study of Thoreau's Harvard education, much of the credit for Thoreau's enthusiasm for and devotion to the classics belongs to C. C. Felton, Eliot Professor of Greek Literature. Felton's pedagogy stressed "that the students should widen their interest beyond the purely linguistic and become aware of 'the whole life of the people whose language was studied.' "¹⁴ Felton also expressed the belief that "the study of antiquity has a noble power to elevate the mind above the low passions of the present, by fixing its contemplation on the great and immortal spirits of the past."¹⁵ This sentiment suggests the role—as an antidote to the burgeoning material culture of nineteenth-century America—that the classics played in Thoreau's Transcendentalism. Additionally, Homeric Greek was attractive, according to Transcendental literary theory, as a "primitive" language that was closer than modern tongues to the poetic and spiritual origins of language. (A confirmation of this view of the classics, as well as his first passing exposure to the significance of the classics of Oriental literature, was provided by Friedrich von Schlegel's *Lectures on the History of Literature*, a key document of Romantic literary crit-

13. Ibid. pp. 14–16.

14. Gruber, "Education," p. 121.

15. "Moore's Lectures on the Greek Language and Literature," *North American Review* 42 (January 1836): 101.

icism which Thoreau read during his junior year.) Felton would probably have been pained to find himself described as a conduit to Transcendentalism (he would later be critical of Emerson's *Essays* for threatening Christianity), but his emphasis on the elevating ideal of classical thought and culture was consonant with Thoreau's own response to the classics. It was Felton's edition of the *Iliad* that Thoreau used at Harvard, and he remained faithful to it, using it during the 1850s for the *Iliad* quotations in drafts of *Cape Cod*.

Yet Thoreau's classical education had considerable gaps, at least by modern standards. Despite his veneration of Homer's *Iliad*, for example, he mentions the *Odyssey* infrequently, and he seems not to have known it except through secondary sources and perhaps Pope's translation.[16] Neither did Thoreau's studies in either philosophy or classics touch directly upon the great philosophical tradition of antiquity, so that he had in college little or no exposure to Platonic or Aristotelian philosophy, or to Roman Stoics such as Marcus Aurelius, whose views he might have found congenial. It should be noted, however, that Cicero's *De Officiis*, read in the sophomore year, does contain an exposition and defense of Stoic doctrines.

The curriculum in mathematics at Harvard was fairly stringent, but the formal study of science, with which it was most closely connected, was still in its infancy. The mathematics course sequence was a combination of pure and "mixed"—that is, applied—subjects, and since its bearing on Thoreau's later development is mainly confined to its usefulness to his work as a part-time surveyor, little needs to be said about his reading in this area. He studied in sequence geometry, algebra, trigonometry, and calculus, followed by the applied subjects of mechanics, optics, electricity, and astronomy. The last four areas were treated in a series of texts called the *Cambridge Natural Philosophy*, prepared for the Harvard course sequence by John Follen.

Thoreau's scientific study in college consisted of one term of natural history recitation and lecture, one term each of voluntary lectures on mineralogy and astronomy (which he may or may not have attended), and the scientific component of his "mixed" mathematics courses. (Had he not missed a term through illness during his junior year, he would also have taken a term of chemistry.) Thus his only formal course work bearing upon his later avocation as a naturalist was the single term of natural history taken at the end of his senior year. It was taught by Thaddeus William Harris, who later became a noted entomologist, but whose principal duties were as college librarian, a fact

16. He owned a copy of Pope's translation; see Bibliographical Catalogue, no. 719.

that may serve to suggest the importance that Harvard attached to instruction in science at this time.

Harris's course consisted of seventeen lectures on botany, based on
Thomas Nuttall's introductory text, *Systematic and Physiological Botany*, and eighteen recitation periods based on William Smellie's *Philosophy of Natural History*.[17] The latter was the principal—indeed the
only—natural history text in the Harvard curriculum, and it was certainly chosen not for its scientific authority but because it harmonized
with the instruction in theology and philosophy. It stressed what was
called the "argument from design," an eighteenth-century concept that
the operations of the natural world provided evidence of a divine and
benevolent plan for the cosmos. "Let him study the works of nature,"
Smellie exhorted the student in the conclusion to his text, "and find in
the contemplation of all that is beautiful, curious, and wonderful in
them, proofs of the existence and attributes of his Creator."[18] Although the edition used at Harvard had been updated by John Ware,
its basic doctrines remained the same as in the first edition of 1790. Its
material was presented not as a subject for rigorous or experimental
inquiry, but essentially as a harmless diversion and amusement, suitable perhaps for country clerics like Smellie to pursue in their spare
time. According to the preface, the study of nature "is a source of interesting amusement, prevents idle or vicious propensities, and exalts
the mind to a love of virtue and of rational entertainment."[19] For his
part, Thoreau displayed few signs of special interest in natural history
while in college. His notebooks record no observations of nature and
little reading in the field, and his only related library withdrawal was
an introduction to botany that was probably required for his class
work for Harris.[20] To judge by his 1837 class book autobiography,
which contained an apostrophe to the woods and streams of Concord
(EEM, 113–114), Thoreau's appreciation of nature at this time was sen-
timentally rather than philosophically Romantic. Likewise, his only
extended composition on a natural history topic, a review of William
Howitt's *The Book of the Seasons* that he wrote toward the end of his
junior year, is conventional in its enthusiastic praise of the pleasures of
solitude and scenery, and approving of the fact that Howitt is "neither
too scientific, nor too much abounding in technical terms" (EEM, 26).

17. Gruber, "Education," pp. 154–158.

18. William Smellie, *The Philosophy of Natural History* (Boston: Cummings, Hilliard & Co., 1824), p. 318.

19. Ibid. p. iii.

20. Cameron, "Books Thoreau Borrowed from Harvard College Library," p. 194;
the volume was James Smith's *Introduction to Physiological and Systematical Botany*.

It might be concluded that this rather dilettantish and casual introduction to natural science hampered Thoreau's development as a naturalist by leaving him untrained in scientific method—especially experimentation and laboratory work.[21] He might be said to have been consigned by his education to amateur status as a naturalist all his life. And had Thoreau attended Harvard just about a decade later, after the arrival of Louis Agassiz and Asa Gray and the foundation of the Lawrence Scientific School, his orientation to natural science might well have been much more rigorous, methodical, and professional. But it should be remembered that scientific education was in its embryonic stage everywhere, and that most of the great nineteenth-century naturalists—Darwin included—were essentially self-taught. The outworn creed that Harvard preached in natural science sent Thoreau away with a vague endorsement of the subject that left him free, really, to explore the diversity of approaches to and theories of nature that were in competition before the triumph of the Darwinian paradigm during the second half of the century. His reading and work in natural science would accelerate in intensity and scope as he grew older, but he was not conditioned by his college training to a particular theoretical bias—there being, in truth, little he had to unlearn. Theory in the natural sciences was in such a state of flux that it was doubtless to his advantage later as a writer and naturalist to be relatively unencumbered by preconceptions. His own ideas would develop through reading in and reflection about diverse scientific and philosophical approaches in the years ahead, and throughout his life he would evince a catholic taste in natural history writing that would range from Aristotle and Pliny to Agassiz and Darwin, and sample approvingly many writers in between.

Thoreau's training in English composition and literature took place in the Department of Rhetoric and Oratory (that august institution the Department of English not yet having come into existence in American colleges). The basic texts for courses in this department, under Edward Tyrrel Channing, Boyleston Professor of Rhetoric and Oratory, were Richard Whately's *Rhetoric* and *Logic*. Whately was an English cleric, Archbishop of Dublin, with Broad Church sympathies, and his views on logic and rhetoric were correspondingly rational and latitudinarian. His work stressed argumentation and proof, and, following George

21. This is essentially the conclusion that Gruber draws ("Education," chap. 6). James McIntosh's study *Thoreau as Romantic Naturalist* (Ithaca: Cornell University Press, 1974) does not treat Thoreau's formal training as a naturalist, while Sherman Paul states forthrightly that "in spite of his gifts for nature study, Thoreau was not a good naturalist" because he never developed a scientific objectivity toward his subject; see *The Shores of America* (Urbana: University of Illinois Press, 1958), p. 277.

Campbell's earlier *Philosophy of Rhetoric*, adopted what might be termed a modestly psychological approach to the subject of style. Employing eighteenth-century epistemological theories derived ultimately from Locke—that ideas are built up in the mind from sense impressions in combination or association—Whately advised the writer or speaker to employ rhetorical devices that served to make strong and clear impressions on the mind of the reader or auditor: perspicuity, concrete diction, and imagery derived from sensory experience, and figurative devices like synecdoche and metonymy.[22] Channing himself had a rather measured conception of the role of rhetoric and, though he could be severe and even caustic in his criticism, strove to help students express their thoughts effectively and not to mold them to a particular way of thinking or writing. He defined rhetoric as

> a body of rules derived from experience and observation, and extending to all communication by language and designed to make it efficient. It does not ask whether a man is to be a speaker or writer,—a poet, philosopher, or debater; but simply,—is it his wish to be put in the right way of communicating his mind with power to others, by words spoken or written. If so, rhetoric undertakes to show him rules or principles which will help to make the expression of his thoughts effective; and effective, not in any fashionable or arbitrary way but in the way that nature universally intends and which man universally feels. For all genuine art is but the helpmate of nature.[23]

The principal work, however, in Channing's courses consisted of themes, forensics, and declamations for which various kinds of outside reading were necessary. He assigned topics requiring no uniform preparation by the class (e.g., "Titles of Books" or "Of Keeping a Journal") as well as topics that demanded detailed knowledge of particular works by classical authors such as Virgil and Horace, and moderns such as Shakespeare and Milton.[24] There were no formal courses in English literature, although Channing read a series of lectures entitled "Rhetoric and Criticism," dealing chiefly with literary issues, to the senior class.[25] More important, however, during Thoreau's junior year Channing also conducted a series of informal evening meetings in his

22. Richard H. Dillman, "Thoreau's Harvard Education in Rhetoric and Composition," *Thoreau Journal Quarterly* 13 (July–October 1981): 54.

23. Edward Tyrrel Channing, *Lectures Read to the Seniors in Harvard College* (Boston: Ticknor and Fields, 1856), pp. 31–32.

24. See Kenneth Walter Cameron, "Thoreau, Edward Tyrrel Channing and College Themes," *Emerson Society Quarterly* 42 (4 Qtr. 1966): 15–34.

25. Cameron, "Chronology of Thoreau's Harvard Years," p. 18.

study devoted to readings and critical discussions of English poetry. Gruber suggests, quite plausibly, that through his lectures and these informal gatherings Channing greatly stimulated Thoreau's interest in English poetry.[26] At any rate, only after he began to study with Channing in his sophomore year did Thoreau begin to withdraw works of English poetry from the library.

Thoreau gradually widened and extended this interest, branching out during his senior year from standard authors such as Chaucer, Shakespeare, and Milton to the collections of Thomas Campbell and Alexander Chalmers (the latter a twenty-one-volume anthology that he read through "without skipping" during this period or, more likely, a few years later).[27] He also read Hazlitt's *Lectures on the English Poets*, the poems of Gray, Johnson's *Lives of the . . . English Poets*, the Robin Hood ballads, some Anglo-Saxon poetry, early Scottish poetry, Burns, and Percy's *Reliques of Ancient English Poetry*.

A stimulus to this literary interest was undoubtedly provided by Longfellow's first course of Harvard lectures on German and Northern literatures during Thoreau's last term in the summer of 1837. These lectures did not begin until May 23, Longfellow missed at least a week in June because of illness, and the term ended on July 2, so Thoreau's acquaintance with the recently installed Smith Professor of Modern Languages was necessarily brief. Nevertheless, Longfellow may have helped significantly to mold Thoreau's taste in Germanic literature. In a "slight sketch of the Course" included in a letter to his father, Longfellow outlined the contents of his dozen lectures (after two introductory periods on the Romance languages):

3. History of the Northern, or Gothic Languages.
4. Anglo-Saxon Literature.
5. and 6. Swedish Literatures.
7. Sketch of German Literatures.
8. 9. 10. Life and Writings of Gothe [*sic*].
11. and 12. Life and Writings of Jean Paul Richter.

Correspondingly, during this term Thoreau withdrew books on Anglo-Saxon poetry and Goethe's *Wilhelm Meister's Apprenticeship* (in Carlyle's translation), and, a few years later, read the saga of Frithiof—doubtless treated by Longfellow in the lectures on Swedish literature, since he praised it in an article in the *North American Review* that

26. "Education," pp. 223–226.
27. See *Walden*, p. 259; also Harding, *Days*, p. 38.

summer.[28] Thoreau would maintain this interest in German and Scandinavian literature, particularly while working on *Cape Cod* during the 1850s when he became fascinated with the records of Norse exploration of the North American coast, but the personal example and stimulus of Longfellow were probably even more important than the content of his lectures. In contrast to the mind-numbing dullness of Greek and Latin recitation, here were warm, effusive, and appreciative lectures on contemporary literature from a dashing—by Cambridge standards—scholar-poet. Longfellow was far too much the Europeanized urban dandy for Thoreau ever to cultivate his society (or be cultivated by him, for that matter), but along with Channing Longfellow provided, by his lively engagement with literary studies, a notable exception to the prevailing pedagogical pattern of rote recitation.

At the same time, Thoreau began to keep a commonplace book in which he copied extracts from many of the poets he was reading.[29] This notebook is a link to his immediate post-Harvard reading, for he continued to fill it with poetry extracts after graduation, and he would fill several more blank books with selections from the English poets during the early 1840s, evidently working toward some literary project.[30] In any event, this interest in English poetry, especially from the fourteenth through the seventeenth centuries, is the most marked taste that Thoreau seems to have developed as an undergraduate. His library withdrawals, his commonplace books, his membership in the Institute of 1770 and the role he played in it as a debater and a book reviewer suggest cumulatively that, however vague his career plans were, he was strongly drawn to a life in letters. The professors who seem to have influenced him most—Felton, Channing, and possibly Longfellow—were all men of letters who wrote on literary subjects for the reviews and did not confine their enthusiasm or their professional activity to the classroom. When Emerson delivered his rousing call for a new age in American letters and his glorification of the scholar's duties in the "American Scholar" address to Thoreau's graduating class in the summer of 1837, its effect on Thoreau must have been confirm-

28. See Cameron, "Books Thoreau Borrowed from Harvard College Library," pp. 193–194, and "Thoreau Discovers Emerson," pp. 326–328; for Longfellow's activities as a lecturer see *The Letters of Henry Wadsworth Longfellow*, vol. 2, *1837–1843*, ed. Andrew Hilen (Cambridge: Harvard University Press, 1966), pp. 16–32.

29. Now in the collection of the Pierpont Morgan Library (MA 594); titled by Thoreau "Miscellaneous Extracts." See William L. Howarth, *The Literary Manuscripts of Henry D. Thoreau* (Columbus: Ohio State University Press, 1974), pp. 289–290, for a description.

30. Robert Sattelmeyer, "Thoreau's Projected Work on the English Poets," in *Studies in the American Renaissance: 1980*, ed. Joel Myerson (Boston: G. K. Hall, 1980), pp. 239–257.

ing and corroborative, for he was already preparing himself to carry out the duties of Emerson's scholar, especially "preserving and communicating . . . melodious verse."

Thoreau's reading in the remaining major area of the Harvard curriculum, religious studies and philosophy, is probably the most difficult to assess, not because the evidence is scant but because the effects of this reading are so difficult to gauge. The subjects involved inevitably raise questions of *how* as well as *what* one thinks, and, carried to their logical extensions, bear upon the ways in which Thoreau's fundamental world view may have been shaped by the philosophical and religious concepts that he came in contact with during these formative years. It can be said with a fair degree of confidence that Thoreau was acquainted with particular religious and philosophical developments of his day, but it can never be argued with equal confidence that he was influenced deeply by them. And there are of course infinite gradations of belief and influence. Nevertheless, the very things that make such judgments difficult also make it necessary to attempt them, for this area of his education was obviously of profound significance in shaping his mature intellectual orientation to the fundamental questions of life. It is possible to trace in some detail Thoreau's college reading in these subjects, and the record suggests that a progressive development of sorts did occur, that Thoreau gradually became familiar with thinkers and schools of thought that led him in fairly well-defined stages from Harvard's rational Unitarian orthodoxy to the radical and revolutionary propositions of Emerson's *Nature*.

During the 1830s, religious education—and indeed preparation for the ministry—was still a major mission of Harvard College. But during the preceding generation its religious orthodoxy had gradually changed from the Calvinism of the institution's founders to a rational and somewhat cerebral Unitarianism that continued to stress the authority of scripture but also emphasized man's capacity for good, the reasonableness of God's laws, and individual moral duty and responsibility. The Unitarians, however, were viewed with suspicion from both the theological left and right. Other established seminaries and colleges, such as those at Andover and Princeton, remained deeply tinctured with Calvinist thought and mistrusted Harvard as far too liberal and rationalistic. The conservatives suspected Unitarianism, with its emphasis on a single godhead, of having abandoned the fundamental Christian doctrines of the Trinity and the divinity of Jesus. A smaller but eventually more troublesome group of opponents came from within Unitarian ranks themselves, objecting to what they perceived to be the sterile and already tradition-bound character of the sect. This chorus of criticism would culminate in Emerson's famous

Divinity School Address (and its ensuing pamphlet war) in 1838, but in the hands of other Unitarian ministers of varying degrees of radicalism—such as W. H. Channing, Theodore Parker, Orestes Brownson, George Ripley, and Frederic Henry Hedge—the controversy had been building for several years.[31]

Thoreau had two terms of instruction in religious and theological studies: a recitation class in his junior year on William Paley's *Evidences of Christianity* and Joseph Butler's *Analogy of Religion*, and a course of lectures on the New Testament during his senior year.[32] Paley's and Butler's texts were both orthodox, rational responses to deism and eighteenth-century skepticism that strove to prove that revealed religion, specifically Christianity, was compatible with the "natural religion" of the deists. Thoreau also had at least some familiarity with Paley's other and better-known religious treatise, *Natural Theology*, for he wrote a theme based upon a passage from it during his senior year (EEM, 101–104). *Natural Theology* contained the classic statement of the "argument from design," in which the existence and attributes of a creator are purportedly proved by the complexity and harmony of the creation. In Paley's famous analogy, a person who found a watch by itself in an uninhabited landscape could infer from an analysis of its construction and operation an intelligent watchmaker; the same conclusion would presumably follow from an analysis of the works of nature, which are infinitely more intricate and complex than a watch and which must therefore have an infinitely more powerful and intelligent creator. Thoreau was familiar enough with this argument to employ it himself a few years later to his own pupils at the Concord Academy.[33]

Both Butler and Paley represent the rational apologist impulse to attempt to prove the truth of Christianity, revelation, and miracles by the very same sort of empirical evidence and inductive reasoning that had given rise to the abstractions of deism and the skepticism of the eighteenth century. In retrospect this impulse seems flawed from its inception, for no matter how skillfully argued and copiously furnished with evidence of the wonders of nature, a case for the authenticity of revelation and miracles based upon natural science and induction is ultimately a step toward the displacement of that religious certainty and scriptural authority by scientific and materialistic criteria for truth.

31. See William R. Hutchison, *The Transcendentalist Ministers: Church Reform in the New England Renaissance* (New Haven: Yale University Press, 1959), esp. chap. 1, "Boston Unitarianism."

32. Cameron, "Chronology of Thoreau's Harvard Years," pp. 16, 18.

33. Harding, *Days*, p. 80, quoting Edward Emerson's notes on Thoreau.

In adopting the tests for truth of their adversaries and attempting to show that Christianity is logical and scientific, Paley's and Butler's works are fundamentally defensive and have about them the aura of a doomed enterprise. Moreover, in their effort to be scientific and logical, they tend to downplay or disregard entirely religious emotions and affections. It would not be surprising if they left unsatisfied such students as actually may have looked to them for spiritual guidance or certainty. Nor would it be surprising if their effect was the opposite of that intended. Benjamin Franklin recalled reading pamphlets against deism and finding himself more persuaded by the arguments that were to be refuted than by those of the Christian apologists.

Henry Ware's lecture course on the New Testament, along with Thoreau's reading of the New Testament for his Greek studies, also reflected indirectly Harvard's post-Calvinist theological orientation. Despite the fact that they deemphasized the divinity of Jesus, the Unitarians naturally reversed the priorities of their Calvinistic forebears and stressed the New Testament's mild laws, its ethics, and its emphasis on man's capacity for regeneration and salvation. They recoiled in distaste from the Old Testament's severe and seemingly arbitrary laws, and from its wrathful and punishing God. Thoreau knew the Bible well,[34] but especially during the early years of his career he drew his allusions and references preponderantly from the New Testament, reflecting perhaps the bias of his education. Generally, he tended to be interested in the Old Testament as primitive myth—comparable in certain ways to the mythology, culture, and religion of the ancient Greeks (PJ 2.183–184)—while he both shared and went beyond the emphasis of the Unitarians on the New Testament as an ethical document. As both *A Week on the Concord and Merrimack Rivers* and *Walden* make plain, Thoreau was far more willing than most of his nominally Christian contemporaries to take seriously and literally the New Testament injunctions to live by faith and to eschew accumulating worldly goods. His Harvard education, as well as his earlier religious training, gave him a command of scripture that served as a keen weapon against what he perceived to be the apologetic and compromised Christianity of his age.

Like his literary reading at Harvard, Thoreau's required philosophical reading provided him with a background and a bridge to independent study that would carry him a great distance beyond conventional ideas enshrined in the curriculum. The curriculum in philosophy was based upon a kind of uneasy truce between the two schools of

34. See John R. Burns, "Thoreau's Use of the Bible," Ph.D. diss., Notre Dame University, 1966.

thought that were dominant in America during the late eighteenth and early nineteenth centuries: the empirical and sensationalist school of John Locke and his followers, and the Scottish "common sense" philosophy advanced to qualify Lockean empiricism by Thomas Reid, Dugald Stewart, and others. Virtually no attempt was made, however, to include in the curriculum European schools of thought that had arisen during the preceding half-century. For post-Kantian French, English, and especially German philosophy, the interested student had to depend on outside reading. And since editions and translations of contemporary European philosophy were scarce (the Reverend James Marsh's edition of Coleridge's *Aids to Reflection*, the first of Coleridge's prose writings to appear in this country, had been published in 1829), the student often had to rely on secondary sources, especially review essays in periodicals.

Thoreau's formal study of philosophy began in his junior year with William Paley's *Moral Philosophy* and Dugald Stewart's *Elements of the Philosophy of the Human Mind.*[35] These texts presented him, respectively and somewhat contradictorily, with a utilitarian ethical system and a common-sense epistemology. Following Locke, Paley denied the existence of innate ideas, including moral ones, and asserted that the general expediency of an action was one's only guide to moral choice.[36] A little more than a decade later, Thoreau would make explicit reference to Paley's doctrine in order to refute it and assert the primacy of a higher moral law in "Resistance to Civil Government" (RP, 67–68). Stewart's philosophy of the mind, on the other hand, like the Scottish philosophy in general, attempted to disprove the Lockean view of mind and thought as merely the product of accumulated sense impressions. Stewart and the other Scots (notably Thomas Reid and Thomas Brown) posited the existence of certain innate principles and ideas in the human mind, among which was the "moral sense," an intuitive guide to right and wrong shared by all men—hence the term "common sense" applied to the school. (It must be stressed that "common" means "shared" and not "ordinary" in this usage.) Such views were popular because they offered a convenient way out of the troublesome extension of Lockean positions represented by the radical skepticism of Hume. There was little appetite in America for abstruse systems of thought that contravened the practical experience of mankind.

All these thinkers, then, were more or less occupied in either extend-

35. Cameron, "Chronology of Thoreau's Harvard Years," p. 16.

36. See Edgley W. Todd, "Philosophical Ideas at Harvard College 1817–1837," *New England Quarterly* 16 (1943): 63–90.

ing or qualifying Locke. But the notion of a common sense that accounted for the intuitive perception of right and wrong represented not only a corrective to but a significant departure from the material and empirical bias of Lockean thought. In fact, by establishing the authority of a common inner sense or conscience, the moral sense, the Scottish school may be said to have prepared the way for Transcendentalism. It takes only a slight shift of emphasis to move from a conception of a common inner sense manifested by individual moral actions to an individual appeal to one's own inner sense. Certainly the moral sense was a familiar concept in Transcendental thought, becoming in Emerson's hands in the Divinity School Address, for example, a powerful weapon against stultified religious orthodoxy.

In any event, after this refutation of Locke during his junior year, Thoreau studied the source of the controversy, Locke's *Essay Concerning Human Understanding*, in the Intellectual Philosophy course during his senior year. Significantly, according to the Harvard catalogue for that year (1836–1837), students were required as a part of their assignment to submit a written critique of Locke's *Essay*, "exhibiting the opinions of other philosophers, on controverted questions."[37] Probably this exercise involved rehearsing the arguments of the Scottish school against Locke's concept of the mind as a *tabula rasa* on which experience inscribed data.

Had Thoreau's philosophical education ended with his class work he would have had a safe grounding in conventional philosophical thought that harmonized with his training in religion and science. But the winds of change were blowing in New England, and in 1836 Thoreau chanced to meet one of the most indefatigable and charismatic spokesmen for reform, Orestes Brownson—a meeting that was to provide the principal catalyst in directing Thoreau's attention to thinkers who led him directly to the "new views" of Transcendentalism.

During his junior year Thoreau took advantage of a new policy that permitted students to leave school for a term to earn money to help pay their college expenses. He secured a teaching position in Canton, Massachusetts, and chanced to board with Brownson, who was at that time minister of the local Unitarian church and serving on the school committee that interviewed Thoreau for the job.[38] Brownson was just then busy on the manifesto of his Transcendental period (he later became a Roman Catholic), *New Views of Christianity, Society and the Church* (1836), a treatise that stressed man's inherent religious nature and argued that the present conditions of both the church and society

37. Cameron, "Chronology of Thoreau's Harvard Years," p. 17.
38. Harding, *Days*, pp. 45–46.

served to retard rather than to advance man's spiritual development.[39]
Thoreau studied German with Brownson, probably for the specific
purpose of reading and discussing German thought: German was the
language of scholarship, philosophy, and the "higher criticism" of the
Bible in the nineteenth century, and many important works in the language were still unavailable in English. In 1837, after he graduated,
Thoreau wrote Brownson for a letter of reference, recalling his stay in
Canton as "an era in my life—the morning of a new *Lebenstag*." In
the same letter, in an apparent reference to their studies together, Thoreau cites his need to earn a living "and not be always keeping up a
blaze upon the hearth within, with my German and metaphysical cat-
sticks" (COR, 19).

In addition to fostering interest in German (an interest, it will be
remembered, that would extend to German literature the next year
under Longfellow), Brownson probably also set Thoreau to reading
French thinkers whom he admired. During his senior year (1836–
1837), after returning to Cambridge, Thoreau read Benjamin Constant
de Rebecque's *De la Religion*, which Brownson had recommended in
the preface to *New Views*.[40] Like Brownson's book, Constant's
stressed the distinction between the universality of religious sentiment
in mankind and the transitory form it happened to take in particular
religious sects. This concept, complementary to the notion of the common moral sense, is one of the cornerstones of Transcendentalism, as
well as the chief source of its quarrel with prevailing religious institutions, which it persisted, to their exasperation, in regarding as merely
temporary and probably distorted manifestations of this vast underlying religious instinct.

More important, Thoreau also read Victor Cousin's *Introduction to
the History of Philosophy*, which he borrowed from the library of the
Institute of 1770 in June 1837 and renewed in July. Cousin was the
leading figure of the French philosophic movement known as Eclecticism, and like Constant's, his work had been championed by Brownson. Thoreau had probably read about Cousin's work before reading
the *Introduction*, for earlier in his senior year he had checked out issues
of the *North American Review* and the *Edinburgh Review* that contained lengthy reviews of that work.[41] French Eclecticism is not remembered today as an important movement in the development of

39. Gruber, "Education," p. 191; Thoreau owned a copy of *New Views* (see Bibliographical Catalogue, no. 209), probably acquired at this time. It is not known just
when it came into his hands or if it came from Brownson himself.

40. *New Views of Christianity, Society and the Church* (Boston: J. Munroe, 1836),
p. viii.

41. Cameron, "Thoreau Discovers Emerson," pp. 326–327.

philosophy, but its tenets were widely disseminated and quite influential in Europe and America during the first half of the nineteenth century. In 1838 George Ripley, for example, made up the first two volumes of his *Specimens of Foreign Standard Literature* with selections from Cousin, his pupil Théodore Jouffroy, and Constant; and he remarked of Cousin in the preface that "there is no living philosopher who has a greater number of readers in this country, and none whose works have met with a more genuine sympathy, a more cordial recognition."[42]

Cousin's system of thought was not an original one. In fact, it consisted essentially of a methodology and an attitude toward truth implied by its title: Truth is not the special province of any particular sect or movement; rather, all systems contain truth, and the proper study of philosophy consists in the historical comparison of various schools in order to discover those truths that have been contributed by each or that are universally agreed upon. Cousin emphasized (and this makes him an important stepping stone to Transcendentalism) the ability of the individual to perceive this truth on his own, through an intuitive faculty quite close to if not indistinguishable from what the Transcendentalists, following Coleridge, called Reason.

Eclecticism was not simply an intellectual smorgasbord, however. Cousin had a dynamic and even dialectic theory of history. He believed that his mode of thought represented a productive synthesis of the mutually exclusive poles of previous systems: "After the subjective idealism of the school of Kant, and the empiricism and sensualism of that of Locke, have been developed and their last possible results exhausted, no new combination is in my opinion possible but the union of these two systems by centering them both in a vast and powerful eclecticism."[43] Eclecticism thus furnished a bridge between the prevailing empiricism and German idealist philosophy by drawing on elements of both and by stressing the ability of the individual to recognize truth intuitively in its various appearances. Like the Scottish commonsense school, it was an attempt to temper the claim of the empiricists—that all information comes to us from without—by positing certain innate and intuitive powers in the mind.

Emerson was also reading Cousin in the 1830s (he owned several of Cousin's works and referred to him frequently in his letters and Jour-

---

42. Quoted in Walter Leighton, *French Philosophers and American Transcendentalism* (Charlottesville: University Press of Virginia, 1908), p. 27.

43. Victor Cousin, *Introduction to the History of Philosophy* (Boston: Hilliard, Gray, Little, and Wilkins, 1832), p. 414.

nal),[44] so that when Thoreau moved back to Concord and began to cultivate his friendship with the older man in 1837 they shared this intellectual interest. They continued to read the works of the Eclectic historians of philosophy during the ensuing years, especially in Gérando's *Histoire Comparée des Systèmes de Philosophie*. The influence of French Eclecticism on Transcendentalism has never been thoroughly explored or assessed,[45] but it seems quite clear that it provided Thoreau and others of his generation with much of the intellectual underpinning of the movement and offered a stepping stone to the bolder pronouncements of the Germans and their chief proponents in English, Coleridge and Carlyle. Emerson R. Marks has cogently summarized Cousin's significance to Transcendentalism as "a purveyor of German transcendental philosophy, in lucid and simplifying French, to Americans put off by . . . the dialectical intricacies of the original texts."[46]

With his interest in the new thought, his acquaintance with Brownson, and his reading in French Eclectic philosophy, Thoreau was well prepared to read the manifesto of American Transcendentalism, Emerson's *Nature*, during his senior year in college, and circumstantial evidence at least suggests that it impressed him deeply. He withdrew it from the library of the Institute of 1770 in April 1837 and again in June. He may have acquired his own copy at this time, and later in the summer he bought a copy as a graduation gift for a friend.[47] More significant, ideas from this new vein of reading begin to appear in his college writing. The theme of May 5, 1837, "Common Reasons," for example, begins with a quotation from Turgot that Emerson had used in *Nature*: "He that has never doubted the existence of matter, may be assured he has no aptitude for metaphysical studies." In the same essay, Thoreau makes the Emersonian distinction between Nature and Spirit, and paraphrases the famous injunction in the last paragraph of *Nature*—"Build, therefore, your own world"—by saying of the philos-

44. See, for example, Walter Harding, *Emerson's Library* (Charlottesville: University Press of Virginia, 1967), pp. 70–71, and *The Journals and Miscellaneous Notebooks of Ralph Waldo Emerson*, ed. William H. Gilman et al., 16 vols. (Cambridge: The Belknap Press of Harvard University Press, 1960–81), 5:458–459, 459–460; 6:355. (Further citations of Emerson's Journals are to this edition and are abbreviated as JMN with volume and page number.)

45. But see Leighton, *French Philosophers and American Transcendentalism*; Georges Joyaux, "Victor Cousin and American Transcendentalism," 1955, rpt. in Brian Barbour, ed., *American Transcendentalism: An Anthology of Criticism* (South Bend: University of Notre Dame Press, 1973), pp. 125–138; and Emerson R. Marks, "Victor Cousin and Emerson," in Myron Simon and Thornton H. Parks, eds., *Transcendentalism and Its Legacy* (Ann Arbor: University of Michigan Press, 1967), pp. 63–86.

46. Marks, "Victor Cousin and Emerson," p. 65.

47. Cameron, "Thoreau Discovers Emerson," p. 328; Harding, *Days*, p. 60.

opher that "he builds for himself, in fact, a new world" (EEM, 101–103).

In early June, in the essay "Barbarities of Civilized States," Thoreau adopts Emerson's definition of art (as the mixture of man's will with nature) in saying of art that man "mingles his will with the unchanged essences around him." In the same essay he employs the expression "Not Me" to stand for nature as opposed to mind or self-consciousness, following both Emerson and Cousin (EEM, 105–110). Thoreau's commencement address, "The Commercial Spirit of the Times," may serve as a final example of the shift in both his vocabulary and his views of man's nature and destiny. In it he sounds a note anticipatory of *Walden*, suggesting that men might reverse the biblical ratio and labor one day out of seven, reserving the other six for "the sabbath of the affections and the soul," during which they would "drink in the soft influences and sublime revelations of Nature" (EEM, 117). These ideas, that man is destined to some higher end than appears in his everyday world and that the way to realize this end lies through the contemplation of nature, show how rapidly and deeply Emersonian thought took root in Thoreau. Still, as Gruber points out, the faith expressed in the address about man's ability to harmonize his material and spiritual needs reflects at the same time Thoreau's debt to Orestes Brownson's *New Views*.[48] If Thoreau was not confirmed in his Transcendental views by the time he left Harvard, his conversion would be complete within a relatively short time. He moved back to Concord after graduation, took up schoolteaching, and began to cultivate his friendship with Emerson. Soon, under the older man's influence, Thoreau would be reading more regularly in the traditional sources of inspiration for Transcendentalists: lyric poetry, ancient and modern idealistic philosophical thought, and Oriental scriptures.

Thoreau's Harvard reading had helped to define and sharpen interests that he would continue to pursue, some of them for the rest of his life. Three of his principal areas of concentration, in fact—classical literature, English poetry, and the new views of contemporary thinkers—would furnish the basis for his first attempts to write for publication during the years following his graduation. At the same time, other of his mature interests had not yet germinated by the time he left college. The most important of these are natural history, the history of early American discovery and exploration, and North American Indians, although he did read a good many travel books—as indeed he would throughout his life—that touched upon these subjects peripherally. Additionally, and somewhat surprisingly, considering his later

48. Gruber, "Education," pp. 193–194.

distaste for fiction, he read a fair amount of it in college too, though here again his taste was toward the historical and the native: Irving, Cooper, Timothy Flint, and Lydia Maria Child.[49]

Perhaps of equal importance to the works that Thoreau read at Harvard were the habits of reading, note taking, and conceptualizing that he developed there. The surviving charging records of the libraries of the college and of his literary society reveal him to have been a regular and frequent borrower of books (withdrawing over eighty volumes during his senior year, for example).[50] Moreover, he developed the habit in college of keeping notebooks of his reading, copying out extracts from works that interested him and brief passages that he might quote in his own writings. One of these college notebooks, which he called the "Index rerum," was indexed alphabetically by subject and also contained a catalogue of his personal library, to which he added titles as he acquired new books. He would continue (albeit with some interruptions) this practice of keeping extracts from his reading for the rest of his life, until he had accumulated more than sixteen manuscript volumes of such notes. The changing contents of these notebooks over the course of his career provide a kind of shorthand notation of shifts in his reading patterns and intellectual interests. The notebooks of the Harvard years, however, are conventional commonplace books, mostly filled with quotable bits of prose and verse from eminent writers, and give little hint of Thoreau's mature style or the interests he would develop over the years. His training and his tastes, in fact, so far as they can be inferred from the record of his reading, fitted him rather well for his first professional pursuits in the years to come as a schoolteacher with high but unfocused ambitions to become a literary man.

49. Cameron, "Books Thoreau Borrowed from Harvard College Library" and "Thoreau Discovers Emerson."

50. Ibid.

2

The Early
Literary Career

Transcendental Apprenticeship, 1837–1844

DURING THE YEARS after his graduation from college, Thoreau grappled with the problem of vocation and felt his way tentatively toward a life in letters. Getting a living was never really a practical problem for him, for he could always (and indeed often did) work at the family pencil and graphite business, which gradually improved despite the economic hard times of the late thirties and early forties. The greater challenge than poverty was success, for he might easily have become prosperous by applying himself consistently rather than intermittently to this work. But the traditional professions open to college graduates—law, the church, business, medicine—failed to interest him, and there was very little of a saleable or even publishable nature he was prepared to write at age twenty-one: His proclivities and training equipped him to be a fair classical scholar and reader of English poetry but little else. And Thoreau was probably too independent, too tinged with Transcendental ideas, and too provincial to make any headway in the literary circles of Boston or New York, as his brief sojourn in the latter city a few years later would demonstrate.

He turned, naturally enough, to the remaining profession traditionally followed by Harvard graduates and practiced by all three of his siblings: teaching school. He first taught briefly in the Concord public school, choosing to resign after a few weeks rather than ferule the students, and then, with his brother John, conducted the Concord Academy from 1838 to 1841. The demanding work of keeping a school was a retarding influence on Thoreau's own reading and writing, and it was not until John's health forced the brothers to close the school in 1841 that Thoreau's reading and literary activity began to gather momentum again. Meanwhile, the founding of *The Dial* in 1840 and his growing intimacy with Emerson gave him an outlet and some direction and stimulus to his rather vague literary ambitions.

Opportunities for study were more limited in Concord at this time than they would later be. The town had no public library yet, only the Concord Social Library of fewer than a thousand volumes. The Fitchburg Railroad, linking Concord to Boston, would not be built for several years, so travel to libraries in the metropolis—later a regular practice for Thoreau—was inconvenient. He depended for the most part on his own and his family's small collection of books, the slender resources of the Social Library, and especially and most importantly on the library of his new friend Emerson. With characteristic generosity, Emerson gave the young schoolteacher access to his books, undoubtedly the finest collection of literature, philosophy, history, and religion in Concord, and even borrowed books for him from the library of the Boston Athenaeum.[1] Under these conditions, Thoreau seems for a time not to have kept up the habit that he had developed in college of making extracts from and careful records of his reading, and it is only from the surviving pages of his early Journal that we can glean any indication of what he was reading at this time.

Generally, this post-college reading tended to extend and develop interests that he had begun to cultivate at Harvard. Foremost among these interests during the fall of 1837 was Goethe, whose *Wilhelm Meister's Apprenticeship* he had read in Carlyle's translation the previous summer during his last term in college, prompted in all probability by Longfellow's enthusiastic lectures on modern German literature. Thoreau now read Goethe in the original, borrowing volumes from Emerson, who owned a fifty-five-volume German edition and who was himself reading and translating Goethe at this time.[2] Thoreau read *Torquato Tasso, Iphigenie auf Taurus*, and *Die Italiänische Reise* that fall, probably in part to keep up and improve his German as well as to acquaint himself with Goethe. His commentary on Goethe in *A Week on the Concord and Merrimack Rivers* faults him for too exclusively regarding life from the artist's vantage point, but Thoreau seems to have been impressed by the fidelity and sensitivity of Goethe's descriptions of his travels in the *Italiänische Reise*, praise that may mark an influence on his own interest in travel writing that was to develop in a few years (PJ 1.6–30; WE, 325–330). It is also possible that Goethe's ideas about the metamorphosis of plants caught Thoreau's

---

1. See Harding, *Emerson's Library*, and Kenneth Walter Cameron, *Ralph Waldo Emerson's Reading* (Hartford: Transcendental Books, 1962). The latter lists Emerson's borrowings from the Boston Athenaeum as well as from other libraries, and Thoreau can frequently be found to be reading a book after Emerson withdrew it. See, for example, Thoreau's reading of the *Laws of Menu* (n. 5, below).

2. Harding, *Emerson's Library*, p. 118; on October 27, for example, Emerson comments on *Torquato Tasso* (JMN 5.415), and Thoreau quotes from the same work on October 26 (PJ 1.6–7).

attention at this time. The *Italiänische Reise* describes Goethe's search for the "protoplant" (*Urpflanze*), an underlying form that would explain the principles of vegetation, and records his excitement upon intuiting that this underlying form was in actuality the leaf.[3] In his Journal for December 1837—at the same time that he is reading *Die Italiänische Reise*—Thoreau speculates in a Goethean fashion on the fundamental law governing ice crystallization and vegetation:

> It struck me that these ghost leaves [of hoarfrost] and the green ones whose forms they assume, were the creatures of the same law. It could not be in obedience to two several laws, that the vegetable juices swelled gradually into the perfect leaf on the one hand, and the crystalline particles trooped to their standard in the same admirable order on the other. (PJ 1.15–16)

Several years would pass before Thoreau would turn his attention seriously to the underlying laws of natural phenomena, but he was acquainted this early, through Goethe, with some of the general ideas of German *Naturphilosophie*.

Much of his other reading from 1837 to 1839 also suggests at least in part an effort to continue and to build upon his training in languages. He read and translated occasionally in the Journal passages from the *Iliad*, Virgil's *Eclogues*, Plutarch's *Morals*, Greek verses purportedly by Anacreon, and Aeschylus's *Prometheus Bound* and *Seven Against Thebes*. His classical training offered him a sort of bridge to writing for publication, too, for his first printed essay would be on the Latin satirist Aulus Persius Flaccus in the inaugural issue of *The Dial* (July 1840), and he would complete translations of Aeschylus and Pindar for the magazine during ensuing years. Not only were the classics a lifelong interest, but translating them was a literary activity that harmonized with his occupation, since he was responsible for the Greek and Latin curriculum of the Concord Academy. His interest in the English literature of earlier periods, on the other hand, is only sporadically noticeable, in quotations from Sharon Turner's *History of the Anglo-Saxons* and occasional allusions to Milton and earlier English poets (PJ 1.1–100).

Early in 1840, however, Thoreau's reading—at least the record of it that he left—and his literary activity began to increase, largely as a result, one suspects, of his growing intimacy with Emerson and the inauguration of *The Dial*. The two most prominent emphases of his reading at this time were a renewed interest in the history of philoso-

---

3. *Goethe's Travels in Italy: Together with His Second Residence in Rome and Fragments of Italy* (London: George Bell and Sons, 1885), pp. 387–390.

phy and the beginning of what would become an intense interest in Oriental thought. Both of these interests reflect the Transcendentalists' eclectic preferences, and both would ultimately be related to the character and contents of *The Dial* and Thoreau's involvement with it as contributor and editor.

The philosophical or quasi-philosophical works that he read between the spring and fall of 1840 included Ralph Cudworth's *True Intellectual System of the Universe*, Gérando's *Histoire Comparée des Systèmes de Philosophie*, and Fénelon's *Abrégé de la Vie des Plus Illustres Philosophes de l'Antiquité* (PJ 1.121–180). All these works reinforced, to a young man tinctured with Transcendentalism, the philosophical idealism and eclecticism that Thoreau had been exposed to in college. Individually and in sum, they offer no sustained or systematic analysis of any school of philosophy, but rather stress the timeless thoughts and wisdom of philosophers of various ages. Gérando's work was an extension of that of Cousin and Jouffroy, which Thoreau had read in college, and although Cudworth's tome intended to demonstrate, in the words of its subtitle, how "the reason and philosophy of atheism [could be] confuted" by a close examination of philosophy, Thoreau doubtless read it as Emerson did, not for its Christian apologia but as "a magazine of quotations, of extraordinary ethical sentences, the shining summits of ancient philosophy."[4]

All three of these works were in Emerson's library, and Thoreau's reading of them at this time suggests that his friendship with the older man had ripened to the stage of sharing not only literary but also philosophical and ethical concerns. Unlike Emerson, however, Thoreau seldom extended his reading of philosophy to original texts (although Emerson himself was by no means a carefully systematic reader of philosophy). Thoreau tended to know philosophy through secondary sources such as these, and his interest in the discipline always tended toward a sort of "practical teleology": Although he was, like the other Transcendentalists, by instinct and training a philosophical idealist, he was especially concerned with how actually to live life according to the dictates of the higher law. He had little appetite for philosophical systems or argument as such, and, as Ellery Channing aptly remarked in his memoir of Thoreau, "metaphysics was his aversion." As he was later to put it in *Walden*, "To be a philosopher is not merely to have subtle thoughts, nor even to found a school, but so to love wisdom as to live according to its dictates, a life of simplicity, independence, magnanimity, and trust. It is to solve some of the problems of life, not only theoretically, but practically" (WA, 14–15).

4. JMN 9.265.

The ancient philosophers provided a heroic ideal, in much the same way that Homer did. The accounts of their lives in Fénelon's work, for example, stressed their simplicity of life, renunciation of wealth, and devotion to truth and learning. Like history, philosophy was always tending to become metamorphosed into biography for the Transcendentalists, as they searched the past for examples of human greatness and potential. Thoreau's notion of the ideal relation between philosophy and life is perhaps best represented by the Stoics—again, as much through the example of their lives as through their doctrines—but except for such snippets as he was exposed to in college (in Cicero's *De Officiis*, for example) and in this post-college period of reading in the history of philosophy where he comments approvingly on Zeno (PJ 1.26–27), he seems to have had relatively little formal or systematic knowledge of this school of philosophers.

Thoreau's reading of Oriental scriptures and philosophy also began at about this time and had a similarly ethical and practical cast. Emerson probably played a role in stimulating this interest, too: He had read and been impressed by the *Institutes of Hindu Law* (or *Laws of Menu*, as they were generally known), and near the end of July 1840 he again withdrew the book from the library of the Boston Athenaeum and lent it to Thoreau, who in August began referring to it in his Journal and making longer extracts from it.[5] Emerson also owned or acquired other orientalia that Thoreau read at this time, including *The Hĕĕtōpădēs of Vĕĕshnŏŏ-Sărmā*, *The Gûlistân* of Sa'dī, and Ockley's *History of the Saracens*. On his own, Thoreau read Murray's history of British India.[6] These titles represent only a smattering of topics on Near and Far Eastern cultures and thought, of course, and Thoreau would do little systematic reading in this field until a few years later. Still, it was another interest that he cultivated with Emerson, and one that would soon have tangible results in the pages of *The Dial*.

Otherwise, Thoreau continued to read widely and eclectically in 1840: essays by Bacon and Sir Thomas Browne, Gibbon's *Memoirs*, Virgil's *Georgics*, the *Odes* of Horace, Plutarch's *Morals*, and, most singular and significant in this otherwise mostly literary and classical list, Charles Lyell's *Principles of Geology* (PJ 1.107–213 passim). Lyell's landmark study was the first work of contemporary hard science Thoreau left evidence of reading, and its importance was not only for uniformitarian geology but also for the biological sciences, estab-

---

5. Cameron, *Emerson's Reading*, p. 25; PJ 1.173; his longer extracts are in his "Miscellaneous Extracts" commonplace book (NNPM, MA 594).

6. Harding, *Emerson's Library*, pp. 301, 236; Cameron, *Emerson's Reading*, p. 25; PJ 1.177.

lishing with what appeared to be incontrovertible proof the great age of the earth—an age to be measured at least in millions rather than the biblical thousands of years—and thus preparing the way for the idea of the gradual change of species through evolution. Whether or not Thoreau sensed the significance of Lyell's conclusions at this time, he began tentatively with this work to lay a foundation for himself in contemporary natural science.

The turn toward a somewhat more focused and intensive reading in particular fields increased in 1841, made possible and prompted in part by two related events that gave Thoreau a great deal more time to pursue his literary studies. On the first of April the Thoreau brothers closed their school, and on the fourteenth of the same month Henry took up residence with the Emersons in the capacity of general handyman.[7] The demands on his time now were fairly light, he had free access to Emerson's library, and not surprisingly he began once more to keep fairly extensive records of his reading. He also turned his energies toward a large-scale reading and literary project, while continuing to think of himself as an aspiring poet and reading selectively in philosophy and Oriental thought.

Already, in December 1840, he had begun to keep a dated list of his reading, and in the same month he began a new commonplace book—the first he had kept since college—in which to make extracts from his reading.[8] The reading itself was still largely eclectic and miscellaneous—ranging from history and biography to natural history, philosophy, and travel literature—but a pattern of increasing interest in contemporary literary issues begins also to be evident. The most obvious signpost of this development is a marked interest in Coleridge's prose writings. A year or so earlier Thoreau had looked into the *Table Talk*, but now between January and April 1841 he read *Aids to Reflection*, *The Statesman's Manual*, and *Confessions of an Inquiring Spirit*.[9] *Aids to Reflection* was especially significant for its careful exposition of the difference between Understanding and Reason, perhaps the key epistemological concept of the Romantic age. The edition that Thoreau is most likely to have read, the one edited by James Marsh in 1829, was

---

7. Harding, *Days*, pp. 87–88, 127–128.

8. The dated reading list was kept from December 5, 1840, to June 3, 1841. It is in the collection of the Huntington Library (HM 13201) and has been transcribed and printed by Kenneth Walter Cameron, "Ungathered Thoreau Reading Lists," pp. 368–371. Thoreau's new commonplace book was also probably begun in December 1840 and was kept until 1848 or 1849; it is currently in the Library of Congress and has been reprinted in a facsimile edition by Kenneth Walter Cameron as *Thoreau's Literary Notebook in the Library of Congress* (Hartford: Transcendental Books, 1964).

9. PJ 1.97, 220, 230; Cameron, "Ungathered Thoreau Reading Lists," p. 368.

one of the most important and influential documents of American Transcendentalism, containing a long preliminary essay by the editor that calls particular attention to this distinction. In addition to providing himself with this background in the chief English exponent of the German philosophical thought that ultimately provided the underpinning of Transcendentalism, Thoreau also dipped into George Ripley's contemporary anthology, *Foreign Standard Literature*, and read Tocqueville's recently published *Democracy in America*. He even displayed what may have been a touch of pride in being especially *au courant*, noting in his reading list that in March and April he read Emerson's *Essays* (First Series) and Carlyle's *On Heroes, Hero-Worship, and the Heroic in History* in proof sheets before publication.[10]

By early 1841, then, Thoreau's grounding in or at least exposure to the major tributaries of Transcendentalism was fairly thorough. Chiefly under Emerson's guidance he had read selections from the idealistic tradition of ancient philosophy, Oriental scriptures, modern eclectic philosophy, Anglicized articulations of German Transcendental thought, and contemporary essayists like Carlyle and Emerson himself. Thoreau had begun this course of reading on his own in college and was primed for it, so to speak, through his acquaintance with Orestes Brownson in 1836. Nevertheless, Emerson's own habits of voluminous and eclectic reading, his impressive library, and his kindness in sharing his books and his thoughts with Thoreau made a powerful impression on the younger man's training and cast of mind.

Beginning in the second half of 1841, however, Thoreau's major reading project took him away from this contemporary focus and back to an interest that he had begun to cultivate at Harvard in the English poetry of earlier periods, especially the fourteenth through the seventeenth centuries. Emerson played a major role in this project, too, but the enterprise seems to have had its origin in Thoreau's desire to turn the freedom of his situation at Emerson's house to some literary account. From the fall of 1841 until shortly after his return to Concord from New York at the end of 1843, he read, copied extensively, and made notes and commentaries on English poetry and verse drama, and the surviving evidence suggests that he envisioned a major literary project of some kind—a book, probably, or a series of articles or lectures—on the subject.[11]

The project had its origins that fall when Emerson lent Thoreau one

---

10. Cameron, "Ungathered Thoreau Reading Lists," p. 368.

11. The account of this project that follows in the text is based on Sattelmeyer, "Thoreau's Projected Work on the English Poets," pp. 239–257, where more extensive documentation may be found.

of his commonplace books containing selections from English poetry (which Emerson used many years later in compiling his own anthology of English verse, *Parnassus*), and Thoreau copied about twenty pages of these quite brief selections into one of his own commonplace books. Later that fall the project grew to a more ambitious scale, for Emerson advanced Thoreau fifteen dollars "in account of his book," as the lender noted, in order for him to go to Cambridge for two weeks, survey the Harvard Library holdings in English poetry, and copy out more extracts. Thoreau obtained a special library privilege by telling President Quincy that he was "engaged in a work . . . for which the aid of [the] Library is requisite," and prevailed upon his friend Charles Stearns Wheeler and another person named Bartlett to check out additional books for him. He bought new blank books, made extensive bibliographical listings of poets and editions, and copied out more than two hundred pages of extracts. He continued the work of transcription and commentary after his return to Concord in December and January, but then only sporadically during 1842. His brother's death in January left him quite ill and despondent for several months, and later in the year he was busy with other literary projects: "Natural History of Massachusetts" and "A Walk to Wachusett."

His second intensive period of work on the English poetry project took place during his sojourn on Staten Island in 1843 while he was tutoring William Emerson's son and trying to write for and (more improbably) get paid by New York magazines. He was largely unsuccessful in this effort, but the experience gave him an opportunity to cultivate libraries and librarians once again. "I read a good deal and am pretty well known in the libraries of New York," he wrote to his family in October, referring to the New York Society Library and the Mercantile Library (COR, 141). The charging records of these libraries do not survive to record all his borrowings, but we know that he discovered Ossian and Francis Quarles, both important to his English poetry project and did other reading in seventeenth-century poetry. His Staten Island Journal is rich in commentary on these poets that suggests critical headnotes or summaries that might precede selections in an anthology.

The precise nature of his collection of English poetry cannot be determined, however, since Thoreau never actually completed the project. It can be said that during this period he read and studied earlier English literature most intensely, and, as the range of his allusion in later works suggests, he read both widely and deeply in major and minor poets and dramatists from the Middle Ages to the end of the seventeenth century. It was this period in his life that he describes in *Walden*, for example, when he speaks of attempting to read through

Chalmers's twenty-one-volume anthology of English poetry "without skipping" (and falling asleep, perhaps forgivably, over Davenant's "Gondibert") (WA, 259). Given the sort of project that he seems to have contemplated, his reading was necessarily far more systematic and intensive in this field than in other of his interests early in his career, and would be matched in scope later in his life only by his study of American Indians, early American history and exploration, and natural history. It would be impractical, in fact, even to attempt to list his reading in English poetry, for the task would involve reproducing the tables of contents not only of Chalmers's massive anthology but also of numerous other collections, editions, and anthologies. (In the Bibliographical Catalogue the editions and anthologies he is known to have read are listed, but only those poets and poems that he quotes directly either in his manuscript notebooks or in his published works are cited.)

Of particular interest to him in this project, however, in addition to such standard authors as Chaucer, Spenser, Shakespeare (whose works he did not need to copy, since there was no scarcity of accessible editions), Jonson, and Milton, were earlier and often less polished works sometimes peripheral to the main development of English verse: Lydgate, such early Scottish poets as Gawin Douglas, Francis Quarles, and the Robin Hood ballads, for example. He also admired James McPherson's Ossian poems, a group of mostly "recreated" ancient Gaelic sagas, and the more scholarly collection of Thomas Percy, *Reliques of Ancient English Poetry*.

What led him to these works, one suspects, was the Transcendental conviction that the most powerful poetic utterance would tend to be located in the rude and primitive beginnings of a poetic tradition. Thoreau generally assented to the theory of art and language sketched by Emerson in *Nature* which affirms that "as you go back in history, language becomes more picturesque, until its infancy, when it is all poetry; or, all spiritual facts are represented by natural symbols."[12] The earliest poets, then, are presumably closest to this magical moment of correspondence between nature and spirit, and, like children, come down to us trailing the clouds of this former glory. Similarly, folk poetry and ballads are also capable of this power. The practical upshot of this theory would lead to a preference for the precursors over the culminators of a poetic tradition, and certainly it led Thoreau to esteem at least in principle (he complained privately to the Journal about

12. *The Collected Works of Ralph Waldo Emerson*, vol. 1, *Nature, Addresses, and Lectures*, introductions and notes by Robert E. Spiller, text established by Alfred R. Ferguson (Cambridge: The Belknap Press of Harvard University Press, 1971), p. 19.

reading "many weary pages of antiquated Scotch") the pre-Chaucerians, early Scottish poets, folk ballads, and the knotty and crabbed verse of Quarles and some other seventeenth-century poets (PJ 1.343). As he expressed the idea himself in a lecture, "Homer. Ossian. Chaucer," delivered to the Concord Lyceum in November 1843 at the end of his work on early poetry, "We cannot escape the impression, that the Muse has stooped a little in her flight when we come to the literature of civilized eras" (EEM, 162).

In a sort of corollary interest to the English poets project during this same time, Thoreau was fascinated with Sir Walter Raleigh. Raleigh was one of the Elizabethan poets whom he most admired, to be sure, and there are numerous extracts from Raleigh's work among his collections of copied verse. But his interest in Raleigh transcended his interest in the poetry, for Raleigh was above all an example of the heroic personality to which Thoreau was so attracted as a young man. Praising him as a soldier, scholar, discoverer, politician, poet, and historian, and even doing his best to sympathize with Raleigh's endeavors as a courtier, Thoreau found in him an embodiment of the sort of well-rounded and robust heroism that he had praised abstractly in his early essay "The Service." He read Raleigh's works (including the *History of the World*) and his biographers, delivered a lecture on him before the Concord Lyceum on February 8, 1843, and revised the lecture (probably shortly thereafter) for an essay that was not published during his life but appears now in the collection of his early and miscellaneous essays (EEM, 178–218).

After concentrating on his English poets project from late 1841 to early 1842, and again in 1843 while he had access to good libraries in New York, Thoreau gradually lost interest in the work. Not coincidentally, perhaps, he stopped thinking of verse as his own primary mode of literary expression at about the same time. And despite his deep and abiding interest in English poetry, he seems from the first to have had a certain amount of ambivalence about collecting and editing poetry as a literary enterprise. In Cambridge in November 1841, at the very beginning of his work, armed with blank notebooks and supported by Emerson's loan, he confided to the Journal that while "running over the catalogue, and collating and selecting" he felt "oppressed by an inevitable sadness" at the gulf between the spirit of poetry he imagined and the "dry and dusty volumes" he was poring over (PJ 1.337–338). For whatever reasons (and they may be as simple as a slackening of interest or as complicated as an unconscious resentment of Emerson's efforts to guide his career), Thoreau gradually gave up work on the project and turned toward both the reading and writing of prose instead.

If Emerson had not been successful in helping Thoreau to make a collection of English poetry in 1841, he was shortly to have better luck in steering his young friend's reading in directions that would help him begin to define his interests as a writer. Early in 1842 Emerson took over the editorship of *The Dial* from a tired and discouraged Margaret Fuller, and he was willing (though reluctantly) to do so perhaps not only because he cared for the success of the journal but also because he could rely on Thoreau for editorial assistance and regular contributions; in fact, Emerson soon referred to Henry as "private secretary to the President of the Dial."[13] The immediate effect of this change on Thoreau was twofold. First, Emerson relied on him for help in making up the "Ethnical Scriptures" department of the magazine, a regular feature that printed excerpts from the religious and ethical writings of other cultures and ages in each issue. Consequently, Thoreau began to extend and amplify his reading of Oriental scriptures and philosophy, and a series of transcripts in his Journal from the *Institutes of Hindu Law* was probably made with a view toward the selections from this work printed in the January 1843 issue of *The Dial* (PJ 1.407–425; EEM, 380–382). Later "Ethnical Scriptures" columns for 1843 and early 1844—"The Sayings of Confucius," "Chinese Four Books" (Confucius and Mencius), and selections from Hermes Trismegistus and the *Gûlistân* of Sa'dî—are of uncertain origin, though Thoreau probably played at least some part in their selection and later demonstrated a knowledge of most of the works selected.[14]

The other and divergent path that his reading took at Emerson's urging was toward natural history. In April 1842, shortly after assuming the editorial reins, Emerson asked Thoreau to prepare a review of a recently published four-volume survey of the flora and fauna of Massachusetts.[15] The result was his first natural history essay, "Natural History of Massachusetts," in the July 1842 issue. Although the essay is in part culled from sketches of natural history in the early Journal, it had apparently not occurred to Thoreau to turn his amateur interest in nature to literary account until Emerson commissioned this review. The essay itself is largely a collection of miscellaneous vignettes of local natural history that bears only the slimmest of relations to the volumes purportedly being reviewed (Thoreau was not professionally qualified

---

13. *The Letters of Ralph Waldo Emerson*, ed. Ralph L. Rusk, 6 vols. (New York: Columbia University Press, 1939), 3.47.

14. See EEM, 382, 383, 385–386, 390, for evidence of Thoreau's participation; but compare Joel Myerson, *The New England Transcendentalists and the "Dial"* (Rutherford, N.J.: Fairleigh Dickinson University Press, 1980), pp. 307–308, who attributes the selections primarily to Emerson.

15. Emerson, *Letters*, 3.47.

to review them in a rigorous way, anyway), but from this modest beginning grew one of the major interests—indeed almost the preoccupation—of his maturity. In 1842 and 1843, however, Thoreau was still uncertain about the direction that his literary career (if he was in fact to have one) would take. He was reading English poetry, trying out various kinds of prose compositions and lectures on literary and miscellaneous topics, and helping unofficially to edit *The Dial*. It would not be until the late 1840s that he would actually begin to record his observations of nature and to study natural history systematically.

Another disappointment to professional ambitions was his brief attempt to write for the New York literary market from May to November of 1843. Living on the edge of New York City, as one might expect, had the effect of making him long ardently for the woods and rivers of Concord, and indeed his best writing that summer was "A Winter Walk," an essay describing in careful detail the sensory and imaginative pleasures of a day's ramble in the environs of his home town. The chief impact of his reading may also have been to make plain to him what he was not suited for. He did his last concerted reading in English poetry in New York, and he also reviewed a utopian Fourierist tract by J. A. Etzler, *The Paradise Within the Reach of All Men*, for the *Democratic Review*. His critique of this fantasy, which promised a sort of new mechanical Eden through labor-saving devices, found Thoreau challenging the communitarian basis of most reform movements of the 1840s and anticipating in a way his reform community of one at Walden two years later:

> Alas! this is the crying sin of the age, this want of faith in the prevalence of a man. Nothing can be affected but by one man. He who wants help wants everything. . . . We must first succeed alone, that we may enjoy our success together. . . . In this matter of reforming the world, we have little faith in corporations; not thus was it first formed. (RP, 42)

His New York experiment ended in late November 1843, when Thoreau returned home for Thanksgiving and apparently decided that there was no point in returning to continue what had been fruitless efforts to earn a living by his pen. Back in Concord for good, but now without any obvious literary prospects, he was again without access to good libraries. Even the faithful *Dial*, which had at least printed his early work, was about to cease publication (the April 1844 number was the last). He would not keep (or at least would not preserve) a regular Journal or record of his reading for the next eighteen months, and he was probably busier with his hands than with his head for a time, working long hours for the pencil business and helping his father build a new family house. The record of his reading does not resume until he declared his personal independence day and moved into his cabin at Walden Pond on July 4, 1845.

Walden and Beyond, 1845–1849

F O R the next several years, Thoreau's life was peripatetic: In 1844, having recently returned from New York, he helped his family build and move into a new house on the outskirts of town; in 1845 he built and then lived for two years in his cabin at Walden Pond; in 1847 and 1848 he lived at the Emersons' again while Waldo was in Europe on an extended lecture tour; and in the summer of 1848 he moved back to the family home for good, though the next year there would be still another house to renovate before the Thoreaus settled permanently in 1850 in their Main Street residence in Concord.[16] These were the busiest and quantitatively the most productive years of Thoreau's literary career, too, for between 1844 and 1849 he wrote and published *A Week on the Concord and Merrimack Rivers*, worked through two or three drafts of *Walden*, and thought of it as virtually ready to print by the time *A Week* appeared. He also wrote and published long articles on his first wilderness excursion to Maine, on the writings of Thomas Carlyle, and "Resistance to Civil Government," the essay on the duties of the individual to himself and the state that would become widely influential in the twentieth century as "Civil Disobedience."

Compared both to his apprentice years and to his later career, however, the period from 1844 to 1849 furnishes relatively little in the way of evidence of Thoreau's reading habits. Part of the scarcity of the record is actually a consequence of the accelerated pace of his literary activities during this time. Not only did writing and the various manual tasks that he was performing—building and remodeling houses and working in the pencil factory—consume much of the time and energy that he might normally have devoted to reading, but this ambitious program of literary projects also quite literally consumed much of the Journal in which Thoreau customarily left allusions to his reading. No Journal survives for nearly all of 1844 and the first half of 1845, and likewise nearly all of 1847 and the first half of 1848 are virtual blanks in the record. The Journal was probably kept only irregularly from 1844 to 1849, and such volumes as have survived are fragmentary, as Thoreau characteristically removed leaves from them for insertion in drafts of literary works in progress.[17] The surviving por-

16. Harding, *Days*, pp. 177–178, 221, 263.
17. PJ 2, "Historical Introduction," pp. 445–447.

tions of the Journal and the literary works themselves, however, do provide sufficient information to sketch at least inferentially the developments in his intellectual and literary interests that his reading patterns mark.

By his own testimony, Thoreau did less reading than usual during the summer of 1845 at Walden: "I did not read books the first summer; I hoed beans" (WA, 111). His only reading, he says, consisted of an occasional passage from the *Iliad*, which he kept open on his desk, and "one or two shallow books of travel" (p. 100). Although he may have thought these travel books shallow (at least for the rhetorical purposes of "Reading" in *Walden*), his reading of them was probably not entirely for purposes of escape or entertainment. He was about to begin writing a kind of travel book himself, by which he hoped to achieve some popular success as a writer. *A Week on the Concord and Merrimack Rivers*, to which he would devote most of his time during that first year, provides a convenient summary of the various tributaries of his reading at the time, since the book itself is a compendium of his early works and interests. But before these various interests that manifest themselves in *A Week* are considered, one other literary project with some significance for developments in Thoreau's career needs to be examined.

During the fall and winter of 1845–1846 Thoreau prepared a lecture on Thomas Carlyle that he delivered in Concord on February 6, 1846. He had known Carlyle's work since his college years, when he read *Sartor Resartus* and the translation of Goethe's *Wilhelm Meister's Apprenticeship*. During the early 1840s he kept in touch with Carlyle's work almost inevitably, since Emerson was so actively engaged in promoting and publishing his Scottish friend's work in America: On at least one occasion, for example, Emerson presented Thoreau with a copy of Carlyle's most recent book. But in 1845 Thoreau read and reread Carlyle intensively for his lecture and for a subsequent essay published in *Graham's Magazine* in 1847, concentrating on Carlyle's historical works *The French Revolution* and his recent edition of *Oliver Cromwell's Letters and Speeches*.[18]

Carlyle represented to Thoreau, as he remarks in the essay, "the hero, as literary man," and like many of his contemporaries he owed a good deal to Carlyle for making accessible and popularizing German thought and literature in the English-speaking world (EEM, 243). Nor was he above capitalizing on Carlyle's most popular pieces; the pas-

18. See Chapter 1 for evidence of his earlier reading of Carlyle, and PJ 2.187–226 passim for his reading of Carlyle in 1845–46.

sages on dress in "Economy" in *Walden*, for example, are clearly indebted to Carlyle's exposition of the philosophy of clothes in *Sartor Resartus*. But the chief influence of Carlyle was at a little lower layer, at the level of Thoreau's development of his mature voice and prose style.

During the second half of 1845, while he was working on the Carlyle lecture, Thoreau was beginning to compose passages in the Journal, based on his life at the pond, of personal belief and social criticism that would form the kernel of "Economy" and "Where I Lived and What I Lived For" in *Walden*. Though he did not begin to write *Walden* itself until somewhat later, a large proportion of the material in the first draft can be found in the fragmentary Journal of 1845–1846.[19] Many of these passages appear to be a response to and an imitation of the features of Carlyle's style that Thoreau found significant and praiseworthy, especially the adoption of a distinctive persona to unify and enliven diverse material, and the deliberate cultivation of a rhetoric of exaggeration. The vigor and force of Carlyle's style, achieved through his characteristic exaggeration and various mannerisms of emphasis, seemed remarkable to Thoreau, whose praise has about it a sense of self-discovery: "One wonders how so much, after all, was expressed in the old way, so much here depends upon the emphasis, tone, pronunciation, style, and spirit of the reading. No writer uses so profusely all the aids to intelligibility which the printer's art affords. You wonder how others had contrived to write so many pages without emphatic or italicised words, they are so expressive, so natural, so indispensable here, as if none had ever used the demonstrative pronouns demonstratively before" (EEM, 229). But these mannerisms and the strategy of deliberate exaggeration made Carlyle something more than the Tom Wolfe of Thoreau's generation, for there was a basis of moral and epistemological truth in the style, as Thoreau—using the trick himself—makes clear in defending it: "Exaggeration! was ever any virtue attributed to man without exaggeration: was ever any vice, without infinite exaggeration? . . . To a small man every greater is an exaggeration. He who cannot exaggerate is not qualified to utter truth. . . . Moreover, you must speak loud to those who are hard of hearing, and so you acquire a habit of shouting to those who are not" (EEM, 264–265).

One need only compare familiar passages from the early pages of *Walden* dating from this same time to glimpse Thoreau putting this theory and these devices into practice: "Talk of divinity in man! Look at the teamster on the highway, wending to market by day or night;

19. PJ 2, "Historical Introduction," p. 456.

does any divinity stir within him? His highest duty is to fodder and water his horses! What is his destiny to him compared with the shipping interests? Does not he drive for Squire Make-a-stir? How godlike, how immortal is he? See how he cowers and sneaks, how vaguely all the day he fears, not being immortal nor divine, but the slave and prisoner of his own opinion of himself, a fame won by his own deeds" (WA, 7). Thoreau was aware of the danger of falling under the influence of a style so distinctive and recognizable (having written "Carlyleish" in the margin next to a passage in his Journal as early as 1838), and he found fault with Carlyle for ultimately "indicat[ing] a depth . . . which he neglects to fathom" (PJ 1.34; EEM, 257). Still, the rhetorical verve and the distinctive—almost aggressive—insistence upon the first personness of the narrator in *Walden* may owe a great deal to Thoreau's immersion in Carlyle when the book was in its embryonic stage. Certainly Carlyle helped Thoreau to liberate his style from the decorum and polite diction that characterize his early work and reflect his training in eighteenth-century rhetorical principles at Harvard.

Thoreau's main literary activity during his first year at the pond, however, was the writing of *A Week on the Concord and Merrimack Rivers*. He had begun collecting material for the book a few years earlier (perhaps as early as 1840), and he would continue to work on it until late 1848 or very early 1849, but by July of 1846 it was complete enough for him to read portions of the manuscript to Emerson, who described it as though it were a finished book: "In a short time," he told Charles King Newcomb, "if Wiley & Putnam smile, you shall have Henry Thoreau's 'excursion on Concord & Merrimack rivers,' a seven days' voyage in as many chapters, pastoral as Isaak Walton, spicy as flagroot, broad & deep as Menu."[20]

A Week was Thoreau's first book, and (typical of first books) it expressed many ambitions and acknowledged many obligations. It was a travel narrative; a tribute—almost a pastoral elegy—to his brother John, the unnamed companion on the voyage; an anthology of Thoreau's own early writings; and an attempt to achieve the sort of synthesis of books, nature, and action that constituted the formative influences on the American Scholar as Emerson had described him to Thoreau's graduating class in 1837. It was also, following naturally from these impulses, a compendium of his reading to date, for the scholar's duty, according to Emerson again, was to be expressed "by

20. Emerson, *Letters*, 3.338; See WE, "Historical Introduction," pp. 433–500, for an account of the book's genesis.

preserving and communicating heroic sentiments, noble biographies, melodious verse, and the conclusions of history."[21]

Many of the areas of Thoreau's reading most prominently represented in *A Week* are those already well defined and developed in his early years—classical literature, English poetry, and Oriental thought—about which little need be said. The wealth of quotation from the English poets in the book represents a carryover from the earlier and more ambitious project on the same subject, and he began in *A Week* to develop his thinking on the Oriental scriptures into a sustained exposition of their virtues that included a fairly sharp critique of Christianity as commonly practiced. In particular, Thoreau added the *Bhăgvăt-Gēētā* to his store of Oriental reading in 1846, and wrote enthusiastically about it in his book, praising its "pure intellectuality" and observing sardonically that it "deserves to be read with reverence even by Yankees" (WE, 135–143).

One relatively new interest evident in *A Week* is history, especially the local and regional history of New England. Once Thoreau returned to Concord from his brief venture to New York at the end of 1843, he seems gradually to have become sensible of the richness of his native region, in much the same way that Faulkner, three-quarters of a century later, would discover the inexhaustible potential of his small corner of Mississippi after a series of early experiments and disappointments. Both *A Week* and *Walden* are suffused with a sense of New England history that enhances by contrast or complement the significance of present events and the undertakings of the protagonists. Thoreau's retelling of the Hannah Duston captivity narrative in *A Week*, for example, suggests a tragic dimension to the New England experience not often apparent in the book, and his description of early New England Indian and settlers' dwellings in *Walden* serves to sharpen his attack on the luxuries to which his contemporaries were wedded (WE, 320–323; WA, 29–30, 38–39).

The precise beginning of Thoreau's careful reading of American history cannot be dated with certainty, but it seems to have had its inception while he was living at Walden and to be roughly contemporaneous with his early work on both *A Week* and *Walden*. Allusions to New England history in his writings and the Journal are sparse before this time, but *A Week*, completed in the beginning of 1849, contained quotations from and fairly detailed references to some dozen or so histor-

21. *Nature, Addresses and Lectures*, p. 62. The definitive study of the composition and genesis of *A Week* is Linck C. Johnson, *Thoreau's Complex Weave: The Writing of "A Week on the Concord and Merrimack Rivers" with a Text of the First Draft* (Charlottesville: University Press of Virginia, 1986).

ical works ranging from town histories of Concord, Dunstable, and Haverhill to such classic firsthand accounts of early settlement as Edward Johnson's *Wonder-Working Providence*, Nathaniel Morton's *New-England's Memorial*, John Smith's "Description of New England," and the histories of John Winthrop and Thomas Hutchinson.[22] Thoreau did not reestablish his library privileges at Harvard until late 1849, and thereafter his charging records and manuscript notebooks furnish a quite comprehensive record of his reading in this area. Nevertheless, relying still on the Social Library's small collection and his own and his friends' books, Thoreau began to develop an interest in American history that would in the future carry him back to the age of exploration and discovery in North America and forward to a critical analysis of the historians of his own day.

Transcendental theory both hampered and encouraged this endeavor, conveying a conflicting message to the would-be historian about the value of his labor that is reflected in *A Week* by a certain ambivalence toward the subject. On the abstract and general level, history was suspect because it suggested a concentration on the past that Americans ought not to have. One of Emerson's signal achievements, after all, had been to assure his readers and listeners that to be born without an extensive history or rich traditions was actually a blessing and not a liability, a healthy condition of life in the New World that would be celebrated in Whitman's "Song of the Open Road," for instance. The well-known complaint that begins *Nature*—"Our age is retrospective"—was only true imaginatively (one could hardly imagine an age less "retrospective" than the Jacksonian) for a generation that wished to set itself above the mere writing of history. To discover the universal in the present moment was the Transcendentalists' aim, and Thoreau pays tribute to this ambition in *Walden* when he speaks of Time as "but the stream I go a-fishing in. . . . Its thin current slides away, but eternity remains" (p. 98). Or when he says of history in *A Week* that "critical acumen is exerted in vain to uncover the past; the *past* cannot be *presented*; we cannot know what we are not. But one veil hangs over past, present, and future, and it is the province of the historian to find out, not what was, but what is" (p. 155).

On the other hand, the literary nationalism that the Transcendentalists also espoused promoted the use of native materials and encouraged the development of American legends, heroes, historical events, and traditions in American literature. More important, "what is" in

22. See William Brennan, "An Index to Quotations in Thoreau's *A Week on the Concord and Merrimack Rivers*," in *Studies in the American Renaissance: 1980*, ed. Joel Myerson (Boston: G. K. Hall, 1980), pp. 259–290.

the most universal sense could only be recovered by the sort of detailed study of primary documents that enabled one to pierce the mask of historical difference and recover the timeless facts that characterized human life in whatever era. As there was ultimately no contradiction, as we shall see, between Thoreau's disparagement of travel and his own travel reading and travel writing, there was finally no contradiction between his orthodox skepticism about a reliance on the past and his increasingly antiquarian researches. To read (and eventually in *Cape Cod* to try to write) history transcendentally was the challenge, and the path to this end led him, predictably, toward the original documents, the first reports, the eyewitness accounts that were history as "what is" rather than history as the discipline of writing about or attempting to *present* the past.

In *A Week* much of the attention to the historical past of the region through which the travelers pass focuses naturally enough on the Indian wars of the seventeenth and eighteenth centuries. If there had ever been a heroic age in New England it was during this epoch, when men and women endured the hardships of primitive settlements, harsh climate, isolation, and years of bloody struggle with Indian foes. Thoreau quotes from Daniel Gookin's account of the Puritans' attempt to convert the Indians and narrates at some length the familiar stories told in the song "Lovewell's Fight" and the various accounts of the captivity and escape of Hannah Duston (WE, 80–83, 119–122, 320–324). A note of awe and surprise is present in all these accounts. Thoreau wonders that such monumental endeavors and conflicts could have taken place so recently in a landscape where in the present day he finds only peace and burgeoning commerce. He also wonders how it was with the Indians, who left no chroniclers of their story. "There is no journal to tell" of their experiences, he muses in the conclusion to the recension of the Lovewell fight, and it takes little extrapolation to see the awakening of his own intense interest in the history of American Indians at the same time as he became more absorbed in the history of New England. Within a few years this interest, which had been a hobby with him since boyhood, would increase exponentially and eventually lead to the most extensive and scholarly program of reading that he would undertake during the last dozen years of his life.

In his retelling of the story of Hannah Duston, who escaped captivity by tomahawking her captors in their sleep, Thoreau goes beyond historical re-creation (though his narrative is vivid and imaginative) to tell a tale with mythic overtones of how the settlers became estranged from nature in the new land, a fable of an "American Paradise Lost," as Robert F. Sayre has aptly termed the episode in *Thoreau and the*

American Indians.[23] Here the historical accounts were not merely sifted and compared to construct an accurate version of the events; rather they were treated as being "instinct with significance," to use Melville's phrase for a factual story he hoped to write about, and it became the writer's task to create a story that would somehow figure forth the deeper significance of the episode.

Thoreau may have gotten his stimulus for this sort of deliberate literary mythmaking from reading Alexander Ross's *Mystagogus Poeticus, or The Muses Interpreter* about this time (PJ 2.184–186). Ross, a seventeenth-century divine, briefly retold the classical myths and followed each with a series of interpretations leading from the most obvious and "historical" to the most allegorical and sometimes improbable, usually culminating in a reading that would cause the myth to conform to some Christian moral, a practice for which he was ridiculed by later writers. But although Thoreau had known the Greek myths since reading Jacobs's *Greek Reader* in his early teens at the Concord Academy, he began to look at mythology in a different light after reading Ross, apparently struck for the first time by the capacity of such unadorned tales from the prehistoric past to hold in suspension several layers of significance. His own mythologizing, consisting of outwardly simple, brief, resonant fables using quasi-historical or legendary figures (the artist of Kouroo in *Walden*, for example), may be related to his meditations on Ross. Like his reading of Cudworth's *True Intellectual System*, his response to Ross seems to have involved discarding the vessel of Christian moralizing and fastening instead upon the implicit suggestiveness of the work for an artist working with historical or legendary materials. He records his rereading of the myths through Ross enthusiastically in the Journal early in 1846, and reworked and expanded the passages for *A Week*, where he concludes:

> The hidden significance of these fables, which is sometimes thought to have been detected, the ethics running parallel to the poetry and history, are not so remarkable as the readiness with which they may be made to express a variety of truths. As if they were the skeletons of still older and more universal truths than any whose flesh and blood they are for the time made to wear. . . . In the mythus a superhuman intelligence uses the unconscious thoughts and dreams of men as its hieroglyphics to address men unborn. (PJ 2.184–186; WE, 61).[24]

23. (Princeton University Press, 1977), p. 52.

24. See Robert D. Richardson, Jr., *Myth and Literature in the American Renaissance* (Bloomington: Indiana University Press, 1978), esp. pp. 92–99, for Thoreau's use of myth in *A Week*.

Thoreau's renewed interest in mythology inevitably sent him back to the classical writers themselves. The fragmentary Journal for 1847–1848 contains translations of the story of Phaeton and Apollo and the creation of the Cosmos out of Chaos from Ovid's *Metamorphoses* (PJ 2.366–369). Robert D. Richardson, Jr., has shown how the climactic thawing-sand-and-clay section of "Spring" in *Walden*, the significance of which phenomenon Thoreau was beginning to realize about this same time, relies heavily on the *Metamorphoses* for its imagery. Moreover, the concept of metamorphosis itself, as Richardson points out, was to Thoreau and his contemporaries analogous to what evolution would be to the second half of the nineteenth century: "a master image of the workings of nature," a paradigm advanced by natural historians (especially Goethe) to account for the various and manifold expressions of life and their relationships to one another.[25] Thus Thoreau's interest in mythology, his allusions to Ovid, and his fable of creation and renewal in "Spring" are all part of a conceptual whole, a vision of the various forms of a single power working through both nature and the imagination. Nature, like history, could best be understood by discovering its primitive, naked forms or ur-phenomena, and in *Walden* Thoreau explicitly links the insight into the creative processes of nature that he receives from the thawing sand and clay to the creative power of mythology within a culture: "This is the frost coming out of the ground; this is Spring. It precedes the green and flowery spring, as mythology precedes regular poetry" (WA, 308).

It was about this time, too, that Thoreau read Coleridge's *Hints Toward ... a More Comprehensive Theory of Life*, a posthumously published treatise arguing for a theory of metamorphosis or evolution and summarizing the laws of nature (polarity and individuation) by which evolutionary change takes place. As I have elsewhere argued, Thoreau's reading of this work in late 1848 may have acted profoundly as a catalyst to his own work as a naturalist, for Coleridge outlined a theory and practice of natural science that were fundamentally in harmony and not in conflict (as Thoreau's earlier exposure to eighteenth-century natural science had been) with the epistemological and aesthetic principles of Romantic thought.[26] Even more important,

25. Ibid. p. 137. See also Ronald Gray, *Goethe: A Critical Introduction* (Cambridge: Cambridge University Press, 1967), p. 120, where Goethe's theory of the metamorphosis of plants is summarized. Thoreau is remarkably close to Goethe's declaration that "alles ist Blatt" ("all is leaf") when he proclaims in "Spring" that "the Maker of this earth but patented a leaf" (p. 308).

26. Robert Sattelmeyer and Richard A. Hocks, "Thoreau and Coleridge's *Theory of Life*," in *Studies in the American Renaissance: 1985* ed. Joel Myerson (Charlottesville: University Press of Virginia, 1985), pp. 269–284.

perhaps, Coleridge linked his *Theory of Life* to a close and detailed study of natural phenomena and showed how a program of careful observation was integral to an understanding of nature's essential principles and processes. Thoreau took unusually careful notes from the *Theory of Life*, extracting its central arguments (a practice that he did not usually follow when taking notes on natural history books), and it may be that Coleridge's book gave him some of the stimulus that he needed to convert his youthful Transcendentalism and love of nature into a meaningful and satisfying life's work. The *Theory of Life* describes a creative force or power working through nature, a view related to and to an extent developed from the *Naturphilosophie* of Schelling, but also attentive, in its dependence upon the exhibits in John Hunter's museum, to the classification, observation, and cataloguing of specimens themselves. The study of nature in the light of this theoretical orientation becomes not an innocent diversion, nor even a way of appreciating the evidence of creation in some former ages (as the preceding age's natural theologians had it), but, as James Engel has recently phrased it, "a huge arena in which the individual human mind can seek the moving spirit of the world, and in which we learn to imitate the divine creative force."[27]

At the same time, Thoreau was also reading a more purely philosophical treatise that summarized the tenets of this school of natural philosophers, J. B. Stallo's *General Principles of the Philosophy of Nature*, a work that contained, in addition to Stallo's exposition of the various "Evolutions" (his term for the various changes of form and development observable in nature), chapters detailing the views of Kant, Fichte, Schelling, Oken, and Hegel. Stallo pays homage to "Father Goethe," as he calls him, as the progenitor of this school of thought, and distinguishes its principles from those of both the natural theologians and the materialists.

The theoretical and methodological grounding that Thoreau absorbed from these works was complemented and amplified by his acquaintance at this time with the man who would soon become the leading natural scientist of his age, Louis Agassiz. The Swiss scientist, already in possession of a distinguished reputation in Europe, arrived in America in the fall of 1846 and quickly became a celebrity in New England intellectual and scientific circles for his series of lectures called "The Plan of the Creation" during the winter of 1846–1847. Thoreau may have attended these lectures (although no direct evidence of his

27. *The Creative Imagination: Enlightenment to Romanticism* (Cambridge: Harvard University Press, 1981), p. 313. Engel is speaking of Schelling's *Naturphilosophie*, but the description is apt for both Coleridge and Thoreau.

having done so exists), for in the spring of 1847 he began collecting specimens of fish and turtles for Agassiz and corresponded with him through his associate, James Elliot Cabot. In 1848 Agassiz would be appointed to a professorship in the fledgling Lawrence Scientific School, from which base he would work tirelessly in the decades ahead to extend, popularize, and professionalize the study of natural science in America. His approach, while it was based on field work, observation, and comparative anatomy, was fundamentally in harmony with Coleridge's *Theory of Life*, for Agassiz too had been influenced by the *Naturphilosophie* of Oken and Schelling during his youth and would never come to accept the materialism of Darwin.[28]

Shortly after his careful reading of the *Theory of Life* and his becoming acquainted with Agassiz, Thoreau began systematically to train himself as a naturalist and to define his principal work as the study of New England natural history. He would retain to the end of his life a view of natural science essentially identical to that outlined by Coleridge, a view fundamentally opposed of course to the growing tide of materialistic and positivistic science of his own day. And, whatever temporary disappointments he would feel and express about the minutiae of scientific observation, the fact is that from 1849 onward he devoted himself happily and energetically to a variety of natural history investigations, especially those having to do with the propagation and dispersal of plants. In 1853, asked by the Association for the Advancement of Science, to which he had been nominated as a member, to describe his specialty in the field, he could proclaim in the Journal with mixed affirmation and exasperation:

> Now, though I could state to a select few that department of human inquiry which engages me, and should be rejoiced to do so, I felt that it would be to make myself the laughing-stock of the scientific community to describe or attempt to describe that branch of science which specially interests me, inasmuch as they do not believe in a science which deals with the higher law. . . . The fact is I am a mystic, a transcendentalist, and a natural philosopher to boot. Now I think of it, I should have told them at once I was a transcendentalist. (J 5.4)

As was his habit during other periods of his life, Thoreau continued to read widely in travel literature during the late 1840s. In fact, his reading of travel books is perhaps the most constant feature among his literary interests from his college years until his final illness. The bibli-

---

28. See the discussion of Agassiz's influence on Thoreau's later natural history writing in Chapter 4, below.

ography of travel works read by Thoreau in John Aldrich Christie's *Thoreau as World Traveler* lists nearly two hundred titles and might well have included many others.[29] And, more important, as Christie shows, this reading in travel literature provided Thoreau with a means of giving his own microcosmic focus on Concord and New England a global resonance. It needs to be kept in mind that the bulk of what Thoreau wrote for publication was either travel narrative or a closely related form of essay (which might without denigration be termed "pedestrian") that was based on traveling by foot and that he usually called the excursion. Thus, the relationship of his travel reading to his literary career is even more fundamental and obvious than Christie suggests.

Travel narrative—specifically, the spatial and temporal dimensions of a journey out and back—gave him both a structure and a level of metaphoric correspondence in which he could objectify the essential Transcendental quest for insight through nature and test his principles and assumptions against society and the external world at large. *A Week on the Concord and Merrimack Rivers, Cape Cod, The Maine Woods,* and such essays as "A Winter Walk," "A Walk to Wachusett," "Walking," and "A Yankee in Canada" are all excursions or outright travel narratives that need to be considered in the context of both Thoreau's wide reading in travel literature and the enormous popularity of the genre in the nineteenth century. Even *Walden*, in many ways the antithesis of a travel book and a celebration of staying home, is quite literally as well as hyperbolically about one who "travel[s] a good deal in Concord." The perspective that Thoreau adopts toward his neighbors and countrymen is very much that of a traveler, a stranger in a strange land describing the curious business and domestic practices of the natives.

The mid nineteenth century was a golden age of travel literature, as Europeans and Americans penetrated the last blank spaces on the globe or reentered regions of the world that had been closed to them for centuries: It saw the great western explorations of Lewis and Clark, Pike, and Frémont; the Arctic expeditions of Kane, Parry, and Franklin; the journeys and archaeological expeditions to the Near East of Layard, Lane, and Chateaubriand; travels and scientific surveys in South America, especially the region of the Amazon, by Lieutenant Herndon for the United States government and by the great German naturalist Humboldt; and the expeditions to unlock the mysteries of

29. (New York and London: Columbia University Press and the American Geographic Society, 1965), pp. 313–333. Christie does not cite books about travel in New England or periodical articles, and he did not have access to the fragmentary Journals of the 1840s that record additional travel reading.

the Nile and central Africa by David Livingstone and Richard Burton. Thoreau knew all these and scores more, for his taste in travel literature was remarkably catholic, if not undiscriminating. He read not only works of sober science and acute observation such as Darwin's *Voyage of a Naturalist Round the World* but also government surveys for railroad routes to the Pacific, women's accounts of travel, books on hunting exotic game in Africa, accounts of gold mining in Australia, and even romanticized and fictionalized books for young people such as Mayne Reid's *The Desert Home; or The Adventures of a Lost Family in the Wilderness*, a sort of book with obvious popular cinematic counterparts in our own age. In fact, what Thoreau says sardonically in *Walden* of his contemporaries' appetite for popular fiction—"There are those who, like cormorants and ostriches, can digest all sorts of this, even after the fullest meal of meats and vegetables, for they suffer nothing to be wasted"—might be said with equal aptness of his taste for travel literature (WA, 104).

It was a fondness for which he occasionally upbraided himself, as in his remark about the "one or two shallow books of travel" that he read his first summer at Walden, but on the whole this reading was nourishing, providing him with a virtually limitless fund of geographical knowledge that enriched his writings about the environs of Concord, as well as a framework and a persona—the journey and the traveler—through which he could give body and outwardness to his personal quests. During the mid to late 1840s his reading in travel literature was characteristically varied, in terms of both quality and locale described: Melville's *Typee* (presumably one of the shallow books that he referred to, and one which, it will be remembered, was published as nonfiction), John Charles Frémont's *Report of the Exploring Expedition to the Rocky Mountains*, Eliot Warburton's *The Crescent and the Cross; or, Romance and Realities of Eastern Travel*, Chateaubriand's *Travels in Greece, Palestine, Egypt, and Barbary*, the Reverend Joseph Wolff's *Narrative of a Mission to Bokhara*, and the Reverend William Ellis's *Polynesian Researches* (also, incidentally, a source for Melville) (PJ 2.168, 315, 349–350; WE, 60, 127).

The experience of being jailed overnight in the summer of 1846, for having refused to pay his poll tax for several years, led Thoreau to crystallize and defend his political views in "Resistance to Civil Government," published in 1849 in Elizabeth Peabody's *Aesthetic Papers*. Typically, the essay was revised from a lecture delivered in 1848, and it would not receive its most famous name, "Civil Disobedience," until the posthumous publication of Thoreau's *A Yankee in Canada, With Anti-Slavery and Reform Papers* in 1866, and this familiar title may well be non-authorial. The sources that influenced this essay, which has of course become enormously influential itself, are perhaps more obvious and at the same time more elusive than the sources, say, of Thoreau's orientation in natural history. The whole body of what may loosely be termed his political writing, in fact, beginning with his favorable notices of the abolitionists Nathaniel Rogers and Wendell Phillips in 1844 and 1845 and culminating with his impassioned defense of John Brown in 1859, is less susceptible of analysis in terms of specific intellectual debts than most other areas of his thought.

The reasons for this difficulty are, in part at least, obvious. "Politics" is a vague term at best, encompassing in everyday usage everything from one's most deep-seated convictions to the grubbiest and most manipulative aspects of governments on every level from the family to the international community. Nor was Thoreau in any sense a student of politics or political theory as he was of natural history, ethnology, the classics, or English poetry. His political ideas, on the one hand, tended to come from a variety of non-political sources, and his articulation of them, on the other, tended to be prompted by immediate and local issues—his night in jail, the well-publicized cases of the fugitive slaves Thomas Sims in 1851 and Anthony Burns in 1854, the John Brown affair. He made no effort to read political philosophy systematically. This is not to say that Thoreau's political thinking did not evolve, of course; it is rather to suggest that it developed in a sort of organic way out of certain political pressure points of his age—the extension of slavery and the question of individual rights versus civil law in particular—coming into conflict with some of his most fundamental and strongly held convictions about the purposes and conduct of life.

Although he knew Jonathan Dymond's *Essays on the Principles of Morality* from a theme assignment during his junior year, Thoreau's formal study of moral philosophy at Harvard had emphasized the dominant authority in the field, William Paley. If they were not so already, Paley's utilitarian and relativistic views became repugnant to Thoreau during the 1840s because they appeared to authorize the compromises of Northern politicians over slavery. In "Resistance to Civil Government" Thoreau deliberately invokes Paley's relativism in order to refute it and replace it with the familiar Transcendental doctrine of the "higher law," the obligation of the individual to obey the severest dictates of conscience, whatever the strictures of civil law might be.

The philosophical and religious sources of this doctrine are well known, and it requires little effort to see how it would lead to the sort of uncompromising stance toward government that Thoreau adopts in his most famous essay. But Thoreau was also sanctioned in his political radicalism by both his family and his cultural forebears in Massachusetts. His mother, sister, and aunts were all active in the Concord anti-slavery society, and abolitionism may be said to have been a part of the very air he breathed. He regularly read such anti-slavery organs as Nathaniel Rogers's *Herald of Freedom* and William Lloyd Garrison's *The Liberator*, participated in abolitionist activities in Concord, and even owned the book *Anti-Slavery Melodies* by Jairus Lincoln. Beginning in 1852, moreover, he subscribed to Horace Greeley's emphatically anti-slavery and pro-temperance *New York Tribune*.

In addition, as Richard Drinnon has pointed out, Thoreau inherited a legacy of political resistance based on conscience: "In his day, the doctrine of a fundamental law still covered Massachusetts like a ground fog."[30] The intellectual and religious legacy of the commonwealth, going back to such figures as Anne Hutchinson and Roger Williams in the early days of the Massachusetts Bay Colony, gave ample precedent for such action as Thoreau took first in resisting the Mexican War and the extension of slavery and then in publicizing his actions and making his own case an occasion for denouncing more widespread evils. The immediate context of the Transcendental movement also furnished authorization and support for his views, as well as examples of individual action based on principle (Alcott too had refused to pay the poll tax). Drinnon credits Emerson's "Politics" as having more direct influence over Thoreau's political views than was exerted by other contemporaries such as Alcott, Channing, or Theodore Parker; and likewise Truman Nelson cites Emerson's "The Transcendentalist" as an important source that served to bridge the gap between the movement's ideals and direct political action.[31] No doubt Thoreau knew these essays, although he does not allude to them in his writing, and they clearly sanction, as "The American Scholar" had done earlier, the need for action on the part of the reformer, raising the specter at least of non-compliance with authority. Emerson himself, however, was slow to come to see the need for direct action, and criticized Thoreau's night in jail as a gesture that was "mean and skulking, and in bad taste."[32]

Ethel Seybold maintained that Sophocles' *Antigone*, a play that Thoreau knew well and that dramatizes an act of what may be termed civil disobedience in its heroine's decision to bury her brother in open defiance of Creon's proscription, was the major inspiration for "Re-

30. "Thoreau's Politics of the Upright Man," in *Thoreau in Our Season*, ed. John H. Hicks (Amherst: University of Massachusetts Press, 1962), p. 155.

31. "Thoreau and John Brown," in *Thoreau in Our Season*, pp. 135–136.

32. *The Journals of Bronson Alcott*, ed. Odell Shepard (Boston: Little, Brown, 1938), pp. 183–184.

sistance to Civil Government": "From it must have come his concept of divine law as superior to civil law, of human right as greater than legal right."[33] Drinnon, while agreeing that *Antigone* is an important source, quite correctly observes that "no single work provided Thoreau with his key concept," and makes the more defensible claim that "there was not a major figure in the classical background of anarchism on whom Thoreau did not draw in some way," citing specifically Zeno's Stoicism and Ovid's nostalgia for a time before there was either a state or the need for one.[34]

Yet it would be difficult to say, in the last analysis, whether Thoreau's civil disobedience was patterned after that of Antigone or anyone else, or whether his acts represent parallel responses from similar principles. After his endorsement of Wendell Phillips and Nathaniel Rogers in the mid 1840s, and his masterful orchestration of argument and rhetoric in "Resistance to Civil Government," Thoreau's political writings during the 1850s became increasingly topical, strident, and negative in the sense that they were predominantly devoted to attacking evil rather than to proposing concrete measures for its eradication. In the newspapers, he followed with a kind of reluctant avidity the escalating crises that eventually led to the Civil War. He also followed the career and writings of Daniel Webster, who became in the course of time the embodiment to Thoreau of what he hated most about politics, the tendency of "statesmen" to compromise principle for expediency. "Slavery in Massachusetts" and his addresses on John Brown illustrate the depth of both his knowledge of political events and his passion about slavery, but they betray no significant new intellectual sources for his own political thought, a subject that still deserves to be accorded more attention by scholars.[35]

Despite the fact that he apparently neglected to keep the sort of detailed records of his reading from 1844 to 1849 that he kept at other times in his life, it is apparent that Thoreau's intellectual, literary, and professional interests developed and shifted significantly during this period of sustained literary labor. The evidence of shifts and developments during this seminal period in his career is to be seen in profound but subtle changes in his stance toward nature and in his style itself, changes attributable at least in part to his renewed interest in Carlyle

33. *Thoreau: The Quest and the Classics*, p. 17.

34. Drinnon, "Thoreau's Politics," pp. 154–155.

35. See Wendell Glick's "Thoreau and Radical Abolitionism," Ph.D. diss., Northwestern University, 1950; Michael Meyer, "Thoreau and Black Emigration," *American Literature* 53 (November 1981): 380–396; and Johnson, *Thoreau's Complex Weave*, esp. pp. 85–121, for a sample of perspectives on Thoreau's interest in reform and politics.

during the early stages of *Walden* and to adding the *Theory of Life* to his earlier reading of Coleridge's philosophical and ethical writings. His interest in belletristic subjects declined at this time, for no evidence survives to suggest that he continued his project of collecting English verse or maintained an interest in translations of Latin or Greek authors. With the composition of *A Week, Walden*, long essays on Carlyle and the Maine woods, and "Resistance to Civil Government," he had begun to find his characteristic forms, subjects, and voice. His reading in the years ahead would lead him to cultivate this ground more intensively and carefully. The history of New England, especially the earliest explorations of the coast, and the history of the American Indians, along with the detailed study of natural history, were newly discovered disciplines that were to prompt and enrich Thoreau's literary projects during the 1850s.

3

From
A Week to *Walden*

Exigencies and Opportunities, 1849–1850

FOLLOWING the publication of *A Week on the Concord and Merrimack Rivers* in May 1849, Thoreau's life began a quiet transformation. Partly as a result of the reception of the book, but partly owing also to the development of new interests and a newfound stability in the routines of his life, his literary habits—his reading, especially—changed and began to settle into patterns that would remain more or less constant for the rest of his life. The failure of *A Week* to generate much critical or popular appreciation and the financial setback that its poor sales caused were both disappointing to Thoreau, but they were offset by other and compensating developments among his literary interests that made the next decade a busy and productive one—although the issue of the significance and value of his projects after *Walden* was published in 1854 is still capable of provoking lively critical debate.[1]

Nevertheless, there is a kind of quiet drama to be inferred from the record of his reading and writing during these years, for his studies of natural history, early American history, and the American Indian did progress far enough to suggest, at least in the essays that he managed to finish or cull from these projects late in life, the directions in which his thought was proceeding. His natural history work may be gauged

---

1. The most authoritative case for Thoreau's "decline" is that made by Sherman Paul in *The Shores of America*, who says that during the 1850s "the sources of [Thoreau's] life began to dry up" and that "nature had become barren, and the method which Thoreau now adopted in order to find her meaning . . . did not bear any significant crop of inspiration" (pp. 272, 274). This view, the culmination of a strain in Thoreau criticism that goes back to Emerson's funeral address, has been challenged recently by the work of scholars more sympathetic to Thoreau's aims as a naturalist and writer. See Sayre, *Thoreau and the American Indians*, p. 101; William L. Howarth, *The Book of Concord* (New York: Viking Press, 1982), pp. 190–208; and John Hildebidle, *Thoreau: A Naturalist's Liberty* (Cambridge: Harvard University Press, 1983), pp. 69–96.

from such late essays as "Wild Apples" and "The Succession of Forest Trees" (extracted from a longer manuscript on the dispersal of seeds); his ideas about American history from "Provincetown" in *Cape Cod*; and his engagement with the American Indian from the contrast between his reading on the subject and his firsthand experience with Joe Polis in Maine in 1857, narrated in "The Allegash and East Branch" in the posthumously published *The Maine Woods*. Before taking up the developments in his reading that helped to shape these late works and that mark his mature intellectual interests, however, it may be useful to consider first the new patterns of stability that began to cohere in his life around 1850 from a concatenation of circumstances as varied as the commercial failure of *A Week* and his partial estrangement from Emerson, the establishment of the Concord Town Library, and his resumption of regular reading notes and detailed, dated Journal entries.

The failure of *A Week* to sell well had at least three significant repercussions for Thoreau. First, since he had agreed to guarantee the costs of production, and since it was soon apparent that royalties from sales would not cover these costs, he incurred a debt of almost $300. He had to rely on other employment, especially surveying and pencil making, to meet his ordinary expenses and to pay off his publisher ("falsely so called," he observed mordantly). It was not until near the end of 1853, four and a half years after the book appeared, that he managed to discharge this obligation (JL 5.521). The extremely slow sales of the book (just over two hundred copies in four years) also dimmed Thoreau's chances of earning at least a nominal living from his pen and of following *A Week* with *Walden*, which he was confident by 1849 was nearly ready for publication.[2] He had to confront more directly than before the stark reality that, after nearly a decade of writing for various magazines, lecturing, and publishing a book, he was unlikely to be even moderately remunerated for his work. Like virtually all other serious American writers of his generation, he had to find some alternative arrangement for making a living if he wished to continue to write, and he also had to find some alternative forms of expression for his writing while his literary career reoriented itself to cultural and economic realities.

This is not to say that Thoreau abandoned the idea of lecturing or of writing for paying publications. Quite the contrary: There were occasional periods of brisk activity in lecturing, and he was, in Emerson's words, in "a tremble of great expectation" when *Walden* appeared in

2. See WE, "Historical Introduction," p. 469.

1854.[3] In 1861 and 1862, he quite literally worked on his deathbed, dictating to his sister Sophia after he became too weak to write himself, in order to prepare as many essays as possible for publication. But in 1850 he had to accommodate himself to the truth that no reliable public outlet for his work existed, and as a consequence he turned increasingly to the Journal as a mode of private expression that served simultaneously as a record of his studies and observations and as a potential storehouse for his occasional public performances. This shift in his primary form of composition is vividly suggested by the proportions of his printed Journal in the 1906 edition: whereas two volumes suffice for the thirteen-year period from 1837 to 1849, twelve are required for the next dozen years, from 1850 to 1861. (The earlier Journal had been much longer, of course; much of it was used up or destroyed by Thoreau in the process of drafting his early literary works.) The summer of 1850 marks the beginning of this later phase of the Journal as a voluminous, regularly kept, and dated document that records in great detail Thoreau's studies—especially of natural history—during the rest of his life. Since he frequently noted his response to books he was reading in his Journal, his interests in the fifties are generally somewhat easier to trace than those of earlier decades.

The third consequence of *A Week* and its reception appears to have been a real rupture in Thoreau's relationship with Emerson. Thoreau's Journal records a deep and disturbed preoccupation with the subject of friendship in 1849, returning again and again to the idea of its failure or end. He goes so far as to associate the crisis and its aftermath with the friend's criticism of *A Week*: "I had a friend, I wrote a book, I asked my friend's criticism, I never got but praise for what was good in it;—my friend became estranged from me and then I got blame for all that was bad, & so I got at last the criticism which I wanted."[4] The critic is never explicitly named, but since Emerson was Thoreau's closest friend, played so dominant a role in his literary apprenticeship, and urged him to publish *A Week* at his own expense, assuring him he would be unlikely to lose financially by so doing, there can be little doubt that he is behind the often anguished passages on friendship from this period.

Thoreau's sense of injury over this criticism was probably only tangentially related to the change in his relationship with Emerson, however, for the roots of their estrangement lay deeper. It was clear that

3. Emerson, *Letters*, 4.460.

4. MS Journal for 1849 (HM 13182); quoted in WE, "Historical Introduction," p. 478.

Thoreau did not and could not fulfill Emerson's expectations of him,[5] and for his part Thoreau could scarcely continue into his mid-thirties as a disciple of anyone, especially of the apostle of self-reliance. Even before this time he had been privately and publicly satirized for his apparent imitation of the older writer, and he must have been acutely self-conscious of his widely perceived position as Emerson's protégé.[6] Ironically, the book that everywhere testified to Emerson's influence was to be at least the apparent occasion of a breach between the two men that would never entirely be healed, although it would be patched over. Painful as it evidently was, the rift probably helped to propel Thoreau in the direction of what he came to view as his proper studies and lightened the pressures that he must have felt to live up to Emerson's expectations.

Another important change in Thoreau's social and domestic life about this time was in his relations with his family. Thoreau moved back to live with his parents and sisters after Emerson's return from Europe in the summer of 1848, and during the following year he helped to carry out extensive renovations in their new house on Main Street, into which the family settled permanently early in 1850.[7] He had lived at home for only about eighteen months during the previous eight years—in 1844 and the first half of 1845 while he was building his cabin at the pond—but now he settled back with the family for good, taking a hand as usual in the graphite business and working independently as a surveyor. He occupied the attic floor of the new house, a spacious finished area that gave him ample space for his belongings, his instruments, his writing desk and bookshelves, and his growing collections of natural history specimens.[8] The new house was near the river, and since Ellery Channing, his friend and frequent companion, now lived almost across the street in a house whose back yard sloped down to the bank, Thoreau had a convenient place to moor his boat for the river excursions that were almost as regular a habit as his walks. This domestic stability helped to shape Thoreau's literary habits and pursuits in the decade to come. His housing since college had been a series of makeshift and temporary arrangements, and now that his

---

5. Emerson's charge, leveled in his funeral address, that Thoreau lacked ambition and failed to accomplish tangible results from all his studies, had been expressed as early as 1842, when he described to Margaret Fuller Thoreau's "perennial threatening attitude" (*Letters*, 3.75) that led to no significant output; and in 1844 he predicted in his Journal that Thoreau would "never be a writer," for he was "as active as a shoemaker" (JMN 9.45).

6. Harding, *Days*, pp. 65–66, 299–300.

7. Ibid. p. 263.

8. Howarth, *The Book of Concord*, pp. 4–5.

life had assumed more or less settled routines he could begin realisti-
cally to devote more time to the long-range projects that now increasingly interested him.

The most important of these new routines was the habit of daily
walks that he began about this time, a habit that he would practice
uninterruptedly all year round in all weathers until the onset of his final
siege of tuberculosis. "Within a year," he wrote to H.G.O. Blake in
November 1849, "my walks have extended themselves, and almost
every afternoon, (I read, or write, or make pencils, in the forenoon,
and by the last means I get a living for my body.) I visit some new hill
or pond or wood many miles distant" (COR, 250–251). About the
same time, in the Journal, he began to record and index "Places to
Walk to," and gradually his settled practice when not engaged in a
large surveying project became to spend the morning at some literary
labor—whether working on a lecture or essay or writing up previous
days' Journal entries from field notes—the afternoon in walking or
boating, and the evening in reading. After narrating in the Journal a
winter day's outdoor activities in December 1856, for example, Thoreau looked forward to a typical evening: "Now for a merry fire, some
old poet's pages, or else serene philosophy, or even a healthy book of
travels, to last far into the night, eked out perhaps with the walnuts
which we gathered in November" (JL 9.173).

His daily walks were not primarily for exercise or recreation but for
discipline. He was training himself to become a careful observer and
recorder of natural phenomena, jotting on small sheets of paper details
which would form the basis of Journal passages that he would later
write up in his study, sometimes composing several days' entries in one
stint. It was about this time, too—1849 or 1850—that he began to
study systematically botany and natural history in general. He describes, again in a Journal entry from December 1856, how "from year
to year we look at Nature with new eyes" and how about a half-dozen
years earlier he had begun to bring home plants in a "botany box"
constructed inside the crown of his hat and busied himself "looking
out the name of each one and remembering it" (JL 9.156–157).

As Thoreau's outward life and pursuits were becoming more regular
and settled, and his literary projects grew more dependent upon reading and research, his access to important sources of books also improved. In September 1849 he petitioned Jared Sparks, president of
Harvard College, for permission to withdraw books from the library,
claiming—surely for the only time in his life—benefit of clergy. Normally, ordained ministers were the only nonresident alumni permitted
to check out books. Thoreau, exercising a characteristic philological
ingenuity turning on the fact that "clergy" and "clerk" (in the medie-

val sense of "scholar") were derived from the same root, argued that he should qualify "*because I have chosen letters for my profession*, and so am one of the clergy embraced by the spirit at least of her rule" (COR, 266–268). Whether or not Sparks found this line of reasoning compelling, he did grant the request, and thereafter Thoreau used the Harvard library regularly, especially for his researches in early American history and American Indian ethnology. The railroad, which had been completed out to Concord in 1844, made it possible to travel conveniently to Boston and return the same day. Thaddeus W. Harris, the librarian, was also an entomologist of note (he had been Thoreau's natural science instructor at Harvard), and Thoreau frequently improved his visits to the library by talking over scientific matters of mutual interest with Harris.

Other Boston libraries were also important to Thoreau's work. In 1850 he was elected a corresponding member of the Boston Society of Natural History, entitling him to charge books from the society's fine library, a privilege that proved to be of immense use to him as his study of natural history became more specialized and expert over the years.[9] The New England metropolis's other renowned library was in the Boston Athenaeum, and despite the fact that he was not a member, Thoreau made at least occasional use of its collections. Emerson had earlier introduced him as a guest and sometimes borrowed books for him on his charging privileges.[10] Non-members, especially if they were students or writers, could consult the catalogue and the collections, and Thoreau took advantage of this policy when he was beginning his extensive bibliographical survey of works on the American Indians: One of his manuscript notebooks contains a lengthy list of books on the subject that is headed "At Athenaeum."[11]

He also added slowly and carefully to his personal library, buying mostly books on natural history, both ancient and modern, and planning each purchase as if it were a military campaign, for the expenditure represented no inconsiderable portion of his earnings. He paid fifteen dollars, for example, for Loudon's *Arboretum et Fruticetum Britannicum*, an eight-volume botanical encyclopedia that was also in the Town Library. According to Ellery Channing's memoir, Thoreau "prized 'Loudon's Arboretum,' of which, after thinking of its purchase and saving up the money for years, he became a master."[12] When he

9. Kenneth Walter Cameron, "Emerson, Thoreau, and the Society of Natural History," *American Literature* 24 (March 1952): 21–30.

10. Harding, *Days*, p. 130.

11. Indian book 4 (NNPM MA 598).

12. *Thoreau: The Poet-Naturalist* (Boston: Roberts, 1873), p. 26.

was in Boston he generally visited Burnham's bookstore, where he would occasionally come across a bargain in old books, such as the three-volume edition of Pliny's natural history that he found in 1859. He jotted down the titles of used books that he found at Burnham's (with their prices) to carry back to Concord with him, obviously to meditate their purchase and plan for the outlay. His personal library never grew much in excess of four hundred volumes (not counting the seven hundred-odd volumes of *A Week* that he included when sardonically recounting the story of the publisher's return of unsold copies), but they were a carefully chosen and compact lot, selected to facilitate his literary and scientific work.

The availability of books in Concord also improved significantly about this time. In 1851 the Concord Town Library, which would become the Concord Free Public Library in 1873 (where many of the books in Thoreau's personal library are housed today), came into being as a public library, absorbing the collection of the old subscription Social Library and thereafter building its collections through regular acquisitions funded by tax revenue.[13] The librarian, Albert Stacy, also owned a stationer's store from which he operated a circulating library of books that could be borrowed for a small rental fee. The circulating library—a target of Thoreau's satire on "easy reading" in *Walden* (WA, 104)—tended to concentrate on popular current literature, especially fiction and travel books, and was the source of much of Thoreau's reading in the latter genre during the 1850s. The Town Library, on the other hand, tended to acquire (in a complementary way that suggests that being town librarian and owning his own circulating library did not constitute a conflict of interest for Stacy) more sober works of nonfiction in fields such as history, religion, and natural and applied science.[14] Its collections were quite important for Thoreau, who took an avid interest in the fledgling institution and even suggested acquisitions to the librarian (JL 5.41). No charging records from the early years of the Town Library have been discovered, but some acquisition records do survive, and they demonstrate that Thoreau frequently read books that came to the library almost as soon as they were accessioned.[15] Many of the books that the library acquired in the

13. Allen French, T. Morris Longstreth, and David B. Little, *A History of the Concord Free Public Library*, pamphlet printed for the centennial of the library by the Library Corporation (Concord: Concord Press Corp., 1973).

14. See the catalogue of the Town Library, reprinted by Kenneth Walter Cameron in *The Transcendentalists and Minerva*, 2.818–828.

15. Acquisition records of Concord Free Public Library. Darwin's *Origin of Species*, for example, was acquired by the library on January 23, 1860, and Thoreau made extracts from it in one of his "fact books" before extracts from a book that he borrowed from Harvard on February 6.

1850s—especially documentary works such as the government surveys of the West and the *Collections* of the Massachusetts Historical Society—were invaluable to Thoreau's natural history and early American history projects. To a certain extent, his criticisms of the literary climate of Concord in *Walden*, the references to the "half-starved Lyceum . . . and the puny beginning of the library" in "Reading," were met by a gradual improvement in the local collections during the decade (WA, 108).

Interestingly, Thoreau seems to have struck a bargain with Stacy to set up a sort of private subscription library that enabled him to read current books not otherwise available. James Spooner, a young man from Plymouth who met Thoreau in the early fifties and wrote fairly extensive accounts of conversations with him, noted on one of these occasions that Thoreau "asked me if we had convenient opportunity for obtaining books. . . . He said that he had made an arrangement with the Concord bookseller to furnish what books he might wish— there were some half dozen others who would read them too & at three or four cts. apiece he would get the price of the book and then sell it afterwards."[16]

Thoreau continued to borrow books from Emerson too, although he did most of his reading from this source in the early 1840s. He also relied on the libraries of other friends: Bronson Alcott had a collection especially rich in philosophy and religion, and Ellery Channing was an inveterate reader with an extensive collection of literary works. After 1855, Thoreau occasionally borrowed books from Franklin Benjamin Sanborn (later to be an editor and biographer of Thoreau), a young abolitionist schoolteacher boarding at the Thoreau house.[17]

He also read newspapers, more often and more regularly than the criticism of the popular press in *Walden* might lead one to expect. Probably because of his friendship with Horace Greeley, its publisher, he took a subscription to the weekly edition of the *New York Tribune* in 1852. Greeley was sympathetic to reform generally and to the temperance and abolitionist movements particularly, and was usually supportive of the Transcendentalists (he had provided jobs on his paper to both Margaret Fuller and the feckless Ellery Channing). The *Tribune*'s editorial policy was thus more palatable to Thoreau than that of most other newspapers, even though it too had its share of lurid stories of crimes and disasters such as Thoreau alludes to in *Walden*. Greeley

16. Francis B. Dedmond, "Thoreau as Seen by an Admiring Friend: A New View," *American Literature* 56 (October 1984): 335–336.

17. Harding, *Days*, pp. 352–355. Thoreau noted, for example, in Indian book 12 (NNPM MA 606) that his source for Henry Youle Hind's report on a Canadian exploring expedition was Sanborn's library.

was moreover a sort of unofficial literary agent for Thoreau, and he saw to it that extracts from *Walden* appeared in his paper and that the book was prominently reviewed, perhaps by Greeley himself.

The *Tribune* was also issued in daily and semi-weekly editions, and Thoreau occasionally refers to articles in these as well as in the weekly edition that he took. As might be expected, most of his references to and clippings from the paper concern either natural history phenomena or the American Indian. But when an event gripped Thoreau, he read all the newspapers that he could get his hands on. Such was the case in the fall of 1859, when John Brown led his abortive raid on Harper's Ferry and was subsequently captured and hanged (JL 12.406ff.). At such a time Thoreau was more likely to become enraged by the timidity of editors than to learn much of value about the event. As had been his custom earlier, he read periodical literature regularly, with an eye especially for essays on developments in natural science or ethnology; the latest books were still not always easy to obtain, and the major monthly and quarterly magazines often provided essay reviews that apprised him of new works in these fields. During the 1850s he kept up with new and emerging American periodicals such as *Harper's*, the *Atlantic*, and *Putnam's* (the last two in which he published), and more intermittently with British magazines, from established journals such as the *Westminster Review* to more recent ventures such as Charles Dickens's *Household Words*.

As a consequence of his more settled habits, his wider and easier access to books, and his shifting literary interests, Thoreau began about this time to keep detailed records of his reading in a series of notebooks designed to facilitate his various literary and scientific projects. He was an almost compulsive note taker by now (Channing describes him as always reading "with pen in hand"),[18] and he quoted extensively from the books he read. The Journal is one of these repositories of information about his reading, although by no means the principal one. Thoreau tried as a rule to preserve the Journal for his own thoughts and his records of natural history observations, and not to use it for extensive extracts from books. Frequently, however, allusions to and quotations from his reading appear in the late Journal and provide a convenient way of dating his acquaintance with a particular work.

The later notebooks strictly devoted to extracts from his reading, all commencing around 1850, consist of the following: two commonplace books, one intended for "facts" and another originally for "poetry"; a notebook on reading related to the history and early exploration of

18. *Thoreau: The Poet-Naturalist*, p. 40.

Canada and Cape Cod; and eleven volumes of "Indian books," as he called them, of extracts on the history and culture of North American Indian tribes.[19] The two commonplace books are perhaps the most interesting of these volumes intrinsically, for they suggest that Thoreau at first tried to distinguish in his reading notes between "poetry" (in the broadest Transcendental sense of any literary material that contained some significant idea, expression, or insight), and "facts"— either striking or interesting phenomena that might be evidence of some process or law of nature, or the sort of data that might someday flower into truth in the manner of the story of the bug that hatched from the apple-tree table in the concluding chapter of *Walden*. Not surprisingly, however, he found it impossible to maintain this distinction, as he confessed in the Journal within a year or so of beginning the parallel notebooks: "I have a commonplace book for facts and another for poetry, but I find it difficult to preserve the vague distinction which I had in my mind, for the most interesting and beautiful facts are so much the more poetry and that is their success" (JL 3.311).

This remark was probably made with specific reference to the *Heimskringla*, historical and legendary accounts of Norse kings that Thoreau was currently reading and ambivalently making extracts from in both notebooks, but in any event he soon ceased to make "poetry" extracts at all, and he used the remaining leaves of the poetry commonplace book to continue his fact notebook when the latter was filled in 1857 or 1858. His professional interest in literary subjects was waning as his interest in history and natural science was waxing, although there is no indication that he considered these more factual disciplines fundamentally less poetic if rightly pursued. It needs to be borne in mind that Thoreau's extracts of "facts" from a particular work do not always register the nature of his interest in the book itself or indicate its significance to him. Oftentimes he noted oddities, colorful details or incidents, or even casual remarks that he might later work into or allude to in his own writing. In *Walden*, for example, when he describes having killed a woodchuck that had been ravaging his bean field, he observes casually that he "effect[ed] his transmigration, as a Tartar would say," and a Tartar does in fact say this in a passage from a travel book that he had copied into the "fact" book.[20] But on the other hand, the entries cannot be categorized as predominantly of this character: Some are clearly made for purposes of study, some express ideas that

19. See the list of abbreviations in this volume, pp. 114–115, for a description of these manuscript notebooks.

20. The source of the Tartar's remark is Évariste Régis Huc's *Recollections of a Journey through Tartary, Thibet, and China* (see Bibliographical Catalogue).

he found congenial, some offer theories or hypotheses about natural phenomena, and others merely describe phenomena that he was interested in. The scattered quotations that Thoreau typically extracted from a given work may thus be misleading, and anyone concerned with the influence of a particular book upon him would be on safe ground to assume that it may not have suited his purposes at the time of reading to quote the passages that ultimately most affected him.

The Canada notebook, whose contents and chronology have been described in detail by Lawrence Willson, had its origins in Thoreau's excursion to Montreal and Quebec in the fall of 1850.[21] He characteristically studied the geography and history of the places he visited, both to intensify the experience of his infrequent travels and to help him prepare to write about the journey and the locale, but his reading on Canada tended to an unusual extent to spill over and extend into other areas of interest. He began the notebook in November 1850, shortly after his return, and made a number of extracts from various works of history and cartography that were useful to him in preparing "An Excursion to Canada" between late 1850 and early 1852, when he sent the essay to Horace Greeley to try to find a publisher.[22]

Other extracts and notes in the volume, however, not all directly related to the Canada excursion, were made between 1850 and 1856 in a separate section. Although varied in nature, this second set of extracts mainly treats the early cartography of New England and Canada and the inadequacy of contemporary historians who failed to take into account (out of an Anglophilic bias, Thoreau implies) the earliest and most accurate French sources for the history and the mapping of the continent. He would treat this subject at great length in the last chapter of *Cape Cod*, "Provincetown," citing many of the sources in the Canada notebook, and the notebook most importantly reflects his growing fascination with the drama of early exploration and his excitement at the parallel discovery of the relatively unknown history of that exploration by nations—especially the French—other than the English.

The Indian notebooks make up Thoreau's largest single repository of extracts from his reading—eleven volumes containing nearly three thousand manuscript pages of text on all aspects of American aboriginal history, culture, and allied subjects. How (or even whether) he intended to employ these notes directly in his literary projects cannot be known with any certainty, but they do represent a monument to a major intellectual interest of the last dozen years of his life. The evo-

21. "Thoreau's Canadian Notebook," *Huntington Library Quarterly* 22 (May 1959): 179–200.
22. Harding, *Days*, p. 282.

lution of this specific interest will be taken up in the next chapter; suffice it to say for the present that the Indian books, like the other notebooks just described, appear to have their inception in the period following the publication of *A Week*. As Linck C. Johnson has argued, the first surviving Indian book appears to have been started (in a manner analogous to the Canada notebook) as a response to or in anticipation of Thoreau's first trip to Cape Cod in October 1849—so that it might with equal aptness be called the "Cape Cod notebook."[23] Thereafter its focus shifted toward the Indian, and its successors continued this emphasis.

In short, by 1850 Thoreau had begun to study in a fairly systematic fashion the three main interests of the second phase of his career—natural history, early American history, and the history of North American Indians before contact with Europeans—and had a series of notebooks and a regularly kept Journal in which he recorded his reading in these and ancillary fields during the remainder of his life. His pursuits were taking an increasingly scholarly and scientific direction, and if he sometimes voiced disappointment with what seemed a corresponding loss of emotional attachment to his inquiries, his intellectual curiosity remained undiminished. This faculty propelled him to work diligently and for the most part happily on these projects over the years, patiently adding information to his records and incorporating it into ongoing literary projects. His life had settled into patterns that normally permitted him to spend a portion of each day on his studies—both out of doors and within—and he had greatly improved access to libraries and to books in general.

The problem of getting a living was always more vexing philosophically and ethically than actually and practically to Thoreau. Countering the fact that he always could (and often did) make a comfortable living in the pencil business are a series of impassioned engagements (in his writing) with the idea of a man's proper calling: in his Harvard commencement address, in "The Service," in the first two chapters of *Walden*, in "Life Without Principle," and in many of his letters, especially to H.G.O. Blake. On a different sort of practical level, though, he shared the dilemma faced by most if not all American writers in the nineteenth century, and like them he had to make concessions to a culture that tended not to acknowledge or reward many of its most serious artists. His solution was characteristic and distinctive: Rather than work at a newspaper or take on editorial piece work, seek a gov-

---

23. "Into History: Thoreau's Earliest 'Indian Book' and His First Trip to Cape Cod," *Emerson Society Quarterly* 28 (2 Qtr. 1982): 75–88. See also Sayre, *Thoreau and the American Indians*, p. 108, who suggests that the first Indian notebooks may have been begun somewhat earlier when Thoreau was at Walden.

ernment clerkship or customs house job, he trained himself to be a surveyor, an occupation that gave him some control over his day and permitted him to work outdoors, and he made his Journal the primary document of his imaginative life. But he remained at heart and in mind a literary man, a writer whose essential tools and stock in trade were books, and the last dozen years of his active life evince an increasing reliance upon them. "Decayed literature," he observed in an almost Jamesian mood while contemplating shelves of early Canadian history at Harvard in 1852, "makes the richest of all soils" (JL 3.353).

Shifting Emphases, 1850–1854

SINCE the surviving records of Thoreau's reading for the 1850s are more extensive than for the earlier decades, it will be best to treat the main areas topically in a separate chapter in order to suggest something of the outline and development of his principal interests. As I have already suggested, these interests involve varieties of history—natural history, the early history of North American discovery and exploration, and the history of American Indian tribes. None of these subjects was new to him, of course, but each assumed a significance in the early fifties that it had not had earlier. At the same time, a number of other interests, more or less related to these principal ones and carried over from the previous decades, need to be considered and briefly assessed as well.

From a literary standpoint, the early fifties culminate in the publication of *Walden* in 1854, and although that book incorporates Thoreau's reading less obtrusively and in more sophisticated ways than had *A Week*, it too is representative of a stage in Thoreau's intellectual maturation, a stage at which his mastery of familiar subjects (poetry, the classics, travel, Oriental scripture) is balanced against his growing absorption in natural history and history of other types as well: the history of New England, of Concord and Walden Pond, and ultimately of himself.

His interest in travel writing, for example, remained strong and in fact is often not to be distinguished from his more formally historical studies. A book such as William Bartram's *Travels* was not only a literary classic of the genre (it had inspired passages in Coleridge's "Kubla Khan" nearly fifty years before Thoreau read it) but also an important source of information about natural history and the customs of Indian tribes in the South. The account of the "busk" or ceremony of purification and renewal in "Economy" in *Walden* is derived from Bartram, and other early travel writers such as John Josselyn, William Wood, and Timothy Dwight provided similar information for

Thoreau's investigations of New England natural and civil history.[24] Prominent scientists like Darwin, Lyell, and Humboldt published accounts of their travels that were rich in information about natural science, and accounts of Arctic and South American explorations furnished details about aboriginal life in those regions that were pertinent to Thoreau's own study of North American Indian cultures. It is typical, then, to find extracts from such travel works in his natural history commonplace books or Indian notebooks.

His interest in other subjects, however, notably Oriental philosophy and religion, diminished perceptibly during the decade. When Thoreau reestablished his borrowing privileges at Harvard in the fall of 1849, among his first withdrawals were a number of Oriental works, from which he made lengthy extracts in an early commonplace book which still had some blank pages. He even translated into English a French translation of "The Transmigration of the Seven Brahmins," a tale he found in *Harivansa, ou Histoire de la Famille de Hari*, an appendix to the Hindu epic the *Mahābhārata*.[25] Since he had told President Sparks that he needed to consult the library for professional purposes, and since his other withdrawals in 1849 were of books that he needed for his Cape Cod lecture, it is possible that Thoreau may have contemplated some literary project on Oriental literature at this time. He had considered the subject for several years, had treated it briefly in *A Week*, and had read James Elliot Cabot's "The Philosophy of the Ancient Hindoos" in the inaugural issue of the *Massachusetts Quarterly Review* the previous year.[26] In November 1849 he told H.G.O. Blake, after quoting passages about the freedom of the yogin absorbed in contemplation and detached from the world, "To some extent, and at rare intervals, even I am a yogin" (COR, 251). This apparent renewal of interest in Eastern philosophy and religion may thus be related to his own adoption of a more settled mode of life and the beginning of the previously described regular rituals of walking, writing, and reading, of which Thoreau speaks in the same letter. It may also reflect an attempt on his part to explain and justify philosophically the retired life that he was to lead henceforth. Whatever the causes, his enthusiasm

24. WA, 68; see Philip F. Gura, "Thoreau and John Josselyn," *New England Quarterly* 48 (December 1975): 505–518, for a suggestive examination of Thoreau's reading of early travel and exploration accounts.

25. See Arthur F. Christy, *The Orient in American Transcendentalism* (New York: Columbia University Press, 1932), pp. 217–279; Thoreau's translation of "The Transmigration of the Seven Brahmins" may be found in *Translations*, ed. Kevin P. Van Anglen (Princeton: Princeton University Press, 1986), pp. 135–142.

26. "Hindoo Scripture" appears on a list of possible topics that Thoreau drew up in the early 1840s; see WE, "Historical Introduction," p. 437. Thoreau made extracts from Cabot's article in his DLC "Literary Notebook."

was relatively short-lived and led to no discernible literary results beyond the translation of the "Seven Brahmins" tale (which he never attempted to publish). In *Walden*, passages from the Eastern scriptures
sharpen Thoreau's critique of his countrymen's modes of life and provide examples and analogues for his own more contemplative path. He
does not tend to wield them, as he had done in *A Week*, as a stick with
which to beat Christianity. The idea of the yogin's life is fully integrated into the perspective of the narrator, so that he can describe quite
naturally in "The Pond in Winter" the interpenetration of East and
West when "the pure Walden water is mingled with the sacred water
of the Ganges" (p. 298). Significantly, the most resonant Eastern fable
in *Walden*, the story of the artist of Kouroo, is apparently a product of
Thoreau's own invention, demonstrating the extent to which he had
internalized and absorbed this material.

By 1851, reading the *Harivansa* again, he could self-deprecatingly
summarize the influence of such works on himself as essentially confirming tendencies already present: "Like some other preachers, I have
added my texts—derived from the Chinese and Hindoo scriptures—
long after my discourse was written" (JL 2.192). In 1854 he withdrew
the *Bhăgvăt-Gēētă* and *Vishńu-Puráńa*, both already familiar to him,
from Harvard, but thereafter he seldom demonstrated an active interest in the subject—no further library withdrawals, infrequent and casual allusions in the Journal, and no extracts in the notebooks. When
his English friend Thomas Cholmondeley sent him a magnificent gift
of forty-four volumes of Oriental works in 1855 he responded warmly
and gratefully, but he does not seem to have been inspired to read or
reread the books themselves to any significant extent. Channing avers,
with uncharacteristic plainness, "After he had ceased to read these
works, he received a collection of them as a present, from England"
(COR, 397–399).[27] Whether he ceased to read them or not, they certainly arrived after his discourse was written, at a time when he had
become absorbed in other books and other interests.

Another field that he cultivated in a desultory fashion in the 1850s
was "literary" nonfiction. (Fiction, of course, he read scarcely at all
during his adult life, although he had had a fair acquaintance with
Irving, Cooper, and Scott, as well as lesser novelists, during his college
years. He apparently read no more of Melville after *Typee* [1846], and
no more of Hawthorne after *Mosses from an Old Manse* [1846],
which he mentions in a rather awkward poem in *A Week* [pp. 18–19].
He owned for a time a copy of *The Scarlet Letter*, probably a gift from
the author, but crossed it off his library catalogue as either lost or given

27. *Thoreau, The Poet-Naturalist*, pp. 40–41.

away.) He also appears not to have continued to read Carlyle avidly
after his 1846 lecture and essay, perhaps because his own abolitionist
convictions were growing stronger as Carlyle was expressing increasingly strident opinions on the other side, but he was quite strongly
attracted during the fifties to both De Quincey and Ruskin.

De Quincey's works were being published for the first time in a uniform edition by Ticknor and Fields (the author having finally acquired
the necessary leisure to collect his works after a lifetime of being jointly
hounded by his creditors and his opium habit), and Thoreau kept up
with and looked forward to new volumes as they appeared at something like yearly intervals. He read *Literary Reminiscences* (containing
anecdotes about Wordsworth and Coleridge, among others) and *The
Caesars* shortly after their publication in 1851, and *Historical and
Critical Essays* and *Theological Essays*, which appeared in 1853 and
1854, respectively. It is probably to *Historical and Critical Essays* that
he refers in a Journal entry in March 1853 that suggests his continuing
interest in and critical concern with Concord libraries: "I told Stacy
the other day that there was another volume of De Quincey's Essays
(wanting to see it in his library). 'I know it,' says he, 'but I shan't buy
any more of them, for nobody reads them.' I asked what book in his
library was most read. He said 'The Wide, Wide World' " (JL 5.43).

He was critical of De Quincey as one of the contemporary writers
(Dickens was another, he thought) who "express themselves with too
great fullness and detail" and "lack moderation and sententiousness"
(JL 2.418), but some quality obviously attracted him as well. Perhaps
it was the high stature that De Quincey claimed for prose composition
itself. In his essay on Herodotus, a passage from which Thoreau copied
into one of his commonplace books, De Quincey makes claims for
prose that Thoreau, then working through the latter stages of revision
on *Walden*, may well have found congenial or even inspiring. Speaking
of Herodotus as the original writer of prose, De Quincey argues: "If
prose were simply the negation of verse . . . indeed, it would be a slight
nominal honour to have been the Father of Prose. But this is ignorance,
though a pretty common ignorance. To walk well, it is not enough that
a man abstain from dancing. Walking has rules of its own the more
difficult to perceive or to practise as they are less broadly *prononcés*.
. . . Numerous laws of transition, connection, preparation, are different for a writer in verse and a writer in prose. Each mode of composition is a great art; well executed, is the highest and most difficult of
arts."[28]

28. De Quincey, *Collected Writings*, 14 vols. (Edinburgh: Adam and Charles Black,
1890), 6.100.

In any event, it is perhaps mildly surprising to find that Thoreau should have preserved a regard for and a continuing interest in De Quincey, a writer known chiefly for *The Confessions of an English Opium Eater*. One doubts that Thoreau, who once told Alek Therien in his cups that he might as well go home and cut his throat, would have much sympathy for De Quincey's longstanding laudanum habit; nor did he approve of what he considered De Quincey's narrow-minded and merely orthodox defense of the English church (JL 4.486). All these objections aside, De Quincey was one of the most gifted and original prose writers of the century, and that is more than enough reason for Thoreau to have read him carefully. And, given all their differences, Thoreau may have been attracted also to De Quincey's methods of handling classical, scholarly, and arcane subject matter in ways that made it lively and readable.

Another unexpected enthusiasm he acquired was for Ruskin. In 1857 he asked H.G.O. Blake: "Have you ever read Ruskin's books? If not, I would recommend you to try the second and third volumes (not parts) of his 'Modern Painters.' I am now reading the fourth, and have read most of his other books lately. They are singularly good and encouraging, though not without crudeness and bigotry. The themes in the volumes referred to are Infinity, Beauty, Imagination, Love of Nature, etc.,—all treated in a very living manner. I am rather surprised by them. It is remarkable that these things should be said with reference to painting chiefly, rather than literature. The 'Seven Lamps of Architecture,' too, is made of good stuff; but, as I remember, there is too much about art in it for me and the Hottentots. We want to know about matters and things in general. Our house is yet a hut" (COR, 497).[29] Once again, as with De Quincey, one suspects that it was the "very living manner" in which Ruskin's subjects, especially nature, were treated that principally attracted Thoreau, for, as he suggests in the passage, he affected to be not much interested in art criticism as such.

The pose of cultural savage ("me and the Hottentots") is one he liked to assume in such circumstances, but if he was not much interested in painting he was very much interested in the artistic depiction of nature and in equipping himself generally with the vocabulary, sense of perspective, and if possible the eye of the painter and the art critic. He had read and written about Burke's ideas of the sublime and the beautiful in college, and early in the 1850s he read carefully several of William Gilpin's popular books on picturesque scenery, so it is appropriate that he should have read Ruskin. In addition to *Modern Painters*

29. According to acquisition records, the Town Library acquired nine volumes of Ruskin's works in August 1857.

and *Seven Lamps of Architecture*, the books he mentions in the letter to Blake, Thoreau made extracts from *The Elements of Drawing* in one of his commonplace books, and his mention of having read "most of his other books lately" suggests that he probably knew Ruskin's most famous work, *The Stones of Venice* (1851–1853), although he does not specifically refer to it or to other of Ruskin's works. In the final analysis, although he found Ruskin "singularly good," he parted company with him as with so many other English writers for having failed (largely as a result of following conventional Christian orthodoxy, Thoreau thought) to carry his love of nature to its ultimate extension as a means to the worship of divinity. In a Journal entry of about the same time as the letter to Blake he says that Ruskin "expresses the common infidelity of his age and race. . . . The love of Nature and fullest perception of the revelation which she is to man is not compatible with the belief in the peculiar revelation of the Bible which Ruskin entertains" (JL 10.147). The Transcendentalists' persistent criticism of orthodox Christianity and established churches was that an insistence on "peculiar" or singular revelation such as Genesis or the gospels announced blinded humanity to the continuous and ever-present revelation that could be found through nature.

In sharp contrast to his interests and tastes in the previous decade, Thoreau's reading of poetry in the 1850s consisted almost exclusively of contemporary English and American verse. His taste was not wonderfully discriminating, by modern standards anyway, but along with Emerson he was among a very small number of his contemporaries who recognized and responded to the genius of Whitman's *Leaves of Grass* in 1855 and 1856. He gave a qualified approbation to Coventry Patmore's recently published *The Angel in the House* in a letter to Blake in 1856, saying, "Perhaps you will find it good for you" (COR, 422). Whether he found it good for himself or not, it is certainly curious to find this unsentimental bachelor celebrant of chastity recommending a poem that extols (albeit with Victorian delicacy and circumlocution) sexual love and marriage. Blake was married, though; perhaps Thoreau thought he might find it instructive. (He had earlier sent Blake copies of his own essays "Love" and "Chastity and Sensuality.") A useful shorthand index to the tone and subject of Patmore's poem, which is no longer widely read, might be his friend Edmund Gosse's praise of its author's handling of the central theme: "He dwells with chaste rapture on the joys which are the prelude to that mystery of immaculate indulgence."[30]

Thoreau also copied verse from William Allingham's *Poems* into

30. 30. Edmund Gosse, *Coventry Patmore* (London: Hadden and Houghton, 1905), p. 98.

one of his commonplace books and owned a copy of Allingham's *The Music Master . . . And Two Series of Day and Night Songs*, whose title poem has been aptly characterized by a recent critic of Allingham as "appealing to the worst side of sentimental Victorian taste," telling as it does the story of two lovers whose exquisitely self-sacrificing reserve keeps them from ever declaring their love.[31] Both Allingham and Patmore were acquaintances of Emerson's (and Allingham had received a review copy of *A Week*), so it may be that their representation in the short list of contemporary poets Thoreau read is to be attributed as much to professional courtesy as to taste.[32]

A more significant volume of verse that he owned was Tennyson's *In Memoriam* (1850). He had some previous acquaintance with Tennyson's earlier work, for he had mentioned Tennyson in a Journal comment that was a part of his English poets project in the early 1840s (PJ 1.436). If he read *In Memoriam*, however (no explicit mention of his having done so is extant), he might well have been attentive to the crisis in belief that Tennyson anatomizes there, for in the 1850s Thoreau's own reading in natural science (discussed in the next chapter) exposed him to the ideas and trends portrayed in *In Memoriam* that were pushing the consciousness of the literate public slowly but inexorably toward the disturbing implications of Darwin's *Origin of Species*.

Thoreau's principal and almost his only voiced enthusiasm for poetry during the decade, however, was for Walt Whitman, and though the circumstances of their acquaintance are well enough known, they are worth describing again as an example of the strengths and limitations of Thoreau's literary judgment.[33] He owned a copy of the 1855 first edition of *Leaves of Grass*, which had probably been recommended to him by Emerson, who had in turn received a copy from Whitman and had praised the book in his famous letter to the poet greeting him "at the beginning of a great career." Bronson Alcott was also enthusiastic about Whitman, and when Thoreau was surveying in Perth Amboy, New Jersey, in late 1856, Alcott, then living in New York City, took him out to Brooklyn to meet Whitman. There passed a wary but apparently not uncongenial interview, and Whitman gave Thoreau a copy of the 1856 second edition of *Leaves of Grass*. Thor-

31. Alan Wainer, *William Allingham* (Lewisburg, Pa.: Bucknell University Press, 1975), p. 26.

32. Harding, *Days*, p. 252.

33. Ibid. pp. 372–376; see also Andrew Schiller, "Thoreau and Whitman: The Record of a Pilgrimage," *New England Quarterly* 28 (1955): 186–197, and Charles Metzger, *Thoreau and Whitman: A Study of Their Aesthetics* (Seattle: University of Washington Press, 1961). Whitman's comments on Thoreau are recorded by Horace Traubel in *With Walt Whitman in Camden*, 3 vols. (New York: Rowman and Littlefield, 1961), 1.212 and passim.

eau's first response to the poet, jotted down in a letter to Blake shortly afterward, was to be "much interested and provoked," and he described Whitman as "apparently the greatest democrat the world has ever seen. . . . A remarkably strong though coarse nature, of a sweet disposition, and much prized by his friends. Though peculiar and rough in his exterior . . . he is essentially a gentleman. I am still somewhat in a quandary about him" (COR, 441). A bit more than a week later, on December 7, Thoreau had had time to sort out his thoughts and to read the copy of the second edition that Whitman had given him, and he again wrote to Blake an assessment that needs to be quoted at some length:

> That Walt Whitman, of whom I wrote to you, is the most interesting fact to me at present. I have just read his 2nd edition (which he gave me) and it has done me more good than any reading for a long time. Perhaps I remember best the poem of Walt Whitman an American & the Sun Down Poem. There are 2 or 3 pieces in the book which are disagreeable to say the least, simply sensual. He does not celebrate love at all. It is as if the beasts spoke. I think that men have not been ashamed of themselves without reason. No doubt, there have always been dens where such deeds were unblushingly recited, and it is no merit to compete with their inhabitants. But even on this side, he has spoken more truth than any American or modern that I know. I have found his poem exhilirating encouraging. As for its sensuality,— & it may turn out to be less sensual than it appeared—I do not so much wish that those parts were not written, as that men & women were so pure that they could read them without harm, that is, without understanding them. One woman told me that no woman could read it as if a man could read what a woman could not. Of course Walt Whitman can communicate to us no experience, and if we are shocked, whose experience is it that we are reminded of?
>
> On the whole it sounds to me very brave & American after whatever deductions. I do not believe that all the sermons so called that have been preached in this land put together are equal to it for preaching—
>
> We ought to rejoice greatly in him. He occasionally suggests something a little more than human. You cant confound him with the other inhabitants of Brooklyn or New York. How they must shudder when they read him! He is awfully good. (COR, 444–445)

Thoreau goes on to praise *Leaves of Grass* as "a great primitive poem" (an extremely approbative term for Thoreau, who persistently complained about the lack of wild or primitive vigor in English verse) and concludes by calling Whitman "a great fellow." In this letter Thoreau brought himself to focus more directly than in the earlier one on Whitman's poems themselves and less on the phenomenon of Whitman the person—the self-conscious advertisement or artifact of his vision. It is clear that Thoreau is still troubled by the "simply sensual" poems, but on the other hand, he allows that "it may turn out less sensual than it appeared," perhaps an inchoate acknowledgment of Whitman's ultimately symbolic and spiritualizing (while still earthy and, for the day, graphic) presentation of sexuality. The second edition did, in fact, contain a number of new poems explicitly treating sexual themes, such as "I Sing the Body Electric," "A Woman Waits for Me," and "Spontaneous Me." And it was a part of Whitman's self-proclaimed program for the second edition, as he told Emerson, to "celebrate in poems the eternal decency of the amativeness of Nature" and not to be one of the "bards of the fashionable delusion of the inherent nastiness of sex, and of the feeble and querulous modesty of deprivation."[34]

Thoreau's sense that the most memorable poems were "the poem of Walt Whitman an American & the Sun Down Poem" ("Song of Myself" and "Crossing Brooklyn Ferry" in later editions) is a judgment certainly affirmed by most later readers. It is difficult to point to any particular effect that reading Whitman had on Thoreau's own work at this stage in his life, but tempting to speculate that Whitman might have exerted a far greater influence if Thoreau could have known *Leaves of Grass* when he was most interested in reading and writing poetry, in his early twenties. What is clear, however, is that Thoreau valued Whitman's poetry highly, despite the limitations imposed upon his taste by prevailing New England and Victorian cultural attitudes toward sex, and it is in some respects remarkable that he was able to see Whitman as clearly as he could since the new poet was in so many ways the opposite of himself: garrulous, urban, expansive, and self-promoting. Only one other contemporary figure stirred his imagination more vividly in this decade, and that was John Brown.

Thoreau, no less than his contemporaries, was always fascinated with the heroic personality—figures like Whitman or John Brown, who devoted themselves at great personal cost to some ideal—and this familiar nineteenth-century preoccupation led naturally enough to a fondness for biography and autobiography. Emerson's *Representative Men* and Carlyle's *Heroes and Hero-Worship* are representative doc-

34. Gay Wilson Allen, *The New Walt Whitman Handbook* (New York: New York University Press, 1975), p. 83.

uments of the age, as are Thoreau's own essays "The Service," "Sir Walter Raleigh," and "Thomas Carlyle and His Works." The "simple and sincere account of his own life" that Thoreau, in the opening passage of *Walden*, requires of every writer, reflects not only the rhetorical strategy of that book but also an active preference for biographical and autobiographical writing among literary genres. This strain in his reading is consistent, going back to his college years, although it never really becomes a major preoccupation.

Not surprisingly, Thoreau read literary biography and autobiography: In addition to De Quincey's *Literary Reminiscences*, already mentioned, he read Wordsworth's *Memoirs* and owned a copy of *The Prelude*, Wordsworth's autobiographical poem, published in 1850. Likewise, the lives of great naturalists attracted him, and he read both Humboldt's own *Personal Narrative* and Klencke's biography of that great German naturalist, as well as Stöver's life of Linneaus. He read a number of other more or less simple and sincere accounts of the lives of people in fields quite distant from his own interests: Benvenuto Cellini's autobiography, the classical historian B. G. Niebuhr's *Life and Letters*, Daniel Webster's *Private Correspondence*, the Italian dramatist Vittorio Alfieri's autobiography, and Henry Morley's life of Bernard Pallissy, a sixteenth-century potter who was also a self-taught natural scientist. Thoreau may have been attracted to Pallissy because he foresaw and wrote against the evils of deforestation and urged the careful management of forest lands. When Thoreau read Pallissy's life in 1859 he was deep in his own studies of plant dispersal and succession, and also concerned, in other late projects such as *The Maine Woods*, with the future of America's forests and the need to preserve wild land.

Most of the foregoing areas of inquiry, as well as Thoreau's developing interest in natural history and history, help to account for the richly allusive and yet concrete texture of *Walden*. *A Week* had been, among other things, a rather obvious compendium of Thoreau's early literary and intellectual interests, a kind of summary of his reading to date, but in *Walden* the relationship of reading to writing is more intricate and subtle. For one thing, in *Walden* Thoreau's reading is much more adroitly integrated into the text and subordinated to his central themes than it was in *A Week*. There are no separable essays on subjects derived from his reading, as in *A Week*, but instead a chapter called "Reading," which demonstrates both by argument and example the nourishing influence of a liberal classical education, and which at the same time contains a somewhat uncharacteristic plea for cooperation and communal action in building libraries and other cultural resources in New England. In his masterpiece, Thoreau confidently tells his audience not just what he has read but how to read.

The descriptive prose of *Walden* differs from that of *A Week* by virtue of its more copious allusion and illustration, the product of Thoreau's several years of careful revision and filling out of the book's structure during the 1850s, a process which involved not only adding to but integrating into his prose the results of his continuing study. This feature and this process are nowhere more evident than in the Conclusion to *Walden*, one of the last sections of the book to be written. The rhetorical and thematic high points of the chapter—the advice to live like a traveler at home and become "expert in home-cosmography," the fable of the artist of Kouroo, and the concluding exemplum of the "strong and beautiful bug which came out of the dry leaf of an old table of apple-tree wood"—are built and based upon his reading in travel literature, Eastern scriptures, and New England history, respectively. Yet each involves a quite different but equally subtle transformation of sources, from the sly humor of travel literature invoked on behalf of staying home, to the original fable of the artist of Kouroo, loosely modeled on Hindu mythology, to the metamorphosis of the story of the bug, in which Thoreau rescues a trivial incident from a "dry leaf" in the historical collections (a characteristic pun that emphasizes the sterility of both mind and nature unless transformed by spirit and imagination) to stand as a triumphant example of regeneration.

Walden's later chapters were generally written or significantly revised late in the book's genesis. Thus, "Economy" and "Where I Lived, and What I Lived For" were relatively complete in the first draft of 1846–1847, while most of "The Pond in Winter" and "Spring," and all of "Conclusion," for example, were written between 1851 and 1854.[35] The greater particularity of these later chapters, especially "The Pond in Winter" and "Spring," with regard to the description of natural phenomena and seasonal changes reflects Thoreau's growing absorption in the study of natural history during this period. His account of the ice on Walden Pond, for example, or the famous and climactic description of the thawing sand and clay foliage of "Spring" are both informed by his recently acquired habits of careful observation and description.

Likewise, the linking of language itself to natural phenomena, so

35. See J. Lyndon Shanley, *The Making of Walden* (Chicago: University of Chicago Press, 1957); Ronald L. Clapper, "The Development of *Walden*: A Genetic Text," Ph.D. diss., UCLA, 1967; and Donald A. Ross and Stephen Adams, "The Endings of *Walden* and Stages of Composition," *Bulletin of Research in the Humanities* 84 (Winter 1981): 451–469.

evident in the sand foliage passage, where the shapes and sounds of various letters are posited to have some primordial meaning as basic as the meaning of the natural forms themselves, is also the product in part of a new development in his reading. From his early schooling onward, Thoreau had always been interested not only in languages but also in language itself, and as he matured his style grew increasingly to reflect his assimilation and extension of the Transcendentalists' language theory as sketched by Emerson in *Nature* and developed by him in greater detail in "The Poet": Like nature itself, language is a path back to spirit and to original unity; it is "fossil poetry" that reveals by its history and the etymology of particular words the original and primal significance of nature itself to mankind. Thoreau's contribution to this theory was to take it seriously and literally as a principle of his style, and consequently we find one of his most characteristic stylistic devices to be the often surprising reattachment of a word to its original sense, as when he describes the sand foliage in *Walden* as "a truly *grotesque* vegetation," calling attention to the original significance of "grotesque" (from the same root as "grotto") as coming from underground. He was assisted in this development—perhaps the key signature of his mature style—by his reading during the early 1850s of Richard Trench's *On the Study of Words* (1851) (itself indebted to Emerson's *Nature* and "The Poet") and especially by Charles Kraitsir's *The Significance of the Alphabet* (1846) and *Glossology* (1852). As the recent work of Michael West and Philip Gura has demonstrated, Thoreau was particularly indebted to Kraitsir for his belief in the primal intrinsic significance of human sounds, a belief manifested most explicitly in his glossological speculations in the "Spring" chapter of *Walden*. As Gura puts it, "What Thoreau offered as his most important 'lesson' from the worlds of matter and spirit was that words were not merely steps to a higher reality but themselves embodied and reflected the reality, a thought initially suggested to him by Kraitsir."[36] In his best work, Thoreau wrote painstakingly according to his fundamental principle of reading—"We must laboriously seek the meaning of each word and line, conjecturing a larger sense than common use permits out of what wisdom and valor and generosity we have"— and much of the perennial vigor of *Walden* is due to Thoreau's theory and practice of recovering the primeval significance of language, of "re-membering" words and of speaking "without bounds."

36. Michael West, "Charles Kraitsir's Influence upon Thoreau's Theory of Language," *Emerson Society Quarterly* 19 (4 Qtr. 1973): 262–274; Philip F. Gura, *The Wisdom of Words: Language, Theology, and Literature in the New England Renaissance* (Middletown, Conn.: Wesleyan University Press, 1981), p. 134.

4

The Later
Literary Career

Natural History

SUCH modest fame as Thoreau possessed during the late nineteenth and early twentieth centuries derived mainly from his natural history writings, especially the four volumes of seasonal selections from his Journal, edited by H.G.O. Blake, that were issued at intervals during the eighties and nineties. Thoreau's public popularity today is likewise maintained by his reputation as the author of pronouncements about the importance of preserving wild nature that have provided, as Roderick Nash has shown, the philosophical and programmatic cornerstones of conservation and preservation movements in this century.[1] But on the whole the rise of Thoreau's literary reputation has tended— among academics, at any rate—to throw his achievements as a naturalist into the shade. Increasingly his artistry and the self-referential sufficiency and integrity of his texts, especially *Walden*, have displaced the propositions of the natural scientist and social critic as centers of critical interest. Whatever the shifts and fluctuations in his reputation during our century, Thoreau's own development during the 1850s, the major phase of his abbreviated career, was clearly in the direction of increasing interest in the study of and writing about nature on the one hand, and on the other the expression of increasingly sharp and outspoken views on sensitive social and political issues of his day, especially the rampant materialism of his culture (e.g., "Life Without Principle") and the complicity of the North in the perpetuation of slavery (e.g., "Slavery in Massachusetts").

Beginning, as we have seen, at the time of his acquaintance with the great naturalist Louis Agassiz and his reading of Coleridge's *Theory of Life* during the late 1840s, the serious and concerted study of natural history gradually became, along with writing itself, his principal avocation. When he died, in May 1862, the town clerk listed his occupa-

---

1. *Wilderness and the American Mind*, rev. ed. (New Haven: Yale University Press, 1973), pp. 84–95.

tion as "Natural Historian,"[2] and this designation reflects not only his status and reputation in the community but one of his major intellectual and literary preoccupations as well. And far from being a retreat and a falling away from the high achievement of writing *Walden*, his natural history studies plunged Thoreau into one of the liveliest and most turbulent intellectual controversies of the nineteenth century.

Not all the books he read, however, bore on his serious theoretical study of the flora and fauna (especially the former) of New England. Thoreau read widely in natural history during this period, and a great deal of this reading was in ephemeral or popular works that, like some of his travel reading, were mainly useful to him in providing illustrative metaphors or allusions that could enliven his own prose. He also had certain basic texts, manuals of botany like Bigelow's and Gray's, that were essential tools for learning taxonomy. "One studies books of science merely to learn the language of naturalists,—to be able to communicate with them," he said (JL 5.42). He knew the natural history portions of the great government surveys of the West, some of them written by eminent scientists; compendiums like Loudon's *Encyclopedia of Plants* or the monumental *Arboretum et Fruticetum Britannicum*; books on such specialized subjects as ornithology, oology, zoology, conchology, herpetology; and popular "light reading" with such titles as *Gleanings in Natural History, Curiosities of Natural History, Leaves from the Notebook of a Naturalist, Illustrated Natural History*, and *Zoological Recreations*. He even knew the popular illustrated book that the young heroine of *Jane Eyre* is reading as the novel opens, Bewick's *British Birds*. Running through this apparently omnivorous reading, however, is a vein of serious theoretical contemporary natural science with direct bearing on Thoreau's own aims as a naturalist and on the history of scientific thought in the nineteenth century.

To be a naturalist during the 1850s—at least if one was as well read in the field as Thoreau—was to witness one of the most exciting and unsettling periods in the history of the discipline. For decades, evidence had been accumulating to undermine theories of creation that were consistent with a literal interpretation of the account rendered in Genesis. The gradual deciphering of the fossil record led to a growing awareness that the age of the earth would have to be measured at least in millions rather than in thousands of years. The earth itself, it was seen, must have been subject to great physical changes in its history to account for such phenomena as the presence of marine fossil beds deep in strata lifted thousands of feet above sea level. A corresponding and apparently confirming astronomical theory, positing vast amounts of

2. Howarth, *The Book of Concord*, p. 3.

time during which matter had become progressively more organized, was offered by Sir William Herschel's nebular hypothesis: that the celestial bodies had been formed out of primordial gas during remote eons—a view not too distant from our present cosmology. The fixity of species, heretofore an unquestioned and unquestionable assumption, was undermined by fossil records of animals that clearly existed no more, and by contemporary testimony from travelers and explorers that other animals—notably the dodo—had become extinct in modern times. In this interregnum between the passing away of the old static and rigidly hierarchic conception of the organization of nature, each of whose elements had been ordained and created from the beginning, and the gradual victory attained by the Darwinian model of development and speciation through *natural* selection (that is to say, through physical laws), Thoreau passed his career as a naturalist.

During this period, every naturalist had to wrestle, if only indirectly, with the great scientific issue of the age: What was the agency or mechanism by which change and development in nature occurred? Change there surely was. Among scientists even the most ardent supporters of special creation no longer defended the static view of nature that Thoreau had been exposed to in college. But how did nature change, how much, in what directions, and what did change portend or signify about humanity's place in nature? Not even the casual classifier or amateur naturalist (which Thoreau was assuredly not, in any case) could entirely escape the controversy and the unsettling questions, for even learning taxonomy required one to choose a system, and a system of classification in turn reflected an attitude toward the arrangement of species, genera, families, and so on that expressed an implicit adherence to some theory of creation or natural development. Thoreau's reading in natural science during this period served to acquaint him with the principal theoretical divisions among contemporary scientists, to provide him with a basic knowledge of the history of the major issues in science during his century, and to prepare him to read and be able to make an informed judgment about Darwin's *Origin of Species* early in 1860, almost immediately upon its publication in America.

At the same time, in his own field studies and writings he practiced a type of natural history that was different in kind from either that of the creationists and scriptural apologists on the one hand, or the more positivistic, proto-evolutionary biologists on the other,[3] a kind of nat-

3. For a more sophisticated system of classifying the orientations of mid-nineteenth-century biologists, see Dov Ospovat, "Perfect Adaptation and Teleological Explanation: Approaches to the Problem of the History of Life in the Mid-Nineteenth Century," *Studies in the History of Biology* 2 (1978): 33–56. See also Neal C. Gillespie, *Charles Darwin and the Problem of Creation* (Chicago: University of Chicago Press,

ural history more closely related to Coleridge, Goethe, and German *Naturphilosophie* than either, but also containing highly distinctive elements of his own, marked by his increasing interest in such ancient natural historians as Aristotle, Pliny, and Herodotus. Thoreau's work as a naturalist during this decade was characterized, as we shall see, by an effort to give equal weight to both the natural and the historical components of *natural history*: that is, understanding the nomenclature and the relationships among phenomena as described by current science (the "natural" part) and at the same time treating those phenomena as having ultimate significance only through the history of their association with humankind. Concomitantly, he found both the orthodox Christian apologias for special creation and the nascent theory of organic evolution tinctured with what he termed "infidelity." To fix the coordinates of his distinctive stance in the lively debate about the origin and development of life, then, it is necessary to sketch in some detail his reading of key documents and his own writing of natural history during the 1850s.

His grounding had been orthodox in the extreme, as I have suggested in the treatment of his natural history education (or lack of it) at Harvard, where he had read a classic apology for the "argument from design" in William Smellie's *The Philosophy of Natural History*. As the nineteenth century progressed, it became increasingly impossible to reconcile, as Smellie and his kindred had tried to do, the Mosaic account of creation with the discoveries of such new sciences as geology, paleontology, embryology, and comparative anatomy. In 1840, for example, Thoreau read one of the key works in the accelerating dismantling of the biblical chronology, Lyell's *Principles of Geology* (a book that, about the same time, was having a profound influence on the young Charles Darwin on board the *Beagle*).[4] Although Lyell was a vigorous opponent of evolution, he argued for a uniformitarian geology whose imaginatively provocative vistas of eons upon eons opening backward in time provided a necessary prerequisite for a serious consideration of evolution. Another such essential prerequisite was the disproof of the fixity of species, and this had been provided principally by Baron Cuvier, another outspoken opponent but unwitting ally of the progressive development view, whose *The Animal Kingdom* Thoreau read in 1851. Cuvier established on a scientific footing the comparative study and classification of fossil fauna and announced the discovery of more than a score of extinct species. He furnished a portion

---

1979), esp. chap. 1, "Special Creation Among British and American Naturalists 1830–59," for an extremely useful overview of the terms of the debate.

4. Loren Eiseley, *Darwin's Century* (Garden City, N.Y.: Doubleday, 1958), p. 99.

of the methodology by which later paleontologists would demonstrate the common ancestry of various species through progressive structural differentiation.[5]

Gradually the old orthodoxy of the natural theologians who had defended for the most part the literal interpretation of Genesis (with some occasional slippage on the score of what a biblical "day" of creation consisted of) gave way to a somewhat awkward new orthodoxy that posited distinctly different periods of creation separated, if need be, by the long stretches of time required by the geologic and astronomical calendars. The large gaps frequently encountered in the fossil record and the appearance of highly developed organisms without the apparent existence of appropriately primitive earlier forms in older strata made it for a time plausible to argue that, although the different major classes of plants and animals had clearly come into existence at different times and not all at once, there was not sufficient evidence to prove that later groups had developed from earlier ones. As Edward Hitchcock, an eminent Massachusetts geologist whose work Thoreau knew well, put it, "Geology shows a divine hand cutting the chain asunder at intervals, and commencing new series of operations."[6]

This theory provided for a carefully circumscribed sort of evolution and a generally beneficent sort of progressionism. If the major subdivisions of organic life had, as the fossil record then suggested, appeared suddenly at different times in the history of the earth, and if some modern animals, including man, bore striking resemblances to earlier forms, then a kind of organic typology was evident in nature. Although the major groups themselves gave indications of progressive development in complexity from the one to the other over time (from invertebrates to vertebrates, for example), such profound gaps existed between them that they could only have been created separately and could not have arisen gradually from a common ancestor. Thus, the argument went, the fossil record revealed creation in steps, with natural laws sufficing to explain development within but not between major groups. Read this way, as it was by many competent scientists, the geological record seemed to reveal an anticipation of man, as the creator gradually and carefully prepared for the apotheosis of creation by successively bringing into existence increasingly sophisticated forms, all ultimately pointing toward the pinnacle that would be reached in *Homo sapiens.*

A refined and idealistic—as opposed to the earlier utilitarian—argument from design was still intact, in other words, one refined to in-

5. Ibid. pp. 80–89.
6. *The Religion of Geology,* quoted in Gillespie, *Charles Darwin,* p. 23.

corporate the results of the new sciences. The scientists who made the discoveries and provided much of the evidence later adduced to support the theory of evolution were often the most vigorous in their defense of what was still called "the plan of the Creator." The principal American apologist of this school of progressive but separate creations was also the most distinguished, popular, and in many ways the most brilliant scientist of his day, Louis Agassiz, with whom Thoreau was personally acquainted and whose works he knew well. It will be remembered that Thoreau's first contact with Agassiz had occurred in 1847, when he began corresponding with Agassiz (through his assistant James Elliot Cabot) and collecting specimens for him. Thoreau also may have attended Agassiz's fashionable "Plan of Creation" lectures in Boston the previous winter. He acquired in 1850 or 1851 as his major zoological text the manual that Agassiz wrote with Augustus A. Gould, *Principles of Zoology*.

This book was considerably more than a mere manual of zoology, however, for in it Agassiz set forth and argued for his particular theory of creation, from which it will be necessary to quote at some length in order to give an idea of the prevailing theoretical climate in which Thoreau worked:

> It is evident that there is a manifest progress in the succession of beings on the surface of the earth. This progress consists in an increasing similarity to the living fauna, and among the Vertebrates, especially, in their increasing resemblance to Man.
>
> But this connection is not the consequence of a direct lineage between the faunas of differing ages. There is nothing like parental descent connecting them. . . . The link by which they are connected is of a higher and immaterial nature; and their connection is to be sought in the view of the Creator himself, whose aim, in forming the earth, in allowing it to undergo the successive changes which Geology has pointed out, and in creating successively all the different types of animals which have passed away, was to introduce Man upon the surface of our globe. Man is the end towards which all the animal creation has tended, from the first appearance of the first Palaeozoic fishes.
>
> To study, in this view, the succession of animals in time, and their distribution in space, is, therefore, to become acquainted with the ideas of God himself.[7]

A graphic synopsis of Agassiz's plan of creation is contained in the diagram that serves as the frontispiece to *Principles* showing the five

7. Louis Agassiz and Augustus A. Gould, *Principles of Zoology*, new revised ed. (Boston: Gould and Lincoln, 1873), pp. 237–238.

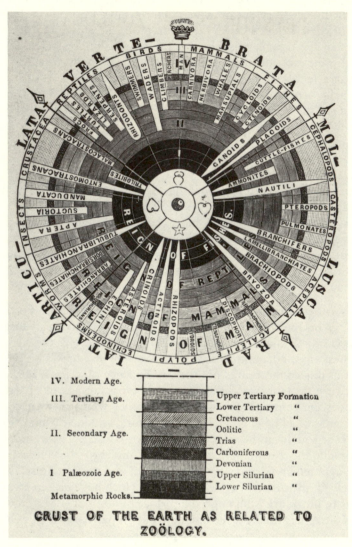

Frontispiece of Agassiz and Gould's *Principles of Zoology*,
illustrating the different epochs of creation.

major groups of fauna and their successive but separate first appearances on the globe.

Thus Agassiz's theory of different epochs of creation required him to posit what he termed in the *Essay on Classification*, another work with which Thoreau was acquainted, "repeated interventions on the part of the Creator," so that he was in the uncomfortable position (for a scientist) of having to argue for and defend not one divine suspension of natural law, but several. Agassiz had been influenced in his youth by the *Naturphilosophie* of Oken and Schelling, and he never lost his belief in the "higher and immaterial" essence of nature, a belief that eventually led him to become the leading spokesman for the opponents of Darwinism in America.[8] Agassiz retained his public popularity, but as a consequence of his opposition to Darwin he and the other proponents of the creationist philosophy gradually lost credibility in the scientific community after 1860.

But before this time he had no real opponents and his theory dominated the field, at least in America. Ironically, Agassiz too was one of the unwitting contributors to the general and eventual triumph of the Darwinian model, for like Lyell and Cuvier he was a brilliant scientist whose work in paleontology and embryology—stressing the tendency of the embryo to pass through successive earlier stages of development (work that played a part in the development of the now-familiar idea that ontogeny recapitulates phylogeny)—Darwin himself cited as a point of support for the theory of natural selection.[9] One of Agassiz's other major contributions to science was a theory of glaciation which solved a major problem in geology and further weakened the biblical explanations that began by assuming the literal truth of the Noachian deluge.

One of the most bizarre offshoots of Agassiz's theory of separate creations was its use by pro-slavery scientists to defend the South's peculiar institution. If the characteristic human races of each part of the globe had been created separately, they might not be intrinsically equal, and it became easier to construct a rationale for the subservience of those supposedly inferior races. Two such works that Thoreau knew were Charles Pickering's *The Races of Man* and Nott and Glidden's *Types of Mankind*, the latter containing a prefatory sketch by Agassiz. Although a patriotic supporter of the North during the Civil War, Agassiz continued to assert the separate creation and physical inferiority of the Negro race.

8. Edward Lurie, *Louis Agassiz: A Life in Science* (Chicago: University of Chicago Press, 1960), pp. 27–28.

9. Ibid. p. 288.

In the passage from the conclusion of *Principles of Zoology* quoted earlier, it will be noted that Agassiz takes pains explicitly to deny the possibility of "parental descent" in the evolution of major groups from a common ancestor, and that he makes this denial well in advance of Darwin's postulation of such a theory of descent. The idea of organic evolution, in other words, was already in the air and being widely discussed by scientists, theologians, and educated persons generally. That it required rebuttal this early was due largely to the controversy beginning in 1844 over an anonymously published book titled *Vestiges of the Natural History of Creation*, by a Scottish journalist and amateur naturalist named Robert Chambers. *Vestiges* put forward for the first time in England a comprehensive and elaborately buttressed theory of organic evolution without the need for a first cause or special creation at any point. Despite the fact that its arguments and evidence were often weak or wrong, and that Chambers himself was not highly qualified in all the branches of natural science from which he adduced evidence, the book made the first really bold and in many ways impressive argument for the creation of organic life out of inorganic materials and for its successive evolution through time into the various classes of flora and fauna that came to populate the globe—all without requiring the direct or indirect intervention of God.[10] Milton Millhouser, in *Just Before Darwin*, his study of Chambers and *Vestiges*, describes the furor that ensued: "For four years now [in 1848] it [*Vestiges*] had been the center of a fierce little storm, the target of a steady fire of philosophic analysis, scientific ridicule, and theological vituperation. Its author was variously denounced as atheist, shallow smatterer, and credulous dupe. The work itself, alarmingly popular despite a merciless critical pounding, was regarded by the orthodox as pernicious in the very highest degree."[11]

It was of Chambers principally that Agassiz was thinking when he denied the possibility of "parental descent," and this cudgel was taken up by numerous other scientists and religious thinkers during the 1850s, the chief among whom was Hugh Miller, another Scotsman who was also an amateur geologist and a polemicist in the Presbyterian Free Church controversy. He published in 1849 a somewhat strident refutation of *Vestiges* with the wonderful title *The Foot-prints of the Creator; or, The Asterolepis of Stromness*, issued in an American edition in 1850 with a laudatory memoir of Miller by Agassiz—which, in

10. Milton Millhouser, *Just Before Darwin* (Middletown, Conn.: Wesleyan University Press, 1959), esp. chap. 4, "Vestiges of the Natural History of Creation," pp. 86–115.

11. Ibid. p. 4.

the climate of the day, amounted to a kind of semi-official imprimatur. In this and other popular works such as *The Old Red Sandstone* and *The Testimony of the Rocks*, Miller became the chief reconciler of orthodox religion with the new geological science, like Agassiz trying to show that the fossil record revealed the creator's progressive plan and that, without a first cause and successive interventions by God, evolution was impossible. Even more important, perhaps, it was greatly to be feared. In *Foot-prints of the Creator*, with characteristic bluntness, Miller let the real cat out of the bag. The "development hypothesis" he says, referring to Chambers's theory of organic evolution, "would fain transfer the work of creation from the department of miracle to the province of natural law, and would strike down, in the process of removal, all the old landmarks, ethical and religious."[12]

The reason that these landmarks would be struck down is quite clear if one carries, as Miller does, the implications of the "development hypothesis" to their logical conclusion:

> If, during a period so vast as to be scarce expressible by figures, the creatures now human have been rising, by *almost* infinitesimals, from compound microscopic cells,—minute vital globules within globules, begot by electricity on dead gelatinous matter— until they have at length become the men and women whom we see around us, we must hold either the monstrous belief that all the vitalities, whether those of monads or of mites, of fishes or of reptiles, of birds or of beasts, are individual and inherently immortal and undying, or that human souls are *not* so.[13]

Thoreau knew not only the principal works of Agassiz but also Chambers's *Vestiges*, Miller's refutation of Chambers in *Foot-prints*, and the other works by Miller named earlier. He knew Agassiz and his work well enough to refer to him frequently in the Journal in the 1850s and to discuss learnedly with him the copulation of turtles and like matters at dinner at Emerson's in 1857 (JL 9.298–299). For the most part in his Journal and notebooks, in fact, he confines himself to such phenomenal or factual matters as these and does not comment directly upon the relative merits of the arguments on either side of the large issue of development versus special creation. A significant exception to this reticence, however, comes in a Journal entry for September 28, 1851, after Thoreau had been reading Miller's *Old Red Sandstone*. Miller had described the beauty of a fossil fish and then ventured to

12. Hugh Miller, *Footprints of the Creator; or, the Asterolepis of Stromness* (Boston: Gould and Lincoln, 1856), p. 36.

13. Ibid. p. 38.

speak of it as *almost* approaching a kind of moral beauty. Thoreau's comment makes clear the grounds of his divergence from both Miller's and Chambers's school of thought: "The hesitation with which this is said—to say nothing of its simplicity—betrays a latent infidelity more fatal far than that of the 'Vestiges of Creation,' which in another work this author endeavors to correct. He describes that as an exception which is in fact the rule. The supposed want of harmony between 'the perception and love of the beautiful' and a delicate moral sense betrays what kind of beauty the writer has been conversant with" (JL 2.30–31). Although he appears to be speaking as much about art and beauty as about nature here, Thoreau's point is that the realms of the beautiful and the good and the natural cannot be separated, and the fatal flaw or "infidelity" in Miller's treatment of nature is simply another manifestation of the flaw of orthodox Christianity generally in fixing creation at some former date. For Thoreau, as for Emerson, morality or virtue was not to be separated from beauty, and creation was not to be assigned to some former era, no matter how ingeniously the fossil record might be interpreted. It was the perception of the divine that rendered nature both beautiful and good and made it live. To treat it as evidence of creation at some former time, whether through science or religion, was to convert it into dead matter. For Emerson, in the Divinity School Address, the duty of the minister was to show not that God was, but is; for Thoreau, the duty of the naturalist was to show not that creation was, but is. The triumphant climax of "Spring" in *Walden*, in this context, is both an assertion of the vital principle animating nature and a fairly explicit refutation of the contemporary squabbles over the meaning of the geologic record:

> The earth is not a mere fragment of dead history, stratum upon stratum like the leaves of a book, to be studied by geologists and antiquaries chiefly, but living poetry like the leaves of a tree, which precede flowers and fruit,—not a fossil earth, but a living earth; compared with whose great central life all animal and vegetable life is merely parasitic. (p. 309)

As Thoreau's comments about the worse "infidelity" of Miller suggest, a thoroughgoing Transcendental naturalist would find it easier to accept organic evolution than special creation. The notion of a universe in a continual state of becoming, where nature is dynamic and evolving, was a world image far more appealing to Transcendentalists than the model of a world of creative starts and stops advanced by the reconcilers of science with Christian orthodoxy. The assumption that Thoreau made—his primary article of faith, as it were—that nature was an externalization of spirit, did not preclude his acceptance of evolution, which dealt really only with nature as phenomena, the "dumb, beautiful ministers" of Walt Whitman's "Sun Down Poem." Scientific evolution might accurately describe the actual, in other words, without touching what was ultimately real; and it was certainly a more powerful paradigm for the study of natural history than the patchwork theory of Agassiz and his allies that required successive episodes of miraculous intervention by God interspersed with eons of uninterrupted natural law in order to account for the diversity of types and species.

Thus, when Darwin's *Origin of Species* appeared in late 1859, Thoreau was not only ready and eager to read it but also inclined to be favorably disposed toward it. He acquired the book from the Town Library early in 1860, immediately upon its accession, it would appear, and made extracts from it in his natural history "fact book." Shortly afterward, he told Franklin Sanborn that he liked the *Origin of Species* very much.[14] Although, characteristically, his extracts do not distill Darwin's thesis directly, but rather consist mostly of curious or significant phenomena that he was interested in, he did note details about the naturalization of plants and the dispersion of seeds that show his careful attention to aspects of the theory that bore on his current project of studying the dispersion and succession of plant species within a given area.

He seems, in fact, to have seized on both the theoretical strength of Darwin and the corresponding weakness of Agassiz. In the spring of 1860, Emerson quotes a remark of Thoreau's that cogently expresses a fundamental difference between the two theories: On being told, apparently, that Agassiz had scoffed at Darwin, Thoreau said, "If Agassiz sees two thrushes so alike that they bother the ornithologist to discriminate them, he insists they are two species; but if he sees Humboldt [the great German natural scientist] and Fred Cogswell [a retarded inmate of the Concord Almshouse], he insists that they come from one ancestor" (JMN 14.350). What Agassiz and his school of scientists were not willing to acknowledge, in other words, was the infinite series of gradations in nature that suggested that species varied naturally. At the same time, they clung to a belief in the uniqueness of human beings— at least Caucasians—despite the evidence that they, too, varied widely, naturally, and in precisely the same ways.

Thoreau's reading of Darwin, as William L. Howarth has suggested, may even have given him considerable impetus for his own natural history writing. He had been interested for several years in the dispersion of seeds and the succession of plants within particular habitats,

14. Harding, *Days*, p. 429.

and in 1860 he began composing a long work on this subject that remained unfinished at his death.[15] He did manage in the fall of 1860 to extract from this work in progress a lecture and an essay titled "The Succession of Forest Trees" that probably gives a fair indication of the direction of the whole. Working in the essay as a self-proclaimed Transcendentalist, one whose interest ultimately is the significance of the seed as expressive of a vital principle of nature, Thoreau nonetheless offers a convincing and scientifically sound analysis of how plant communities—in this case oaks and pines—progress toward what botanists would later call the climax phase of vegetation. The image of the natural world that he depicts is in certain senses compatible with the Darwinian view—one of constant competition, struggle, and change— but on the other hand still expressive of the integral and dynamic whole that speaks to humanity of nature's vital spiritual center.

At the same time that he was following the developments in contemporary natural science that culminated in the *Origin of Species*, however, Thoreau was also discovering another world of natural history of equal fascination and importance to him in the works of ancient Greek and Latin naturalists and earlier English natural historians and herbalists. He began reading Aristotle, Aelianus, Theophrastus, Herodotus, and Pliny in earnest in 1859 and made rather extensive extracts from their works in his notebooks and frequent allusions to them in his Journal. He also began working references to them into his current natural history writings. Ellery Channing, who knew Thoreau's current interests better than anyone, believed that "he meant probably to translate and write on the subject [natural history] as viewed by the ancients."[16] Whether or not Channing was correct, it is nevertheless true that Thoreau devoted a great deal of time and care to reading the ancient natural history writers and the earlier English herbalists and natural historians—Gerard for example, and Evelyn, and Edward Topsell's sixteenth-century translation of *The Historie of Foure-Footed Beasts*. Thoreau found in these earlier writers a freshness of language and a vividness of description that were a pleasing antidote to contemporary scientific writing and nomenclature:

> The most poetic and truest account of objects is generally by those who first observe them, or the discoverers of them, whether a sharper perception and curiosity in them led to the discovery or the greater novelty more inspired their report. Accordingly, I love most to read the accounts of a country, its natural produc-

15. Howarth, *The Book of Concord*, pp. 195, 203–208.
16. *Thoreau: The Poet-Naturalist*, p. 61.

tions and curiosities, by those who first settled it, and also the earliest, though often unscientific, writers on natural science. (JL 9.232)

In another sense these writers were less a restorative contrast to the dryness of modern scientific writing than they were a necessary complement to it and an essential component of the true natural history of any phenomenon, because their very words, according to Thoreau's extension of the Transcendental theory of language, were literally as well as figuratively true to life:

> As in the expression of moral truths we admire any closeness to the physical fact which in all language is the symbol of the spiritual, so, finally, when natural objects are described, it is an advantage if words derived originally from nature, it is true, but which have been turned (tropes) from their primary signification to a moral sense, are used, i.e., if the object is personified. The one who loves and understands a thing the best will incline to use personal pronouns in speaking of it. To him there is no neuter gender. Many of the words of the old naturalists were in this sense doubly tropes. (JL 13.145–146)

As words generally reveal their full meaning only if one is acquainted with their etymologies, so particular natural facts disclose their real significance only through the history of their association with man. Thoreau's appreciation of the old natural history writers marks his belief that the meaning of nature is dependent upon man, the perceiver, and that natural *history* must indeed have a historical component: To know a natural object—the apple tree in "Wild Apples," for example—requires more than fixing its genus and species and being able to identify its varieties; it involves tracing, as Thoreau does in the beginning of that essay, the history of the apple tree's association with man, giving the sum of its histories, so to speak, and attempting to write a diachronic natural science in which the discoveries of the present day do not invalidate but rather take their place in succession with those of the past.[17] As "The Succession of Forest Trees" is part of a longer unfinished manuscript on the dispersion of seeds, "Wild Apples" is part of a longer unfinished work on wild fruits, only one other part of which, a lecture on huckleberries, Thoreau was able to put into something like finished form before he died.[18] These few pieces, however, all show the coalescence of his careful observation, acquaintance

17. Robert Sattelmeyer, "Introduction," to Henry David Thoreau, *The Natural History Essays* (Salt Lake City: Peregrine Smith Press, 1980), pp. xxx–xxxiv.

18. Howarth, *The Book of Concord*, pp. 184–186.

with contemporary scientific work, and incorporation of the work of the ancients into what was—inchoately, perhaps—a distinctive mode of natural history writing in America, one that placed equal emphasis on the natural and the historical.

Civil History

IN APRIL 1858, Emerson reported to a correspondent, H. S. Randall, that "[Thoreau's] study seems at present to be equally shared between Natural and Civil History; . . . he reads both with a keen and original eye."[19] The "Civil History" Emerson refers to is the history of the early exploration and discovery of the North American continent, especially the northeast coast of New England and Canada, and his observation that this interest was equally shared with natural history is accurate, for Thoreau's preoccupations with the two types of history did indeed develop together and with equal strength during the last decade of his life. And like his absorption in natural science, his fascination with regional and early American history began to be concerted and serious during the period of stabilization and redirection in his career around 1850. He had explored local New England and Concord history earlier for *A Week* and in the elegiac account "Former Inhabitants" in *Walden* (much of which was drafted in the Journal as early as 1845–1846), but history first became a major intellectual preoccupation following his visits to Cape Cod in 1849 and 1850 and his trip to Montreal and Quebec in 1850. These excursions stimulated his interest in the wider field of early American history by presenting him with certain intellectual problems and opportunities that he attempted to work out and capitalize upon during the ensuing decade. The most important of these discoveries was the realization that the story of early exploration and colonization was much more complex, varied, and problematic than he had realized, and that Cape Cod itself offered a unique ground upon which to practice the discipline of history. A cape, as he described its etymology in the beginning of his narrative, was "that part by which we take hold of a thing," and the "thing" that Thoreau had in mind was ultimately no less than the historical evolution of the idea of America itself.

Since Thoreau traveled infrequently, he customarily tried to make his excursions as intense and concentrated as possible by reading as much as he could lay his hands on about the history of the object of

19. Partial transcription of letter in sale catalogue of *The Stephen H. Wakeman Collection of Books of Nineteenth-Century American Writers* (New York: American Art Association, 1924), item 211.

his journey before, during, and after the trip. He and his brother had carried John Hayward's *New England Gazetteer* with them on the Concord and Merrimack in 1839, and when Thoreau and Ellery Channing first visited Cape Cod ten years later, he read "some short notices of the Cape towns" in the eighth volume of the first series of Massachusetts Historical Society *Collections* while the stagecoach passed through the various villages described (WE, 221; CC, 20). After (and possibly before as well) the trip to the Cape and his trip to Canada the next year, Thoreau began to compile a bibliography and take notes on documentary and secondary sources for the history of both Canada and Cape Cod in his Canada notebook.[20]

These two reading projects at first overlapped and then became differentiated from one another over the years. Thoreau was fascinated by Cape Cod, so much so that he was able to compose and deliver a quite popular lecture on the Cape within a few months of his first visit. He took pains to return to gather more impressions and information the following summer. He remained interested in the Cape, its history, and its people, returning again in 1855 and 1857 and adding information to the unpublished portion of his manuscript of *Cape Cod* until shortly before his death.[21] The Canadian excursion, on the other hand, failed to arouse much enthusiasm in him. Thoreau responded somewhat chauvinistically to French Canadian civilization, the British military presence there, and the Roman Catholicism of the inhabitants. His account of the excursion in "A Yankee in Canada," which was suspended part way through its serialization in *Putnam's* when Thoreau refused to excise or tone down what the genteel George William Curtis considered to be "heresies" in the essay,[22] is probably the least inspired of his travel essays. He himself confessed to being strangely unmoved by this trip—his only one outside the United States—and largely indifferent to the literary project that developed from it.[23]

Yet imaginatively his visit to French Canada was perhaps the key to his sustained interest in Cape Cod and in early American history, for in the process of researching the early history of French settlement and exploration in North America, he began to piece together the threads of a story that he would devote much of his attention in *Cape Cod* to

20. See Willson, "Thoreau's Canadian Notebook."

21. Harding, *Days*, pp. 270–272, 359–361, 382–385; see also "Historical Introduction," *Cape Cod*, ed. Joseph J. Moldenhauer (Princeton: Princeton University Press, 1988).

22. Harding, *Days*, pp. 282–283.

23. In a letter to Blake (COR, 299), he said frankly of "An Excursion to Canada," "I do not wonder that you do not like my Canada story. It concerns me but little, and probably is not worth the time it took to tell it."

chronicling: the extent and richness of what he came to call the "Ante-Pilgrim" history of the New World.

The Canada notebook itself gives physical testimony to this bifurcation of interest. It divides into two sections, one commencing at each end of the notebook (that is, Thoreau wrote one series of notes starting from the front of the notebook and then, turning the notebook upside down, another series starting from the back). The first section, as Lawrence Willson has described it, was made "from late 1850, just after his return from Canada, until he wrote his lecture and presented 'A Yankee in Canada' for publication early in 1852," and consisted mostly of information that would help fill out and embellish the narrative—details about the St. Lawrence River, statistics about the population of Canada, early settlement, the climate (especially the effects of extreme cold), and so forth.[24] The sources quoted are not, for the most part, historical, although Thoreau does extract primary material on early voyages to New France by Cartier and Jean Alphonse from a volume of the *Transactions* of the Literary and Historical Society of Quebec and from Charlevoix's *Histoire . . . de la Nouvelle France* (1744), both of which would be important sources for him. In general, however, this material does not suggest a depth of historical interest growing out of the Canada trip.

The other section of the notebook begins in parallel with the first section of notes as far as chronology is concerned—commencing in November 1850 and running to 1855 or 1856—but consists of quite different though related material. Thoreau's first entry in the section suggests the nature of his interests:

> November 18, 1850
> Saw at Cambridge . . . the following old books containing
> maps.
> 1570 to 84. Ortelius
> 1597 Wytfliet
> 1612 1st ed
> 1609 . . . Lescarbot [etc.][25]

The notes that he took on these early maps of the New World pay special attention to the depiction of Canada and the St. Lawrence, so they are related to the Canadian project, but they opened for him a much more interesting subject than could be subsumed or contained in the account of his rather disappointing excursion. The progress of cartography, starting with the very earliest sixteenth-century sources in which the ratio of wishful thinking and fantasy to accurate depiction

24. "Thoreau's Canadian Notebook," p. 189.
25. Ibid. p. 190.

is especially high, provided him literally with a graphic representation of the evolution of the idea of America in the European mind in the sixteenth, seventeenth, and eighteenth centuries. The phenomenon of America, he was discovering, was a much wider and more important subject to the Western mind than the rather narrow range of events described by American historians generally suggested, since that version emphasized British exploration and settlement.

Soon he began making notes from Samuel de Champlain's *Voyages*, taking pains to describe to himself the material contained in different early editions of Champlain's work, and also from Marc Lescarbot's *Histoire de la Nouvelle-France*. These primary sources, especially Champlain, who quickly became Thoreau's standard by which to judge other explorers' accounts, opened his eyes for the first time to the superiority as well as the chronological precedence of the French explorers. He continues the notebook with a "general denunciation, by implication," as Willson terms it, "of English writers on America for their neglect of the French source books [and maps] he has consulted."[26]

This discovery was leading him in a direction that was at odds with the atmosphere and themes of his Canada story, in which he portrayed the French-based civilization of Quebec as derivative, decadent, and marked by feudal anachronisms repugnant to a Yankee. The subject belonged, more naturally, with his story of Cape Cod, an isolable American geographical entity that could serve to represent the developments and the vicissitudes in American history. Accordingly, at some point in the composition of both works he made a decision to integrate the results of his historical researches into the Cape Cod narrative. In the manuscript of "An Excursion to Canada" there survives a portion of an early draft that indicates this decision clearly: In the midst of a discussion about Champlain he notes on the blank portion of a leaf, "Missing pages transferred to Cape Cod," and the next surviving leaf has several reworkings of a passage on Champlain and Lescarbot, praising their "instructive & interesting" accounts and taking to task the contemporary American historian George Bancroft, who "appears never to have heard of" Champlain's early *Voyages*. The polemic concludes: "It is remarkable that so interesting & particular an account of the coast of New England should have been written and given to the world—as early as 1613 several editions of which are to be found at Cambridge—& yet no Historian[s] of America have even seen them!"[27]

The upshot of this discovery and the consequent professional deci-

26. Ibid. p. 194.
27. CSmH (HM 953).

sion to integrate the subject into the *Cape Cod* manuscript was that that work, especially the last chapter, "Provincetown," gradually expanded to become a detailed exposition and critique of early American history in both senses of the word—that is, the events of the past and the discipline of writing about them. Like "An Excursion to Canada," *Cape Cod* originally contained a fair number of historical references in addition to topographical, descriptive, social, and statistical information that fleshed out the narrative of Thoreau's 1849 journey. But "Provincetown" in this early (pre-1855) state probably contained for its historical theme mainly Thoreau's sarcastic running commentary on the difference between his and Channing's experiences of the Cape and those of the Pilgrims as described in Mourt's "Relation," a sort of collective journal of the Plymouth colony founders. (He counters, for example, the Pilgrim's assertion that the land of the Cape was "excellent black earth" to "a spit's depth" by observing that he and Channing "did not see enough black earth in Provincetown to fill a flower-pot").[28]

But like "An Excursion to Canada," *Cape Cod* was suspended in the midst of its serialization in *Putnam's* in August 1855, and the remainder of the manuscript, including "Provincetown," was not published until Ticknor and Fields brought out a posthumous edition of the book in 1865. During the years after 1855, however, Thoreau continued to revise the manuscript, especially the Provincetown chapter, and so broadened and deepened the historical focus of the book that it grew to be a meditation on American history in which the Cape itself becomes metonymically the ground for examining the adequacy of contemporary American historiography. Like *Walden*, which benefited enormously from the enforced prolongation of its genesis as a result of the commercial failure of *A Week* in 1849, *Cape Cod* emerged the better—at least the more serious and scholarly—book for its interruption. And like *Walden*, which derives its simultaneously dramatic and retrospective character from the fact that Thoreau added during the 1850s details of natural history and reflection about the significance of his experiences at the pond, *Cape Cod* absorbed its influx of historical material into the framework of the original 1849 narrative in such a way as to make the resulting product a blend of narrative immediacy and historical reflection. The depth and the extent of the reading that went into this late revision can best be gauged by two important paragraphs in "Provincetown" in which Thoreau develops in great detail a theme first articulated in the draft of the Canada excursion, the su-

---

28. CC, 199; see also CC, "Historical Introduction."

periority of French explorers over the English and the weakness of contemporary American historians:

> It is remarkable that there is not in English any adequate or cor-
> rect account of the French exploration of what is now the coast
> of New England, between 1604 and 1608, though it is conceded
> that they then made the first permanent European settlement on
> the continent of North America north of St. Augustine. If the
> lions had been the painters it would have been otherwise. This
> omission is probably to be accounted for partly by the fact that
> the *early edition* of Champlain's "Voyages" had not been con-
> sulted for this purpose. This contains by far the most particular,
> and, I think, the most interesting chapter of what we may call the
> Ante-Pilgrim history of New England, extending to one hundred
> and sixty pages quarto; but appears to be unknown equally to
> the historian and the orator on Plymouth Rock. Bancroft does
> not mention Champlain at all among the authorities for De
> Monts' expedition, nor does he say that he ever visited the coast
> of New England. Though he bore the title of pilot to De Monts,
> he was, in *another sense*, the leading spirit, as well as the histo-
> rian of the expedition. Holmes, Hildreth, and Barry, and appar-
> ently all our historians who mention Champlain, refer to the edi-
> tion of 1632, in which all the separate charts of our harbors, etc.,
> and about one half the narrative, are omitted; for the author ex-
> plored so many lands afterward that he could afford to forget a
> part of what he had done. Hildreth, speaking of De Monts' ex-
> pedition, says that "he looked into the Penobscot [in 1605],
> which Pring had discovered two years before," saying nothing
> about Champlain's extensive exploration of it for De Monts in
> 1604 (Holmes says 1608, and refers to Purchas); also that he
> followed in the track of Pring along the coast "to Cape Cod,
> which he called Malabarre." (Haliburton had made the same
> statement before him in 1829. He called it Cape Blanc, and Malle
> Barre—the Bad Bar—was the name given to a harbor on the east
> side of the Cape.) Pring says nothing about a river there. Belknap
> says that Weymouth discovered it in 1605. Sir F. Gorges says, in
> his narration, 1658, that Pring in 1606 "made a perfect discovery
> of all the rivers and harbors." This is the most I can find. . . .

> John Smith's map, published in 1616, from observations in
> 1614–1615, is by many regarded as the oldest map of New Eng-
> land. It is the first that was made after this country was called
> New England, for he so called it; but in Champlain's "Voyages,"
> edition 1613 (and Lescarbot, in 1612, quotes a still earlier ac-

count of his voyage), there is a map of it made when it was known to Christendom as New France, called *Carte Geographique de la Nouvelle Franse faictte par le Sieur de Champlain Saint Tongois Cappitaine ordinaire pour le Roy en la Marine,— faict l'en 1612*, from his observations between 1604 and 1607; a map extending from Labrador to Cape Cod and westward *to the Great Lakes*, and crowded with information, geographical, ethnographical, zoological, and botanical. (pp. 179–181)

Pride in his own ancestry may account in some measure for Thoreau's allegiance to the French explorers, but his critique is really directed against the narrowness of conception and the lack of imagination that characterized both the English explorers and later American historians. From his reading of the early voyages and explorations he concluded that "the most distinguished navigators of that day were Italians, or of Italian descent, and Portuguese. The French and Spaniards, though less advanced in the science of navigation than the former, possessed more imagination and spirit of adventure than the English, and were better fitted to be the explorers of a new continent even as late as 1751" (CC, 184–185). His principal criteria for judging the adequacy of the explorers' accounts were not only accuracy and truth but also an adequacy of imagination and something like that capacity for wonder before the New World that Nick Carraway lyrically describes at the end of *The Great Gatsby*. The historical analysis in "Provincetown," based as it is on the careful comparison of early accounts to later historians, is perhaps somewhat tedious and tendentious at times. But it is no mere groping among the dry bones of the past; it is a re-creative activity that strives to inculcate a wider, more catholic, and hospitable attitude toward the richness and the plenitude of American discovery than contemporary historians had displayed.

From these early-seventeenth-century explorations Thoreau gradually works his way further back in time, citing first various sixteenth-century sources—including Verrazzano, Hakluyt, Diego Ribero (a Spanish cartographer), and Jean Alphonse, the pilot for Roberval in 1542. Then he extends his range of reference even farther by way of C. C. Rafn's *Antiquitates Americanae*, an edition of Norse (Icelandic) sagas with historical and geographical introduction and notes that provided information about the Norse exploration of the New England coast in the eleventh century. (He had briefly encountered this tradition in Samuel Laing's translation of the *Heimskringla* of Snorri Sturluson a few years earlier.) He goes on to cite Lescarbot on the probability that French sailors had frequented the Newfoundland banks "from time immemorial," and Postel, a sixteenth-century

French writer quoted by Lescarbot, who averred that this area had been visited by Gauls since about the time of Christ. "But let us not laugh at Postel and his visions," Thoreau concludes. "He was perhaps better posted up than we; and if he does seem to draw the long-bow, it may be because he had a long way to shoot,—quite across the Atlantic. If America was found and lost again once, as most of us believe, then why not twice? . . . Consider what stuff history is made of,—that for the most part it is merely a story agreed upon by posterity" (CC, 196–197).

The revision of "Provincetown" from 1855 to around 1860 (the last dateable additions of historical material to the manuscript) suggests that Thoreau was attempting to conceive and write history in rather the same way that he was attempting to write natural history, that is, by familiarizing himself not only with the theories and conclusions of contemporary writers (i.e., Romantic historians such as Bancroft) but also with the oldest, sometimes legendary, accounts of the same events and places. The purpose of this process and the incorporation of these findings in his writing were not merely to debunk the more or less official "Pilgrim version" of early American history currently being promulgated by such orators on Plymouth Rock as Edward Everett (although this was surely a part of his aim) but rather to create a different historical conception of America as the gradual unfolding of a drama of discovery and imaginative appropriation of the continent by the European mind. Cape Cod became the logical locus for this effort because it was both the point of first contact for many explorers and an isolable geographical entity that could stand for the whole sweep of American history. "A man may stand there," he concludes in "Provincetown," stating a natural fact that simultaneously expresses an intellectual one, "and put all America behind him" (CC, 215).

Aboriginal History

THE remaining historical interest that occupied Thoreau during the 1850s—the history of North American Indian tribes before or just at the point of their first contact with white men—was perhaps even more difficult than early American history to pursue and to disentangle from the legends and myths that grew up around it. As in his early employment of historical material in *A Week*, his mature interest in Indian history grew out of or grew up simultaneously with his interest in American history in general, constituting in fact a sort of alternate or counter-history, attractive to him both because its subject was shrouded in mystery and because it was by definition tantalizingly *pre*-historic. At the same time that he was interested in Indians as the shadowy figures who flitted through the annals of early New England, however, he was more fascinated by what he came to perceive as their potential for guiding him toward some wisdom gained through the apprehension of nature that had been lost by civilized people.

His studies in this area included not only what was known of the history and prehistory of Indian tribes but also natural history (their pharmacopeia, for example, or their uses and names for other natural products), ethnology, anthropology, linguistics, and other related disciplines, mostly in their infancy at the time. The material that he amassed in his studies was extensive—eleven volumes of notes on and extracts from his reading—but it proved to be relatively unmalleable as far as his own literary pursuits were concerned. He certainly entertained for a time, at least, the notion of writing a book on the Indians, but precisely what form it might have taken is difficult to say.[29] His reading in this field is relatively easy to chart, however, since he kept such careful extracts over the years. Its principal relation to his literary career appears to have been to provide a context in which to establish his growing capacity to appreciate and extract significance from his own rapprochement with a series of Indian guides on his Maine wilderness expeditions. The state of knowledge about Indian cultures in the 1850s was sketchy and inexact by modern standards, and like his contemporaries Thoreau was never able completely to overcome his predisposition to divide humanity into "civilized" and "savage" or "barbarian" categories. Nevertheless, in his Indian reading he attempted, albeit with limited success, to accomplish in a general way what his natural history and historical studies were also calculated to achieve: to humanize the discipline and to seek a way of expressing the results of his research that would preserve and communicate the personal immediacy of the act of knowing, and that would demonstrate the relatedness of facts discovered to other facts in the observer's (or the reader's) experience.

So intertwined are all Thoreau's studies during this period that his series of Indian books containing the extracts from his reading seem to grow initially out of the reading he did for *Cape Cod* in 1849; and just as the reading he did for "An Excursion to Canada" eventually spilled over to the historical essay in *Cape Cod*, his notes on the history of Indians on Cape Cod eventually became the first surviving volume of his eleven-volume set of extracts and notes covering all aspects of Indian history and culture.[30] Moreover, the subject of Indians was inex-

29. Sayre, *Thoreau and the American Indians*, chap. 4, "A Book About Indians," pp. 101–122.

30. Johnson, "Into History: Thoreau's Earliest 'Indian Book' and His First Trip to Cape Cod."

tricably bound up with American history and natural history, Thoreau's other major areas of interest during the 1850s. One of the most sensitive and important issues in natural science at this time, for example, was the ancestry and origins of the various races, and Thoreau's reading in the primitive anthropological speculations of his day took him over some of the same ground that he covered in following the debates among biologists about the origins and ancestry of other species—with the significant difference that theories about the ancestry and inherent characteristics of people were not solely academic or religious issues. They were sometimes used to justify social and political decisions (the removal of Indian tribes to the West, for example) affecting the lives and the very survival of so-called primitive peoples. For obvious reasons, it is even more difficult to separate Indian history from early American history when, as in the case of Thoreau, the researcher's interest centers upon early exploration and discovery by Europeans and upon the period of first contact with Europeans by the Indians. The two subjects are merely different versions of or ways of looking at the same historical and cultural moment.

Thoreau's general interest in Indians dates back to his youth, when he had some familiarity with local legends and collected, as he continued to do for the rest of his life, arrowheads and other Indian artifacts.[31] At this time, his reading consisted mainly of such popular collections of Indian lore and biography as Samuel Drake's *Indian Biography* and B. B. Thatcher's *Indian Traits*, miscellaneous compilations of legend, hearsay, travelers' reports, and information of varying degrees of accuracy, all regarded from a perspective of Romantic and nostalgic lament for the inevitable passing away of the race. Thatcher, for example, in a passage that is representative of this sort of literature, describes Indian life before the coming of the Europeans as blissful and even edenic:

> But generally they lived in circumstances of health, security and ease. The woods and the waters supplied them with their abundant livelihood, almost without effort. The hunter's game was all around him, and above him, in the streams, forests and skies of his native land. And, above all, he was not only hardy, patient and brave, able to encounter the elements, and fearless to meet his foe in the field of battle; but he was *a free man*. The mountain eagle that screamed over the slow-soaring smoke of his wig-

31. See, for example, COR, 16–18, 24–25; also Kenneth Walter Cameron, "Books on Indians Which Thoreau Knew or Might Have Known by November, 1837," *Emerson Society Quarterly* 1 (4 Qtr. 1956): 10–12.

wam, was not freer than him who dwelt beneath that humble room. . . .

We find the cellars of their wigwams in our old pastures, moss-grown and yawning. We decipher their rude inscriptions on the rocks of the forest. The farmer's plough, perhaps, turns up the mouldering relics of their ancient dead. . . .

The time will come but too soon, we fear, when the history of the Indians will be the history of a people of which no living specimen shall exist upon the earth;—too soon will the places that now know them know them never again. Their council-fires will have gone out upon the green hills of the South. Their canoes shall plough no more the bosom of the Northern Lakes. Even the prairies and mountains of the far West will cease to be their refuge from the rushing march of civilization.[32]

This curious but typical mixture of Rousseau-like admiration for the noble savage in the unfallen natural state and an almost gothic taste for melancholy reminders of the Indians' decline (Freneau's "Indian Burying Ground" is perhaps the most notable expression of the latter) may be detected in the background of Thoreau's early treatment of New England's Indian history in *A Week*. At this stage in his life, he conceived of the Indians largely as a race either extinct or on its way to extirpation. However sad or melancholy this fact, it was inevitable. Thus his treatment in "Ktaadn" (1848) of Louis Neptune, the Indian who was to guide him on his first wilderness trip to Maine, concludes with an apostrophe to the passing of the Indian that was actually quite conventional: "In a bark vessel sewn with the roots of the spruce, with horn-beam paddles he dips his way along. He is but dim and misty to me, obscured by the aeons that lie between the bark canoe and the batteau. . . . He glides up the Millinocket and is lost to my sight, as a more distant and misty cloud is seen flitting by behind a nearer, and is lost in space. So he goes about his destiny, the red face of man" (MW, 79). As the title of Cooper's *The Last of the Mohicans* suggests, early-nineteenth-century American books typically depict the Indian as passing away, a portent of the gradual disappearance of his race from the continent itself.

As he began his mature study of the subject, Thoreau started collecting—in a manner similar to the change in his natural history reading habits about the same time—more precise and concrete information about Indian customs, especially from the various contributors' accounts in the *Collections* of the Massachusetts Historical Society,

32. *Indian Traits*, 2 vols. (New York: Harper & Brothers, 1854) 1.17–18, 21.

extracts from which make up the bulk of the first surviving Indian book, compiled in 1849–1850. He was still confined at this stage, however, to the New England tribes (who *were* largely extinct) and to mostly descriptive and anecdotal material that was strongly colored by the theological biases of the early informants.

With Indian book 4, however, compiled in 1850-1851 after his trip to Canada, Thoreau began to expand his Indian reading to the same primary French sources—Champlain, Roberval, Cartier, Lescarbot—that he had begun to draw upon for his American historical researches. The French explorers and even their missionaries he would find more useful than the English in providing reliable and even sympathetic descriptions of Indian life, for they were more prone to regard the Indians as human beings, to adopt their habits and mode of life, and actually to live among them. At the same time, he consulted writers in other fields who could provide corroborating or complementary information: Jacob Bigelow's *American Medical Botany* for the Indians' uses of medicinal plants, Charles Darwin's account of the voyage of the *Beagle* for the characteristics of the Indians of South America, and E. G. Squier's early work on Indian religion, *The Serpent Symbol*. He continued to collect miscellaneous information from the accounts of travelers, naturalists, missionaries, and explorers, but there was beginning to be a somewhat more scientific and comparative cast to the extracted material. At the same time that the subject thus began to open up to Thoreau it was also so enormous and simultaneously so embryonic (with vast amounts of new information appearing annually) that no real discernible shape or focus is evident in his note taking.

By 1852, with his sixth notebook, Thoreau had begun to make his major discoveries of important primary sources and to grasp the underlying social and political issues that made the "Indian question" so vexing to his culture. Behind all the collections and descriptions of Indian manners and customs was an extraordinarily touchy problem: Were the Indians a separate variety of humans, and if so, how had they gotten that way, and when? Were their differences to be ascribed to external conditions of environment or the hand of Providence? The contemporary literature on Indians thus participated in the larger ongoing debate about variation in nature, the fixity of species, and the plan of the Creator, if there was one, that characterized the natural sciences during the decade. Additionally, the 1840s and the 1850s were a period of explosive westward expansion, bringing the United States and its doctrine of manifest destiny into conflict with large numbers of potentially hostile tribes in Texas, the Great Plains, and the Far West. It was a period that saw, in Wilcomb Washburn's words, "the greatest real estate transaction in history," as tribe after tribe was induced by "wars, treaties, and a mass population movement" to cede its traditional lands to the onrushing Americans and retreat to reservations.[33] All the ethnographic and ethnologic information collected and disseminated by individual scientists and the government was necessarily adduced as evidence in the debate over Indian origins and Indian rights.

A key document in the scientific debate was Samuel G. Morton's *Crania Americana*, a massive comparative study of aboriginal skulls from the Americas that Thoreau read in 1852. It was prefixed by an important essay, "On the Varieties of Human Species," that described the supposed physical and mental characteristics of the various races. Typical of the age, Morton assigns differences in physical types to the aftermath of the biblical flood, when the Creator fitted each variety of the human species for its particular niche: "Each race was adapted from the beginning to its peculiar local destination," Morton argues. "In other words, it is assumed that the physical characteristics which distinguish the different Races, are independent of external causes."[34] This theory of special creation or providential adaptation harmonized neatly with Agassiz's prevalent theory of separate epochs of creation in the natural world. Such differences as may be observed between races would thus be God-given and immutable, and Morton proceeds to class the various races according to such characteristics. The Caucasian race, not unexpectedly, is "distinguished for the facility with which it attains the highest intellectual endowments," and the Indian, as one might also predict from the foregoing, is characterized as "averse to cultivation, and slow in acquiring knowledge; restless, revengeful, and fond of war."[35] Such ostensibly scientific conclusions, buttressed by scores of plates and tables of various skulls and their dimensions, constituted the state of knowledge and theory about human origins and capacities at the time, and were taken over and assumed by most mid-nineteenth-century writers on the Indian.

The most important of these was Henry Rowe Schoolcraft, who between 1851 and 1857 published a massive six-volume folio series titled *Historical and Statistical Information Respecting the History, Condition, and Prospects of the Indian Tribes of the United States,* under the auspices of the government's Bureau of Indian Affairs. Containing much miscellaneous material, randomly organized, and finally more literary than scientific (Longfellow drew upon it for *Hiawatha*), Schoolcraft's work nonetheless had a kind of authority, if only because

33. *The Indian in America* (New York: Harper & Row, 1975), p. 196.
34. Morton, *Crania Americana* (see Bibliographical Catalogue no. 1012), p. 3.
35. Ibid. pp. 5–6.

of its bulk and its government sponsorship. Thoreau read the volumes consecutively as they appeared and made extensive extracts from them in his Indian notebooks. Schoolcraft's avowed purpose was to educate white people about Indians so they could help to "reclaim such a race to the paths of virtue and truth; to enlighten the mind which has been so long in darkness." Beginning from the biblical account of the dispersal of various races of men, Schoolcraft saw the Indians' "barbarism" as a "lapsed state" (since God had provided all men with the capacity for agricultural life in antediluvian times) to be accounted for by the seductiveness of the wilderness in which they lived: "Wandering in the attractive scenes of the temperate and tropic zones . . . must have proved a powerful stimulus to erratic and barbaric notions."[36] Similarly, the stated intention of Lewis H. Morgan's *League of the Iroquois* (1851), a pioneering work of ethnology that was highly laudatory of the Iroquois's social and political institutions, was "To encourage a kinder feeling toward the Indian . . . and of his capabilities for future elevation."[37] Even the most ardent advocates of an "enlightened" policy toward the Indian—and perhaps the most eminent authorities on the subject before the Civil War—still assumed that the Indians were a lapsed race who might by herculean efforts on the part of whites make some progress toward civilization.

In 1852 Thoreau began reading the *Jesuit Relations*, an enormous body of firsthand information that would serve for him, along with Schoolcraft's compendium, as a major source of facts about the cultures and customs of Indian tribes in the northeastern part of North America. These annual reports of the Jesuits' missionary activity in the New World were a treasure trove of details for Thoreau, who read all the volumes of the *Relations* that were available at Harvard—those covering the years from 1632 to 1694. And despite his general anticlericalism and his Yankee suspicion of Roman Catholicism, one can imagine that he found the reports themselves engaging as well as informative, for they detailed heroic individual exertions, sacrifice, and perseverance, as well as being full of direct, homely, and ingenuous accounts of life among Indian tribes that had had relatively little contact with European civilization. Between 1852 and 1858, he copied over three hundred pages of extracts from this source.

This period from 1852 to 1858 also marks the time of his most extensive reading and note taking on the subject of Indians, and the time

36. Schoolcraft, *Historical and Statistical Information* (see Bibliographical Catalogue no. 1218), I.X, 47.

37. *League of the Ho-Dé-No-Sau-Nee or Iroquois* (New York: Dodd, Mead and Company, 1901), p. ix.

during which he was most actively considering writing his own book on the Indians. A leaf laid in one of his early notebooks but dating from 1858 contains a list of the subjects in Schoolcraft's and in two other Indian histories, followed by a list of what Thoreau headed "My Own" subjects—some thirty-five titles ranging from "Ante Columbian History" to "Arts & uses derived from the Indians."[38]

He apparently did not pursue this structure or outline any further. Perhaps it was becoming evident to him from the voluminous data rapidly coming into print through government surveys and as a result of the westward movement generally that a book on "the Indian" was an impossible task conceptually: There were simply too much variation and diversity among various Indian tribes to permit valid generalizations about the Indian as a homogenous race or culture. By this time, he had looked over the seven volumes of government reports of the surveys for the Pacific railroad route, the report on the survey of the United States—Mexico boundary, a report of an exploring expedition to Saskatchewan, and similar documents containing information about Western tribes. How to assess and organize the masses of raw data about Indians that were accumulating so rapidly during the 1850s, without possessing a coherent anthropological methodology or theory, was certainly a serious obstacle to writing a book about the Indian.

Another very likely possibility, suggested by Robert F. Sayre, is that Thoreau lacked the extensive firsthand experience with the subject that his literary imagination required: A project essentially dependent upon research in secondary material was unsuited to his particular talents and capacities as a writer.[39] In any event, although he continued to read and make notes on works about Indians until 1861, the Indian books from the last few years of his life increasingly tend to reflect his reading in other areas of interest at that time, especially natural science, the ancient natural historians, and travel: books such as Gerard's *Herball*, Richard Owen's *Palaeontology*; Pliny, Aristotle, and Aelianus; Isaac Hayes's *Arctic Boat Journey*; and Richard Burton's *The Lake Region of Central Africa*. These are interspersed with entries from more typical sources such as Samuel Penhallow's *History of the Wars of New England*, Jefferson's *Notes on the State of Virginia*, and John Halkett's *Historical Notes Respecting the Indians of North America*. Thoreau made direct use of all this information about Indians only occasionally in his writings, and with the advantages of hindsight it is perhaps possible to understand why the project remained

38. Sayre, *Thoreau and the American Indians*, p. 120.
39. Ibid. pp. 121–122.

chiefly at the stage of collecting and compiling—intellectual activities that, as Sayre points out, were satisfying in themselves.[40]

Thoreau's trip to Minnesota in 1861, which gave him a long-delayed opportunity to observe the flora and some of the Indian tribes of the northern plains, came too late in his life (he was already suffering from his final siege of tuberculosis) to provide such an autobiographical experiential framework for him. Additionally, however, the nature of his specific interest created a problem for him that was, given the state of cultural anthropology in his day, extraordinarily difficult if not impossible to solve. He was chiefly interested, as he wrote on his Association for the Advancement of Science membership form in 1853, in "The Manners & Customs of the Indians of the Algonquin Group previous to contact with the civilized man." There were two imposing obstacles to the fulfillment of this interest, one cultural and the other methodological. The cultural prohibition is the one previously mentioned: Thoreau carried with him to some extent the unquestioned assumption of his era that the Indian was a "savage" and that there existed an almost unbridgeable gap between him and the "civilized" person;[41] it was not in the intellectual vocabulary of mid-nineteenth-century people to conceive of humanity as a broad spectrum of cultures—or indeed to think of "culture" itself as we do today as a descriptive rather than a normative term—subject to dispassionate descriptions and analysis. "What a vast difference between a savage & a civilized people," Thoreau observed in a note to Indian book 7 in 1852, and several years later, in 1858, he could only draw the conclusion from all his reading that "the fact is, the history of the white man is a history of improvements, that of the red man a history of fixed habits of stagnation" (JL 10.252). In the same way that he seems to have been at least partially caught up by the euphoria of westward expansion and manifest destiny in portions of "Walking," Thoreau here betrays, perhaps unconsciously, certain of his era's racist assumptions about the fundamental cultural, physiological, and mental differences between whites and Indians.

The methodological difficulty that he faced in trying to assess Indian culture "previous to contact with the civilized man" was that all he had to rely upon were the reports of civilized man. Such a task, to paraphrase a remark of William James's, is rather like trying to study the dark by turning the light up quickly. There were few techniques available for reconstructing, as an anthropologist might today, the pre-

40. Ibid. p. 122.

41. See Roy Harvey Pearce, *Savages and Civilization* (Baltimore: Johns Hopkins University Press, 1965).

history of the tribes that he was interested in, and so Thoreau was forced to depend upon the testimony of observers whose very presence of necessity altered the state of the culture they described. The component of Indian culture that came closest to providing clues to prehistory was language, a subject in which Thoreau already had, by natural proclivity, a great deal of interest. He took notes from such early writers on Indian languages as Roger Williams and Jonathan Edwards, as well as from contemporary works such as Peter Dupenceau's "The General Character and Forms of the Languages of the American Indians" and John Pickering's notes to Father Rasles's *Dictionary of the Abnaki Language.* Had he pursued this inquiry further, it is conceivable that he might have been able to see how relationships among languages and dialects could indicate cultural affinities among tribes and aid in the ethnographical study of origins and migration patterns, but such developments lay rather far in the future; the state of knowledge about Indian languages at the time was often confined to fairly primitive word lists and dictionaries of the sort that missionaries compiled for purposes of religious instruction. Theories that did exist were highly conjectural and generally contradictory, and Thoreau's notes indicate that he was acutely aware of the widely divergent views of contemporary writers about the origins and dispersion of North American Indian tribes.[42]

Ultimately, however, this interest in the prehistory of American Indians was really an interest in the possibility of recovering whatever primal wisdom and knowledge the Indian might have possessed and that civilized man had lost, and Thoreau was able to approach this understanding only through his own very limited personal contact with Indians, especially Joe Polis, his guide on the last of his expeditions to Maine in 1857. As he tells the story in "The Allegash and East Branch," he was able for the first time to get some direct experiential confirmation of the Indian's superior powers to understand and accommodate himself to nature—a relationship that could finally only be demonstrated physically, as it was by Polis, and that was not susceptible of analysis and translation into literary terms with which a white audience would be comfortable. He wrote to H.G.O. Blake on his return from this trip to Maine:

> Having returned, I flatter myself that the world appears in some respects a little larger, and not, as usual, smaller and shallower, for having extended my range. I have made a short excursion into

42. Lawrence Willson, "Thoreau: Student of Anthropology," *American Anthropologist* 61 (April 1959): 279–289; see esp. pp. 283–287 for a discussion of Thoreau's reading in such philological studies and speculations.

the new world which the Indian dwells in, or is. He begins where we leave off. It is worth the while to detect new faculties in man,—he is so much the more divine; and anything that fairly excites our admiration expands us. The Indian, who can find his way so wonderfully in the woods, possesses so much intelligence which the white man does not,—and it increases my own capacity, as well as faith, to observe it. I rejoice to find that intelligence flows in other channels than I knew. It redeems for me portions of what seemed brutish before. (COR, 491)

No experience in all his reading about Indians over the years had produced a moment of insight of this magnitude, although it was clearly what he had been searching for all along. His literary and intellectual heritage had actually led him away from this sort of expansive experience, and one suspects that he was finally unable to integrate it into the framework of received knowledge that he had so painstakingly collected in the Indian books.

In his last years Thoreau turned more regularly toward reading and writing about natural history, as we have seen, for there the state of theory was sufficiently advanced and in flux to permit at once a wider and more informed field for speculation; and he had of course in this field a multitude of those direct observations that he had so few of about Indians. If he seriously considered a book about Indians, it was likely that he gave it up by 1859 as his attention became more engrossed by the problems of the dispersal of plants and allied botanical phenomena, a subject in which his reading encompassed both ancient writers and contemporary theory, and about which he was able to collect data and perform experiments in the Concord environs that he knew so well. It is significant, perhaps, that the Indian remained a problem for him to the end of his life. He declined to print his "Allegash and East Branch" narrative during his lifetime, telling James Russell Lowell that he would not be able to face his guide Joe Polis again if he did so, even though Polis's portrait in the narrative is on the whole a favorable one. The subject may even have occupied his dying thoughts, for according to one tradition the last words that he is supposed to have uttered as his sister sat reading to him on the morning of his death were "Moose" and "Indian."[43]

Significant and symmetrical it is too that his last words should have been a response to his reading, even if that reading was performed by someone else during his last days. Only the legendary Thoreau—the half-mythic though in part self-created persona who comes down to us

43. Channing, *Thoreau: The Poet-Naturalist*, p. 319.

as the dweller by Walden Pond, the inmate of Concord jail, and the saunterer walking westward—epitomizes the Emersonian injunction that books are for the scholar's idle times. The historical Thoreau who had adopted letters as his profession, as he told Harvard's President Sparks, depended as all literary persons do upon books as a major part of his stock in trade. He was by inclination as well as long habit a bookish man with scholarly instincts, and a writer for whom the act of reading was the diastole to the systole of composition. Rightly conceived, his reading was the sort of heroic activity that he characterizes in *Walden* as "a noble exercise, and one that will task the reader more than any exercise which the customs of the day esteem." It was also the channel through which his intellectual and professional interests grew and evolved over the course of his career. This evolution—from a fairly conventional focus in the classics of antiquity and English literature to an absorption in American history, the American Indian, and natural history—bears witness to Thoreau's active participation in many of the liveliest intellectual problems of his age and demonstrates the extent to which his life was a fulfillment of Emerson's prophecy in "The American Scholar" that the revolution in American literature was "to be wrought by the gradual domestication of the idea of Culture."

Bibliographical
Catalogue

W O R K S in the catalogue are listed alphabetically by author, or by title when no author has been identified or the work is anonymous. Titles and publication information for books are taken from the *National Union Catalogue of Pre-1956 Imprints* (and on a few occasions from the *British Museum Catalogue of Printed Books* and the catalogue of the Bibliothèque Nationale), and minor variations in the forms of reporting these data have not been normalized. Whenever verifiable, the edition cited is the one Thoreau used; otherwise, publication data for the most recent and readily accessible edition are listed.

On the line following the publication data, Thoreau's probable source for the item, if known, is identified by one of a series of abbreviations expanded below. For books whose source is the catalogue of Thoreau's personal library, I have noted those items that carry the autograph of another member of his family and that may therefore not have been of particular use or interest to him. If his source for a given work is unknown, this line is blank.

Following the source line is a listing of Thoreau's references to the work in both his published writings and unpublished manuscript notebooks, again identified by abbreviations that are expanded below. References in his published works come first, in the approximate order of their composition, followed by references in the Journal, and then by references in the manuscript notebooks. With the exception of his late essay "Huckleberries" and his correspondence, citations to his published writings are either to the definitive Princeton University Press edition of his writings currently in progress, or—for volumes not yet superseded by those in the Princeton series—to the previously standard Walden edition (Houghton Mifflin, 1906). References to the Journal are listed by date and by volume and page number, so that passages may be located in either edition. References to the previously unpublished portions of the forthcoming third volume of the Journal in the Princeton edition are identified by "PJ 3" and date.

Exact dates for many entries are provided by dated library charging records, Journal entries, or correspondence. In cases where no such precise date is established for an entry in a manuscript notebook, a conjectural date is supplied, based on the item's position with respect to other, dateable entries. A brief comment on the item—its use to Thoreau, its relation to other items in the catalogue, or a special problem connected with it—may follow the list of references. Occasionally these notes refer by author and short title to previous studies of various aspects of Thoreau's reading, expanded citations of which may be found in the bibliography of secondary sources that follows the catalogue.

113

Abbreviations Used in Bibliographical Catalogue

Sources

A L	Amos Bronson Alcott's Library
B A	Boston Athenaeum Library
C L	Concord Town Library (Concord Social Library before 1851)
E L	Ralph Waldo Emerson's Library
F B S	Franklin Benjamin Sanborn's Library
H L	Harvard College Library
I N	Institute of 1770 (Harvard)
R W E	Library withdrawal by Ralph Waldo Emerson
S L	Stacy's Circulating Library, Concord
S N H	Society of Natural History Library, Boston
T X	Required text at Concord Academy or Harvard College
T L	Thoreau's Personal Libary

References
Published Works and Correspondence

C C	*Cape Cod* (Princeton, 1987)
C O R	*The Correspondence of Henry David Thoreau* (1958)
E E M	*Early Essays and Miscellanies* (Princeton, 1975)
E X	*Excursions* (1906)
H U	"Huckleberries," in *Henry David Thoreau: The Natural History Essays,* ed. Robert Sattelmeyer (Salt Lake City: Peregrine Smith, 1980)
J L	*Journal* (1906) (followed by volume number and date)
M W	*The Maine Woods* (Princeton, 1972)
P J	*Journal* (Princeton, 1981–) (followed by volume number and date)
R P	*Reform Papers* (Princeton, 1973)
T M J	*Thoreau's Minnesota Journey,* ed. Walter Harding (Geneseo, N.Y.: Thoreau Society, 1962)
T R	*Translations,* ed. K. P. Van Anglen (Princeton: Princeton University Press, 1986)
W A	*Walden* (Princeton, 1971)
W E	*A Week on the Concord and Merrimack Rivers* (Princeton, 1980)

Major Commonplace Books and Notebooks (with repository and MS *designation)*

C N	Canadian Notebook, 1850–1856 (NNPM, MA 595)
C P B 1	Commonplace Book, 1841–1851 (NYPL, Berg)
C P B 2	Commonplace Book, 1856–1861 (NYPL, Berg)
F B	Fact Book, 1851–1857 (MH, Widener)

HM 13201	Dated Reading List, 1840–1841 (CSmH)
IB 2–12	Indian Books, 1849–1861 (NNPM, MA 596–606)
LN	Literary Notebook, 1840–1848 (DLC)
ME	Miscellaneous Extracts, 1836–1840 (NNPM, MA 594)

Miscellaneous Notebooks and Fragmentary Notes (identified in the catalogue by their designations in William L. Howarth, The Literary Manuscripts of Henry David Thoreau [Columbus: Ohio State University Press, 1974])

F2a	"Index rerum," partial index of college reading, 1833–1837 (CSmH HM 945)
F5	Partial early commonplace book, 1841–1842 (CSmH HM 957)
F6a	Extracts from Francis Quarles (NBu)
F1b–e, F6	Miscellaneous reading notes, 1836–1842 (ViU)
F6d	Partial early notebook, 1841–1842 (RPB)

1. ABERCROMBIE, John. *Inquiries concerning the intellectual powers and the investigation of truth.* New-York: J. & J. Harper, 1832.
   TL
   COR, 29 (10–6–38)

2. ABOUT, Edmond François V. *Greece and the Greeks of the present Day.* Trans. by authority. New-York: Dix, Edwards and Co., 1857.
   BA 12–31–57 (by RWE)
   JL 10.234–235 (1–3–58)

3. "Acclimatization of Animals." *Littel's Living Age* 64 (March 1860): 719–734.

   CPB2

   Reprinted from *Edinburgh Review*; mentions controversy over Darwin's *Origin of Species* (q.v.), which T was reading in early 1860.

4. ACHARIUS, Erik. *Methodus qua omnes detectos lichenes....* Stockholmiae: impensis F.D.D. Ulrich, typis C. F. Marquard, 1803.
   HL 3–16–52

5. ADAIR, James. *The history of the American Indians; particularly those nations adjoining to the Mississippi, East and West Florida, Georgia, South and North Carolina, and Virginia. ...* London: E. and C. Dilly, 1775.
   HL 12–10–55
   IB 10

6. ADAM, Alexander. *Adam's Latin Grammar, with some improvements and the following additions: rules for the right pronunciation of the Latin language; metrical key to the odes of Horace; a list of Latin authors arranged according to the different ages of Roman literature....* Boston: Hilliard, Gray, Little and Wilkins; and Richardson and Lord, 1829.
   TX

7. ADAM, Alexander. *Roman Antiquities; or, An account of the manners and customs of the Romans. ...* New-York: Collins and Hannay [etc.], 1833.
   TX

8. ADAM, Alexander. *The rudiments of Latin and English Grammar; designed to facilitate the study of both languages, by connecting them together. ...* 2d New York, from the 9th English ed. New-York: E. Duyckinck and G. Long, 1820.
   TL, TX

9. ADAMS, Mrs. Abigail (Smith). *Letters of Mrs. Adams, the
    wife of John Adams. With an introductory memoir by her
    grandson, Charles Francis Adams.* Boston: C. C. Little and
    J. Brown, 1840.

    HM 13201 (3–2–41)

10. ADDISON, Joseph. In Chalmers (q.v.), vol. 9.
    Cato: A Tragedy
    WA, 7

    T's remark on the teamster in *Walden*—"Does any divinity
    stir within him?"—appears to be a paraphrase of a line from
    Cato, V, i: "It's the divinity that stirs within us."

11. ADDISON, Joseph, and Richard STEELE. See *The Spectator.*

12. ADELUNG, Johann Christoph. *Mithridates, oder Allgemeine
    sprachkunde.* . . . Berlin: vossische buchhandlung, 1807–
    1817.

    IB 9 (*c.* 1855)

13. *Adventures with animals, zoological notes and anecdotes.* . . .
    London: Dean & Son, 1857.
    TL

14. AELIANUS, Claudius. *Aeliani De natura animalum libri XVII.
    Graece et Latine cum priorum interpretum et suis animadver-
    sionibus edidit Io. Gottlab Schneider.* Lipsiae: E. B. Schwick-
    ert, 1784.
    HL 4–9–60
    CC, 169; IB 12

15. AELIANUS, Claudius. *Aeliani sophistae variae historiae libri
    XIV.* . . . [n.p.]: Editio postrema curante John. Henrico Le-
    derlino, 1613.
    HL 2–6–60
    CPB 2

16. AESCHYLUS. *Tragoediae. Ad exemplar glasgvense accurate
    expressae.* Lipsiae: Tauchnitii, 1819.
    EL
    Prometheus Bound
    TR, 3–53; CC, 51, 140; PJ 1.82–85 (11–39)
    Seven Against Thebes
    TR, 63–110; RP, 3; PJ 1.91 (12–39), 106 (1–40), 165 (7 & 8–
    40)

17. AESOP. *The fables of Aesop, and others. With designs on
    wood, by Thomas Bewick.* Newcastle: Printed by E. Walter,
    for T. Bewick, 1818.

JL 3.240 (1–28–52); 5.411 (9–1–53); 7.90 (1–20–54), 469 (10–1–55)

This edition, owned by Daniel Ricketson, is described by T in the JL 7.469 entry; his source for other references to Aesop is unknown, but the fables were of course widely familiar and available.

18. *Aesthetic Papers*. See Peabody, Elizabeth.

19. AGARDH, Carl Adolf. *Systema algarum*. In Loudon, *Encyclopedia of Plants* (q.v.).

    FB (*c.* 1852)

20. AGASSIZ, Louis. *Contributions to the natural history of the United States of America*. 2 vols. Boston: Little, Brown, & company, 1857.
    CL
    CPB2 (*c.* 1858)

    Includes Agassiz's "Essay on Classification."

21. AGASSIZ, Louis. *Etudes sur les glaciers. . . . Ouvrage accompagné d'un atlas de 32 planches*. Neuchâtel: Jent et Gassmann, 1840.
    HL 3–13–54

22. AGASSIZ, Louis. *An introduction to the study of natural history. . . .* New York: Greeley & McElrath, 1847.
    JL 10.399 (5–4–58)

23. AGASSIZ, Louis, and A. A. GOULD. *Principles of zoology: touching the structure, development, distribution, and natural arrangement of the animals, living and extinct, with numerous illustrations. Part 1. Comparative physiology. For the use of schools and colleges. . . .* Boston: Gould, Kendall, and Lincoln, 1848.
    TL

24. AGASSIZ, Louis, and A. A. GOULD. *Principles of zoology. . . .* Revised ed. Boston: Gould & Lincoln, 1851.
    SNH 8–11–51
    JL 3.71–72 (10–14–51); CC, 127

25. AIKIN, John. *The arts of life. . . .* Boston: Carter & Hendee, 1830.
    CL
    JL 7.460 (9–24–55)

26. AIKIN, John, ed. *Select works of the British poets, in a chronological series from Ben Jonson to Beatie. With biographical*

and critical notices. Philadelphia: T. Wardle, 1840.
TL

27. AINSWORTH, Robert. *An abridgement of Ainsworth's diction-
    ary, English & Latin, by Thomas Morell. . . .* Philadelphia:
    U. Hunt, 1829.
    TL

28. ALCOTT, Amos Bronson. *Conversations with children on the
    Gospels, conducted and edited by A. Bronson Alcott.* Boston:
    J. Munroe and company, 1836–37.
    TL

29. ALDEN, Timothy, Jr. *A collection of American epitaphs and
    inscriptions.* 5 vols. New York, 1819.

    CC, 126

    T's source for this work was probably John Barber's *Histori-
    cal Collections* (q.v.), which quotes the passage used in CC.

30. ALDEN, Timothy, Jr. "Memorabilia of Yarmouth." *Collec-
    tions of the Massachusetts Historical Society*, 1st ser., vol. 5
    (1798; rpt. 1835): 54–60.

    CC, 4; JL 9.448–449 (6–20–57); IB 2

    This article, which begins "Cape Cod may be well represented
    by a man's arm bent into a certain position," is probably T's
    source for the description of the Cape at the beginning of CC.

31. ALEXANDER, William. In Chalmers (q.v.), vol. 5. "A Paraensis
    to Prince Henry"
    WE, 85

32. ALFIERI, Vittorio. *The Autobiography of Vittorio Alfieri, the
    tragic poet. . . . Trans., with an original essay on the genius
    and times of Alfieri by C. Edwards Lester.* New York: Paine
    and Burgess, 1845.

    COR, 478 (4–26–57)

    Likely edition, unless T read the work in Italian, in which
    there are many possible editions.

33. ALISON, Archibald. *History of Europe from the commence-
    ment of the French revolution in 1789 to the restoration of
    the Bourbons in 1815.* 4 vols. New York: Harper, 1846–.

    EEM, 248

34. ALLEN, Wilkes. *The history of Chelmsford, from its origin in 1653, to the year 1820. . . .* Haverhill, Mass.: Printed by P. N. Green, 1820.

WE, 253

35. "The Alligator." *Harper's Magazine* 10 (Dec. 1854): 37–49.

JL 9.100 (10–4–56)

36. ALLINGHAM, William. *The music master: a love story. And two series of day and night songs. . . .* London: G. Routledge & co., 1855.
TL

37. ALLINGHAM, William. *Poems.* London: Chapman and Hall, 1850.

CPB1 (*c.* 1850)

38. ALLSTON, Washington. *Lectures on art and poems . . . edited by Richard Henry Dana, Jr.* New York: Baker and Scribner, 1850.

LN (*c.* 1850)

39. ALPHONSE, Jean. See *Voyages de découverte au Canada.*

40. AMERICAN ACADEMY OF ARTS AND SCIENCES, Boston. *Memoirs of the American academy of arts and sciences.* Vols. 1–4; new ser., v. 1–. Boston: [etc.] 1785–19–.
SNH 7–9–51, 8–1–51; HL 2–15–58
CC, 122; JL 2.45 (1850); JL 14.224 (11–8–60); CPB2; IB 12

T's exact borrowings of the Academy's *Memoirs* are unclear from charging records. See entries for Cutler, Rev. Manasseh, and Davis, Charles Henry, for works he cites specifically.

41. *American almanac and repository of useful knowledge for 1830–61.* Boston: Grey & Bowen: [etc., etc.].
TL (1846, 1849, 1850, 1851 issues)
JL 13.211 (3–23–60); CN; CPB2

42. "American Ethnological Society." *New York Tribune,* April 4, 1854, pp. 5–6.

IB 8

On migration of Aztecs and distribution of Indians in the Great Basin.

43.   *American Monthly Magazine.* New ser., 1 (Nov. 1836).
      IN 12–5–36

      For contents see Cameron, "Thoreau Discovers Emerson,"
      327.

44.   AMERICAN PHILOSOPHICAL SOCIETY, Philadelphia. *Transac-
      tions of the American philosophical society, held at Philadel-
      phia, for promoting useful knowledge.* Philadelphia, 1771–.
      New ser., vol. 1. Philadelphia: Abraham and Small, 1819.
      HL 9–17–55
      JL 8.203–204 (3–10–56); IB 9

45.   "An American Survey of the Basin of the La Plata." *Littel's
      Living Age* 63 (Oct. 1859): 308–312.

      IB 12

      Anonymous review of Thomas Page, *La Plata, the Argentine
      confederation, and Paraguay: being a narrative of the explo-
      ration of the tributaries of the river La Plata and adjacent
      countries during the years 1853, '54, '55 and '56. . . .*

46.   ANACREON. See *Carminum Poetarum Novem.*

47.   "Ancient and Modern Artillery." *Harper's Magazine* 10
      (March 1855): 458–469.

      IB 10 (*c.* 1855)

48.   "Ancient Persian Poetry." *Foreign Quarterly Review* 18 (Oct.
      1836): 119–158.

      ME (*c.* 1837)

49.   ANDERSON, Robert. *The works of the British poets. With
      prefaces, biographical and critical, by Robert Anderson. . . .*
      14 vols. London: Printed for J. Arch, 1795–[1807?].

      LN (*c.* 1843)

      T copied poems by Drummond of Hawthornden, Carew,
      Peele, Daniel, Lovelace, Lawrence Minot, and Donne from
      vols. 4 and 5 of Anderson's anthology.

50.   ANDERSSON, Karl Johan. *Lake Ngami: or, Explorations and
      discoveries during four years' wanderings in the wilds of
      south western Africa, by Charles John Andersson. . . .* New
      York: Harper & brothers, 1856.
      CL
      IB 10; FB (*c.* 1857)

51.   ANDREWS, E. A. *A copious and critical Latin-English lexicon, founded on the larger Latin-German lexicon of Dr. W. Freund.* . . . New York: Harper & bros., 1856.
      TL

      Edition uncertain; many available both before and after this date.

52.   ANDREWS, Israel D. See United States Congress. 32nd Congress.

53.   *Annual of scientific discovery; or, Year-book of facts in science and art, for [1850]–71, exhibiting the most important discoveries and improvements in mechanics, useful arts, natural philosophy.* . . . Boston: Gould and Lincoln; [etc., etc.] 1851.

      CC, 124; JL 2.348 (7–25–51); CN; IB 8

54.   "Another of the Same Nature, Made Since." In *England's Helicon* (q.v.).
      HL 12–8–41
      PJ 1.10 (11–9–37)

55.   ANTAR. *Antar, a Bedoueen romance. Translated from the Arabic, by Terrick Hamilton. Part the first.* London: J. Murray, 1820.
      HL 3–12–34

56.   ANVILLE, Jean Baptiste Bourguinon. *Complete body of ancient geography.* . . . London: R. Laurie and J. Whittle, 1802.
      HL 9–5–36

57.   *Appleton's dictionary of machines, mechanics, engine-work and engineering.* 2 vols. New York: D. Appleton and company, 1857–58.
      CL
      CPB2 (*c.* 1859)

      T's extracts are from the article "Hydrodynamics" and have to do with the velocity and carrying power of river currents.

58.   ARCHER, Gabriel. "The Relation of Captain Gosnold's Voyage to the North Part of Virginia, Begun the Six-and-Twentieth of March, Anno 42 Elizabethae Reginae, 1602, and Delivered by Gabriel Archer, a Gentleman in the Said Voyage." *Collections of the Massachusetts Historical Society*, 3d ser., vol. 8 (1843): 72–81.

      CC, 190–191, 192–193, 194; IB 2 (*c.* 1850)

59.   ARIOSTO, Ludovico. *Orlando Furioso: translated from the Italian of Ludovico Ariosto, with notes; by John Hoole.* London: Printed for the author and sold by C. Bathurst, 1783.
TL

60.   ARISTOTLE. *Histoire des animaux d'Aristote, avec la traduction françoise par M. Camus.* . . . Paris: Chez la veuve Desaint, 1783.
HL 12–16–59
JL 13.55, 77–78 (12–26–59 & 1–5–60); CPB2

61.   ARISTOTLE. *Meteorologica.* Quoted in Thomas Stanley, *History of Philosophy* (q.v.)

WE, 128

62.   ARNIM, Bettina (Bretano) von. *Günderode.* Boston: E. P. Peabody, 1842.
TL

63.   ARNOLD, Benedict. "Arnold's Letters on his Expedition to Canada in 1775." *Collections of the Maine Historical Society,* 1st ser., vol. 1 (1831): 341–387.

MW, 130, 132, 246

Article also includes a journal of a 1761 expedition by a Col. Montresor.

64.   ARNOLD, Samuel Greene. *History of the state of Rhode Island and Providence plantations.* New York: D. Appleton & co., 1859.

IB 12 (c. 1859)

65.   ASIATIC SOCIETY OF BENGAL. *Bibliotheca Indica. A collection of Oriental works, published under the patronage of the hon. court of directors of the East India Company, and the superintendence of the Asiatic Society of Bengal.* Vol. 14, nos. 41–42. Calcutta, 1853.
TL
JL 10.54 (9–30–57)

66.   ATKINSON, James. *Epitome of the art of navigation.* London: Mount, 1758.
TL

67.   ATKINSON, Thomas Witlam. *Oriental and Western Siberia: A narrative of seven years' explorations and adventures in Siberia, Mongolia, the Kirghis Steppes, Chinese Tartary, and*

part of Central Asia. . . . New York: Harper & brothers,
1858.
SL
JL 7.480 (10–3–55); IB II; CPB2

68.   ATKINSON, Thomas Witlam. *Travels in the regions of the upper and lower Amoor and the Russian acquisitions on the
confines of India and China.* . . . New York: Harper, 1860.

IB 12 (*c.* 1860)

69.   AUBREY, John, et al. *Letters written by eminent persons in the
seventeenth and eighteenth centuries: to which are added,
Hearne's journeys to Reading and to Whaddon Hall, and the
lives of eminent men.* London: Longman, Hurst, Rees, Orme,
and Brown [etc., etc.], 1813.
EL
WE, 109; PJ 1.287–288 (3–13–41), 338 (11–30–41)

70.   AUDUBON, John James. *Ornithological biography, or An ac-
count of the birds of the United States of America.* . . . 5 vols.
London: A. Black [etc., etc.] 1831–49.
HL 2–20–37
EX, 123; PJ 1.353 (12–31–41)

71.   AUDUBON, John James. *A synopsis of the birds of North
America.* Edinburgh: Adam and Charles Black; London:
Rees, Brown, Green, and Longman, 1839.

JL 5.3 (3–5–53)

72.   AUDUBON, John James, and Rev. John BACHMAN. *The vivipa-
rous quadrupeds of North America.* Vol. 1. New-York: J. J.
Audubon, 1851.
TL
PJ 3 (1849); JL 4.434 (12–30–52); 7.202–203 (2–21–55),
239–241 (3–10–55), 244 (3–12–55), 267 (3–23–55); FB;
IB 7

73.   BABSON, John James. *History of the town of Gloucester,
Cape Ann, including the town of Rockport.* Gloucester,
[Mass.]: Procter brothers, 1860.

CC, 194n

74.   BACHE, A. D. See United States. Coast and Geodetic Survey.

75.   BACHI, Pietro. *A comparative view of the Italian & Spanish
languages, or an easy method of learning the Spanish tongue.
For those who are already acquainted with the Italian.* Boston: Cottons and Barnard, 1832.
TL, TX

76.   BACHI, Pietro. *A grammar of the Italian language.* . . . Boston: Hilliard, Gray, Little and Wilkins, 1829.
TL, TX

77.   BACHI, Pietro. *Scelta di prose italiane, tratte da' più celebri scrittori antichi et moderni, per uso degli studiosi di questa lingua.* Cambridge, [Mass.]: per Carlo Folsom, 1828.
TL, TX

78.   BACHI, Pietro. *Teatro scelto italiano.* . . . Cambrigia, Mass.: Hilliard & Brown, 1829.
TL, TX

79.   BACK, Sir George. *Narrative of the Arctic land expedition to the mouth of the Great Fish River and along the shores of the Arctic Ocean, in the years 1833, 1834, and 1835.* . . . Philadelphia: E. L. Carey and A. Hart, 1836.
HL (4–24–37)

80.   BACKUS, Rev. Isaac. "An Historical Account of Middleborough, in the County of Plymouth." *Collections of the Massachusetts Historical Society,* 1st ser., vol. 3 (1794; rpt. 1810): 148–153.

JL 7.472, 478 (10–2–55)

81.   BACON, Sir Francis, viscount St. Albans. *Essays. Moral, economical, and political.* Boston: Joseph Greenleaf, 1807.
TL
PJ 1.107 (2–11–40)

82.   BACON, Sir Francis, viscount St. Albans. In Wotton, Sir Henry, *Reliquiae Wottonianae* (q.v.).
"The World" ("Humane Life Characterized")
CPB1 (*c.* 1841)

83.   BACON, Sir Francis, viscount St. Albans. *Of the proficience & advancement of learning.* . . . London: W. Pickering, 1825.

COR, 145 (10–17–43)

84.   BACON, Oliver N. *A history of Natick, from its first settlement.* . . . Boston: Damrell & Moore, 1856.

JL 8.118 (1–19–56)

85.   BACQUEVILLE de la POTHERIE, Claude C. le Roy. See *Voyages de découverte au Canada.*

86.   BADHAM, Charles David. *A treatise on the esculent funguses of England.* London: Reeve brothers, 1847.
HL 10–6–59

87.   BAILEY, Ebenezer. *First lessons in algebra, being an easy introduction to that science.* . . . Boston: Carter, Hendee & co., 1833.
TL, TX

88.   BAILEY, Jacob Whitman. "Account of an Excursion to Mount Katahdin in Maine." *American Journal of Sciences and Arts* 32 (1837): 20–34.

MW, 4, 67

89.   BAILEY, Nathan. *A new universal etymological English dictionary: containing not only explanations of the words in the English language . . . but also their etymologies from the ancient and modern languages.* . . . London: Printed for T. Osborne and J. Snipton etc., 1755.
TL
JL 4.468 (1–20–53); 6.112 (2–9–54); 7.183 (2–13–55)

Edition uncertain; many available. Possibly also one of T's sources for his etymology of "Cape" and "Cod" at the beginning of CC.

90.   BAILEY, Philip James. *The angel world, and other poems.* Boston: Ticknor, Reed and Fields, 1850.

CPBI (c. 1850–51)

91.   BAILEY, Philip James. *Festus; a poem.* London: W. Pickering, 1839.

WE, 95, 292; LN

92.   BAILEY, Samuel. *Essays on the formation and publication of opinions, and on other subjects.* The 2d edition, revised and enlarged. London: R. Hunter, 1826.
HL 9–16–34, 1–9–37.

93.   BAINES, Edward. See "Review of Edward Baines's *A History of the Cotton Manufacture in Great Britain.*"

94.   BAIRD, Spencer Fullerton. "American Ruminants. On the Ruminating Animals of North America and Their Susceptibility of Domestication." In U.S. Patent Office. Report. Pt. 2. Agriculture. 1851, pp. 104–128. Washington: 1852.
TL
JL 5.406 (8–31–53)

95.   BAIRD, Spencer Fullerton. *Directions for making collections in natural history.* Washington: Smithsonian institution, 1853.

TL
COR, 310 (12–19–53)

96.   BAIRD, Spencer Fullerton. *Mammals of North America; The descriptions of species based chiefly on the collections in the museum of the Smithsonian Institution.* Philadelphia: J. B. Lippincott & Co., 1859.

COR, 592 (10–13–60)

97.   BALLANTYNE, R. H. *The young fur traders.* Edinburgh: T. Nelson, 1856.

IB 10 (*c.* 1857)

98.   BANCROFT, George. *A history of the United States, from the discovery of the American continent.* . . . 10 vols. Boston: Little, Brown, and company, 1834–75.
EL, CL
CC, 179–194 passim; JL 9.75 (9–10–56); IB 9; HM 13201 (1–17–40)

99.   BANKS, John. *A new history of the life and reign of the Czar Peter the Great, emperor of all Russia, and father of his country.* . . . Montpelier, [Vt.]: Printed by Wright & Silbey, for P. Merrifield, & co., Windsor, Vt., 1811.
HL 9–18–33

100.   BARBER, John Warner. *Connecticut historical collections, containing a general collection of interesting facts, traditions, biographical sketches, anecdotes, etc., relating to the history and antiquities of every town in Connecticut, with geographical descriptions.* New Haven: Durrie & Peck and J. W. Barber, 1836.

IB 10 (*c.* 1857)

101.   BARBER, John Warner. *Historical collections, being a general collection of interesting facts, traditions, biographical sketches, anecdotes, &c., relating to the history and antiquities of every town in Massachusetts, with geographical descriptions. Illustrated by 200 engravings.* Worcester, Mass.: Dorr, Howland, & co., 1839.

WE, 197; WA, 164; CC, 175; JL 8.163–165 (2–3–56); IB 2

Several editions available; possibly also T's source for the story of the "strong and beautiful bug" in "Conclusion," WA.

102.   BARBOUR, John. *The Bruce; or, the history of Robert I. King of Scotland. Written in Scottish verse by John Barbour.* . . . London: Printed by H. Hughes for G. Nicol, 1790.
HL 1–10–42

Borrowed at T's request by Charles Stearns Wheeler; letter by T dated 6–15–42 (not in COR) asks Wheeler to return the volume.

103.   BARD, Samuel A. (pseudonym). See Squier, E. G.

104.   BARNEY, Mary. *A biographical memoir of the late Commodore Joshua Barney: from autobiographical notes and journals in possession of his family and other authentic sources.* Edited by Mary Barney. Boston: Gray & Bowen, 1832.
HL 3–5–34

105.   BARNFIELD, R. In *England's Helicon* (q.v.).
HL 12–8–41
"The Unknown Shepherd's Complaint"
CPB1

Attributed to Barnfield; printed under pseudonym "Ignoto."

106.   BARROW, Sir John. *A voyage to Cochinchina, in the years 1792 and 1793.* . . . *To which is annexed an account of a journey made in the years 1801 and 1802, to the residence of the chief of the Booshuana nation.* . . . London: T. Cadell and W. Davies, 1806.
HL 9–30–34

107.   BARRY, John Stetson. *The history of Massachusetts . . . By John Stetson Barry.* Boston: Phillips, Sampson, and company, 1857.

CC, 179

108.   BARTH, Heinrich. *Travels and discoveries in North and Central Africa. From the journal of an expedition undertaken under the auspices of H.B.M.'s government in the years 1849–1855 . . . and a sketch of Denham and Clapperton's expedition, by the American Editor.* Philadelphia: J. W. Bradley, 1860.
SL
IB 12 (*c.* 1860)

109.   BARTLETT, John Russell. *Dictionary of Americanisms. A glossary of words and phrases, usually regarded as peculiar to the United States.* New York: Bartlett and Welford, 1848.
TL

110. BARTON, Benjamin Smith. *New views of the origin of the tribes and natives of America.* Philadelphia: Printed for the author, 1798.
HL 3–4–56
IB 10

The copy of this work T borrowed was bound with George Burder's *The Welch Indians . . .* and Jonathan Edwards's *Observations on the Language of the Muhhakeneew Indians* (q.v.).

111. BARTON, Bernard. *Poetic vigils.* London: Baldwin, Cradock, and Joy, 1824.

LN (*c.* 1841)

112. BARTRAM, John. *Observations on the inhabitants, climate, soil, rivers, productions, animals, and other matters worthy of notice. Made by Mr. John Bartram, in his travels from Pensilvania to Onondago, Onego, and the Lake Ontario, in Canada. To which is annexed a curious account of the cataracts at Niagra. By Mr. Peter Kalm, a Swedish gentleman who travelled there.* London: printed for J. Whiston and B. White, 1751.
HL 3–24–56
CC, 185; IB 10

113. BARTRAM, William. *Travels through North and South Carolina, Georgia, East and West Florida, the Cherokee country, the extensive territories of the Muscogulges, or Creek confederacy, and the country of the Chactaws. . . .* Philadelphia: Printed for Jones & Jonson, 1791.
SNH 8–1–51
WA, 68; EX, 199; JL 2.376–378 (8–6–51); IB 4

114. BAUER, Juliette, trans. See Klencke, Hermann.

115. BAYFIELD, Captain Henry W., et al. *Sailing directions for the island and banks of Newfoundland . . . compiled chiefly from the surveys made . . . by Captains Henry W. Bayfield, F. Bullock, etc.* London: J. Imray, 1851.

CN (*c.* 1852)

116. BAYLY, Anselm Yates. *The advantage of a settlement upon the Ohio in North America.* London: J. Riddley, 1763.
HL 3–24–56
CC, 235

Bound with John Bartram's *Observations* (q.v.) in the copy T borrowed.

117.   "Bears and Bear-Hunting." *Harper's Magazine* 11 (Oct. 1855): 591–607.

       IB 10 (*c.* 1856)

118.   BEAUMONT, Francis. In Chalmers (q.v.), vol. 6.
       HL 1–17–44 (by RWE)
       "The Honest Man's Fortune"
       LN

119.   BEAUMONT, Francis, and John FLETCHER. *The Faithful Shep-herdess.*

       PJ 2.333 (Fall 1846)

120.   BEAUMONT, Francis, and John FLETCHER. *Nice Valour; or The Passionate Madman.*

       ME (*c.* 1837)

121.   BEAUMONT, Sir John. In Chalmers (q.v.), vol. 6.
       HL 1–17–44 (by RWE)
       "Bosworth Field . . ."
       LN

122.   BEAURIEU, Gaspard Guillard de. *Cours d'histoire naturelle; ou, Tableau de la nature considérée dans l'homme, les quad-rupédes, les oiseaux, les poissons. . . .* Paris: Lacombe, 1770.
       TL

       Conjectural title; see Harding, *Thoreau's Library,* pp. 57–58.

123.   BECHSTEIN, Johann Matthous. *Cage and chamber-birds; their natural history, habits, food, diseases, management, and modes of capture. Incorporating the whole of Sweet's British Warblers.* London: H. G. Bohn, 1853.
       TL
       JL 13.246 (4–13–60)

124.   BECK, Lewis Caleb. *Botany of the northern and middle states. . . .* Albany: Printed by Webster and Skinners, 1833.

       TMJ

125.   BECK, Lewis Caleb. *Botany of the United States north of Vir-ginia.* 2d ed., rev. and enl. New York: Harper & Brothers, 1856.

       JL 8.466 (8–13–56)

126.   BECKFORD, William. *Italy; with sketches of Spain and Portugal.* 2 vols. London: R. Bentley, 1834.
       IN 12–8–36

127.   BECKWOURTH, James Pierson. *The life and adventures of James P. Beckwourth, mountaineer, scout, and pioneer, and chief of the Crow nation of Indians. With Illustrations. Written from his own dictation, by T. D. Bonner.* New York: Harper & brothers, 1856.

       IB 10; FB (*c.* 1856)

128.   BEESON, John. *A plea for the Indians; with facts and features of the late war in Oregon.* New York: J. Beeson, 1857.
       TL

129.   BELKNAP, Jeremy. *American biography: or, an historical account of those persons who have been distinguished in America, as adventurers, statesmen, philosophers, divines, warriors, and other remarkable characters. . . .* Vol. 2. Boston: Isaiah Thomas and E. J. Andrews, 1798.

       CC, 179–180, 191, 194; CN

130.   BELKNAP, Jeremy. *The history of New-Hampshire. Comprehending the events of one complete century and seventy-five years from the discovery of the river Poscataqua to the year one thousand seven hundred and ninety. . . .* Boston: Published by Bradford and Read, 1813.

       WE, 88, 123, 179–180, 191, 220, 221, 246; JL 11.5 (7–2–58), 58–59 (7–19–58); IB 11

131.   BELL, Thomas. *A history of British quadrupeds, including the Cetacea. Illustrated by nearly 200 woodcuts.* London: J. Van Voorst, 1837.
       TL
       CC, 115; JL 10.437 (5–20–58)

132.   BELL, Thomas. *A history of British reptiles . . . Illustrated by more than 40 woodcuts.* London: J. Van Voorst, 1839, 1849.
       SNH 5–27–58
       CPB2

133.   BELLENDEN, John. "Allegorie of Vertue and Delyte." In Sibbald, James, *Chronicle of Scottish Poetry* (q.v.).

       COR, 65 (3–11–42)

134.   BELLOWS, Henry Whitney. *Historical sketch of Col. Benjamin Bellows, founder of Walpole . . . with an appendix relating his descendants.* New York: J. A. Gray, 1855.

JL 9.77–78 (9–11–56)

135.   BELON, Pierre. *L'histoire de la natvre des oyseavx, avec levrs descriptions; & naïfs portraicts retirez dv naturel: escrit en sept livres. . . .* Paris: G. Cauellat, 1555.
HL 2–6–60
CPB2

136.   BELTRAMI, Giacomo Constantino. *La découverte des sources du Mississippi et de la rivière Sanglante. . . .* Nouvelle-Orléans: Impr. par B. Levy, 1824.
TL, SNH 10–23–52

The work T withdrew from SNH may have been a translation of the French original he owned, or an anonymous tract defending Beltrami. See Cameron, "Emerson, Thoreau, and the Society of Natural History," p. 25.

137.   BENJAMIN, Asher. *The American builder's companion; or, a new system of architecture: particularly adapted to the present style of building in the United States of America. . . .* Boston: Pub. by Etheridge and Bliss, S. Etheridge, printer, Charleston, 1806.
TL

138.   BENLOWES, Edward. *Theophila, or loves sacrifice. A divine poem. . . .* London: Printed by R.N., sold by Henry Seile and Humphrey Mosely, 1652.
HL 12–9–41

139.   BENNET, Nehemiah. "Description of the Town of Middleborough, in the County of Plymouth. With Remarks." *Collections of the Massachusetts Historical Society*, 1st ser., vol. 3 (1794; rpt. 1810): 1–3.

140.   BERKELEY, George (Bishop). "Verses on the Prospect of Planting Arts and Learning in America."

EX, 223

141.   BERNÁLDEZ, Andrés. "Extract from the History of the Catholic Sovereigns, Ferdinand and Isabella." *Collections of the Massachusetts Historical Society*, 3d ser., vol. 8 (1843): 5–69.

WE, 391; PJ 2.124 (Spring 1845); IB 2

142.   BERNARD, Jean Frédéric. *Recueil de voyages au nord, divers mémoirs très utiles au commerce & à la navigation. . . .* 8 vols. Amsterdam: J. F. Bernard, 1715–27.

HL 12–7–58
IB 11

143. BEVERLY, Robert. *The history of Virginia, in four parts. . . .*
London: F. Fayram and J. Clarke, and T. Bickerton, 1722.
HL 1–26–57
CC, 12n, 80; JL 9.274 (2–20–57); FB; IB 8

144. BEWICK, Thomas. *The History of British birds. The figures
engraved on wood by T. Bewick.* 2 vols. New Castle: Beilby
& Bewick, 1794–1804.
HL 1–16–55
COR, 369; JL 7.126–127 (1–20–55); IB 9

145. *Bhagavad-Gītā.* See Mahābhārata. *The Bhagavad-gītā.*

146. Bible. Boston: Sold by Lincoln, Edmunds, & co., [etc.] 1834.

This and the following editions were owned by T or his family and listed in his library catalogue. The most complete listing of his references and allusions to the Bible is Burns,
"Thoreau's Use of the Bible."

147. Bible. Edinburgh: Mark and Charles Kerr, 1793.
TL

148. Bible. New York: White for the American Bible Society,
1829.
TL

149. Bible. Philadelphia: L. Coffin or Shattuck & Company, 1788.
TL

Either edition possible.

150. Bible, New Testament. *Novum Testamentum. Juxta exemplar
Joannis Millii accuratissime impressum. . . .* Worcester:
Thomas, 1800.
TL

151. BIDDLE, Richard. *A memoir of Sebastian Cabot: with a review of the history of maritime discovery. Illustrated by documents from the rolls, now first published.* Philadelphia: Carey
and Lea, 1831.
HL 9–17–55
CC, 183, 184, 185, 187; CN; IB 9

152. BIGELOW, Jacob. *American medical botany, 1817–21, being a
collection of the native medicinal plants of the United States,
containing their botanical history and chemical analysis,
properties and uses. . . .* Boston: Published by Cummings and
Hilliard, at the Boston bookstore, no. 1 Cornhill. University
press. . . . Hilliard and Metcalf, 1817–20.

HL 4–30–51
JL 2.219–222 (5–29–51), 228 (6–6–51), 261 (6–14–51); IB 4

153.   BIGELOW, Jacob. *Elements of technology, taken chiefly from a course of lectures delivered at Cambridge, on the application of the sciences to the useful arts.* . . . Boston: Hilliard Gray, Little and Wilkins, 1829.

COR, 23 (2–10–38)

154.   BIGELOW, Jacob. *Florula bostoniensis, A collection of plants of Boston and its vicinity.* . . . Boston: Cummings, Hilliard, & co., 1824.
TL
JL 2.273 (6–29–51), 414 (8–21–51); 3.130 (11–24–51); 4.95 (6–13–52), 129–130 (6–23–52); 5.219 (6–2–53), 276 (6–18–53); 6.404 (7–18–54); 8.337 (5–15–56), 406 (7–10–56), 432 (7–28–56); 9.156 (12–4–56); 10.9 (8–22–57), 14 (8–25–57), 15 (8–27–57); 11.281 (11–3–58); 12.208 (6–19–59)

In the 12–4–56 Journal entry T identifies this as his first botany book, purchased about twenty years earlier.

155.   *Biographie universelle, ancienne et moderne, ou, Histoire, par ordre alphabétique, de la vie publique et privée de tous les hommes, qui sunt fait remarquer par leurs écrits, leurs actions, leurs talents, leurs vertus ou leurs crimes.* . . . 52 vols. plus suppléments. Paris: Michaud frères [etc.], 1811–62.

CC, 187

156.   BION. See *Greek Pastoral Poets.*

157.   BIRKENHEAD, Sir John. In Chalmers (q.v.), vol. 6.
HL 1–17–44 (by RWE)
"On the Happy Collection of Beaumont and Fletcher's Works"
LN

158.   BLAIR, Hugh. *An abridgement of lectures on rhetoric . . . to which are added, Questions, adapted to the above work, for the use of schools and academies, by an experienced teacher of youth.* Exeter: Printed and published by John J. Williams, 1822.
TL

Autograph of Helen Thoreau.

159.   BLAIR, Hugh. *Sermons.* Philadelphia: From the Press of M. Carey, 1794.
TL

Autograph of John Thoreau, Sr.

160. BLAIR, Hugh. *Sermons.* 2 vols. Boston: I. Thomas & E. T. Andrews, 1799.
      TL

161. BLAKE, John Lauris. *A biographical dictionary; comprising a summary of the lives of the most distinguished persons of all ages, nations, and professions, including more than two thousand articles of American biography.* Philadelphia: H. Cowperthwait & co., 1856.
      TL

162. BLANCHARD, Samuel Laman. *Sketches from life.* . . . London: H. Colburn, 1846.
      TL

163. BLODGET, Lorin. *Climatology of the United States, and the temperate latitudes of the North American continent.* . . . Philadelphia: J. B. Lippincott, 1857.

      JL 14.335 (4–6–61); COR, 611 (4–10–61); CPB2

164. BLOODGOOD, S. Dewitt. See Hogg, James.

165. BODAEUS, Johannes. *Theophrasti Eresii De historia plantarum libri decem, graece et latine.* . . . Amsteldami: apud H. Laurentium, 1644.

      EX, 317

166. BODE, Georg Heinrich. *Orpheus, poetarum graecorum antiquissimus. Auctore Georgio Henrico Bode . . . commentario praemio ornata.* Gottingae: Typis Dieterichianis, 1824.

      HM 13201

      Possible edition; see Cameron, "Ungathered Thoreau Reading Lists," pp. 365, 370.

167. BOLTON, Edmund. In *England's Helicon* (q.v.).
      HL (12–41)
      "A Pastoral Ode to an Honorable Friend," "The Shepherd's Song: A Carroll or Himme for Christmas"
      CPB1

168. BONAPARTE, Charles Lucien Jules Laurent, prince de Canino. *American Ornithology.* 4 vols. Philadelphia: Carey, Lea & Carey, 1825–33.

      JL 12.198 (6–2–59)

169.   BOND, Henry. *Family memorials. Genealogies of the families and descendants of the early settlers of Watertown, Mass.* . . . Boston: Little, Brown & Co., 1855.

         JL 8.187–188 (2–25–56)

170.   BOND, John Wesley. *Minnesota and its resources; to which are appended Campfire sketches, or, Notes of a trip from St. Paul to Pembina and Selkirk settlements on the Red river of the North.* New York: Redfield, 1853.

         TMJ

171.   BONNER, T. D. See Beckwourth, James.

172.   BOSSU, Jean Bernard. *Nouveaux voyages aux Indes Occidentales; contenant différens peuples qui habitent les environs due grand Fleuve Saint-Louis, appelé vulgairement le Mississippi; leur religion, leur gouverment, leur moeurs, les guerres, & leur commerce.* Paris: Le Jay, 1768.
         HL 4–26–59
         IB 12

173.   BOSSU, Jean Bernard. *Nouveaux voyages dans l'Amérique Septentrionale, contenant une collection de lettres écrites sur les lieux, par l'auteur; à son ami, M. Douin . . . ci-devant son camarade dans le Nouveau monde.* Amsterdam: Changuion, 1777.
         HL 4–26–59
         IB 12; CPB2

174.   BOSSU, Jean Bernard. *Travels through that part of North America formerly called Louisiana. Tr. from the French, by John Reinhold Forster, F.A.S. Illustrated with notes relative chiefly to natural history.* . . . 2 vols. London: Printed for T. Davies, 1771.
         HL 4–26–59
         IB 12

175.   *Boston Daily Journal.*

         T mentions reading an editorial on John Brown in this newspaper ("Who Is Brown, the Leader?" [q.v.], reprinted from the *New York Herald*) in JL 12.407 (10–19–59); also a notice about a lecture on the word "schooner" on May 3, 1859—see CC, 157.

176.   *Boston Quarterly Review.*

         In a letter to Orestes Brownson, the editor (COR, 20), T mentions having read the first issue of this magazine.

177. BOSTON SOCIETY OF NATURAL HISTORY. *Proceedings.*

T read widely in the *Proceedings* of the Natural History Society, of which he was elected a corresponding member in
1850. See individual articles, mostly brief communications or
citations of specimens donated, under the following names:
Brewer, T. M.; Burnett, W. I.; Giraud, Charles; Jackson,
Charles T.; Kneeland, Samuel, Jr.; Sprague, Charles J.; Storer,
H. R.; Winslow, C. F.

178. BOSWELL, James. *The Life of Samuel Johnson.* London:
Jones, 1827.

PJ 1.92 (12–39)

179. BOSWORTH, Joseph. *Elements of Anglo-Saxon grammar, with
copious notes, illustrating the structure of the Saxon and the
formation of the English language.* . . . London: Printed for
Harding, Mauor, and Lepard, 1823.
HL 6–22–37
PJ 1.339 (11–30–41); ME

180. BOTTA, Paul Émile. See "Review of Paul Émile Botta's *Travels
in Arabia.*"

181. BOUCHER, Pierre. *Histoire véritable et naturelle des moeurs et
productions dú pays de la Novvelle France, vulgairement dite
la Canada.* Paris: F. Lambert, 1664.
HL 10–6–59
EX, 91; IB 12

182. BOUCHETTE, Joseph. *The British dominions in North Amer-
ica; or, A topographical and statistical description of the
provinces of lower and upper Canada, New Brunswick, Nova
Scotia, the islands of Newfoundland, Prince Edward, and
Cape Breton.* . . . London: Longman, Rees, Orme, Brown and
Green, 1831.

EX, 39, 94–95; CC, 184; CN

183. BOUCHETTE, Joseph. *A topographical description of the province of Lower Canada, with remarks on Upper Canada, and
on the relative connexion of both provinces with the United
States of America.* . . . London: Printed for the author and
published by W. Faden, 1815.

EX, 41, 42–43, 63–64, 92; CN

184. BOURNE, Vincent. *Miscellaneous poems: consisting of origi-
nals and translations.* London: W. Ginger, 1772.

"Hymn," "On the Feast of Pentecost"
CPBI (12–41)

185.   B[OWRING], J[OHN]. "German Epigrams." *London Magazine*
       9 (March, April, May 1824).
       LN (12–41)

186.   BOYER, Abel. *Boyer's French dictionary; comprising all the
       additions and improvements of the latest Paris and London
       editions, with a very large number of useful words and
       phrases.* Boston: T. Bedlington, and Bradford & Peaslee,
       1827.
       TL

187.   BRACKENRIDGE, Henry Marie. *Journal of a voyage up the
       river Missouri, performed in eighteen hundred eleven.* . . .
       Baltimore: Pub. by Coale and Maxwell, Pomeroy & Joy,
       printers, 1815.
       HL 1–16–37
       ME

188.   BRADFORD, William. *History of Plymouth plantation. By
       William Bradford.* . . . *Now first printed from the original
       manuscript.* . . . Boston: Little, Brown and company, 1856.

       CC, 201–202; JL 9.164, 169–170, 177 (12–6 & 8 & 10–56);
       12.182 (5–5–59); IB 8; IB 10; FB

       This first complete printing of Bradford's *History*, edited by
       Charles Deane, was also published in the 3d ser., vol. 3, of
       Collections of the Massachusetts Historical Society; the ear-
       lier references to Bradford are from Nathaniel Morton's
       New-England's Memorial (q.v.).

189.   BRAND, John. *Observations on popular antiquities: chiefly il-
       lustrating the origin of our vulgar customs, ceremonies, and
       superstitions. Arranged and rev., with additions by Henry El-
       lis.* 2 vols. London: F. C. and J. Rivington, 1813.
       HL 12–1–41
       CC, 124; EX, 297; JL 13.159 (2–23–60), 240 (4–2–60); ME; IB
       12; CPB2

       T cites a 1795 edition in IB 12 and CPB2, but neither the Na-
       tional Union nor British Museum catalogue lists an edition
       for 1795.

190.   BREBEUF, Jean de. In *Jesuit Relations* (q.v.) for 1636.
       HL 11–11–52
       IB 7; IB 8

191.   BRERETON, John. *A briefe and true relation of the discoverie of the north part of Virginia, being a most pleasant, fruitfull, and commodious soile: made this present yeere 1602, by Captaine Bartholomew Gosnold, Captaine Bartholomew Gilbert, and divers other gentlemen . . . Whereunto is annexed a treatise, of M. Edward Hayes. . . . Collections of the Massachusetts Historical Society*, 3d ser., vol. 8 (1843): 82–123.

CC, 190–194; IB 2

192.   BREWER, T. M. Untitled contribution to *Proceedings of the Boston Natural History Society* 4 (1851–54): 324.

CPB2 (*c.* 1858)

193.   BREWER, T. M. See Wilson, Alexander (no. 1440).

194.   BREWERTON, George D. "A Ride with Kit Carson through the Great American Desert and the Rocky Mountains." *Harper's Magazine* 7 (Aug. 1853): 306–334.

IB 8 (*c.* 1854)

195.   BREWSTER, Sir David. *Letters on natural magic. Addressed to Sir Walter Scott, bart.* N.Y.: Harper & bros., 1836.
CL
FB (*c.* 1857)

196.   BREWSTER, Sir David. *The life of Sir Isaac Newton.* New-York: J. & J. Harper, 1831.
TL
JL 8.362–363 (6–2–56)

197.   BRIDGMAN, William. *Translations from the Greek, viz, Aristotle's synopsis of the virtues and vices. The similitudes of Demophilus. The golden sentences of Democrites. And the Pythagoric symbols, with explanations of Jamblichus . . . to which are added the Pythagoric sentences of Demophilus, by Mr. Thomas Taylor.* London: Printed for W. Bridgman, by R. Wilks, 1804.
EL
LN (*c.* 1841)

198.   *British Drama: a collection of the most esteemed tragedies, comedies, operas, & farces in the English language.* 2 vols. Philadelphia: Lippincott, 1822.
TL

199.   BRODERIP, W. J. *Leaves from the notebook of a naturalist.* Boston: Published by E. Littel & co. New York: G. P. Putnam, 1852.

TL
FB (c. 1852)

200.   BRODERIP, W. J. *Zoological recreations*. London: H. Col.-
        burn, 1847.

        FB (c. 1855)

201.   BROOKE, Fulke Greville, 1st baron. *Certain learned and ele-
        gant workes, of the right honorable Fulke Lord Brooke, writ-
        ten in his youth, and familiar exercise with Sir Phillip Sidney.*
        . . . London: Printed by E. P. Curslow, for H. Seyle, 1633.
        HL 12–1–41
        "The Worth That Worthiness Should Move"
        CPB1

202.   BROOKS, Charles. *Elements of Ornithology*. Boston: J. Mun-
        roe & Co., 1847.

        JL 5.93 (4–5–53); FB

203.   BROOKS, Charles. *History of the Town of Medford, Middle-
        sex County, Massachusetts, from its first settlement, in 1630
        to the present time, 1855.* Boston: J. M. Usher, 1855.

        IB 10; FB (c. 1856)

204.   BROSSES, Charles de. *Terra australis cognita: or Voyages to
        the terra australis, or southern hemisphere, during the six-
        teenth, seventeenth, and eighteenth centuries.* 3 vols. Edin-
        burgh: Printed for the author and sold by Hawes, Clark, and
        Collins, London, 1766–67.
        HL 1–19–37 (vol. 1)

205.   BROWN, Thomas. *Lectures on the philosophy of the human
        mind.* 2 vols. Hallowell [Me.]: Glazier, Masters & co. 1833.
        TL

206.   BROWNE, Sir Thomas. *Miscellaneous works.* Ed. Alexander
        Young. Cambridge, Mass.: Hilliard and Brown, 1831.

        RP, 14, 36; PJ 1.107–108 (2–40)

207.   BROWNE, Sir Thomas. *Works, including his life and corre-
        spondence.* Ed. Simon Wilkins. 4 vols. London: W. Pickering,
        1835–36.
        EL
        WE, 68; PJ 1.446–447 (1–3–43); 2.354 (Fall 1846)

208.   BROWNE, William. In Chalmers (q.v.), vol. 6.
        HL 1–17–44 (by RWE)
        "Britannia's Pastorals"

LN
"The Shepherd's Pipe"
WE, 117

209. BROWNSON, Orestes. *New views of Christianity, society, and the church*. Boston: J. Munroe and company, 1836.
TL

210. BRY, Theodore de. *Collectiones peregrinationum in Indiam Orientalem et Indiam Occidentalem, XXV partibus comprehensae, a Theodoro, Joan: Theodoro de Bry, et a Matheo Merian pulicatae.* 3 vols. Francofurti ad moenum: typis Ioanis Wecheli, sumtibus vero Theodoro de Bry, 1590–1634.
HL 2–9–53

211. BRYANT, William Cullen. "The Fringed Gentian."

JL 4.391 (10–19–52)

T also refers to Bryant's poetry in PJ 1.459 (8–25–43) but does not quote or allude to specific poems.

212. BRYANT, William Cullen. *Letters of a Traveller; or, Notes of things seen in Europe and America.* New York: G. P. Putnam [etc., etc.], 1850.

IB 8; FB (*c.* 1853)

213. BUCHANAN, James. *Sketches of the history, manners, and customs of the North American Indians with a plan for their melioration.* New York: W. Borradaile, 1824.
TL

214. BUCKINGHAM, James. *Canada, Nova Scotia, New Brunswick, and other British provinces in North America; with a plan of national colonization.* London: Fischer, son, & co., [1843].

CN (*c.* 1852)

215. BUCKLAND, Francis Trevelyan. *Curiosities of natural history.* New York: Rudd & Carleton, 1859.
CL
CC, 65–66; IB 12; CPB2 (*c.* 1859)

216. BUCKLE, Henry Thomas. *History of Civilization in England.* New York: D. Appleton and company, 1858.

IB 11 (*c.* 1858)

217. BUFFON, Count Georges Louis LeClerc, comte de. See Lelarge de Lignac, Joseph Adrien.

218.   BULLOCK, William. *Six months' residence and travels in Mexico, containing remarks on the present state of New Spain, its natural productions, state of society, manufactures, trade, agriculture, and antiquities, &c.* 2 vols. London: J. Murray, 1825.
       HL 3–19–34 (vol. 2)

219.   BULWER-LYTTON, Edward George, 1st baron Lytton. See Lytton, Edward George Earle Bulwer-Lytton.

220.   BUNSEN, Christianus Carlus Josias. *Christianity and mankind, their beginnings and prospects.* 7 vols. London: Longman, Brown, Green and Longmans, 1854.
       TL

221.   BUNSEN, Christianus Carlus Josias. *Egypt's place in universal history: an historical investigation in five books. . . . Translated from the German by Charles H. Cottrell.* London: Longman, Brown, Green, and Longmans, 1848.
       TL

222.   BUNYAN, John. *The pilgrim's progress from this world to that which is to come, delivered under the similitude of a dream.* . . . New-York: Published by John Tiebout, 238 Water-street, Paul & Thomas, printers, 1811.
       TL
       LN (*c.* 1847–48)

223.   BURDER, George. *The Welch Indians; or, a Collection of papers, respecting a people whose ancestors emigrated from Wales to America, in the year 1170, with Prince Modoc . . . and who are now said to inhabit a beautiful country on the west side of the mississippi.* London: Printed for Chapman [1797].
       HL 3–4–56
       IB 10

       Bound with Barton, Benjamin Smith, *New Views* (q.v.).

224.   BURGH, James. *The dignity of human nature. Or, A brief account of the certain and established means for attaining the true end of our existence. In four books . . . a new edition.* 2 vols. London: Printed for J. Johnson and J. Payne [etc.], 1767.
       HL 2–17–35

225.   BURKE, Edmund. *Philosophical inquiry into the origin of our ideas of the sublime and beautiful. The 6th ed. with an introductory discourse concerning taste, and several other additions.* London: J. Dodsley, 1770.
       HL 3–23–37
       EEM, 93–99

226. BURKE, Edmund. *The works of the Right Honourable Edmund Burke.* 8 vols. London: F. and C. Rivington, 1801.
IN 7–11–37

227. BURNETT, W. I. Untitled contribution to *Proceedings of the Boston Natural History Society* 4 (1851–54): 352.

CPB2 (*c.* 1858)

228. BURNOUF, Eugène. See Saddharmapuṇḍarīka.

229. BURNS, Robert. *The poetical works of Robert Burns.* 2 vols. London: G. Jones & co., 1829.
TL
"For A' That and A' That"
PJ 2.221 (winter, 1845–46)
"My Heart's in the Highlands," "Scenes of Woe"
EEM, 114, 115

T also withdrew an unidentified volume of Burns's poetry from the IN on 5–1–37, probably for use in composing his classbook autobiography in EEM.

230. BURRITT, Elijah Hinsdale. *The geography of the heavens. . . . New ed. rev. and illus. by Hiram Mattison.* New York: Huntington and Savage, Mason and Law, 1850.

JL 3.9 (9–21–51)

Many earlier editions available.

231. BURTON, Richard F. *The lake region of Central Africa, a picture of exploration.* New York: Harper & brothers, 1860.

JL 14.296–297 (12–30–60); IB 12

232. BURTON, Richard F. *Personal narrative of a pilgrimage to el Medinah and Meccah.* New York: G. P. Putnam & co., 1856.

EX, 228; JL 9.251–252 (2–10–57); IB 10

233. BURTON, Robert. *The anatomy of melancholy, what it is, with all the kindes, causes, symptomes, prognosticks, and severall cures of it. . . . To which is now first prefixed, an account of the author.* 3 vols. London: J. & E. Hodson, 1804.
EL
PJ 1.4 (1837)

234. *The business man's assistant and legal guide, containing the laws of Michigan, Indiana, Illinois, Iowa, and Wisconsin. . . .* Chicago: R. Blanchard, 1858.
TL

235. BUTEUX, Jacques. In *Jesuit Relations* (q.v.) for 1652.
HL 1–26–57
JL 9.297–298 (3–18–57)

236. BUTLER, Charles. *The life of Erasmus; with historical remarks on the state of literature between the 10th and 16th centuries.* London: J. Murray, 1825.
HL 9–3–33

237. BUTLER, Joseph. *The analogy of religion, natural and revealed, to the constitution and course of nature.* Boston: Hilliard and Brown, 1830.
TL

238. BUTTMAN, Phillip Karl. *Greek grammar for the use of schools, from the German of Phillip Buttman.* Boston: Cummings, Hilliard, and company, 1826.
TL

239. BYRD, William. In *England's Helicon* (q.v.).
HL 12–8–41
"The Heard-Man's Happie Life"
CPBI

240. BYRON, George Gordon Noel Byron, 6th baron. *The works of Lord Byron, in verse and prose; including letters, journals, etc. With a sketch of his life.* New-York: George Dearborn, 1835.
TL
Don Juan
COR, 66–67 (3–14–42); LN

241. CABOT, James Elliot. "The Philosophy of the Ancient Hindoos." *Massachusetts Quarterly Review* 1 (Sept. 1848): 401–422.

WE, 382–383; EX 241; LN (*c.* 1848)

242. CADALSO, José. *Cartas marruecas y poesias selectas. Por el coronel don José Cadalso. Nueva edición con notas y acentos de prosodia.... Preparado, revisado, y corregido. Por F. Sales....* Boston: De la Imprenta de Munroe y Francis, 1827.
TL

243. CAESAR, Julius. *Commentarii....* Lipsiae: Weidman; Londini: I. Payne et Mackinlay et W. Lynn, 1805.
TL, TX

244. CALIDAS. *Sacontala, or the fatal ring.* In Jones, Sir William, *Works* (q.v.), vol. 9.
HL 1–28–50
WE, 175; WA, 319; CPBI

245.   CAMOENS, Luis de. *The Lusiad; or, the discovery of India.* Tr.
       William Julius Mickle. In Chalmers (q.v.), vol. 21.

       PJ 1.175 (11–29–41)

246.   CAMPBELL, Thomas. *Poetical works of Thomas Campbell: in-
       cluding Theodoric, and many other pieces not contained in
       any former edition.* Philadelphia: J. Crissy, and J. Grigg,
       1826.
       EL
       "Hohenlinden"
       WE, 173; PJ 1.132 (6–19–40); 2.13 (1842–44)

247.   CAMPBELL, Thomas. *Specimens of the British poets, with bio-
       graphical and critical notices and an essay on English poetry.*
       7 vols. London: J. Murray, 1819.
       HL 3–9–37
       ME

248.   CANADA. GEOLOGICAL SURVEY. *Report of progress for 1845–
       50.* [Montreal; Toronto, ?].
       SNH 4–7–52

249.   CANADA. GEOLOGICAL SURVEY. *Report of progress for 1853–
       56.* [Toronto, ?].
       FBS
       CPB2 (*c.* 1860)

250.   *The Canadian guide book, with a map of the province.* Mon-
       treal: Armour & Ramsey; [etc., etc.], 1849.
       TL
       EX, 3–101 passim

251.   CANDOLLE, Alphonse Louis Pierre Pyramus de. *Géographie
       botanique raisonnée; ou, Exposition des faits principaux et
       des lois concernant la distribution géographique des plantes
       de l'époque actuelle.* . . . 2 vols. Paris: V. Masson; [etc., etc.],
       1855.

       IB 12 (*c.* 1861)

252.   CANDOLLE, Augustin Pyramus de, and Kurt Polycarp SPREN-
       GEL. *Elements of the philosophy of plants.* . . . *Tr. from the
       German.* Edinburgh: W. Blackwood, 1821.

       PJ 1.18 (12–16–37)

253.   CAREW, Thomas. *A selection from the poetical works of
       Thomas Carew.* . . . London: [n.p.], 1810.
       HL 12–8–41

254.   CAREW, Thomas. *The Works of Thomas Carew*. Edinburgh:
       W. & C. Tait, 1824.

       PJ 1.466 (9–43)
       "The Pretensions of Poverty"
       WA, 80
       "A Divine Mistress," "Disdaine Returned," "To Saxham," "A
       Pastorall Dialogue," "Epitaph on the Lady Mary Villers,"
       "Jealousie," "An elegie Upon the Death of Dr. Donne, Deane
       of St. Paul's," "On the Duke of Buckingham," "A Song,"
       "The Primrose" (att. to Herrick, T says), "Coelum Britanni-
       cum," "Unfading Beauty"
       LN (*c.* 1843)

255.   CARLYLE, Thomas. *Critical and miscellaneous essays*. 4 vols.
       Boston: J. Munroe and company, 1838–39.
       TL
       EEM, 233, 240–241; PJ 2.217 (Winter 1845–46)

256.   CARLYLE, Thomas. "Cruthers and Jonson; or, The Outskirts
       of Life." *Fraser's Magazine* 2, no. 12 (Jan. 1831): 691–705.

       PJ 2.205 (Summer 1845)

257.   CARLYLE, Thomas. *The French revolution: a history*. 2 vols.
       Boston: C. C. Little and J. Brown, 1838.
       TL
       EEM, 247–248; PJ 2.206, 217, 219, 221

258.   CARLYLE, Thomas. *The life of Frederick Schiller. Compre-
       hending an examination of his works. . . . From the London
       ed. . . .* New York: G. Dearborn & co., 1837.
       TL
       EEM, 232

259.   CARLYLE, Thomas. *Oliver Cromwell's letters and speeches.
       With elucidations*. 2 vols. New York: Wiley & Putnam, 1845.

       EEM, 258–262; PJ 2.131–132 (*c.* 1845), 187–188 (after 12–
       23–45), 224–225 (before 2–22–46), 226 (after 2–22–46),
       253 (after 2–20–46)

260.   CARLYLE, Thomas. *On heroes, hero-worship, and the heroic
       in history. Six lectures. Reported, with emendations and addi-
       tions*. London: J. Fraser, 1841.
       EL
       EEM, 262–263; HM 13201 (1841)

       T's source for his first reading of *On Heroes*, he noted on his
       1841 reading list, was proof sheets sent to RWE from Eng-
       land.

261.   CARLYLE, Thomas. *Past and present.* Boston: C. C. Little & J. Brown, 1843.
TL
EEM, 235, 247

262.   CARLYLE, Thomas. *Sartor resartus. In three books.* London: J. Fraser, 1834.
EL
EEM, 244–245, 254–255; F2a

T was probably also familiar with the first American edition edited by RWE (Boston: J. Munroe, 1836).

263.   *Carminum Poetarum Novem.* In Pindar, *Olympia, Pythia, Nemea, Isthmia. Graece & Latine* . . . and *Carminum Poetarum Novem, Lyricae Poesas Principum, Fragmenta.* 2 vols. in 1. [Heidelbergae]: Apud Hieronymum Commelinum, Elect. Palat. Typographum, 1598.

TR, 55–62; WE, 225–231; PJ 1.62, 65 (12–38); 2.233 (4–17–46)

T's source for the Anacreontics, Greek lyrics once thought to be by Anacreon; see TR, 164–168.

264.   CARPENTER, William. *Scripture natural history; or a descriptive account of the zoology, botany and geology of the Bible . . . with improvements by the Rev. G. D. Abbott.* Boston: Lincoln, Edmonds & Co., 1841.
TL

265.   CARPENTER, William. *Vegetable physiology, and systematic botany. . . .* London: H. G. Bohn, 1858.
CL
EX, 250; JL 12.23–24 (3-7-59), 33 (3-10-59), 143 (4-15-59); CPB2; IB 12

266.   CARTER, James G. *A map of New Hampshire, for families and schools.* Portsmouth, N.H.: Nathaniel March, [183?].
TL

267.   CARTIER, Jacques. See *Voyages de découverte au Canada.*

268.   CARVER, Jonathan. *Three years travels throughout the interior parts of North America, for more than five thousand miles, containing an account of the Great Lakes, and all the lakes, islands, and rivers. . . . Together with a concise history of the genius, manners, and customs of the Indians inhabiting the lands adjacent to the heads and to the westward of the great river Mississippi. . . .* Charlestown: Printed for Samuel

Etheridge, for West and Greenleaf, no. 56, Cornhill, Boston,
1802.
TL
JL 4.97 (6–13–52); IB 6

269.   CASS, Lewis. "Indians of North America." *North American
Review*, new ser., vol. 13 (1826): 53–119.

IB 12 (*c.* 1861)

Review of Halkett, John, *Historical Notes Respecting the Indians of North America* (q.v.), and Hunter, John D., *Manners
and Customs of Several Indian Tribes* (q.v.).

270.   CATESBY, Mark. *The natural history of Carolina, Florida, and
the Bahama Islands, containing the figures of birds, beasts,
fishes, serpents, insects, and plants . . . with their descriptions
in English and French. . . .* Vol. 1. London: Printed for
B. Whilte, 1771.

IB 6 (*c.* 1852)

271.   CATO, Marcus Portius. In *Scriptores Rei Rusticae* (q.v.).
AL
WA, 63, 84, 163, 166, 243; PJ 2.270 (Summer 1846); JL
2.442–445 (9–2–51); 3.61 (10–9–51); 6.68–69 (1–14–54),
71–73 (1–15–54), 106 (2–8–54)

272.   CATO, Marcus Portius. *M. Portius Cato concerning agricul-
ture. Trans. Thomas Owen.* London: J. White, 1803.
AL
WA, 84

Most of T's quotations from Cato are from *Scriptores Rei
Rusticae* (q.v.), also borrowed from Alcott.

273.   CELLARIUS, Christoph. *Geographia antiqua: being a complete
sett of maps, of antient geography. . . .* London: Printed for
John and Paul Knapton, 1747.
TL

274.   CELLINI, Benvenuto. *Memoirs of Benvenuto Cellini, a Floren-
tine artist; written by himself. Containing a variety of infor-
mation respecting the arts and the history of the sixteenth
century. With notes and observations of G. P. Carpani.
Translated by Thomas Roscoe.* 2 vols. New York: Wiley &
Putnam, 1845.
CL
WA, 202; JL 2.494–495 (9–11–51); FB

275.   CERVANTES SAAVEDRA, Miguel de. *History of the renowned
Don Quixote de la Mancha; from the Spanish. Translated by*

several hands, and published by the late Mr. Motteaux. 7th ed., rev. . . . London: Printed for D. Midwinter, 1743.

JL 10.344–345 (4–2–58)

This is the edition owned by the Harvard library, but T's source is unknown; he also makes passing references to Cervantes in EEM, 180, 240.

276.   CHALKHILL, John. *Thealma and Clearchus. A pastoral romance.* Chiswick: from the press of C. Whittingham, 1820.
HL (1–5–42)

Withdrawn by Charles Stearns Wheeler for T.

277.   CHALMERS, Alexander, ed. *The works of the English poets, from Chaucer to Cowper; including the series edited with prefaces, biographical and critical, by Dr. Samuel Johnson: and the most approved translations. The additional lives, by Alexander Chalmers.* . . . 21 vols. London: J. Johnson etc., 1810.
HL 1–9–37, 3–13–37, 11–29–41, 12–6–41

Chalmers's anthology was T's principal source for his reading in English poetry through the 18th century. He speaks in WA of reading Chalmers through "without skipping" (p. 259). Quotations from poets he is most likely to have read in Chalmers are cited under their names in the catalogue.

278.   CHAMBERS, Robert. *Ancient sea-margins, as memorials of changes in the relative level of sea and land.* Edinburgh: W. & R. Chambers; [etc., etc.], 1848.
HL 5–9–54

279.   CHAMBERS, Robert. *Vestiges of the natural history of creation.* 2nd ed., *from the 3rd London ed., greatly amended by the author. And introduced by George P. Cheever.* New York: Wiley & Putnam, 1845.
EL
JL 3.31 (9–28–51)

280.   CHAMPLAIN, Samuel de. *Des savvages, ou, Voyage de Samvel Champlain, de Brovage, faict en la France nouuelle, l'an mil six cens trois.* . . . A Paris: Chez C. de Monstreoil, 1604.
HL 1–11–59
IB 12

281.   CHAMPLAIN, Samuel de. *Voyages de la Novvelle France occidentale, dicte Canada; faits pour le Sr de Champlain Xainctogeois, capitaine pour le roy en la marine du Ponant, & toutes les descouuertes qu'il a faites en ce pais depuis l'an 1603; jusques en l'an 1629.* . . . Paris: C. Collet, 1632.

HL 10–28–50, 12–27–50, 9–4–55
CC, 66, 122, 181–201 passim; COR, 524 (11–6–58); IB 4; CN

282.   CHAMPLAIN, Samuel de. *Les voyages dv sievr de Champlain Xainctogeois, capitaine ordinaire pour le Roy, en la marine. Divisez en devx livres. ou, Iovrnal tres fidele des observations faites és descouuertures de la Nouuelle France.* . . . A Paris: Chez Iean Berjon, . . . 1613.
HL 11–18–50, 9–4–55
EX, 8; CC, 37, 156, 227–255 passim; IB 4; CN

283.   CHANNING, Walter. *New and old.* . . . Boston: [n.p.], 1851.
TL

284.   CHANNING, William Ellery. *Discourses, reviews, & miscellanies.* Boston: Carter and Hendee, 1830.
TL

285.   CHANNING, William Ellery (the younger). *Near home; a poem.* Boston: James Munroe and company, 1858.
TL

286.   CHANNING, William Ellery (the younger). *Poems.* Boston: C. C. Little and J. Brown, 1843.
TL
"Boat Song"
WE, 43, 46
"The River"
WE, 45, 317

287.   CHANNING, William Ellery (the younger). *Poems. Second series.* Boston: J. Munroe and company, 1847.
TL

288.   CHANNING, William Ellery (the younger). *The Woodman, and other poems.* Boston: J. Munroe & company, 1849.
TL
"Baker Farm"
WA, 203–204, 208
"Old Sudbury Inn"
PJ 3 (Fall 1849)
"Walden Spring"
WA, 115

289.   CHAPIN, Loring Dudley. *Vegetable kingdom; or, Handbook of plants and fruits. With one hundred and forty illustrations, a copious glossary, etc.* . . . 2 vols. in 1. New York: J. Lott, 1843.
TL

290.   CHAPMAN, George. *The Tragedy of Caesar and Pompey.*

WE, 379; WA, 33

291. CHARLEVOIX, Pierre-François-Xavier de. *Histoire et descrip-
      tion générale de la Nouvelle France, avec le Journal historique
      d'un voyage fait par ordre de roi dans l'Amérique septen-
      trionale. . . .* 3 vols. A Paris: Chez la Veuve Ganeau, Libraire
      . . . , 1744.
      HL 11–5–51
      CC 183, 190; EX, 18, 43, 52, 65, 66; JL 3.282–283 (2–6–52),
      285–286 (2–7–52), 350 (3–14–52); IB 3; IB 5; IB 10; CN

292. CHATEAUBRIAND, François Auguste René, vicomte de.
      Oeuvres complètes. 28 vols. Paris: Ladvocat, 1826–31.
      HL 4–28–36 (vol. 6); 5–5–36 (vol. 7)

293. CHATEAUBRIAND, François Auguste René, vicomte de. *Travels
      in Greece, Palestine, Egypt, and Barbary, during the years
      1806 and 1807. Trans. F. Shoberl.* New York: Van Winkle
      and Wiley, 1814.

      PJ 2.349–350, 352–353 (Fall 1846)

294. CHATTO, William Andrew. *The angler's souvenir, by
      P. Fischer, esq. pseud. . . . Assisted by several pescatory char-
      acters, with illustrations by Beckwith & Topham.* London:
      C. Tilt, 1835.

      PJ 1.151 (7–7–40)

295. CHAUCER, Geoffrey. *The Canterbury tales of Chaucer; with
      an essay on his language and versification, an introductory
      discourse, notes and a glossary by Tho. Tyrwhitt, esq. . . .*
      London: W. Pickering, 1830.
      HL 9–3–35, 11–30–41

      For specific references to Chaucer's works, see next entry.

296. CHAUCER, Geoffrey. In Chalmers (q.v.), vol. 1.
      HL 12–41
      The Canterbury Tales: "General Prologue"
      EEM, 167–168; WA, 212; EX, 159–160; PJ 1.399–400 (4–2–
      42); LN
      "The Man of Law's Tale"
      EEM, 169; LN
      "The Nun's Priest's Tale"
      EEM, 168; PJ 1.351 (12–30–41); LN
      "The Prioress's Tale"
      WE, 372; EEM, 168; PJ 1.351 (12–30–41)
      "The Canon Yeoman's Tale," "The Clerk's Tale," "The
      Franklin's Tale," "The Knight's Tale," "The Manciple's
      Tale," "The Pardoner's Tale," "The Parson's Tale," "The
      Squire's Tale," "The Wife of Bath's Tale"
      LN
      "Chaucer's Dream" (attrib.)
      WE, 317, 331; LN
      "The Court of Love" (attrib.)

WE, 371; EEM, 167
"The Legend of Good Women"
EEM, 170; WE, 373; PJ 2.175 (8–23–45)
"The Parliament of Fowls"
WE, 276; LN
"The Romance of the Rose"
WE, 276
"The Testament of Love"
EEM, 165; WE, 370; LN
"A Treatise on the Astrolabe"
EEM, 165; WE, 367–370
"Troilus and Criseyde"
WE, 11, 24; PJ 2.85 (1842–44); LN
"Balade de Bon Conseyle" ("Truth"), "The Cuckoo and the Nightingale" (attrib.), "The House of Fame"
LN

T's essay "Homer. Ossian. Chaucer" appeared in the January 1844 issue of *The Dial* (EEM, 154–173). The Chaucer section was later revised for WE, 367–374.

297.   CHESTERFIELD, Philip Dormer Stanhope. *The beauties of Chesterfield, consisting of selections from his works. By Alfred Howard.* . . . Boston: C. Ewer, 1828.
TL

298.   CHILD, Lydia Maria (Francis). *Hobomok, a tale of early times. By an American.* Boston: Cummings, Hilliard, 1824.
HL 2–19–34

299.   CHILD, Lydia Maria (Francis). *Philothea: A Romance.* Boston: Otis, Broaders, 1836.

FId (*c.* 1836)

300.   CHILD, Lydia Maria (Francis). *The Rebels; or, Boston before the revolution.* Boston: Cummings, Hilliard, 1825.
HL 2–19–34

301.   CHOLMONDELEY, Thomas. *Ultima Thule; or, Thoughts suggested by a residence in New Zealand.* London: J. Chapman, 1854.
TL
COR, 376–377 (6–27–55)

302.   CHORLEY, Henry Fothergill. *Memorials of Mrs. Hemans, with illustrations of her literary character from her private correspondence.* 2 vols. New York and London: Saunders and Otley, 1836
IN 7–14–37

303.   CHURCH, Benjamin. *The history of King Philip's war; also of expeditions against the French and Indians in the eastern parts of New England, in the years 1689, 1690, 1692, 1696, and 1704.* Boston: Howe and Norton, printers, 1825.
TL
PJ 1.167–168 (*c.* 8–40); COR, 470 (3–28–57)

304.   CHURCHMAN, John. *An account of the Gospel labors, and Christian experiences of a faithful minister of Christ, John Churchman, late of Nottingham in Pennsylvania, deceased. . . .* Philadelphia: Printed by J. Cruikshank, 1779.
TL

305.   CICERO. *De Divinatione.*

EEM, 59

Source unknown. The quotation from *De Divinatione* (1.122) is in a college theme assignment on "fate," so T's source may have been some compendium of classical quotations on the subject.

306.   CICERO. *De officiis, libri tres. Ex editionibus Oliveti et Ernesti.* Cambridge, [Mass.]: Brown, Shattuck & Co., 1833.
TX

307.   CICERO. *De Oratore.*

EEM, 83

Edition and source unknown.

308.   CICERO. *M. T. Ciceronis orationes quaedam selectae notis illustratae. In usum Academiae Exoniensis. Editio sterotypa, tabulis analyticis instructa.* Bostoniae: Sumtibus Hilliard, Gray, Little, et Wilkins, 1831.
TL, TX

309.   CLAPPERTON, Hugh. See Denham, Dixon.

310.   CLARK, William. See Lewis, Meriwether.

311.   CLARKE, James Freeman. *Eleven weeks in Europe, and what may be seen in that time.* Boston: Ticknor, Reed, and Fields, 1852.
CL
FB (*c.* 1853)

312.   CLARKSON, Rev. David. *A discourse of the saving grace of God, by the late Reverend and learned David Clarkson, min-*

ister of the Gospel. London: Printed by J. Astwood, for Tho. Parkhurst, 1688.
TL

313.   CLAUDIAN. "De Sene Veronesi."

WA, 322; RP, 194; PJ 1.310 (5–41)

Source unknown.

314.   CLEVELAND, Charles Dexter. *An epitome of Grecian antiqui-ties. For the use of schools*. Boston: Hilliard, Gray, Little and Wilkins, 1827.
HL 2–12–34

315.   COCHRANE, Charles Stuart. *Journal of a residence and travels in Colombia during the years 1823, and 1824*. 2 vols. London: Printed for H. Colburn, 1825.
HL 3–5–34 (vol. 1)

316.   *A code of Gentoo laws, or, Ordinations of the Pundits, from a Persian translation made from the original, written in the Shanscrit language. . . . The english translation by Nathaniel Brassey Halhed*. London: [n.p.], 1786.
TL

317.   COFFIN, George W. *A plan of the public lands in the State of Maine surveyed under instructions from the commissioners and agents of the States of Massachusetts and Maine. . . .* Boston: 1835.
TL

318.   COLBURN, Warren. *An introduction to algebra upon the in-ductive method of instruction*. Boston: Hilliard, Gray, Little, & Wilkins, 1826.
TL

319.   COLDEN, Cadwallader. *History of the five Indian nations of Canada which are dependent on the province of New York, and are a barrier between the English and the French. . . .* London: Printed for T. Osborne, 1747.
HL 12–7–54
IB 8

320.   COLEBROOKE, Henry Thomas. *Miscellaneous essays by H. T. Colebrooke. . . .* 2 vols. London: W. H. Allen and co., 1837.
TL

321.   COLEMAN, William Stephen. *British butterflies, figures and descriptions of every native species, with an account of but-terfly development, structure, habits, localities, mode of cap-*

ture, and preservation. . . . London: Routledge, Warnes &
Routledge, 1860.
TL

322. COLEMAN, William Stephen. *Our woodlands, heaths &
hedges. A popular description of trees, shrubs, wild fruits, etc.
With notices of their insect inhabitants.* . . . *Illustrated by the
author.* London: Routledge, Warnes & Routledge, 1859.
TL
HU, 224

323. COLERIDGE, Henry Nelson. *Introductions to the study of the
Greek classic poets. Designed principally for the use of young
persons at school and college.* London: J. Murray, 1830.
HL 9–15–36
EEM, 50–58; F2a

324. COLERIDGE, Samuel T., Percy B. SHELLEY, & John KEATS.
*The poetical works of Coleridge, Shelley, and Keats, complete
in one volume. Stereotyped by John Howe.* Philadelphia:
[J. Grigg], 1832.
TL

325. COLERIDGE, Samuel Taylor. *Aids to reflection. With an ap-
pendix, preliminary essay, and additional notes, by James
Marsh.* Burlington, Vt.: Chauncey Goodrich, 1829.
AL
PJ 1.222 (1–41); HM 13201 (2–21–41)

326. COLERIDGE, Samuel Taylor. *Confessions of an inquiring spirit
. . . edited from the author's ms. by Henry Nelson Coleridge.*
London: W. Pickering, 1840.

HM 13201 (4–14–41)

327. COLERIDGE, Samuel Taylor. *Hints toward the formation of a
more comprehensive theory of life.* . . . *Ed. by Seth B. Wat-
son.* Philadelphia: Lea and Blanchard, 1848.
AL
LN (*c.* 1848)

328. COLERIDGE, Samuel Taylor. *Letters, conversations, & recol-
lections of S. T. Coleridge.* . . . 2 vols. London: Edward
Moxon, 1836.
IN 7–14–37
ME

329. COLERIDGE, Samuel Taylor. *Specimens of the table talk of the
late Samuel Taylor Coleridge.* . . . New York: Harper &
brothers, 1835.
EL
PJ 1.97 (12–39)

330.   COLERIDGE, Samuel Taylor. *The statesman's manual; or, the Bible, the best guide to political skill and foresight: a lay sermon, addressed to the higher classes of society.* Burlington, Vt.: Chauncey Goodrich, 1832.
EL
PJ 1.230 (1–41)

331.   *Collections, historical and miscellaneous.* See Farmer, John, ed.

332.   COLLIE, David. *The Chinese classical work, commonly called The Four Books.* Malacca: The Mission Press, 1828.
EL
EEM, 147–153

Source for "Chinese Four Books" in *The Dial*'s "Ethnical Scriptures" column for October 1843; extracts can only tentatively be ascribed to T. See EEM, 385–386.

333.   COLLIER, John P., ed. *Old ballads, from early printed copies of the utmost rarity. Now for the first time collected.* London: Printed for the Percy Society by C. Richards, 1840.

LN (*c.* 12–41)

334.   COLLINS, William. In Chalmers (q.v.), vol. 13.
"Eclogue II. Hassan; or the Camel-Driver"
EX, 139–140
"Oriental Eclogues," "Ode to Evening," "Ode on the Death of Mr. Thomas," "Ode on the Popular Superstitions of the Highlands; Considered as the Subject of Poetry"
CPBI (*c.* 1841)

335.   COLMAN, Henry. *Report on the agriculture of Massachusetts.* Boston: Dutton and Wentworth, 1838–41.

WA, 158–162; PJ 2.129 (*c.* 1845–46)

336.   COLTON, Walter. *The land of gold; or, three years in California.* New York: D. W. Evans, 1850.
SL
JL 2.73 (10–17–50)

337.   COLUMELLA. In *Scriptores Rei Rusticae* (q.v.).
AL
JL 6.111 (2–9–54), 125 (2–16–54); 8.52 (12–16–55), 56–57 (12–21–55), 245 (4–3–56), 312 (4–26–56)

338.   COLUMELLA. *L. Junius Moderatus Columella Of husbandry. In twelve books: and his book concerning trees. Tr. into English, with several illustrations from Pliny, Cato, Varro, Pal-*

ladius, and other antient and modern authors. London: Printed for A. Millar, 1745.
HL 3–4–56

See previous entry for T's references.

339.   COMBE, George. *Lectures on moral philosophy.* . . . Boston: Marsh, Capen, & Lyon; New York: D. Appleton & Co., 1836.
IN 12–8–36

340.   *Complete railway map to accompany the American Railway Guide.* New York: Dinsmore, n.d.
TL

341.   [CONCORD, Mass.]. *Reports of the selectmen and other officers of the town of Concord, from March 5, 1860, to March 4, 1861.* . . . Concord: Printed by Benjamin Tolman, 1861.
TL

342.   CONFUCIUS. See also Pauthier, Jean-Pierre-Guillaume, and Collie, David.

Most of T's quotations from Confucius are from Pauthier's *Confucius et Mencius* (q.v.).

343.   CONFUCIUS. *The Morals of Confucius.* In *The Phenix* (q.v.).

EEM, 140–142; ME

344.   CONFUCIUS. *The works of Confucius; containing the original text, with a translation. Vol. 1st. To which is prefixed a dissertation on the Chinese language and characters. By J. Marshman.* Serampore: Printed at the Mission Press, 1809.
EL
EEM, 140–142

See also Collie, David, and Pauthier, Jean-Pierre-Guillaume, for specific references.

345.   CONSTANT DE REBECQUE, Henri Benjamin. *De la religion, considérée dans sa source, ses formes et ses développements.* 5 vols. Paris: Bosange, 1824–31.
HL 4–27–37 (vol. 1); 6–1–37 (vols. 2, 3)
EEM, 108

346.   CONYBEARE, John Josias. *Illustrations of Anglo-Saxon poetry. Edited, with additional notes, introductory notices, &c., by his brother William Daniel Conybeare.* London: Harding and Lepard, 1826.
HL 6–22–37, 11–29–41
ME

347.   CONYBEARE, William Daniel. See Conybeare, John Josias.

348.   COOK, James. *The three voyages of Capt. James Cook round the world.* 7 vols. London: Printed for Longman, Hurst, Rees, Orme, and Brown, 1821.
CL
WA, 13; CC, 169–170; PJ 2.143 (*c.* 1845–46); FB; IB 12

349.   COOPER, James Fenimore. *The headsman; or, the Abbaye des Vignerons. A tale. By the author of the "Bravo", &c.* . . . Philadelphia: Carey, Lea, & Blanchard, 1833.

F1b (*c.* 1835)

350.   COPWAY, George. *Traditional history and characteristic sketches of the Ojibway nation. Illustrated by Darley.* Boston: Sanborn, Carter, Basin, [1855].
TL

351.   CORNUT, Jacques. *Jac. Cornut . . . Canadensium plantarum . . . aliarumque nondum editarum historia.* . . . Parisiis: venundatur apud Simonem Le Monye, 1635.
HL 5–2–60

352.   COTTON, Charles. In Chalmers (q.v.), vol. 6.
HL 1–17–44 (by RWE)
"The Morning Quatrains," "The World"
WE, 130, 235; LN
"The Tempest"
PJ 2.106 (*c.* Fall 1844); LN
"Evening Quatrains," "On the Death of the Most Noble Thomas Earl of Ossory," "Contentment"
LN

353.   COULTAS, Harland. *What may be learned from a tree.* New York: D. Appleton & company [etc. etc.], 1860.

JL 14.120 (10–14–60); CPB2

354.   COURT DE GÉBELIN, Antoine. *Monde primitif, analysé et comparé avec le monde moderne.* . . . Nouvelle éd. 9 vols. Paris: Durand, 1787–88.

ME (*c.* 1836)

355.   COUSIN, Victor. *Introduction to the history of philosophy. . . . Translated from the French by Henning Gotfried Linberg.* Boston: Hilliard, Gray, Little, and Wilkins, 1832.
IN 6–25–37, 7–14–37

356.   COWLEY, Abraham. *Prose works of Abraham Cowley esq., including his essays in prose and verse.* London: Pickering, 1826.

LN; HM 13201 (4–15–41)

357.   COWPER, William. *The life and posthumous writings of William Cowper, Esq. with an introductory letter to the Right Honorable Earl Cowper. By William Hayley, Esq.* 2 vols. Boston: W. Pelham, Manning & Loring, and E. Lincoln, 1803.
TL

Autograph of John Thoreau.

358.   COWPER, William. *Poems of William Cowper, Esq., with a new memoir compiled from Johnson, Southey and other sources.* New York, Leavitt & Allen, [1850].
TL
"Verses Supposed To Be Written by Alexander Selkirk"
WA, 82

359.   COWPER, William. *The task.* (1 vol.)
TL

Edition unknown.

360.   COWPER, William. *The works of the late William Cowper, Esq. of the Inner Temple. [Edited by John Johnson. With portraits.] 10 vols. London: Baldin, Cradock & Joy, 1817.*
HL 11–10–36 (vol. 3)

361.   COX, Ross. *Adventures on the Columbia river, including the narrative of a residence of six years on the western side of the Rocky mountains among various tribes of Indians hitherto unknown: together with a journey across the American continent.* New-York, J. & J. Harper, 1832.
HL 9–25–33, 1–12–37

362.   CRANZ, David. *The history of Greenland: containing a description of the country, and its inhabitants: and particularly a relation of the mission, carried on for above these thirty years. . . .* London: Printed for the Brethren's society for the furtherance of the gospel among the heathen and sold by J. Dodbley [etc.], 1767.
HL 11–1–60
EX 166; CC, 60–61, 72, 149; JL 13.395 (7–7–60); CPB2; IB 12

363.   CRASHAW, Richard. In Chalmers (q.v.), vol. 6.
HL 1–17–44 (by RWE)

"Sospetto d'Herode"
LN; ME

364. CRATES OF THEBES. Untitled fragment.
WE, 98
In *Greek Anthology* 7.326; T's source unknown.

365. CROLY, George. *Life and times of His late Majesty George the Fourth. With anecdotes of distinguished persons of the last fifty years.* . . . New and improved ed. New York: J. & J. Harper, 1831.
TL

366. CUDWORTH, Ralph. *The true intellectual system of the universe: wherein all the reason and philosophy of atheism is confuted, and its impossibility demonstrated . . . and an account of the life and writings of the author: by Thomas Birch.* 4 vols. London: R. Priestly, 1820.
EL
WE, 226, 361; PJ 1.123, 127 (4–40), 140–141 (6–40); ME

367. CULBERTSON, Thaddeus A. "Journal of an Expedition to the Mauvaises Terres and the Upper Missouri, 1850." *Smithsonian Institution. 5th Annual Report of the Board of Regents.* Washington: Smithsonian Institution, 1851. Pp. 84–145.
SNH 12–29–52
IB 6; FB

368. CUMMINGS, R. Gordon. See Gordon-Cummings, Roualeyn George.

369. CUNNINGHAM, Allan. *Some account of the life and works of Sir Walter Scott.* . . . Boston: Stimpson & Clapp, 1832.

EEM, 42–44; F2a (5–3–36)

370. CUNNINGHAM, John William. *A world without souls.* Boston: Manning & Loring, 1810.

F2a (c. 1836)

371. CURTIUS RUFUS, Quintus. *Historia Alexandri Magni. Adiecta sunt Supplementa Freinshemii. Ed. stereotypa ex nova tabularum impressione emendatissima.* Lipsiae: Sumtibus et typis C. Tauchnitii, 1829.
TL

372. CUSICK, David. *David Cusick's Sketches of ancient history of the Six nations.* . . . Lockport, N.Y.: Turner & McCollum, printers, 1848.

HL 3–4–56
IB 10

373.   CUTLER, Rev. Manasseh. "An Account of Some of the Vegeta-
ble Productions, Naturally Growing in this Part of America,
Botanically Arranged." *Memoirs of the American Academy of
Arts and Sciences*, 1st ser., vol. 1 (Boston, 1785): 396–493.

JL 14.224 (11–8–60); IB 12; CPB2

374.   CUVIER, Georges Léopold Chrétien Frédéric. *The animal
kingdom, arranged in conformity with its organization . . .
with additional descriptions of all the species hitherto named,
and of many not before noticed, by Edward Griffith . . . and
others. . . .* 16 vols. London: Printed for G. B. Whittaker,
1827–32.
SNH 8–11–51
CC, 169–170; JL 2.402 (4–19–51)

375.   CUVIER, Georges Léopold Chrétien Frédéric. *A discourse on
the revolutions of the surface of the globe, and the changes
thereby produced in the animal kingdom. . . .* Philadelphia:
Carey & Lea, 1831.
EL
CC, 204–205

376.   DABLON, Claude. In *Jesuit Relations* (q.v.) for 1670–72.
HL 12–7–58
IB 11

377.   DACIER, André. *The life of Pythagoras, with his symbols and
golden verses. Together with the life of Hierocles, and his
commentaries upon the verses. . . .* London: Printed for
J. Tonson, 1707.
AL
LN (*c.* 1841)

378.   DANA, Richard Henry, Jr. *The seaman's friend: containing a
treatise on practical seamanship, with plates; a dictionary of
sea terms; customs, and usages of the merchant service; laws
relating to the practical duties of master and mariners.* Boston: Published by Thomas Groom & co., 1857.
TL
JL 7.452 (8–9–55)

Journal reference is obviously to an earlier edition, of which
there were many; first edition was 1841.

379.   DANIEL, Samuel. In Chalmers (q.v.), vol 3.
Philotas
WE, 102; LN
Musophilus

WE, 102, 103, 128; LN
"To the Lady Margaret, Countess of Cumberland"
WE, 381; RP, 135; LN
"Ulysses and the Syren," "History of the Civil Wars," "To
Lucy Countess of Bedford," "To the Lady Anne Clifford,"
"To Henry Wrothesly, Earl of Southampton," "Hymen's
Triumph to the Queen"
LN

380.   DANTE ALIGHIERI. *La divina commedia. Con argomenti, ed
annotazioni scelte da' migliori commentatori. Nuova edizione
coll'accento di prosodia.* 3 vols. Avignone: F. Sequin aîné,
1816.
TL
EX, 230; PJ 1.212 (12–40)

T's reference in the Journal is nonspecific.

381.   DANTE ALIGHIERI. *Divine comedy: the inferno. A literal
prose translation with the text of the original collated from
the best editions, and explanatory notes. By John A. Carlyle.*
New York: Harper & brothers, 1849.
TL

382.   DARBY, William. *View of the United States, historical geographical, and statistical. . . .* Philadelphia: H. S. Tanner,
1828.

EX, 93–94

T's quotation in "An Excursion to Canada" does not corre-
spond precisely to the relevant passage in *View*; his source
was probably some other of Darby's many works on geography.

383.   DARTMOUTH COLLEGE, Plaintiff. *Report of the case of the
trustees of Dartmouth College against William H. Woodward. Argued and determined in the Superior Court of Judi-
cature of the state of New Hampshire, November, 1817. And
on error in the Supreme Court of the United States, February,
1819. By Timothy Farrar. . . .* Portsmouth, N.H.: Published
by John W. Foster, 1819.
TL

384.   DARWIN, Charles. *Journal of researches into the natural his-
tory and geology of the countries visited during the voyage of
H.M.S. Beagle round the world, under the command of Capt.
Fitz Roy, R.N.* 2 vols. New York: Harper & brothers, 1846.

WA, 13–14; CC, 31, 95–96; EX, 77, 226; JL 2.240–248 (6–11–
51), 261–264 (6–14–51); IB 4

Spine title is *Voyage of a Naturalist round the World.*

385. DARWIN, Charles. *On the origin of species by means of natural selection, or The preservation of favoured races in the struggle for life*. New York: D. Appleton, 1860, or London: J. Murray, 1859.
CL
CPB2 (*c.* 1860)

T may have commented on Darwin's evolutionary theory in a letter to Thomas Cholmondeley that has not survived; see COR, 613.

386. DARWIN, Charles. *Voyage of a Naturalist round the World*. See Darwin, *Journal of researches*.

387. DAVENANT, William. In Chalmers (q.v.), vol. 6.
HL 1–17–44 (by RWE)
Preface to *Gondibert*
WA, 260; LN

388. DAVIES, Charles. *Elements of surveying and navigation; with a description of the instruments and the necessary tables*. Rev. ed. New York: A. S. Barnes, 1847.
TL

389. DAVIES, Charles. *Grammar of arithmetic; or, An analysis of the language of figures and science of numbers*. New York: A. S. Barnes & co., 1850.
TL

390. DAVIS, Charles Henry. "A Memoir upon the Geological Action of Tidal and Other Currents of the Ocean." *Memoirs of the American Academy of Arts and Sciences* (Boston), 4th ser., pt. 1 (1849–50): 117–156.

CC, 122; JL 2.45 (1850)

391. DAVIS, E. H. See Squier, E. G.

392. DAVIS, John. In Thatcher, James T., *History of the town of Plymouth* (q.v.).
"Ode for the 22nd of December"
CC, 143

393. DAVIS, Wendell. "Description of Sandwich in the County of Barnstable, 1802." *Collections of Massachusetts Historical Society*, 1st ser., vol. 8 (1802): 119–126.

CC, 16–17

394. DE BRY, Theodore. See Bry, Theodore de.

395. DE CANDOLLE, Alphonse. See Candolle, Alphonse Louis Pierre Pyramus de.

396. DE KAY, James Ellsworth. *Zoology of New-York, or the New-York Fauna; comprising detailed descriptions of all the animals hitherto observed within the state of New York.* . . . 5 vols. Albany: Printed by Carroll and Cook . . . , 1842–44.
SNH 5–24–52 (Part 1, "Mammalia")
CC, 111, 114; JL 4.82 (6–5–52); 7.463–464 (9–29–55); 9.134 (10–25–56), 485 (7–20–57); 10.443–444 (5–27–58); 12.198 (6–2–59); FB; IB 9

T consulted later volumes of De Kay at the Society of Natural History library in Boston and at the Astor Library in New York in 1856.

397. DE QUENS, Jean. See Quens, Jean de.

398. DE QUINCEY, Thomas. *The Caesars.* Boston: Ticknor, Reed, and Fields, 1851.

JL 2.173–174 (3–19–51)

399. DE QUINCEY, Thomas. *Confessions of an English opium eater, and Suspira de profundis.* Boston: Ticknor, Reed, and Fields, 1852.
CL
PJ 1.446 (1–43); COR, 478 (4–26–57)

Source of Journal reference is obviously an earlier edition.

400. DE QUINCEY, Thomas. *De Quincey's writings.* 23 vols. Boston: Ticknor, Reed, and Fields, 1850–59.
CL

T read widely in De Quincey's *Writings* as they appeared; for references see individual titles.

401. DE QUINCEY, Thomas. *Essays on philosophical writers and other men of letters.* 2 vols. Boston: Ticknor, Reed, and Fields, 1854.
CL
"Analects from Richter"
CPB2 (c. 1854)

402. DE QUINCEY, Thomas. *Historical and critical essays.* 2 vols. Boston: Ticknor, Reed, and Fields, 1853.
CL
"Philosophy of Herodotus"
FB (c. 1854)

T also mentions not yet having read this volume in JL 6.76 (1–24–54).

403. DE QUINCEY, Thomas. *Literary reminiscences.* Boston: Ticknor, Reed, and Fields, 1851.

CL
JL 2.418 (8–22–51)
"Coleridge's Conversations," "Education of Genius"
CPB2

404. DE QUINCEY, Thomas. *Narrative and miscellaneous papers.* 2 vols. Boston: Ticknor, Reed, and Fields, 1853.
CL
"System of the Heavens as Revealed by Lord Rosse's Telescopes"
JL 5.254 (6–14–53)

405. DE QUINCEY, Thomas. *Theological essays and other papers.* Boston: Ticknor, Reed, and Fields, 1854.
CL
"The Toilette of the Hebrew Lady"
IB 9 (*c.* 1855)

406. DE SMET, Pierre Jean. See Smet, Pierre Jean de.

407. DE SOTO, Hernandez. See Irving, Theodore.

408. DE STAËL, Madame. See Staël-Holstein, Anna Louise Germaine.

409. DE VRIES, David Peterson. "Voyages from Holland to America, A.D., 1632 to 1644. . . . Translated by Henry C. Murphy." *Collections of New York Historical Society,* 2nd ser., vol. 3, pt. 1 (1857): 9–136.
HL 1–13–58
IB 11

410. DEANE, Charles. See Bradford, William.

411. *Dearborn's map of Massachusetts . . . carefully revised and additions made in 1848.* Boston: Dearborn, 1848.
TL

412. DECKER, Thomas. *The Honest Whore.*

RP, 175

T probably found the line from *The Honest Whore* that he quotes in "Life Without Principle" in Charles Lamb, *Specimens of English Dramatic Poets* (q.v.).

413. DEFOE, Daniel. *The life and suprising adventures of Robinson Crusoe.* . . .

MW, 68; PJ 1.196 (11–9–40), 271 (2–22–41), 329 (9–3–41)

Source and edition unknown.

414.   DEGÉRANDO, Joseph Marie, baron. See Gérando, Joseph
       Marie de, baron.

415.   DENHAM, Dixon, and Hugh CLAPPERTON. *Narrative of trav-
       els and discoveries in Northern and Central Africa, in the
       years 1822, and 1824, extending across the great desert to the
       tenth degree of northern latitude, and from Kouka in Bornou,
       to Sackatoo. . . .* 2 vols. London: J. Murray, 1826.
       HL 4–23–34 (vol. 1)

416.   DENHAM, Sir John. In Chalmers (q.v.), vol. 7.

       "Cooper's Hill"
       WE, 12; LN

417.   DENTON (Maryland) *Journal.*

       CC, 91

       The source of an anecdote describing a certificate of church
       membership found in a fish. T's source unknown.

418.   "Description of Cape Cod, and the County of Barnstable."
       Massachusetts Magazine; or, Monthly Museum 3 (Feb.,
       March 1791): 73–76, 149–152.

       CC, 119–120, 175

419.   "Description of Carver." *Collections of the Massachusetts
       Historical Society,* 2d ser., vol. 4 (1796; rpt. 1846): 271–279.

       JL 7.484 (10–5–55)

420.   "Description of Holliston." *Collections of the Massachusetts
       Historical Society,* 1st ser., vol. 3 (1794; rpt. 1810): 18–21.

       IB 2 (c. 1849)

421.   DESOR, Edward. "The Ocean and Its Meaning in Nature."
       Massachusetts Quarterly Review 2 (June 1849): 308–325.

       CC, 100

422.   DEWEY, Chester, and Ebenezer EMMONS. *Report on the her-
       baceous plants and on the quadrupeds of Massachusetts.
       Massachusetts Zoological and Botanical survey. Pub. agreea-
       bly to an order of the legislature. . . .* Boston: Folsom, Wells
       and Thurston, printers, 1840.
       TL
       EX 104–131; CC, 111, 115, 158; PJ 1.306 (4–41); JL 3.469
       (4–25–52); 4.28 (5–6–52), 421 (12–2–52); 8.367 (6–6–56),

408–409 (7–12–56); 9.74 (9–9–56); 10.437 (5–20–58); 14.80–81 (9–11–60)

423.   *The Dial: a magazine for literature, philosophy, and religion.* 4 vols. Boston: Weeks, Jordan, and company [etc.], 1841–44.

424.   D'ISRAELI, Isaac. *Curiosities of literature.* New York: Leavitt & Co., 1851.
TL
EEM, 70 (12–16–36)

425.   DOANE, Heman. See Pratt, Enoch.

426.   "The Dodo and Its Kindred." *Blackwood's Edinburgh Magazine* 65 (Jan. 1849): 81–98.

PJ 3 (*c.* 1849)

Anonymous review of Hugh Strickland, *The dodo and its kindred; or, The history, affinities, and osteology of the dodo, solitaire, and other extinct birds of the islands Maritius, Rodriguez, and Bourbon.* London: Reeve, Benham, and Reeve, 1848.

427.   DODSLEY, Robert, ed. *A collection of poems in six volumes. By several hands.* London: Printed for J. Dodsley, in Pall Mall, 1775.

"Upon a Small Building in Gothic Taste"
CPBI (12–41)

428.   "Does the Dew Fall?" *Harper's Magazine* 7 (Sept. 1853): 504–506.

JL 5.513 (11–20–53)

429.   DOMENECH, L'Abbé Emmanuel Henri Dieudonné. *Seven years residence in the great deserts of North America.* London: Longman, Green, Longman and Roberts, 1860.

COR, 611 (4–10–61)

Conjectural title; T's reference is to "Six Years in the Deserts of North America." I have been unable to locate a work by that title, but the work above was a recently published book at the time of T's citation.

430.   DONNE, John. In Chalmers (q.v.), vol. 5.
"An Anatomy of the World. The First Anniversary"
WE, 334; ME
"Elegy 18"

WE, 380
"Obsequies on the Lord Harrington, etc., To the Countess Bedford"
WE, 132
"Of the Progress of the Soul. The Second Anniversary"
WE, 297; ME
"To the Countess of Bedford" ("Honour Is So Sublime Perfection")
PJ 1.165 (7 & 8–40); ME
"To the Countess of Huntington"
WE, 267
"To Sir Edward Herbert"
WA, 220; PJ 2.304 (Fall 1846)
"A Letter to the Lady Carey and Mrs. Essex Rich, from Amiens," "Satire II," "Song" ("Sweetest Love I Do Not Go"), "The Sun Rising"
ME
"The Service"
RP, 4

431.   DONNE, John. *Poems on several occasions. . . . With elegies on the author's death. To this edition is added some account of the life of the author.* London: Printed for Jacob Tonson, sold by W. Taylor, 1719.
EL

For T's references to specific Donne poems, see preceding entry. The source of T's extracts from Donne probably varied, and the extracts in his ME commonplace book also include several untitled fragmentary passages.

432.   DOUGLAS, Gawin. *The Aeneid of Virgil translated into Scottish verse by Gawin Douglas.* 2 vols. Edinburgh: [T. Constable, printer], 1839.

PJ 1.343 (11–14–41)

433.   DOUGLAS, Gawin. "Consider it Warilie . . ."

CPBI (12–41)

434.   DOWNING, A. J. *The fruits and fruit trees of America; or, The culture, propagation, and management in the garden and orchard, of fruit trees generally; with descriptions of all the finest varieties of fruit, native & foreign, cultivated in this country.* New York and London: Wiley and Putnam, 1845.

EX, 309

435. DRAKE, Edward Cavendish. *A new and universal collection of authentic and entertaining voyages and travels, from the earliest accounts to the present time. Judiciously selected from the best writers in the English, French, Spanish, Italian, Dutch, German, and other languages. . . .* London: J. Cooke, 1768.

EX, 235; JL 4.226 (7–14–52)

436. DRAYTON, Michael. In Chalmers (q.v.), vol. 4.
"To My Dearly Loved Friend, Henry Reynolds, Esq. Of Poets and Poesy"
WE, 68; PJ 1.457 (6–19–43)
"Description of Morning, Birds, and Hunting the Deer"
ME

437. DRUILLETTE, Gabriel. "Narrative of a Voyage made for the Abnaquiois Missions. . . ." Trans. J. G. Shea. *Collections of the New York Historical Society*, 2d ser., part 1, vol. 3 (1857): 309–322.
HL 1–13–58
IB 11

438. DRUMMOND, William, of Hawthornden. In Chalmers (q.v.), vol. 5.
"Icarus"
WA, 197; LN
"A Pastoral Elegy on the Death of S.A.A."
WE, 337; PJ 2.81 (1842–44)
"No Trust in Time"
WE, 390; LN
"Contente and Resolute," "The Instability of Mortal Glory," "The River of Forth-Feasting," "Tears on the Death of Moeliades"
LN

439. DRUMMOND, William, of Hawthornden. *Poems of William Drummond of Hawthornden.* London: Printed for J. Jeffrey, 1790.
EL

Also availble at the Mercantile Library in New York, this edition was possibly T's source for comments on Drummond in September 1843 (PJ 1.466); see preceding entry for listing of specific references to Drummond's works. T's source for his extracts in LN was probably Robert Anderson, *The Works of the British Poets* (q.v.).

440. DRYDEN, John.

T copied scattered phrases from Dryden's poems, including "The Character of the Good Parson," *Palamon and Arcite,*

Annus Mirabilis, Religio Laici, and "The Wife of Bath's Tale" in F2a in 1836.

441. Du Buat, Pierre Louis Georges, comte. *Principes d'hydraulique; et de pyrodynamique vérifiés par un grand nombre d'expériences.* . . . 3 vols. Paris: F. Didot, 1816.
HL 8–15–59

442. Dubartas, Guillame de Saluste. *Devine weeks and works* (many eds. available).

"Probability of the Celestial Orbs Being Inhabited"
CPB1 (*c.* 1841)

443. Dublin, New Hampshire. *The History of Dublin, N.H., containing the address by Charles Mason, and the proceedings at the centennial celebration, June 17, 1852; with a register of families.* Boston: J. Wilson, 1855.

CPB2 (*c.* 1860)

444. Duhamel du Monceau, Henri Louis. *Traités des arbes et arbustes qui se cultivent en France en pleine terre.* Paris: H. L. Guerin & L. F. Delatour, 1755.
IB 6 (*c.* 1852)

445. Dumont, Étienne. *Recollections of Mirabeau, and of the two first legislative assemblies of France.* London: E. Bull, 1832.
HL 1–13–35

446. Duplessy, F. S. *Des végétaux résineux.*

CC, 81

T's source for Duplessy was Loudon, *Arboretum* (q.v.), 4.2058.

447. Duponceau, Peter S. "The General Character and Forms of the Languages of the American Indians." In American Philosophical Society *Transactions* (q.v.).
HL 9–17–55
IB 9

448. Dwight, Timothy. *Travels in New England and New York.* 4 vols. New Haven: T. Dwight, 1821–22; London: Printed for W. Baynes and son; [etc. etc.], 1823.
AL
CC, 163, 167, 177; JL 9.75 (9–10–56)

449. Dyer, Sir Edward. In Percy, Thomas, *Reliques of Ancient English Poetry* (q.v.).

"My Mind to Me a Kingdom Is"
ME (c. 1837)

450. DYMOND, Jonathan. *Essays on the principles of morality, and
      on the private and political rights of mankind.* New York:
      Harper & brothers, 1834.

      EEM, 99–101 (4–28–37)

      T was asked in Channing's theme assignment to refer to Mrs.
      Opie's opinions as well as Dymond's, but he refers to and
      quotes only the latter in his theme.

451. EASTMAN, Mary (Henderson). *Dahcotah; or, Life and legends
      of the Sioux around Fort Snelling. . . .* New York: J. Wiley,
      1849.

      IB 8 (c. 1854)

452. EATON, Amos. *Manual of botany, for North America. . . . 5th
      ed., rev., cor., and much extended.* Albany: Websters and
      Skinners, 1829.
      EL
      JL 10.31 (9–11–57)

453. "Ecclesiastical History of Massachusetts." *Collections of the
      Massachusetts Historical Society,* 1st ser., vol. 10 (1809): 1–
      37.

      PJ 3 (Fall 1849)

454. *Edinburgh review, or critical journal.* Edinburgh: A. and C.
      Black [etc. etc.], 1803–29.
      HL 3–17–35 (vols. 35, 48)

455. EDWARDS, Bela Bates. See Park, Edwards Amasa.

456. EDWARDS, Frank S. *Doniphan's campaign. A campaign in
      New Mexico with Colonel Doniphan.* Philadelphia: Carey
      and Hart, 1847.

      IB 3

457. EDWARDS, Jonathan. *Observations on the language of the
      Muhhekaneew Indians. . . . A new edition with notes, by John
      Pickering. As published in the Massachusetts historical collec-
      tions.* Boston: Printed by Phelps and Farnham, 1823.
      HL 3–4–56.

      Bound with Barton, Benjamin Smith, *New Views* (q.v.).

458.   EDWARDS, Richard. See Evans, Thomas, *Old Ballads*.

459.   EDWARDS, Richard. *The paradise of dainty devices*. . . . See *England's Helicon*.

460.   *Elegant extracts*. See Knox, Vicesimus.

461.   ELLIOT, Ebenezer. *The poetical works of Ebenezer Elliot, the Corn-law rhymer*. Edinburgh: W. Tait, 1840.

       PJ 1.315 (8–4–41)

       Gift of RWE; see Rusk, ed., Emerson's *Letters* 2.433.

462.   ELLIOT, Stephen. *A sketch of the botany of South-Carolina and Georgia*. 2 vols. Charleston, S.C.: J. R. Schenk, 1821–24.

       JL 9.291 (3–13–57); IB 10

463.   ELLIOT, William. *Carolina sports by land and water; including incidents of devil-fishing, [wild-cat, deer and bear hunting, etc.] . . . &c.* . . . Charleston: Burges and James, 1846.
       SL
       JL 14.315–319 (2–21–61)

464.   ELLIS, Rev. William. *Polynesian researches, during a residence of nearly six years in the South Sea Islands; including descriptions of the natural history and scenery of the islands*. . . . London: Fischer, Son, & Jackson, 1829.

       WE, 55, 65; PJ 3 (*c.* 1848)

465.   ELLIS, Rev. William. *Three visits to Madagascar during the years 1853–1856. Including a journey to the capital; with notices of the natural history of the country and of the present civilization of the people*. Philadelphia: J. W. Bradley, 1859.
       SL
       IB 12 (*c.* 1859)

466.   EMERSON, Benjamin Dudley. *First class reader: a selection for exercises in reading, from standard British and American authors, in prose and verse* . . . Boston: Russell, Odiorne and Metcalf, 1833.
       TL

467.   EMERSON, Frederick. *Key to the North American arithmetic, part second and part third. For the use of teachers*. Philadelphia: Hogan & Thompson, 1845.
       TL

468. EMERSON, Frederick. *North American [arithmetic]. Part first, containing elementary lessons.* Boston: Lincoln & Edmonds, 1832.
TL

469. EMERSON, George B. *A report on the trees and shrubs growing naturally in the forests of Massachusetts. Published agreeable to an order of the Legislature, by the Commissioners on the zoological and botanical survey of the state.* Boston: Dutton and Wentworth, printers, 1846.
TL
WE, 159; JL 4.48 (5–13–52); 5.481 (11–6–53); 6.154 (3–6–54); 8.118 (1–19–56), 402 (7–6–56); 9.35 (8–30–56), 55 (9–2–56), 61 (9–5–56), 68 (9–8–56); 10.11 (8–24–57); 11.53 (7–16–58), 348 (11–27–58)

470. EMERSON, Ralph Waldo. *The conduct of life.* Boston: Ticknor & Fields, 1860.
TL

471. EMERSON, Ralph Waldo. *Emancipation in the West Indies.* Boston: James Munroe and Company, 1844.

PJ 2.310 (Fall 1846)

472. EMERSON, Ralph Waldo. *Essays* [First Series]. Boston: J. Munroe and Company, 1841.
TL
HM 13201

473. EMERSON, Ralph Waldo. *Essays: second series.* Boston: James Munroe and Company, 1845.
TL

474. EMERSON, Ralph Waldo. *The method of nature. An oration, delivered before the Society of the Adelphi, in Waterville College, in Maine, August 11, 1841.* Boston: S. G. Simpkins, 1841.
TL

475. EMERSON, Ralph Waldo. "Mr. Channing's Poems." *Democratic Review* 13 (Sept. 1843): 309–314.

PJ 1.459 (8–25–43)

476. EMERSON, Ralph Waldo. *Nature. . . .* Boston: J. Munroe and company, 1836.
TL, IN 4–3–37, 6–25–37
EEM, 101–103

477. EMERSON, Ralph Waldo. *Nature: addresses, and lectures.*
Boston: James Munroe and Company, 1849.
TL

478. EMERSON, Ralph Waldo. *Poems.* Boston: James Munroe and
company, 1847.
TL
"The Problem"
WE, 101; EX, 277; PJ 2.370 (Winter 1846–47); ME
"Ode to Beauty"
WE, 100; PJ 2.369 (Winter 1846–47)
"Each in All"
ME
"The Rhodora"
EX, 303
"Musketaquid"
WE, 5
"Concord Hymn"
WE, 17
"Woodnotes"
WE, 298
"The Sphinx"
WE, 218; PJ 1.279–286 (3–7 to 3–10–41)

479. EMERSON, Ralph Waldo. *Representative men: seven lectures.*
Boston: Phillips, Sampson and company, 1850.
TL

480. "Emerson." Unsigned review in *Blackwood's Edinburgh
Magazine* 62 (Dec. 1847): 643–657.

COR, 204 (1–12–48)

481. *Eminent British Statesmen.* Ed. Dionysius Lardner. 7 vols.
London: Longman, Rees, Orme, Brown, and Green, 1831–
41.

PJ 1.176 (8–40)

482. EMMONS, Ebenezer. *Insects of New-York.* Albany: C. Van
Benthuysen, 1854. (Vol. 5 of the author's *Agriculture of New-
York*)

JL 9.319 (4–6–57)

T withdrew this book from the New Bedford library while
visiting Daniel Ricketson in 1857.

483. EMMONS, Ebenezer. See Dewey, Chester.

484. EMORY, W. H. See United States. Army. Corps of Topographical Engineers (no. 1360), and United States. Dept. of the Interior.

485. *England's Helicon.* In *The paradise of dainty devices, reprinted from a transcript of the first edition. . . . and England's helicon. A collection of pastoral and lyric poems. . . . To which is added a biographical and critical introduction.* 2 vols. in 1. London: T. Bensley, for Robert Triphook, 1812.
HL 12–8–41
CBPI

486. ETZLER, J. A. *The paradise within the reach of all men, without labor, by powers of nature and machinery. Second English Edition.* London: J. Cleave, 1842.
EL
RP, 19–47

In his textual introduction to "Paradise (To Be) Regained," T's review of Etzler (RP, 275), Wendell Glick notes that T's copy was loaned to him by RWE, who in turn had received it from Bronson Alcott in England.

487. EULER, Leonhard. *An introduction to the elements of algebra, designed for the use of those who are acquainted only with the first principles of arithmetic. Selected from the algebra of Euler [by John Farrar], 3rd ed.* Boston: Hilliard, Gray, Little and Wilkins, 1828.
TL, TX

488. EURIPIDES. *Alcestis . . . edit., diatriba recognita, et annotatione perpetua illustravit Gottlob Adolph Wagner.* Lipsiae: sumtibus Engelh. Beniam. Svicqvertii, 1800.
HL 2–10–35

489. EURIPIDES. *Euripidis. Tragoediae cum fragmentis. Ad optimorum librorum fidem recognovit Augustus Witzschel. Nova ed. stereotypa. . . .* 4 vols. Lipsiae: sumtibus et typis C. Tauchnitii, 1841.
TL
Orestes
RP, 43; PJ 1.127 (6–14–40)

490. EVANS, Thomas. *Old ballads, historical and narrative, with some of modern date. . . . A new ed., rev. and considerably enl. from public and private collections, by his son, R. H. Evans.* 4 vols. London: Printed for R. H. Evans, by W. Bulmer and co., 1810.
HL 12–2–41
"The Lordling Peasant"

WE, 130; CPBI
"Description of a Most Noble Lady"
PJ 2.56 (1842–44); CPBI
"The Renuing of Love" (by Richard Evans)
WE, 274; CPBI
"The Shepherd's Love for Philliday," "King Alfred and the Shepherd," "The Banishment of the Dukes of Hereford and Norfolk . . ." "A Praise of Her Lady," "The Lamentable Fall of the Dutchess of Gloucester . . ." "The Lamentable Song of the Lord Wigmore . . ." "Sonnet Sung Before Queen Elizabeth," "The Murder of Prince Arthur . . ." "The Lady and the Palmer," "Hirlas Owain or the Drinking-horn of Owain," "Venus's Search for Cupid"
CPBI

491.   EVELYN, John. *Sylva, or a discourse of forest-trees. . . . To which is annexed Pomona. . . . Also Kalendarium Hortense. . . . 3d. ed.* London: Printed for Jo. Martyn, and Ja. Allestry, 1679.
SNH 4–6–52
WA, 9–10, 162; EX, 211, 308, 311; JL 4.84–88 (6–9–52); FB

492.   EVELYN, John. *Terra: a philosophical discourse of earth. . . .* York: Printed by A. Wood for J. Dodsley [etc.], 1778.

WA, 162

493.   EVERETT, Edward. "Biographies of Anthony Wayne and Sir Henry Vane." *North American Review* 42 (Jan. 1836): 116–148.

EEM, 36–37

494.   EVERETT, Edward. "The Discovery of America by the Northmen." *North American Review* 46 (1838): 161–203.

CC, 195, 196

495.   EVERETT, Edward. *An oration delivered at Plymouth, December 22, 1824.* Boston: Cummings, Hilliard, & co., 1825.

Conjectural edition; source for a declamation by T at the Concord Academy in 1830.

496.   *Everyman.*

PJ 1, 261 (2–8–41)

497.   EWBANK, Thomas. *Life in Brazil; or, A journal of a visit to the land of the cocoa and the palm. With an appendix, con-*

taining illustrations of ancient South American arts. . . . New-York: Harper & brothers, 1856.

IB 10 (*c.* 1856)

498. EWBANK, Thomas. See United States. Navy. *Naval astronomical expedition.*

499. "Extract from an Indian History." *Collections of the Massachusetts Historical Society*, 1st ser., vol. 9 (1804; rpt., 1857): 99–102.

IB 2 (*c.* 1849)

500. FARMER, John. *Map of the states of Michigan and Wisconsin, embracing a great part of Iowa and Illinois.* Detroit: [n.p.], 1854.
TL

501. FARMER, John, ed. *Collections, historical and miscellaneous and monthly library journal*, vol. 3, Concord, N.H.: Hill and Moore, 1824.
TL
WE, 119–122, 161, 168

502. FARRAR, John, comp. *An elementary treatise on astronomy, adapted to the present improved state of the science, being the fourth part of a course of natural philosophy, compiled for the use of the students of the University of Cambridge, New England.* Cambridge, N.E.: Printed by Hilliard, Metcalf, and co., 1827.
TL, TX

503. FARRAR, John, comp. *An elementary treatise on mechanics, comprehending the doctrine of equilibrium and motion, as applied to solids & fluids, chiefly compiled, and designed for the use of students of the university at Cambridge, N.E.:* Printed by Hilliard & Metcalf, at the university press, sold by W. Hilliard [etc.], 1825.
TL, TX

504. FARRAR, John, comp. *Elements of electricity, magnetism, and electromagnetism, embracing the late discoveries and improvements, digested in the form of a treatise; being the second part of a course of natural philosophy, compiled for the use of students of the University at Cambridge, N.E.* Cambridge, N.E.: Printed by Hilliard & Metcalf, 1826.
TL, TX

505. FARRAR, John, comp. *An experimental treatise on optics, comprehending the leading principles of the science, and an*

explanation of the more important and curious optical instruments and optical phenomena; being the third part. . . . Cambridge, N.E.: Printed by Hilliard & Metcalf, 1826.
TL, TX

506.   FARRAR, Timothy. See Dartmouth College, Plaintiff.

507.   FAY, Theodore Sedgwick. *Norman Leslie. A tale of the present times.* . . . New-York: Harper & brothers, 1836.

        F2a

508.   FELCH, Walton. *A comprehensive grammar, presenting some new views of the structure of the language; designed to explain all the relations of words in English syntax, and make the study of grammar and composition one and the same process. Abridged from a work preparing for publication.* Boston: Otis, Broaders & co., 1837.
        TL

509.   FELTON, C. C., trans. See Menzel, Wolfgang.

510.   FÉNÉLON, François de Salignac de la Mothe. *Abrégé de la vie des plus illustres philosophes de l'antiquité.* . . . Nouv. ed. Paris: Delalain, 1822.
        AL
        PJ 1.152–153 (7–8–40), 156–158 (7–11 & 12–40), 164 (7–31–40)

511.   FÉNÉLON, François de Salignac de la Mothe. *Les aventures de Télémaque, fils d'Ulysse.* . . . Bensançon: V. Cabuchet, 1823.
        TL

512.   FERGUSON, Adam. *The history of the progress and termination of the Roman republic. New ed.* 5 vols. Edinburgh: [n.p.], 1813.
        HL 9–12–36, IN 9–12–36, 10–24–36, 12–8–36
        EEM, 63–66; PJ 1.466 (9–24–43)

513.   FERNE, Sir John. *The Blazon Of Gentrie.* . . . *for the instruction of all Gentlemen bearers of Armes, whome and none other this work concerneth.* London: John Windet, for Toby Cooke, 1586.

        JL 11.357 (11–30–58)

514.   FERRIS, Benjamin G. *Utah and the Mormons. The history, government, doctrines, customs, and prospects of the Latter-day saints from personal observation during a six months' residence at Great Salt Lake City.* New York: Harper & brothers, 1854.

SL
JL 6.490 (8–31–54)

515.   FESSENDEN, Thomas Green. *Terrible tractoration, and other*
        poems. By Christopher Caustic [pseud.]. 3rd American ed.
        Boston: Russell, Shattuck & co., 1836.
        IN 12–8–36

516.   FIELD, George. *Chromatography: or, A treatise on colours.*
        . . . New ed., improved. London: Tilt and Bogue, 1841.

        JL 10.99 (10–15–57)

517.   FINLEY, Anthony. *A new general atlas, comprising a complete*
        set of maps, representing the grand division of the globe, to-
        gether with several empires, kingdoms, and states in the
        world; compiled from the best authorities, and corrected by
        the most recent discoveries. Philadelphia: Anthony Finley,
        1824.
        TL

518.   "First Thunder-Storm in 1855." *New York Tribune*, April 19,
        1855, p. 4.

        JL 7.328 (4–21–55)

519.   FISCHER, P. (pseudonym). See Chatto, William Andrew.

520.   FISK, Benjamin Franklin. *A grammar of the Greek language.*
        Second edition. Boston: Hilliard, Gray, Little, and Wilkins,
        1831.
        TX

521.   FISK, Benjamin Franklin. *Greek exercises; containing the sub-*
        stance of the Greek syntax. . . . Boston: Hilliard, Gray, Little,
        and Wilkins, 1831.
        HL 2–5–34

522.   FITCH, Asa. *First and second reports on the noxious, benefi-*
        cial, and other insects, of the state of New-York. Made to the
        state Agricultural society. . . . Albany: C. Van Benthuysen,
        printer, 1856.
        TL

523.   FLACCUS, Aulus Persius. See Persius Flaccus, Aulus.

524.   FLAGG, Wilson. "Birds of the Garden and Orchard." *Atlantic*
        Monthly 2 (Oct. 1858): 592–605.

        CPB2 (*c.* 1858)

525. FLAGG, Wilson. "Birds of the Night." *Atlantic Monthly* 4
      (Aug. 1859): 171–184.

      JL 12.258 (7–25–59)

526. FLETCHER, Giles. In Chalmers (q.v.), vol. 6.
      HL 1–17–44 (by RWE)
      "Christ's Victory"
      WE, 189, 190, 378; LN
      "Christ's Triumph After Death"
      JL 5.305 (6–26–53)

527. FLETCHER, Phineas. In Chalmers (q.v.), vol. 6.
      HL 1–17–44 (by RWE)
      "The Purple Island"
      WE, 388; LN

528. FLINT, Charles L. *Culture of the grasses. An extract from the
      fourth annual report of Charles L. Flint, secretary of the state
      board of agriculture. Pub. under the direction of the Massa-
      chusetts state board of agriculture.* . . . Boston: W. White,
      printer to the state, 1860.
      TL

529. FLINT, Timothy. *The Shoshone valley; a romance.* . . . *By the
      author of Francis Berrian.* 2 vols. Cincinnati: E. H. Flint,
      1830.
      IN 11–17–36

530. FLORIAN, Jean Pierre Claris de. *Gonzalve de Cordove, ou
      Grenade reconquise.* 3 vols. Paris: Guillaume de cie., 1828.
      TL
      PJ 1.148 (7–40)

531. FOLLEN, Charles T. C. *A German reader.* . . . *A new ed., with
      additions, by G. A. Schmitt.* Boston: Hilliard, Gray, Little,
      and Wilkins, 1831.
      TL, TX

532. FOLLEN, Charles T. C. *A practical grammar of the German
      language.* Boston: Hilliard, Gray, Little & Wilkins, 1828.
      TL

533. FONTENEAU, Jean. See *Voyages de découverte au Canada.*

534. FORBES, James David. *Travels through the Alps of Savoy and
      other parts of the Pennine chain, with observations on the
      phenomena of glaciers.* Edinburgh: A. and C. Black; [etc.,
      etc.], 1843.
      SNH 3–13–54
      JL 6.226 (4–27–54); FB

535. FORD, John. *Dramatic works; with an introduction and notes critical and explanatory.* 2 vols. New York: J. & J. Harper (Harper's Family Library), 1831.
IN 7–14–37

Conjectural edition; see Cameron, "Thoreau Discovers Emerson."

536. FORDYCE, James. *Addresses to young men.* 2 vols. in 1. Boston: Printed by Manning & Loring [etc., etc.], 1795.
TL

Autograph of John Thoreau, Sr.

537. FORESTER, Frank [pseud.]. See Herbert, Henry William.

538. FORSHEY, Caleb G. "Physics of the Mississippi River. . . ." Abstracted from "An American railroad journal" in the *Annual of Scientific Discovery* . . . for 1851 (q.v.).

CN (*c.* 1851)

539. FOSTER, John. *Essays in a series of letters, on the following subjects: On a man writing memoirs of himself. On decision of character. On the application of the epithet romantic. On some of the causes by which evangelical religion has been rendered less acceptable to persons of cultivated taste. . . . 5th American from the 8th London edition.* Boston: J. Loring, 1833.
TL

540. FOSTER, John Wells. See United States. General Land Office.

541. Fox, Charles James. *History of the old township of Dunstable, including Nashua, Nashville, Hollis, Hudson, Litchfield, and Merrimac, N.H.; Dunstable and Tyngsborough, Mass.* Nashua: C. T. Gill, 1846.
TL
WE, 43, 64, 110, 111, 112, 120, 122, 161, 167, 220, 254

542. FRANCHÈRE, Gabriel. *Narrative of a voyage to the northwest coast of America, in the years 1811, 1813 and 1814; or, The first American settlement on the Pacific. . . . Tr. and ed. J. V. Huntington.* New York: Redfield, 1854.
TL

543. FRANKLIN, Benjamin. *The life of Dr. Benjamin Franklin. Written by himself.* Salem: Printed for Cushing and Carlton, 1796.
TL
COR, 478 (4–26–57)

544.   FRANKLIN, Sir John. *Narrative of a journey to the shores of the polar sea, in the years 1819, 20, 21 & 22. . . . With an appendix containing geognostical observation, and remarks on the aurora borealis. . . .* Philadelphia: H. C. Carey & I. Lea [etc.], 1824.
CL
CC, 136; IB 9; FB

545.   FREEMAN, James ["r. s."]. "A Description and History of Eastham, in the County of Barnstable. September, 1802." *Collections of the Massachusetts Historical Society*, 1st ser., vol. 8 (1802): 154–186.

CC, 28–44 passim

546.   FREEMAN, James ["r. s."]. "A Description of Chatham, in the County of Barnstable, September, 1802." *Collections of the Massachusetts Historical Society*, 1st ser., vol. 8 (1802): 142–154.

CC, 20–42 passim

547.   FREEMAN, James ["r. s."]. "A Description of Dennis, in the County of Barnstable, September, 1802." *Collections of the Massachusetts Historical Society*, 1st ser., vol. 8 (1802): 129–140.

CC, 20–21, 22, 42

548.   FREEMAN, James ["r. s."]. "A Description of Orleans, in the County of Barnstable. September, 1802." *Collections of the Massachusetts Historical Society*, 1st ser., vol. 8 (1802): 186–195.

CC, 26–28, 59; IB 2

549.   FREEMAN, James ["r. s."]. "A Description of Provincetown, in the County of Barnstable. September, 1802." *Collections of the Massachusetts Historical Society*, 1st ser., vol. 8 (1802): 196–201.

CC, 172, 175–176

550.   FREEMAN, James ["r. s."]. "A Description of the Eastern Coast of the County of Barnstable, from Cape Cod or Race Point . . . to Cape Malebarre, or Sandy Point of Chatham. . . ." *Collections of the Massachusetts Historical Society*, 1st ser., vol. 8 (1802): 110–119.

CC, 49–63 passim

551. [FREEMAN, James]. "A Topographical Description of Truro, in the County of Barnstable, 1794." *Collections of the Massachusetts Historical Society*, 1st ser., vol. 3 (1794): 195–203.

    CC, 104–105, 106, 111, 119, 124–125, 177

552. FREEMASONS. *By-laws of Corinthian lodge, of ancient, free and accepted masons, of Concord, Mass. . . . To which is added an historical sketch of masonry.* Concord: Printed for B. Tolman, 1859.
    TL

553. FRÉMONT, Capt. John C. *Report of the exploring expedition to the Rocky Mountains in the year 1842, and to Oregon and North California in the years 1843–'44.* Washington: Blair and Rives, 1845.

    PJ 2.247 (5–15–46)

554. FRENCH, B. F., ed. and intro. *Historical collections of Louisiana. . . .* 4 vols. New York: Wiley & Putnam, 1846–53.
    HL 12–7–58 (vol. 4)
    IB 11

555. "Friar Rush and the Frolicsome Elves of Popular Mythology." *Foreign Quarterly Review* 18 (Oct. 1836): 180–202.

    ME (*c.* 1837)

556. FROISSART, Jean. *Chronicles of England, France, Spain, and the adjoining countries. . . .* 2 vols. London: H. G. Bohn, 1855.
    TL

    Mentioned casually in JL 2.429 (8–29–51).

557. FULLER, Thomas. *The holy and profane states. With some account of the author and his writings.* Cambridge, Mass.: Hilliard and Brown, 1831.
    EL
    WE, 250, 388; PJ 1.40 (4–15–38)

558. GALBRAITH, William. *Mathematical and astronomical tables for the use of students of mathematics, practical astronomers, surveyors, engineers, and navigators; with an introduction containing the explanation and use of the tables illustrated by numerous problems and examples.* Edinburgh: Oliver & Boyd, 1834.
    HL 4–26–50
    JL 2.3 (6–9–50)

559.   GARCIN DE TASSY, Joseph Héliodore. *Histoire de la littérature hindoui et hindoustani.* 2 vols. Paris: Oriental translation committee of Great Britain and Ireland, 1839–47.
HL 9–11–49
WA, 99, 325; PJ 3 (*c.* 1849)

560.   GARLICK, Theodatus. *A treatise on the artificial propagation of certain kinds of fish.* . . . Cleveland: T. Brown, 1857; New York: A. O. Moore, 1858.

JL 10.379 (4–21–58)

561.   GARVE, Christian. "Sur la Manière d'Écrire l'Histoire de la Philosophie."
ME (*c.* 1838)

Source unknown.

562.   GÉBELIN, Antoine. See Court de Gébelin, Antoine.

563.   *Gentleman's Magazine.* New ser., vol. 5 (1836).
HL 1–30–37

564.   GÉRANDO, Joseph Marie de, baron. *Histoire comparée des systèmes de philosophie, considérés relativement aux principes des connaissances humaines.* 2d. ed., rev., cor. et augm. 4 vols. Paris: A. Eymery [etc.], 1822–23.
EL
PJ 1.178 (9–21–40), 180 (9–26–40)

The PJ 1.180 passage is also transcribed in PJ 2.17.

565.   GÉRANDO, Joseph Marie de, baron. *Self-education; or, The means and art of moral progress. Tr. from the French of M. le baron Degerando.* Boston: Carter and Hendee, 1830.
TL

566.   GÉRARD, Cécile Jules Basile. *The adventures of Gerard, the lion killer, comprising a history of his ten years' campaign among the wild animals of Northern Africa. Tr. from the French by Charles E. Whitehead.* New York: Derby & Jackson, 1856.
SL
JL 8.403–404 (7–8–56), 421 (7–21–56)

567.   GERARD, John. *The herball of generall historie of plantes. Gathered by John Gerarde of London, master in chirurgerie. Very much enlarged and amended by Thomas Johnson, citizen and apothecarye of London.* London: Printed by Adam Islip, Joice Norton and Richard Whitakers, anno 1633.
HL 9–10–60

CC 162–163; JL 13.29–30 (12–16–59); 14.92 (9–22–60), 114 (10–13–60); CPB2; IB 12

In the JL 13.29–30 entry T says he read Gerard at Harvard at that time but did not withdraw the book; he also reports having made extracts from the preface in October 1859.

568.   GERSTAEKER, Frederick. *Wild sports in the far west. Translated from the German. With eight crayon drawings, executed in oil colors, from designs by Harrison Weir.* Boston: Crosby, Nichols and co., 1859.

IB 12 (*c.* 1860)

569.   GESNER, Conrad. See Topsell, Edward.

570.   GIBBON, Edward. *The history of the decline and fall of the Roman empire. New ed.* 12 vols. London: W. Allason etc., 1821.
IN 3–13–37, 4–3–37, EL

PJ 1.206–207 (12–18–40), 384 (3–20–42)

571.   GIBBON, Edward. *Miscellaneous works of Edward Gibbon, Esq. With memoirs of his life and writings, composed by himself: illustrated from his letters, with occasional notes and narrative, by John, Lord Sheffield.* London: B. Blake, 1837.
EL
PJ 1.196 (11–9–40), 206–207 (12–18–40)

572.   GIBBON, Lardner. See Herndon, Lieut. William L.

573.   GILCHRIST, John. comp. *A collection of ancient and modern Scottish ballads, tales, and songs, with explanatory notes and observations.* Edinburgh, and London: W. Blackwood, 1815.
EL
CPB1 (*c.* 12–41)

574.   GILFILLAN, George. *Sketches of modern literature, and eminent literary men (being a gallery of literary portraits).* Vol. 1. New York: D. Appleton & Co., 1846.

EEM, 219–222; PJ 2.216–217 (Winter 1845–46)

575.   GILLISS, James M. See United States. Navy. *Naval astronomical expedition.*

576.   GILPIN, William. *Observations on several parts of England, particularly the mountains and lakes of Cumberland and Westmoreland, relative chiefly to picturesque beauty, made in*

the year 1776. 3rd ed. London: Printed for T. Cadell and
W. Davies, 1788.
HL 7–26–52
JL 4.283–284 (8–6–52); FB

577.   GILPIN, William. *Observations on several parts of Great Brit-
ain, particularly the high-lands of Scotland, relative chiefly to
picturesque beauty, made in the year 1776. 3rd ed.* 2 vols.
London: Printed for T. Cadell and W. Davies, 1808.
HL 7–26–52
WA, 287; JL 4.335, 338–340 (9–1–52)

578.   GILPIN, William. *Observations on several parts of the counties of Cambridge, Norfolk, Suffolk and Essex. Also on several parts of North Wales; relative chiefly to picturesque
beauty, in two tours, the former made in 1769, the latter in
the year 1773.* London: Printed for T. Cadell and W. Davies,
1809.
HL 5–24–52

579.   GILPIN, William. *Observations on the coasts of Hampshire,
Sussex, and Kent, relative chiefly to picturesque beauty: made
in the summer of the year 1794.* London: Printed for T. Cad-
ell and W. Davies, 1804.
HL 11–28–53
CC 93–94; FB

580.   GILPIN, William. *Observations on the River Wye, and several
parts of South Wales, relative chiefly to picturesque beauty:
made in the summer of the year 1770. 5th ed.* London:
Printed by S. Strahan, for T. Cadell and W. Davies, 1800.
HL 5–24–52
FB

581.   GILPIN, William. *Observations on western parts of England,
relative chiefly to picturesque beauty: to which are added, a
few remarks on the picturesque beauties of the Isle of Wight.
2nd ed.* London: Printed for T. Cadell and W. Davies, 1808.
HL 10–5–52
MW, 152; JL 4.394 (10–21–52)

582.   GILPIN, William. *Remarks on forest scenery and other wood-
land views, relative chiefly to picturesque beauty illustrated
by the scenes of New Forest, in Hampshire. . . . 3rd ed.* London: Printed for T. Cadell & W. Davies, 1808.
HL 5–22–52
WA, 250; JL 3.366 (3–31–52), 369–370, 373 (4–1–52), 404,
407–409 (4–12–52), 414–416, 419 (4–15–52), 426–427 (4–
17–52); FB

583.   GILPIN, William. *Three essays: On picturesque beauty; On
picturesque travel; and On sketching landscape: with a poem*

on landscape painting. To these are now added, Two essays giving an account of the principles and mode in which the author executed his own drawings. 3rd ed. 2 vols. London: T. Cadell and W. Davies, 1808.
HL 11–28–53
JL 6.53, 55–59 (1–8–54); FB

584.   GIRAUD, Charles. Untitled contribution to *Proceedings of the Boston Society of Natural History* 5 (1854–56): 39–42.

JL 11.348 (11–27–58)

585.   GIRAUD, Jacob Post. *The birds of Long Island.* New-York: Wiley & Putnam, 1844.
TL
IB 9; FB (*c.* 1855)

586.   GLEASON, F. *Gleason's pictorial drawing-room companion.* Boston: F. Gleason, 1851.

IB 10 (*c.* 1857)

587.   GLIDDON, George R. See Nott, Josiah Clark.

588.   "The Gnawers." *Harper's Magazine* 12 (May 1856): 756–763.

IB 10 (*c.* 1856)

589.   GODWIN, William. *Life of Geoffrey Chaucer, the early English poet: including memoirs of his near friend and kinsman, John of Gaunt, duke of Lancaster; with sketches of the manners, opinions, arts and literature of England in the fourteenth century. . . . 2nd ed.* 4 vols. London: Printed by T. Davison, for R. Phillips, 1804.
HL 5–5–35
F1b

590.   GOETHE, Johann Wolfgang von. *The autobiography of Goethe. Truth and poetry. From my life.* Ed. Parke Godwin. 4 vols. in 2. New York: Wiley and Putnam, 1846.
AL
WE, 327–328; PJ 2.356, 357 (after 12–2–46)

591.   GOETHE, Johann Wolfgang von. *Goetz of Berlichingen, with the iron hand. Tr. from the German by Walter Scott.* New-York: A. H. Innskeep, 1814.

IN 7–14–37

Conjectural; see Cameron, "Thoreau Discovers Emerson."

592.   GOETHE, Johann Wolfgang von. *Iphigenie auf Tauris*. In Goethe, *Werke* (q.v.).

PJ 1.20 (12–18–37)

593.   GOETHE, Johann Wolfgang von. *Die Italiänische reise*. In Goethe, *Werke* (q.v.).

WE, 326–329; PJ 1.11–12 (11–15–37), 16 (12–8–37), 30 (2–27–38).

594.   GOETHE, Johann Wolfgang von. *Torquato Tasso*. In Goethe, *Werke* (q.v.).

PJ 1.6–7 (10–25 & 26–37)

T also owned a copy of *Torquato Tasso*, impossible to identify now because the title page is missing. See Harding, *Thoreau's Library*.

595.   GOETHE, Johann Wolfgang von. *Werke: Vollstandige ausgabe letzer hand*. 55 vols. Stuttgart und Tübingen: J. G. Cotta, 1828–33.
EL

See specific titles for T's references to the volumes in this edition, the primary source for his reading of Goethe.

596.   GOETHE, Johann Wolfgang von. *Wilhelm Meister's apprenticeship. Trans. by Thomas Carlyle*. 3 vols. Boston: Wells and Lilly, 1828.
TL, IN 4–13–37

597.   GOLDSBURY, John. *A sequel to the common school grammar. . . .* Boston: J. Munroe and company, 1842.
TL

598.   GOLDSMITH, Oliver. *The History of England, from the earliest times to the death of George the Second. . . . With a continuation to January, 1814. Embellished with portraits from medals, elegantly and accurately engraved by Mr. Willis. 1st Am. ed., corr.*, 2 vols. Boston: Chester Stebbins, 1814–15.
HL 4–30–34

599.   GOLDSMITH, Oliver. *Miscellaneous works*. 4 vols. London: Richardson & Co., [etc., etc.], 1821.
HL 3–3–35 (vol. 3)

600.   GOLDSMITH, Oliver. *The miscellaneous works of Oliver Goldsmith—with an account of his life and writings. Stereotyped from the Paris edition, ed. by Washington Irving. . . .* Philadelphia: J. Crissy, 1834.

TL
"The Deserted Village"
EEM, 70 (12–16–36)

601.   GOLDSMITH, Oliver. *The Roman history, from the founda-tion of the city of Rome, to the destruction of the Western empire. By Dr. Goldsmith. A new ed., cor.* . . . 2 vols. London: Printed for Leigh and Sotheby, J. Sotheby [etc.], 1805.
HL 3–3–35

602.   GOOKIN, Daniel. *An historical account of the doings and suf-ferings of the Christian Indians in New England, in the years 1675, 1676, 1677.* American Antiquarian Society, Worcester, Mass. Archaeologia Americana. Transactions and Collec-tions. Vol. 2. Cambridge, 1836.

WE, 82, 111, 161, 168, 252, 253; IB 3.

603.   GOOKIN, Daniel. "Historical Collections of the Indians in New England, of Their Several Nations, Numbers, Customs, Manners, Religion, and Government, Before the English Planted There. Also, a True and Faithful Account of the Pres-ent State and Condition of the Praying Indians. . . ." *Collec-tions of the Massachusetts Historical Society*, 1st ser., vol. 1 (1792; rpt. 1806): 141–227.

WA, 29–30; WE, 80–81; CC 48–49; PJ 2.48 (1842–44), 180 (after 12–6–45)

604.   GORDON-CUMMINGS, Roualeyn George. *Five years of a hunt-er's life in the far interior of South Africa. With notices of the native tribes, and anecdotes of the chase of the lion, elephant, hippopotamus, giraffe, rhinoceros, &c.* 2 vols. New York: Harper & brothers, 1850.
SL
EX 225; JL 2.130–132 (12–30–50), 161 (2–14–51), 171 (be-tween 2–27 and 3–14–51)

605.   GORGES, Sir Ferdinando. "A Brief Description of Laconia, a Province in New England." *Collections of the Maine Histori-cal Society* 2 (Portland, 1847): 66–69

CC, 186

606.   GORGES, Sir Ferdinando. "A Briefe Narration of the Originall Undertakings for the Advancement of Plantations in Amer-ica." *Collections of the Maine Historical Society* 2 (Portland, 1847): 1–65.

CC, 186

607.   GOSNOLD, Bartholomew. See Archer, Gabriel.

608.   GOSSE, Philip Henry. *The Canadian naturalist. A series of conversations on the natural history of Lower Canada.* London: J. Van Voorst, 1840.
HL 5–2–60
EX, 91

609.   GOSSE, Philip Henry. *Letters from Alabama (U.S.) chiefly relating to natural history.* London: Morgan & Chase, 1859.

JL 14.311 (1–14–61); IB 12

610.   GOTAMA, called Aksapáda. *The aphorisms of the Nyáya philosophy, with illustrative extracts from the commentary by Viśwanatha, in Sanscrit and English. 1st ed. Printed for the use of Benares College.* Allahabad: Printed at the Presbyterian Mission Press, 1850.
TL

611.   GOULD, Augustus A. *Report on the invertebrata of Massachusetts. Published agreeably to an order of the legislature, by the commissioners on the zoological and botanical survey of the state.* Cambridge: Folsom, Wells and Thurston, 1841.
TL
EX, 129; CC, 65, 67, 85, 86–87

612.   GOULD, B. A., Jr. "The Progress of Astronomy During the Last Half Century." *Boston Daily Evening Traveller* (newspaper), Feb. 2, 1852, p. 1.

FB

613.   GOWER, John. In Chalmers (q.v.), vol. 2.
Confessio Amantis.

WE, 57, 117; PJ 1.437–438 (after 8–23–42); 2.73–74 (1842–44)

614.   GRAGLIA, C. *Italian pocket dictionary: in two parts: I. Italian and English:—II. English and Italian. Preceded by an Italian grammar. . . . 1st American, from the 14th London ed., with corrections and additions.* Boston: Hilliard, Gray, and company, 1835.
TL

615.   GRAHAM, James Duncan. See United States. Topographical Bureau.

616.   GRAY, Asa. *The botanical text-book, an introduction to scientific botany, both structural and systematic. For colleges,*

schools, and private students. 4th ed. . . . . New York: G. D.
Putnam & Co., 1853.
TL

See next entry.

617.   GRAY, Asa. *A manual of the botany of the northern United
States, from New England to Wisconsin and south to Ohio
and Pennsylvania inclusive (the mosses and liverworts by
Wm. S. Sullivant), arranged according to the natural system.*
. . . Boston: J. Munroe and company, 1848; New York: G. P.
Putnam & co., 1856.
TL

T owned both of these editions, in addition to the *Botanical
Textbook* listed above. His references to Gray in the Journal
are so frequent as to preclude listing them all, and it is impossible always to distinguish which volume is being cited. See
also the Appendix to MW, 298–316, for further references to
Gray.

618.   GRAY, Hugh. *Letters from Canada, written during a residence
there in the years 1806, 1807, and 1808, showing the present
state of Canada, its productions, trade, commercial importance and political relations.* . . . London: Printed for Longman, Hurst, Rees, and Orme, 1809.

EX, 94; CN

619.   GRAY, Thomas. *Poems of Mr. Gray. To which are added
memoirs of his life and writings, by Mason, M.A.* 4 vols. New
York: Printed by A. Ward, and sold by J. Dodsley, 1778.
HL 4–24–37
EEM, 76 (1–37); WE, 296
"Elegy Written in a Country Churchyard"
MW, 18; WA, 130; PJ 1.435 (8–8–41); CPBI
"From Some Verses Upon Beauty . . ." "From a Fragment on
the 'Pleasure Arising from Vicissitude,' " "Ode on the
Spring," "Ode on the Progress of Poesy," "Ode on a Distant
Prospect of Eton College"
CPBI

620.   GRAY, Thomas. *The Vestal; or, A tale of Pompeii.* Boston:
Gray & Bowen, 1830.
HL 3–26–34

621.   *Greek Anthology.*

Edition unknown. T's quotations from the *Greek Anthology*
in WE are from Crates of Thebes (98) and Simonides' "Epi-

gram on Anacreon" (225). RWE owned *Anthologia Graeca. The Greek Anthology . . . tr. George Burges, etc.* London: Bohn, 1852, an edition which postdates T's quotations.

622.   *The Greek pastoral poets: Theocrites, Bion, and Moschus. Done into English by M. J. Chapman.* London: J. Fraser, 1836.

COR, 150 (*c.* 11-1-43)

Withdrawn from the Mercantile Library of New York while T was living on Staten Island.

623.   Greek Testament. See Bible.

624.   GREEN, George W. "Life and Voyages of Verrazano." *North American Review* 45 (1837): 293–311.

IB 9 (*c.* 1855)

625.   GREENE, Robert. *The dramatic works of Robert Greene, to which are added his poems. With some account of the author, and notes, by the Rev. Alexander Dyce.* 2 vols. London: W. Pickering, 1831.

LN (*c.* 1843)

626.   GREENLEAF, Moses. *A Survey of the State of Maine.* Portland, Me.: Shirley and Hyde, 1829.

MW, 123

627.   GREGG, Josiah. *Commerce of the prairies; or, The journal of a Santa Fe trader, during eight expeditions across the great Western prairies, and a residence of nearly nine years in northern Mexico.* 2 vols. New York: H. G. Langley, 1844.

IB 8 (*c.* 1854)

628.   GREVILLE, Fulke [supposed author]. "Another of His Cynthia."

WE, 271

629.   GREY, Richard. *Memoria technica; or, A new method of artificial memory . . . applied to . . . chronology, history, etc.* 2nd ed. London: C. King, 1732.
       HL 3–16–57

630.   GRIMANI, Gasparo. *New and improved grammar of the Italian language, with a copious collection of exercises.* London: [n.p.], 1820.
       HL 9–16–34, 10–5–35

631.   GRUND, Francis J. *Elements of chemistry, with practical exercises.* Boston: Jenks & Palmer, [n.d.]
       TL

632.   GRUND, Francis J. *Geometry.* Boston: Jenks & Palmer, [n.d.].
       TL

       Harding (*T's Library*, p. 55) notes that Grund published both a plane and a solid geometry, and is unsure which T owned.

633.   GUIZOT, François Pierre Guillaume. *Essay on the character and influence of Washington in the revolution of the United States of America.* Boston: J. Munroe and company, 1840.
       TL
       PJ 1.209 (12–25–40)

634.   GUROWSKI, Adam. *America and Europe.* New York: D. Appleton, 1857.
       BA 2–1–58 (by RWE)
       IB 10

635.   GUTHRIE, William. *A new geographical, historical, and commercial grammar; and present state of the several kingdoms of the world. . . . The astronomical part by James Ferguson. Illustrated with a correct set of maps, engraved by Mr. Kitchin. The 10th ed., corr. . . .* London: Printed for C. Dilly [etc.], 1787.
       TL

636.   GUYOT, Arnold Henry. *The earth and man: lectures on comparative physical geography, in its relation to the history of mankind. Trans. C. C. Felton, 3rd ed., rev.* Boston: Gould & Lincoln, 1851.
       EL
       CC, 97–98; EX, 93–94, 220, 221, 229–230; JL 2.147–148 (*c.* 1–51); CN

637.   HABINGTON, William. In Chalmers (q.v.), vol. 6.
       HL 1–17–44 (by RWE)
       "Nox Nocti Indicat Scientiam"
       LN
       "Roses in the Bosome of Castara"
       WE, 56; LN
       "To My Honored Friend Sir Edward P. Knight"
       RP, 195; WA, 320; LN

"To My Honored Friend and Kinsman, R. St. Esquire"
WE, 100

638.   HAKLUYT, Richard. *Divers voyages touching the discovery of America and the islands adjacent. Collected and published by Richard Hakluyt in the Year 1582.* . . . London: Hakluyt Society, 1850.

CC, 188

639.   HALIBURTON, Thomas Chandler. *An historical and statistical account of Nova-Scotia.* 2 vols. Halifax, N.S.: [n.p.], 1829.

CC, 180, 190

640.   HALKETT, John. *Historical notes respecting the Indians of North America: with remarks on the attempts made to convert and civilize them.* . . . London: Printed for A. Constable, and co., 1825.
HL 2–28–59
IB 12

641.   HALL, Col. Francis. *Travels in Canada and the United States, in 1816 and 1817.* Boston: Wells and Lilly, 1818.
HL 9–11–33

642.   HALL, S. C., ed. *The book of gems. The poets and artists of Great Britain.* 3 vols. London: Saunders and Otley, 1836–38.

PJ 1.74–75 (7–4–39); LN; ME

643.   HALLAM, Henry. *Introduction to the literature of Europe in the fifteenth, sixteenth, and seventeenth centuries.* 4 vols. London: John Murray, 1837.

PJ 2.188 (before 3–26–46)

644.   HAMILTON, Robert. In *The Naturalist's Library,* ed. Sir Wm. Jardine. Vol. 26, *Mammalia. Whales, etc.* Edinburgh: W. H. Lizars; London: Henry G. Bohn, 1852.

CC, 112, 114; JL 7.464 (9–29–55)

645.   HAMMOND, Samuel H. *Hunting adventures in the northern wilds; or, A tramp in the Chataugay woods, over hills, lakes, and forest streams.* New York: Derby & Jackson, 1856.

FB (c. 1856)

646.   HANBURY, Barnard. See Waddington, George.

647. HARDY, Robert Spence. *A manual of Budhism, in its modern development; translated from Singhalese mss.* London: Partridge & Oakley, 1853.
TL

648. HARIOT, Thomas. *A brief and true report of the new found land of Virginia.* . . . . Francoforti ad Moenum: Typis I Wecheli, sumtibus vero Theodori de Bry [London], 1590.

IB 10 (*c.* 1858)

649. *Harivansa.* See *Mahābhārata* (no. 926).

650. HARLAN, Richard. *Fauna americana, being a description of the mammiferous animals inhabiting North America.* Philadelphia: A. Finley, 1825.
SNH 10–3–52, TL
JL 4.401 (10–26–52); IB 6; FB

651. HARRIS, Thaddeus William. "Larvae of the Crane Fly." *New England Farmer* 6 (May 1854): 210.

JL 6.181 (4–1–54)

652. HARRIS, Thaddeus W. *A report on the insects of Massachusetts, injurious to vegetation.* Cambridge, Mass.: Folson, Wells and Thurston, 1841.

EX, 105–131

This is the edition T used for "Natural History of Massachusetts"; he later owned Harris's *Treatise* (q.v.).

653. HARRIS, Thaddeus William. *A treatise on some of the insects of New England which are injurious to vegetation.* 2d ed. Boston: Printed by White & Potter, 1852.
TL
MW, 223; JL 6.349 (6–14–54); 7.463 (9–27–55)

654. HARTSHORNE, Charles Henry, ed. *Ancient metrical tales: printed chiefly from original sources.* London: W. Pickering, 1829.
HL 12–7–41

655. *Harvardiana. 1834–1837.* 2 vols. Cambridge & Boston: J. Munroe and company [etc. etc.] 1835–37.
TL

656. HARVEY, William Henry. "Nereis Boreali-Americana; or Contributions to a History of the Marine Algae of North

America: Part I." In *Smithsonian Contributions to Knowl-edge*, vol. 3, art. 4. Washington: Smithsonian Institution, 1852.

CC, 52; FB

657.   HARWOOD, Rev. Thomas. *Grecian antiquities; or, An account of the public and private life of the Greeks . . . chiefly de-signed to explain words in the Greek classics, according to the rites and customs to which they refer. To which is added, a chronology of remarkable events in the Grecian history. . . .* London: T. Cadell & W. Davies, 1801.
        HL 1–29–34

658.   HASTINGS, Warren. "Introductory Epistle," *Mahābhārata. Bhăgvăt-gēētā* . . . trans. Charles Wilkins (q.v.).

        WE, 137–138

659.   HAWES, Joel. *Lectures addressed to the young men of Hart-ford and New Haven, and published at their united request.* Hartford: O. D. Cooke & co., 1828.
        TL

660.   [HAWKINS, Alfred.] *Hawkins's picture of Quebec; with his-torical recollections.* Quebec: [A. Hawkins], 1834.
        HL 2–10–51
        CC, 184; CN

661.   HAWLEY, Gideon. "A Letter from Rev. Gideon Hawley of Marshpee, Containing an Account of his Services Among the Indians of Massachusetts and New York, and a Narrative of his Journey to Onahoghwage, July 31, 1794." *Collections of the Massachusetts Historical Society*, 1st ser., vol. 4 (1795; rpt. 1835): 50–67.

        IB 2 (*c.* 1849)

662.   HAWTHORNE, Nathaniel. *Mosses from an old manse.* New York: Wiley and Putnam, 1846.

        WE, 19

        T's reference to *Mosses* in WE indicates only that he knew the title, not necessarily that he had read it.

663.   HAWTHORNE, Nathaniel. *The scarlet letter, a romance.* Bos-ton: Ticknor, Reed & Fields, 1850.
        TL

        T crossed this volume off his library catalogue, suggesting that it was either lost or given away.

664. HAYDON, Benjamin Robert. *Life of Benjamin Robert Haydon, historical painter, from his autobiography and journals, ed. and comp. by Tom Taylor. . . .* London: Longman, Brown, Green, and Longmans, 1853.
EL
COR, 312 (12–19–53), 478 (4–26–57)

665. HAYES, Isaac I. *An arctic boat journey, in the autumn of 1854.* Boston: Brown, Taggard & Chase, 1860.

IB 12 (*c.* 1860)

666. HAYLEY, William. *The life and posthumous writings of William Cowper. With an introductory letter to the Right Honorable Earl Cowper.* Boston: Published by W. Pelham, Manning & Loring, and E. Lincoln, 1803.
TL

667. HAYWARD, John. *New England gazetteer . . . alphabetically arranged.* Concord, N.H.: L. S. Boyd and W. White, 1839.
TL
WE, 237, 254–255; CC, 20; COR, 603 (*c.* 1860); JL 10.474 (6–3–58); 14.44 (8–9–60)

668. HAZLITT, William. *Lectures on the English poets. Delivered at the Surrey institution.* London: Printed for Taylor and Hessey, 1818.
HL 3–23–37, IN before 3–23–37
LN

669. HEAD, Sir Francis B. *The Emigrant. . . . 5th ed.* London: J. Murray, 1847.

EX 47, 221–222; JL 3.268–269 (2–2–52), 278–279 (2–4 & 5–52); IB 5; CN

670. HEADLEY, Henry. *Select beauties of ancient English poetry. With remarks.* 2 vols. in 1. London: T. Cadell, 1787.
HL 12–2–41

671. HEARNE, Samuel. *A journey from Prince of Wale's Fort in Hudson's Bay to the North Ocean. Undertaken by order of the Hudson's Bay company. For the discovery of copper mines, a North West passage, & c., in the years 1769, 1770, 1771, & 1772.* London: A. Strahan and T. Cadell, 1795.

EX, 100–101

672. HECKEWELDER, Rev. John. "An Account of the History, Manners and Customs of the Indian Nations, Who Once Inhabited Pennsylvania, and the Neighboring States." In *American*

Philosophical Society Transactions (q.v.), vol. 1 (1819): 3–347.

IB 9 (*c.* 1855)

673.   HECKEWELDER, Rev. John. "A Correspondence Between the Rev. John Heckewelder . . . and Peter S. Duponceau . . . Respecting the Languages of the American Indians." In *American Philosophical Society Transactions* (q.v.), vol. 1 (1819): 351–448.

IB 9 (*c.* 1855)

674.   HECKEWELDER, Rev. John. *A narrative of the mission of the United Brethren among the Delaware and Mohegan Indians, from its commencement in the Year 1740, to the close of the Year 1808. . . .* Philadelphia: M'Carty & Davis, 1820.
HL 5–9–54
IB 5; IB 8; FB

675.   HEDERICH, Benjamin. *Graecum lexicon manuale, primum a Benjamine Hederico institutum, mox assiduo labore Sam. Potticii auctum myriade amplius verborum, postremo innumeris vitiis repurgatum plurimisque novis significatibus verborum locupletatum cura J. Augusti Ernesti, atque iterum recensitum et quamplurimum in utraque parte auctum a T. Morell. . . .* Londini: impensis C. et J. Rivington [etc.], 1821.
HL 10–28–34

676.   HEINE, Heinrich. *Letters auxiliary to the history of modern polite literature in Germany. Tr. from the German by G. W. Haven.* Boston: J. Munroe, 1836.

IN 11–19–36

677.   HEMANS, Mrs. Felicia. *The poetical works of Mrs. F. Hemans.* 2 vols. Philadelphia: Thos. T. Ash, 1832.
TL
"The Landing of the Pilgrim Fathers in New England"
WE, 52
"The Voice of Music"
WE, 175

678.   HENNEBERT, L'Abbé J. B. See Beaurieu, Gaspard Guillard de.

679.   HENNEPIN, Louis. *Description de la Louisiane, nouvellement decouverte au sud'oüest de la Nouvelle France par ordre du roy. Avec la carte dy pays: Les moeurs et la maniere de vivre des sauvages. . . .* A Paris: Chez la veuve Sebastian Huré, 1683.
HL 5–27–58
IB 11

680.   HENNEPIN, Louis. *Voyages curieux et nouveau de Messieurs Hennepin et de La Borde, ou l'on voit une description très particuliere d'un grand pays dans l'Amerique, entre le Nouveau Mexique, et la mer Glaciale, avec une Relation curieuse des Caraibes sauvages des isles Antilles de l'Amerique, leur moeurs, coutumes, religion, &c. Le tout accompagné des cartes & figures necessaires.* Amsterdam: Aux depens de la Compagnie, 1711.
HL 12–7–58
CC, 12; IB 11; IB12

681.   HENRY, Alexander. *Travels and adventures in Canada and the Indian territories between the years 1760 and 1776.* New York: I. Riley, 1809.
CL
WE, 218–219, 275; PJ 2.15 (1842–44), 101–102 (after 8–1–44), 261–262 (after 6–20–46); JL 14.136 (6–23–52); IB 2

682.   HENTZ, Nicholas Marcellus. "Descriptions and Figures of the Araneides of the United States." *Boston Journal of Natural History*, vols. 4–6 (1843–55).

JL 5.109 (4–11–53)

Author mistranscribed as "Hassley" in JL; article continued intermittently in volumes 4, 5, and 6.

683.   HERBERT, George. *The works of George Herbert. Together with his life. The thirteenth edition corrected, with the addition of an alphabetical table.* 2 vols. London: J. Pickering, 1835–36.

"Affliction"
WE, 373
"Bitter-Sweet"
PJ 1.371 (3–11–42)
"The Church Porch"
PJ 1.4 (1837)
"Constancy"
EEM, 113 (6–30–37)
"The Elixir"
WE, 48
"Man"
PJ 1.254 (2–7–41)
"Virtue"
WE, 314
"The Windows," "Man's Medley," "Life"
ME

T's source for Herbert is unknown; Harvard owned this edition.

684. HERBERT, Henry William. *Complete manual for young sportsmen: with directions for handling the gun, rifle, and the rod; the art of shooting on the wing; the breaking, management, and hunting of the dog; the varieties and habits of game; river, lake, and sea fishing, etc., etc., etc. Prepared for the instruction and use of the youth of America. By Frank Forester [pseud.].* New York: Stringer & Townsend, 1856.

JL 7.440 (7–12–55); FB

685. HERBERT, Henry William. *Frank Forester's field sports of the United States, and British provinces, of North America.* 2 vols. New York: Stringer and Townsend, 1849.

JL 4.495 (2–27–53); IB 8; FB

686. HERIOT, George. *The history of Canada, from its first discovery, comprehending an account of the original establishment of the colony of Louisiana.* London: Printed for T. N. Longman and O. Rees, 1804.

JL 4.491 (2–9–53); IB 8; CN

687. HERNDON, Lieut. William L., and Lardner GIBBON. *Exploration of the valley of the Amazon, made under the direction of the Navy department. . . . Maps and plates.* 2 vols. Washington: R. Armstrong [etc.], public printer, 1853–54.
TL
RP, 176–177; JL 6.335–336 (6–8–54); IB 8

688. HERODOTUS. *Herodotus. A new and literal version. From the text of Baehr, with a geographical and general index. By Henry Cary, M.A.* London: H. G. Bohn, 1854.

CC, 170; IB 12; CPB2 (*c.* 1861)

689. HERRICK, Robert. *The poetical works of Robert Herrick.* 2 vols. London: William Pickering, 1825.
EL
"To Fortune"
RP, 7; PJ 1.98 (12–39); ME
"Another" in the series "Ceremonies for Christmas"
EX, 298
"Corinna's Going a Maying," "The Lily in a Christal," "To Live Merrily and Trust to Good Verses," "To the Rose," "Mrs. Eliz. Wheeler, Under the Name the Lost Shepherdess," "Casualties," "The Christian Militant," "The Rainbow; or Curious Covenant," "His Grange, or Private Wealth," "The Night-Piece. To Julia," "His Prayer to Ben Jonson," "To Sir Clipsbey Crew," "To His Verses," "Rural Charms"
ME

690.   HESIOD. *Works and Days.* In Winterton, Ralph, *Fragmenta* (q.v.).
       WE, 63

691.   HEWITSON, William Chapman. *British oology; being illustrations of the eggs of British birds. With the figures of each species as far as practicable, drawn and coloured from nature & accompanied by descriptions of the materials and situation of their nests, number of eggs, &c.* 2 vols. Newcastle-upon-Tyne: Published for the author by C. Empson, 1833–38.
       SNH 6–21–58
       CPB2

692.   HEYWOOD, Jasper. "Looke on Yon Leafe."

       CPB1 (*c.* 1841)

693.   HEYWOOD, Thomas. *The hierarchy of the blessed angels.* In Lamb, *Specimens of English dramatic poets* (q.v.).

       PJ 2.349 (Fall 1846)

694.   HEYWOODE, John. "A Praise of Her Ladye."

       CPB1 (*c.* 1841)

695.   HIGGINSON, Francis. *New England's plantation. Or, A short and true description of the commodities and discommodities of that country.* London: Printed by T.C. and R.C. for M. Sparke, 1630.
       HL 1–11–59
       IB 12

696.   "Highly Interesting from Canada." *New York Tribune*, Nov. 29, 1860, p. 6.

       JL 14.293 (12–4–60)

       Concerns a fugitive slave in Toronto.

697.   HILDRETH, Richard. *History of the United States of America.* 3 vols. New York: [n.p.], 1849.
       CL
       CC, 179–180; CN; IB 9

698.   HIND, Henry Youle. *Northwest territory. Reports of progress; together with a preliminary and general report on the Assiniboine and Saskatchewan exploration expedition, made under instruction from the provincial secretary. . . . Printed by order of the Legislature Assembly.* Toronto: Printed by J. Lovell, 1859.
       FBS
       JL 13.305 (5–20–60); CPB2; IB 12

699. HIND, Henry Youle. *Rapport sur l'exploration de la contrée situé entre le Lac Supérieur et les établissements de la Rivière Rouge.* . . . Toronto: S. Derbishire & G. Desbarats, 1858.
FBS
CPB2 (*c.* 1860)

700. *Hindu Laws.* See *Code of Gentoo laws.*

701. "The History and Mystery of Tobacco." *Harper's Magazine* 11 (June 1855): 1–18.

IB 10 (*c.* 1855)

702. *History of the erection of the monument on the grave of Myron Holley.* Utica, N.Y.: H. H. Curtis, 1844.

PJ 2.310 (Fall 1846)

703. HITCHCOCK, Edward. See Massachusetts. Geological Survey (nos. 952–953).

704. *Hitopadésa. The Hĕĕtōpădēs of Vĕĕshnŏŏ-Sărmā, in a series of connected fables, interspersed with moral, prudential, and political maxims. Tr.* . . . *by Charles Wilkins.* Bath: R. Cruttwell, 1787.
EL
WE, 124, 203, 209, 224, 275, 284; WA, 121; RP, 46; PJ 1.387–389 (3–24–42); 2.40 (1842–44); LN

705. HITTELL, Theodore. *The adventures of James Capen Adams, mountaineer and grizzly bear hunter, of California.* Boston: Crosby, Nichols, Lee and company, 1861.

IB 12 (*c.* 1861)

706. HOCCLEVE, Thomas. *Poems never before printed by Thomas Hoccleve: selected from a ms. in the possession of George Mason. With a preface, notes and glossary.* London: Printed by C. Roworth, for Leigh and Sotheby, 1796.
HL 12–1–41

707. HODGE, James Thacher. *Second annual report on the geology . . . of Maine and Massachusetts.* Augusta, Me.: Severance, 1838.

JL 9.494 (7–28–57)

708. HOGG, James. *Familiar anecdotes of Sir Walter Scott.* . . . *With a sketch of the life of the Shepherd, by S. Dewitt Bloodgood.* New York: Harper & Brothers, 1834.

EEM, 42–44; F2a

709.   HOLBROOK, John Edwards. *North American herpetology; or, A description of reptiles inhabiting the United States.* Vol. 4 of 5 vols. Philadelphia: J. Dobson, 1842.
       SNH 5–24–52
       JL 4.70 (5–24–52), 97 (6–13–52); 9.484–485 (7–20–57)

710.   HOLLAND, Josiah Gilbert. *History of western Massachusetts. The counties of Hampden, Hampshire, Franklin, and Berkshire. Embracing an outline, or general history, of the section, an account of its scientific aspects and leading interests, and separate histories of its one hundred towns.* 2 vols. Springfield: S. Bowles and company, 1855.

       JL 7.416 (6–11–55); IB 9; FB

711.   HOLMES, Abiel. *The annals of America, from the discovery by Columbus in the year 1492, to the year 1826. 2nd ed. . . .* Vol. 1 of 2 vols. Cambridge: Hilliard and Brown, 1829.

       CC, 179, 183; CN

712.   HOLT, Sestericus. *Zoological notes, and anecdotes.* London: R. Bentley, 1852.
       TL

713.   HOLTON, Isaac Farwell. *New Granada: twenty months in the Andes.* New York: Harper & brothers, 1857.

       IB 10; FB (*c.* 1857)

714.   HOMER. *Homeri Ilias cum brevi annotatione curante C. G. Heyne.* Lipsiae: in Libraria Weidmannia . . . , 1804.
       HL 9–3–35

715.   HOMER. *The Iliad and Odyssey of Homer, translated into English blank verse by the late William Cowper, esq.* Boston: Printed and published by Joseph T. Buckingham, 1814.
       IN 9–12–36

716.   HOMER. *The Iliad of Homer, from the text of Wolf with English notes, and Flaxman's designs. Edited by C. C. Felton, A.M., Eliot Professor of Greek in Harvard University.* 2d ed. Boston: Hilliard, Gray and company, 1834.
       TL, TX
       WE, 65, 66, 92, 93, 94; WA, 144; CC, 51, 94, 117, 141, 156, 166; EX, 181–182; PJ 1.31 (3–3–38), 34 (3–4–38), 57–58 (10–24–38); 2.160 (7–14–45), 172–173 (after 8–6–45), 234 (4–17–46), 332 (Fall 1846); JL 3.245 (1–28–52)

717.   HOMER. *The Iliad of Homer, translated from the Greek by Alexander Pope, in two volumes.* Baltimore: Published by

Philip H. Nicklin, Fielding Lucas, Jun. and Samuel Jefferis; also New York: M. & W. Ward, 1812.
TL

For T's references, see preceding entry.

718.   HOMER. *The Iliads and Odysses of Homer. Translated out of Greek into English by Tho. Hobbes of Mamsbury. The 2nd edition.* London: Printed for Will. Crook, at the Green Dragon, without Temple-Barre, 1677.
HL 4–28–36

719.   HOMER. *The Odyssey. Translated from the Greek by Alexander Pope.* Georgetown, D.C., and Philadelphia: Richards & Mallory & Nicklin, 1813.
TL
EX, 291

720.   *Homes of American authors; comprising anecdotical, personal, and descriptive sketches, by various writers.* . . . New-York: G. P. Putnam and co., 1853.
AL
JL 4.427 (12–9–52); 1B7

721.   HOOKER, Sir William Jackson. *Flora Boreali Americana.* . . . 2 vols. London: H. G. Bohn, 1850–51.

JL 5.49 (3–24–53); 8.458 (8–9–56); 12.202 (6–13–59)

T saw this work at the Astor Library in New York in 1856.

722.   HOOPER, Ellen. "The Wood-Fire." *The Dial* 1 (Oct. 1840): 193.

WA, 254–255

723.   HORACE. *Quinti Horatii Flacci Opera. Accedunt clavis metrica et notae anglicae juventuti accomodatae. By B. A. Gould.* Bostoniae: sumptibus Hilliard, Gray, Little et Wilkins, 1833.
TX

724.   HORACE. *Quinti Horatii Flacci Opera omnia ex editione J. C. Zeunii, cum notis et interpretatione in usum delphini, variis lectionibus, notis variorum, recensu editionum et codicum et indice locupletissimo accurante recensita.* . . . Londini: curante et imprimente A. J. Valpy, A.M., 1825.
TL, TX
RP, 7; PJ 1.98 (12–39); ME

725. HORNE, Richard Henry. *A new spirit of the age.* 2 vols. London: Smith, Elder and Co., 1844.

PJ 2.189 (after 12–23–45)

726. HOUGHTON, Jacob, Jr., and T. W. BRISTOL. *Reports of Wm. A. Burt and Bela Hubbard, esqs., on the geography, topography, and geology of the U.S. surveys of the mineral region of the south shore of Lake Superior, for 1845; accompanied by a list of mineral locations and a correct map of the mineral region . . . also a chart of Lake Superior, reduced from the British admiralty survey. . . .* Detroit: Printed by C. Wilcox, 1846.
TL

727. HOWARD, Alfred, ed. See Chesterfield, Philip Dormer Stanhope.

728. HOWARD, Henry, earl of Surrey. In Hall, S.C., *The book of gems* (q.v.).
"Description of Spring"
ME (*c.* 1837)

729. HOWITT, William. *The book of the seasons, or The calendar of nature.* London: Henry Colburn and Richard Bentley, 1831.

EEM, 26–36 (3–31–36); JL 5.106 (4–9–53); 6.112 (2–9–54); CPB2

730. HOWITT, William. *A boy's adventures in the wild of Australia; or, Herbert's notebook.* Boston: Ticknor and Fields, 1855.
CL
JL 9.291 (3–13–57); IB 10

731. HOWITT, William. *Land, labor and gold; or, Two years in Victoria; with visits to Sidney and Van Diemen's Land.* 2 vols. Boston: Ticknor and Fields, 1855.
CL
RP, 164–166; JL 7.491–496 (10–19–55), 500–501 (10–20–55); IB 9; FB

732. HOY, P. R. "Notes on the Ornithology of Wisconsin." *Transactions of the Wisconsin State Agricultural Society* 2 (1852): 341–364.

TMJ

733. HUBBARD, William. *A general history of New England, from the discovery to MDCLXXX. . . . 2nd ed., collated with the original ms. . . .* Boston: C. C. Little and J. Brown, 1848.

IB 2 (*c.* 1849)

734. HUBBARD, William. *A Narrative of the Indian wars in New England, from the first planting thereof in the year 1607, to the year 1677, containing a relation of the occasion, rise, and progress of the war with the Indians, in the southern, western, eastern, and northern parts of the said country.* Worcester, Mass.: Printed by Daniel Greenleaf for Joseph Wilder, 1801.
TL

735. HUC, Évariste Régis. *A journey through the Chinese empire.* 2 vols. New York: Harper & brothers, 1855.
CL
CN; FB (*c.* 1855)

736. HUC, Évariste Régis. *Recollections of a journey through Tartary, Thibet, and China, during the years 1844, 1845, and 1846 . . . a reprint of the translation by Mrs. Percy Sinnett.* New York: D. Appleton & company, 1852.

WA, 59; EX, 218, 228; JL 3.474 (4–28–52), 485 (4–30–52); 4.15 (5–3–52)

737. HUDSON, Henry. "Extract from the Journal of the Voyages of the Half-Moon, Henry Hudson, Master, from the Netherlands to the Coast of North-America, in the Year 1609." *Collections of the New York Historical Society,* 2d ser., vol. 1 (1841): 317–322.

IB 5 (*c.* 1851)

738. HUGHES, William. *An atlas of classical geography . . . with a sketch of ancient geography and other additions by the American editor. Containing fifty-two maps and plans in twenty-six plates, with an index of places.* Philadelphia: Blanchard & Lea, 1856.
TL

739. HUMBOLDT, Alexander, Freiherr von. *Cosmos; sketch of a physical description of the universe. Translated under the superintendence of Edward Sabine [by Mrs. Sabine].* 4 vols. London: H. G. Bohn, 1849.

LN (*c.* 1849)

740. HUMBOLDT, Alexander, Freiherr von. *Views of nature; or, Contemplations on the sublime phenomena of creation. With scientific illustrations. Tr. from the German. By C. W. Otte and Henry G. Bohn.* London: H. G. Bohn, 1849.

CC, 95; MW, 151; EX, 92; PJ 3 (Fall 1849)

741. HUMBOLDT, Alexander, Freiherr von, and Aimé BONPLAND. *Personal narrative of travels to the equinoctial regions of America, during the years 1799–1804. Tr. and ed. by Thomasina Ross.* 3 vols. London: H. G. Bohn, 1852.
CL
FB (*c.* 1852)

742. HUME, Alexander. In Sibbald, *Chronicle of Scottish poetry* (q.v.).
"Thanks for a Summer Day"
WE, 89–90

743. HUNNIS, William. In *England's Helicon* (q.v.).
"Wodenfride's Song in Praise of Amargana," "Another of the Same"
CPBI (*c.* 1841)

744. HUNT, Robert. *The poetry of science. . . .* Boston: Gould, Kendall, & Lincoln, 1850.

EX, 238; JL 2.165 (2–18–51)

745. HUNTER, John D. *Manners and customs of several Indian tribes located west of the Mississippi, including some account of the soil, climate, and Indian materia medica. . . .* Philadelphia: Printed and published for the author by J. Maxwell, 1823.
TL
FB (*c.* 1856)

746. HUNTER, John D. *Memoirs of a captivity among the Indians of North America, from childhood to the age of nineteen; with anecdotes descriptive of their manners and customs. . . .* London: Printed for Longman, Hurst, Rees, Orme, and Brown, 1823.
HL 12–7–54
IB 8; FB

747. HUTCHINSON, Thomas. *The history of the colony of Massachusetts-Bay, from the first settlement thereof in 1628, until its incorporation with the colony of Plimouth, province of Main, &c. by the charter of King William and Queen Mary, in 1691. . . .* 3d ed. Boston, New-England: Printed by Thomas John Fleet at the Heart and Crown in Cornhill, 1764.

CL
WE, 82, 252; JL 2.354 (7–27–51); IB 2

748. *Indian narratives: containing a correct and interesting history of the Indian wars, from the landing of our pilgrim fathers, 1620, to Gen. Wayne's victory, 1794.* Claremont, N.H.: [n.p.], 1854.
TL

749. "Indians of North America." *North American Review* 22 (Jan. 1826): 53–119.

IB 12 (*c.* 1859)

Anonymous review of John D. Hunter, *Manners and Customs of Several Indian Tribes* (q.v.), and John Halkett, *Historical Notes Respecting the Indians of North America* (q.v.).

750. "Interesting Discovery." *Littel's Living Age* 63 (Oct. 1859): 146.

IB 12 (*c.* 1861)

Anonymous article on the discovery of the tomb of a Celtic chieftain near Paris.

751. IRIARTE Y OROPESA, Tomás de. *Fábulas literarias de D. Tomas de Iriarte. Conteniendo todas las fábulas literarias póstumas del autor. Reimpreso de la edicion de Madrid de 1830. . . . En seguida se hallará la obra maestra dramática, intitulada El sí de las niñas, de D. Leandro Fernandez de Moratin. Reimpresa de la última edicion corregida por el autor. . . . Preparado . . . por F. Sales. . . .* Boston: S. Burdett y cía., 1833.
TL

752. IRVING, Theodore. *The conquest of Florida, by Hernando de Soto.* New York: G. P. Putnam, 1851.

IB 8 (*c.* 1854)

753. IRVING, Washington. *A chronicle of the conquest of Granada, From the mss. of Fray Antonio Agapida.* 2 vols. London: J. Murray, 1829.
HL 2–12–34

754. IRVING, Washington. *The Crayon miscellany. No. 2 containing: Abbotsford and Newstead Abbey.* 3 vols. Philadelphia: Carey, Lea and Blanchard, 1835.

F1b (*c.* 1835)

755.   IRVING, Washington. *History of the life and voyages of Christopher Columbus.* 4 vols. London: J. Murray, 1831.
        HL 1–8–34

756.   IRVING, Washington. *Mahomet and his successors.* 2 vols. New York: George P. Putnam, 1850.

        JL 2.180 (4–21–51)

757.   IRVING, Washington. *The Rocky mountains; or, Scenes, incidents, and adventures in the far west; digested from the journal of Capt. B.L.E. Bonneville.* . . . 2 vols. Philadelphia: Carey, Lea, and Blanchard, 1837.

        HM 13201

758.   IRVING, Washington. *Voyages and discoveries of the companions of Columbus.* Philadelphia: Carey & Lea, 1831.
        HL 1–22–34

759.   IŚVARAKRSNA. *The Sánkhya Káriká; or, Memorial verses on the Sánkhya philosophy, by Iswara Krishna. Translated from the Sanscrit by Henry Thomas Colebrooke. Also the Bháshya or commentary of Gaurapáda* . . . . Oxford: Printed for the Oriental Translation Fund of Great Britain and Ireland by S. Collingwood; London: A. J. Valpy, 1837.
        TL; HL 1–28–50
        WE, 382–383; JL 2.192 (5–6–51); CPBI

760.   IVIMEY, Joseph. *John Milton: his life and times, religious and political opinions; with an appendix containing animadversions upon Dr. Johnson's Life of Milton, etc., etc.* New York: D. Appleton & co., 1833.
        IN *c.* 11–36 & 6–25–37

761.   JACKMAN, William. *The Australian captive; or, an authentic narrative of fifteen years in the life of William Jackman.* . . . Auburn: Derby & Miller; Buffalo: Derby, Orton, & Mulligan, 1853.

        IB 8 (*c.* 1854)

762.   JACKSON, Charles T. Untitled contribution to *Proceedings of the Boston Society of Natural History* 4 (1851–54): 241.

        CPB2 (*c.* 1858)

763.   JACKSON, Charles T. See Maine. Report of the State Geologist.

764.   JACKSON, Robert Montgomery Smith. *The mountain.* Phila-
        delphia: J. B. Lippincott & co., 1860.
        TL

765.   JACOBS, Friedrich. *The Greek reader, by Frederic Jacobs....
        From the 7th German ed., adapted to the translation of Butt-
        man's Greek grammar.* 3d Boston ed. Boston: Hilliard, Gray,
        Little, Wilkins, 1829.
        TX

766.   JAEGER, Prof. Benedict, and H. C. PRESTON. *The life of North
        American insects, illustrated by numerous colored engravings
        and narratives. By Prof. B. Jaeger assisted by H. C. Preston,
        M.D.* 8 vols. Providence: Sayles, Miller and Simons, printers,
        1854.
        TL

767.   JAIMINI. *Aphorisms of the Mímánsá philosophy, by Jaimini.
        With extracts from the commentaries. In Sanscrit and Eng-
        lish....* Allahabad: Presbyterian mission press, 1851.
        TL

768.   JAMBLICHUS, of Calchis. *Jamblichus' Life of Pythagoras, or,
        Pythagoric life. Accompanied by fragments of the ethical
        writing of certain Pythagoreans in the Doric dialect; and a
        collection of Pythagoric sentences from Stobaeus and others,
        which are omitted by Gole in his Opuscula mythologica, and
        have not been noticed by any editor. Tr. from the Greek. By
        Thomas Taylor....* London: Printed by A. J. Valpy, and sold
        by the author, 1818.

        WE, 71, 176, 317; PJ 1.395 (3–28–42); LN

769.   JAMES, George Payne Rainsford. *The history of Charlemagne.*
        New York: J. & J. Harper, 1833.
        TL

770.   JAMES THE FIRST, King of Scotland. *The works of James I,
        king of Scotland, Containing The kings quair, Christis kirk of
        the grene, and Peblis to the play....* Perth: Printed by
        R. Morison, junior, for R. Morison and son, and sold by
        G.G.J. and J. Robinson, London, 1786.
        HL 12–8–41

771.   JAMIESON, Robert. *Popular ballads and songs, from tradition,
        manuscripts and scarce editions; with translations of similar
        pieces from the ancient Danish language, and a few originals
        by the editor.* 2 vols. Edinburgh: A. Constable and co.; [etc.
        etc.], 1806.
        HL 12–8–41
        ME

772.   JARDINE, Sir William, ed. *The naturalist's library.* 40 vols. Edinburgh: W. H. Lizars [etc., etc.], 1845–60.

JL 6.183 (4–3–54)

See also Hamilton, Robert.

773.   JEFFERSON, Thomas. *Notes on the state of Virginia. With an appendix.* 8th American ed. Boston: Printed by David Carlisle, for Thomas & Andrews, 1801.
HL 11–7–60
IB 12

774.   JENNINGS, C. *The eggs of British birds, displayed in a series of engravings, copied and coloured from nature, with descriptions of British birds. . . . The illustrations by Dickes.* 2d ed. Bath [Eng.]: Binns and Goodwin, [etc., etc.], 1853.
TL

775.   JESSE, Edward. *Gleanings in natural history.* Second series. London: J. Murray, 1834.
SNH 12–10–58
CPB2

776.   *Jesuit Relations. Relation de ce qui s'est passé en la Nouvelle France, en l'années 1633–1672.* Paris: [imprint varies], 1633–72. [Issued irregularly; title varies.]

T probably read all the *Jesuit Relations* that HL owned. Cameron, in "Books Thoreau Borrowed," was unable to determine HL's exact holdings, but T withdrew or consulted all the volumes for the period 1633–72 between 1852 and 1857, and made extensive extracts in his IBs. Authors of individual relations are cited, with T's references, by name. See Brebeuf, Buteux, Dablon, Lallemant, Le Jeune, Le Mercier, Perrault, Quens, Rageneau, and Vimont.

777.   JĪMŪTAVĀHANA. *Two treatises on the Hindu law of inheritance, tr. by H. T. Colebrooke.* Calcutta: Hindoostanee press, 1810.
TL

778.   JOGUES, Isaac. See Shea, John G. (no. 1234).

779.   JOHNSON, Anna C. *The Iroquois; or, The bright side of Indian character. By Minnie Myrtle (pseud.).* New York: D. Appleton and company, 1855.

IB 11 (c. 1857)

780.   JOHNSON, Edward. *A history of New-England. From the English planting in the yeere 1628. Untill the yeere 1652. Declaring the form of their government, civill, military, and ecclesiastique.* . . . London: Printed for Nath. Brooke, 1654.
HL 3–13–54
WE, 10–11; WA, 38–39; JL 6.198 (4–15–54); IB 8

Popular title is *Wonder-Working Providence of Sion's Savior in New England.*

781.   JOHNSON, Samuel. *Life of Sir Thomas Browne.* In Browne's *Works* (q.v.), vol. 1.
WE, 68

782.   JOHNSON, Samuel. *The lives of the most eminent English poets; with critical observations on their works. In four volumes. A new edition, corrected.* London: Printed for C. Bathurst, J. Buckland, [etc., etc.], 1783.
HL 3–30–37 (vol. 1)

783.   JOHNSON, Samuel. "Preface," *The plays of William Shakespeare. With the corrections and illustrations of various commentators. To which are added, notes by Samuel Johnson and George Steevens. The 4th ed. Rev. and augm. (with a glossarial index) by the editor of Dodsley's collection of old plays.* 15 vols. London: T. Longman, B. Law and son, [etc.] 1793.

F1b (*c.* 1835)

784.   JOHNSON, Samuel. *Works. New ed., with an essay on his life and genius, by Arthur Murphy.* 12 vols. London: Hanford, Strahan and Preston, etc., 1806.
EL
EEM, 71, 75

T also refers to *Rasselas,* though only in passing, in EX, 135.

785.   JOHNSON, Samuel, and John WALKER. *A dictionary of the English language: by Samuel Johnson and John Walker. With the pronunciation greatly simplified, and on an entirely new plan; and with the addition of several thousand words. By R. S. Jameson. Second edition, revised and corrected.* London: J. O. Robinson, 1828.
TL

786.   JONES, Sir William. See Manu. *Institutes of Hindu Law.*

787.   JONES, Sir William. *The Works of Sir William Jones. With a life of the author, by Lord Teignmouth.* . . . 13 vols. London: Printed for J. Stockdale [etc.], 1807.
HL 1–28–50 (vol. 9)
CPB1

T's extracts are from Calidas's *Sacontala, or The Fatal Ring* (q.v.); see also no. 796.

788.   JONES, William. "A Topographical Description of Concord." *Collections of the Massachusetts Historical Society*, 1st ser., vol. 1 (1792; rpt. 1806): 237–242.
WA, 198; PJ 3 (Fall 1849)

789.   JONSON, Ben. *The works of Ben Jonson . . . adorn'd with cuts. . . . 6 vols.* London: Printed for J. Walthoe, M. Wotton, J. Nicholson [etc.], 1716.
EL
HM 13201
Cataline
PJ 1.254–261 (2–41)
Every Man in His Humor
PJ 1.334 (9–20–41)
Hymenaei
WE, 105; PJ 1.295 (3–30–40)
"Love Freed from Ignorance and Folly"
EX, 226; LN
"To My Muse"
PJ 1.261 (2–9–41)
"To Thomas Lord Chancellor"
PJ 1.262 (2–10–41)
"On Gut"
PJ 1.278 (3–4–41)
"To Sir Ralph Shelton"
PJ 1.278 (3–4–41)
"On Lucy, Countess of Bedford," "To Elizabeth, Countess of Rutland," "An Epitaph on S.P. a Child of Queen Elizabeth's Chapel," "Epitaph on Elizabeth, L.H.," "To John Donne," "To Benjamin Rudyerd," "The Masque of Queens," "The Golden Age Restored. In a Masque at Court, 1615"
LN

790.   JOSSE, M. Augustin Louis. *A grammar of the Spanish language. With practical exercises. Revised, emended, improved and enlarged by F. Sales.* 7th American ed. Boston: Munroe and Francis, [etc., etc.] 1836.
TL

791.   JOSSELYN, John. *An account of two voyages to New England. . . . A large chronological table of the most remarkable passages, from the first discovering of the continent of America, to the year 1673.* 2d ed. London: Printed for G. Widdows, 1675.
HL 1–19–54
MW, 141, 148; CC, 76; JL 2.273 (6–9–51); 3.34 (9–28–51); 6.74 (1–19–54), 76 (1–23–54), 108 (2–8–54); 7.108 (1–9–55); FB; IB 8

T also knew Josselyn's work in the version reprinted in the *Collections of the Massachusetts Historical Society*, 3d ser., vol. 3 (1833): 211–354.

792. JOSSELYN, John. *New Englands rarities discovered: in birds, beasts, fishes, serpents, and plants of that country. Together with the physical and chryurical remedies wherewith natives constantly use to cure their distempers, wounds and sores.* . . . London: Printed for G. Widdowes, 1672.
HL 1–14–51
IB 4

793. *Ju-kiao-li: or, The two fair cousins. A Chinese novel. From the French version of Jean Pierre Abel Rémusat.* London: Hunt and Clark, 1827.

JL 11.65–66 (7–29–58), 81 (8–7–58)

794. JUVENAL. *D. Junii Juvenalis et A. Persii Flacci satirae. Interpretatione ac notis illustravit Ludovicus Prateus . . . jussu christianissimi regis, in usum serenissimi delphini.* Ed. prima americana. Philadelphia: impensis M. Carey, 1814.
TL

For references to Persius, see Persius Flaccus, Aulus.

795. JUVENAL. *D. Junii Juvenalis Satirae expurgatae. Accedunt notae anglicae. In usum scholae bostoniensis. Cura F. P. Leverett.* Bostoniae: Hilliard, Gray, Little, et Wilkins, 1828.
TX

796. KĀLIDĀSA. *Śakoontalá; or The lost ring: an Indian drama, translated into English prose and verse, from the Sanskrit of Kálidása: by M. Williams.* Hertford: S. Austin, 1855.
TL

Part of the collection of orientalia given to T by Thomas Cholmondeley. T had earlier (in 1850) read and taken notes on the version translated by Sir William Jones (q.v.).

797. KALM, Per. See Bartram, John.

798. KALM, Pehr. *Travels into North America; containing its natural history, and a circumstantial account of its plantations and agriculture in general, with the civil, ecclesiastical and commercial state of the country, the manners of the inhabitants, several curious and important remarks on various subjects. . . . Translated into English by John Reinhold Forster.* 3 vols. London: The editor, 1770–71.
HL 8–11–51
EX, 21, 30, 39, 49, 65–66; CC, 99, 158; JL 2.463 (9–5–51), 466 (9–6–51); CN; IB 4; IB 5

799.   KALM, Peter. See Kalm, Pehr.

800.   KANE, Elisha Kent. *Arctic explorations: the second Grinnell*
        expedition in search of Sir John Franklin, 1853, '54, '55 . . .
        illustrated by upwards of three hundred engravings, from
        sketches by the author. . . . 2 vols. Philadelphia: Childs & Pe-
        terson, [etc., etc.] 1856.
        TL
        JL 9.192–193 (12–21–56), 200 (12–28–56); 11.16–61 pas-
        sim; (7–6 to 7–19–58); IB 10; FB

801.   KANE, Elisha Kent. *The U.S. Grinnell expedition in search of*
        Sir John Franklin. A personal narrative. New York: Harper &
        brothers, 1853.
        CL
        WA, 321; EX, 197; JL 6.139–140 (2–26–54); IB 8; FB

802.   KEACH, Benjamin. *The glorious lover. A divine poem, upon*
        the adorable mystery of sinners redemption. By B.K., author
        of War with the Devil. . . . London: Printed by J.D. for
        C. Hussey, 1679.
        HL 12–9–41

803.   KEATS, John. See Coleridge, Samuel T. (no. 324).

804.   KEMBLE, Frances Ann (Fanny). *A year of consolation. By*
        Mrs. Butler, late Fanny Kemble. 2 vols. in 1. New York:
        Wiley & Putnam, 1847.

        LN (*c.* 1848)

805.   KENNEDY, Grace. *Dunallan; or, Know what you judge.* . . .
        By the author of "The decision," "Father Clement," etc., etc.
        . . . Exeter: Printed for the publishers, 1828.
        TL

        Autograph of Helen Thoreau.

806.   KING, Henry. In Campbell, Thomas, *Specimens of the British*
        poets (q.v.).
        "Sic Vita"
        ME (*c.* 1837)

807.   KIP, William Ingraham, ed. *The early Jesuit missions in North*
        America, compiled and translated from the letters of the
        French Jesuits, with notes. New York: Wiley and Putnam,
        1846.

        IB 3 (*c.* 1849)

808.   KIRBY, William, and William SPENCE. *Introduction to ento-*
        mology: or, Elements of the natural history of insects; with

plates. 4 vols. London: Longman, Hurst, Rees, Orme, and Brown, 1815–26.
SNH 10–3–52 (vol. 1) and 11–11–52 (vol. 2)
WA, 215, 231–232; JL 5.465, 467 (10–31–53)

T later owned a one-volume London 1856 edition.

809.   KIRKHAM, Samuel. *A compendium of English grammar; accompanied by an appendix.* . . . Baltimore: [n.p.], 1823.
TL

810.   KLENCKE, Hermann. *Lives of the brothers Humboldt, Alexander and William. Translated and arranged from the German . . . by Juliette Bauer.* . . . New York: Harper & brothers, 1853.

JL 5.117 (5–1–53), 120–121 (5–4–53)

811.   KNAPP, John Leonard. *The journal of a naturalist.* . . . Philadelphia: Carey & Lea, 1831.
TL
JL 7.224 (3–1–55); 10.5 (8–8–57)

812.   KNEELAND, Samuel, Jr. "On the Birds of Keweenaw Point, Lake Superior." In *Proceedings of the Boston Society of Natural History* 6 (1857): 231–241.

JL 10.248 (1–15–58)

813.   KNOX, Vicesimus. *Elegant extracts; or, useful and entertaining passages in prose.* 2d ed. Dublin: P. Byrne, 1793.
TL

T also withdrew a two-volume London 1800 edition from HL on 4–23–34.

814.   KRAITSIR, Charles V. *Glossology: being a treatise on the nature of language and on the language of nature.* New York: G. P. Putnam, 1852.
EL
FB

815.   KRAITSIR, Charles V. *The significance of the alphabet.* Boston: E. P. Peabody, 1846.
TL

816.   KRAPF, Ludwig. *Travels, researches, and missionary labours during an eighteen years' residence in eastern Africa.* . . . *With an appendix respecting the snow-capped mountains of eastern Africa; the sources of the Nile; the languages and litera-*

ture of Abessinia and eastern Africa, etc., etc. . . . . Boston: Ticknor & Fields, 1860.

CPB2 (*c.* 1860)

817. LA FONTAINE, Jean de. *Fables.*
TL

Edition unknown.

818. LA HONTAN, Louis Armand, Baron de. *Voyages du baron de La Hontan dans l'Amerique Septentrionale, qui contiennent une rélation des différens peuples qui y habitent; la nature de leur gouvernement; leur commerce; leurs coûtumes* . . . *2nd éd., revue, corigée, & augmentée.* 2 vols.; vol. 2 has the title "Memoires de l'Amerique Septentrionale. . . ." Amsterdam: Chez F. l'Honoré, 1705.
HL 2–2–52
EX, 43, 67; COR, 621 (6–25–61); JL 3.287 (2–7–52), 337 (3–6–52); IB 5; FB

819. LA POTHERIE, Claude C. le Roy Bacqueville de. See Bacqueville de la Potherie, Claude C. Le Roy.

820. LABAUME, Eugène. *Circumstantial narrative of the campaign in Russia.* . . . *Tr. from the French.* Hartford, Conn.: S. Andrus and Son, 1852.
SL
JL 8.27–28 (11–17–55)

821. LA BORDE, Sieur de. *Relation des Caraibes.* In Hennepin, *Voyages curieux* (q.v.).
HL 12–7–58
CC, 122–123

822. LACROIX, Silvestre François. *An elementary treatise on arithmetic.* . . . 4th ed., rev. and cor. Boston: Hilliard, Gray, and company, 1834.
TX

823. LAET, Joannes de. "Extracts from the New World or a Description of the West Indies." *Collections of the New York Historical Society,* 2d ser., vol. 1 (1841): 281–316.
HL 8–11–51
CN; IB 5

824. LAET, Joannes de. *Novis orbis, seu Descriptionis Indiae Occidentalis, libri XVII. Authore Joanne de Laet Antwerp. Novis tabulis geographicis et variis animantium, plantarum fructu-*

umque icontibus illustratii cum privilegio. Ludg. Batav.: apud Elzevirios, A., 1633.
HL 1–14–51
CN

825.   LAING, Malcolm. "Dissertation on the Poems of Ossian." In Macpherson, James, *The Genuine Remains of Ossian* (q.v.).
CPBI (*c.* 1843)

826.   LAING, Samuel. *Journal of a residence in Norway during the years 1834, 1835, & 1836; made with a view to enquire into the moral and political economy of that country . . . and the condition of its inhabitants. . . .* 2d ed. London: Printed for Longman, Orme, Brown, Green and Longmans, 1837.

WA, 27

827.   LAING, Samuel. See Sturluson, Snorri.

828.   LALLEMANT, Jérôme. In *Jesuit Relations* (q.v.) for 1647–48.
HL 1–26–57
EX, 22, 96; MW 34n, 104; IB 10

829.   LALLEMANT, Jérôme. In *Jesuit Relations* (q.v.) for 1661–62.
HL 1–13–58
MW 282–283; IB 10; IB 11

830.   LAMB, Charles. *Elia. Essays which have appeared under that name in the London magazine.* Philadelphia: Carey, Lea, & Carey, 1828.

"Distant Correspondents"
COR, 9 (8–5–36)

831.   LAMB, Charles. "Specimens from the Writings of Fuller." In *The prose works of Charles Lamb.* 3 vols. London: Edward Moxon, 1838.

WE, 250, 388; PJ 2.351 (Fall 1846)

832.   LAMB, Charles. *Specimens of English dramatic poets, who lived about the time of Shakespeare.* New York: Wiley and Putnam, 1845.
EL
PJ 2.349 (Fall 1846); LN

833.   LANDOR, Walter Savage. *Imaginary conversations of literary men and statesmen. 2nd ed., corr. and enl.* 3 vols. London: Henry Colburn, 1826–28.
EL
PJ 2.189 (after 12–23–45); JL 7.160–161 (2–1–55)

834.   LANE, Edward William. *An account of the manners and cus-toms of the modern Egyptians, written in Egypt during the years 1833, '34, and '35, partly from notes made during a former visit to that country in the years 1825, '26, '27, '28. Reprinted from the third edition containing large additions and improvements.* 3 vols. London: Charles Knight & co., 1846.
CL
IB 12; CPB2 (*c.* 1860)

835.   LANGLAND, Robert. *Piers Ploughman.*

EEM, 90 (3–17–37)

836.   LANGTOFT, Peter. See Peter of Langtoft.

837.   LAPHAM, I. A. "Flora and Fauna of Wisconsin." *Transactions of the Wisconsin State Agricultural Society* 2 (1852): 337–419.

TMJ

838.   LARDNER, Dionysius. *Popular lectures on science and art; de-livered in the principal cities and towns of the United States.* 15th ed. New York: H. W. Law, 1856.
TL
CPB2 (*c.* 1857)

839.   LAVATER, Johann Caspar. *Aphorisms on man. . . .* 3d ed. London: J. Johnson, 1794.

ME (*c.* 1840)

840.   LAWRENCE, Rev. Nathaniel. "Historical Sketch of Tyngsboro, Middlesex, Mass." *Collections of the Massachusetts Histori-cal Society*, 2d ser., vol. 4 (1846): 192–198.

WE, 197

841.   LAWSON, John. *The history of Carolina.* In Stevens, John, *A New Collection of Voyages and Travels* (q.v.).
HL 12–22–56
JL 8.308 (4–24–56); 9.451 (6–21–57); IB 10; FB

T also cites a "London 1714" edition in a list at the end of IB 5.

842.   LAYARD, Sir Austen Henry. *Discoveries among the ruins of Nineveh and Babylon; with travels in Armenia, Kurdistan, and the Desert; being the results of a second expedition un-dertaken for the trustees of the British museum.* New York: Harper & brothers, 1853.

COR, 313 (12–22–53); JL 6.9 (12–3–53), 11 (12–5–53), 15 (12–9–53); 9.214 (1–11–57), 261 (2–15–57); 12.92–93 (3–28–59), 340 (9–22–59); CPB2.

843.   LAYARD, Sir Austen Henry. *Nineveh and its remains; with an account of a visit to the Chaldean Christians of Kurdistan, and the Yezidis, or Devil-Worshippers; and an inquiry into the manner of arts of the ancient Assyrians.* 2 vols. New York: G. P. Putnam, 1849.
    TL
    CC, 41; JL 2.35 (between 6–9 and 6–20–50)

844.   LE CONTE, John. "Observations on a Remarkable Exudation of Ice from the Stems of Vegetables." In *Annual of Scientific Discovery*, 1851 (q.v.).

    FB (*c.* 1853)

845.   LE JEUNE, Paul. In *Jesuit Relations* (q.v.) for 1633.
    HL 10–5–52
    JL 4.388 (10–15–52); CN; IB 6

846.   LE JEUNE, Paul. In *Jesuit Relations* (q.v.) for 1634.
    HL 10–5–52
    IB 6; IB 7

847.   LE JEUNE, Paul. In *Jesuit Relations* (q.v.) for 1635.
    HL 11–11–52
    IB 7

848.   LE JEUNE, Paul. In *Jesuit Relations* (q.v.) for 1636.
    HL 11–11–52
    JL 4.442 (1–2–53), 456 (1–7–53); IB 7

849.   LE JEUNE, Paul. In *Jesuit Relations* (q.v.) for 1637.
    HL 12–30–52
    IB 8

850.   LE JEUNE, Paul. In *Jesuit Relations* (q.v.) for 1638.
    HL 12–30–52
    IB 8

851.   LE JEUNE, Paul. In *Jesuit Relations* (q.v.) for 1639.
    HL 12–7–54
    IB 8

852.   LE JEUNE, Paul. In *Jesuit Relations* (q.v.) for 1640.
    HL 2–9–53
    IB 8

853.   LE JEUNE, Paul. In *Jesuit Relations* (q.v.) for 1656–57.
       HL 1–26–57
       IB 10

854.   LE MERCIER, François. In *Jesuit Relations* (q.v.) for 1652–53.
       HL 1–26–57
       IB 10

855.   LE MERCIER, François. In *Jesuit Relations* (q.v.) for 1653–54.
       HL 1–26–57
       IB 10

856.   LE MERCIER, François. In *Jesuit Relations* (q.v.) for 1664–65.
       HL 1–13–58
       IB 11

857.   LE MERCIER, François. In *Jesuit Relations* (q.v.) for 1667–68.
       HL 4–25–58
       IB 11

858.   LE MERCIER, François. In *Jesuit Relations* (q.v.) for 1669–70.
       HL 4–25–58
       IB 11

859.   "Lecture on Central Africa." *New York Tribune*, Oct. 8,
       1858, p. 8.

       IB 11

860.   LEGENDRE, Adrien Marie. *Elements of geometry. Tr. from the
       French for the use of the students of the University at Cam-
       bridge, New England . . . by John Farrar. . . .* Boston: Hil-
       liard, Gray, Little & Wilkins, 1831.
       TL

       Autograph of John Thoreau, Jr.

861.   LELARGE DE LIGNAC, Joseph Adrien. *Lettres à un Amériquain
       sur l'histoire naturelle générale et particuliere de monsieur de
       Buffon. . . . 9 pts. in 4 v. . . .* A Hambourg, et se trouve à
       Paris chez Duchesne, 1751–56.

       EX, 222.

862.   LEMPRIERE, John. *A classical dictionary, containing a copious
       account of all the proper names mentioned in ancient authors,
       with the value of coins, weights, and measures among the
       Greeks and Romans, and a chronological table. . . .* 6th ed.,
       cor. London: T. Cadell, 1806.

TL
PJ 1.26–27 (2–7–38); FB

Many editions available.

863.   LEONARD, Levi Washburn. *The literary and scientific class book, embracing the leading facts and principles of science. . . . Selected from John Platts' literary and scientific class book. . . .* Keene, N.H.: J. Prentiss, 1826.
TL

Autograph of Helen Thoreau.

864.   LESCARBOT, Marc. *Histoire de la Novvelle-France. Contenant les navigations, déscouvertes, & habitations faites par les François és Indes Occidentales & Nouvelle-France souz l'avoeu & authorité de noz roys tres-chrétiens. . . . Seconde édition, revevuë, corrigée, & augmentée par l' autheur.* A Paris: Chez Jean-Millot, 1612. Avec privilege du roy.
HL 11–18–50
CC, 190–191; MW, 60; CN; IB 4

865.   LESCARBOT, Marc. "The Voyage of Monsieur de Monts." In Purchas, Samuel, *Purchas his Pilgrimes* (q.v.).

MW, 54; CC, 189–190

866.   LESLEY, J. Peter. *Manual of coal and its topography. Illustrated by original drawings, chiefly of facts in the geology of the Appalachian region of the United States of North America.* Philadelphia: J. B. Lippincott, 1856.
TL

867.   LEVETT, Christopher. "A Voyage into New England, Begun in 1623 and Ended in 1624." *Collections of the Massachusetts Historical Society,* 3d ser., vol. 8 (1843): 59–90.

IB 2 (c. 1849)

868.   LEWIS, Meriwether, and William CLARK. *History of the expedition under the command of Captains Lewis and Clark to the sources of the Missouri, thence across the Rocky mountains, and down the Columbia to the Pacific Ocean. Performed during the years 1804, 1805, and 1806, by order of the government of the United States. Prepared for the press by Paul Allen, esquire. . . .* 2 vols. Philadelphia: Pub. by Bradford and Inskeep, 1814.
TL

869.   *The Liberator* (Boston).

RP, 122; JL 12.407 (10–19–59)

T read the accounts of John Brown's raid on Harper's Ferry and its aftermath in the issues for October 1859.

870.   *Liberty and anti-slavery songbook.* Boston: King, 1842.
TL

871.   LIEBER, Francis. "Vocal Sounds of Laura Bridgeman. . . ." *Smithsonian contributions to knowledge,* vol. 2. Washington: Smithsonian Institute, 1851.

IB 8 (*c.* 1852)

872.   LIEBIG, Justus von. *Animal chemistry: or Organic chemistry and its applications to physiology and pathology. . . .* New York: Wiley and Putnam, 1842.

WA, 13; PJ 2.143 (Fall–Winter 1845–46)

873.   "Life and Doctrine of Geoffroy St. Hilaire." *Westminster Review* 61 (1854): 84–100.

JL 6.178–179 (3–30–54)

Anonymous article which describes St. Hilaire's theory of "unity of composition" in nature, and contrasts his views to those of his more famous pupil Cuvier.

874.   LINCOLN, Mrs. Almira H. See Phelps, Mr. A. Hart Lincoln.

875.   LINCOLN, Jairus. *Anti-slavery melodies: for the friends of freedom. Prepared for the Hingham anti-slavery society by Jairus Lincoln.* Hingham, Mass.: E. B. Gill, 1843.
TL

876.   LINDLEY, John. *A natural system of botany; or, A systematic view of the organization, natural affinities, and geographical distribution of the whole vegetable kingdom. . . . 2nd ed., with numerous additions and corrections, and a complete list of genera, with their synonyms.* London: Longman, Rees, Orme, Brown, Green, and Longman, 1836.
SNH 2–2–52, 5–9–52
IB 8; FB

877.   LINDSEY, William Lauder. *A popular history of British lichens. . . .* London: L. Reeve, 1856.
TL
CC 26

878.   LINNAEUS, Carl von. See Linné, Carl von.

879.   LINNÉ, Carl von. *Amoenitates academicae; seu dissertationes variae, physicae, medicae, botanicae. Antehac seorsim editae nunc collectae et auctae cum tabulis aeniis.* 7 vols. Holmiae: [n.p.], 1749–69.
HL 5–24–52 (vol. 2)
IB 4; FB

880.   LINNÉ, Carl von. *Caroli Linnaei . . . Philosophia botanica, in qua explicantur fundamenta botanica cum definitionibus partium, exemplis terminorum, observationibus, rariorum, adjectis figuris aeniis. Edition altera.* Viennae Austriae: typis J. T. Trottner, 1763.
HL 2–2–52
CC (title page motto); JL 3.307–309 (2–16–52), 324 (2–29–52), 326 (3–1–52), 346–348 (3–12–52)

881.   LINNÉ, Carl von. *Lachesis lapponica; or, A tour of Lapland, now first published from the original manuscript journal of Linnaeus; by James Edward Smith.* London: White and Cochrane, 1811.
BA 11–1–39 (by RWE)
EX, 107; PJ 1.86 (11–22–39)

882.   "The Lion and His Kind." *Harper's Magazine* 10 (May 1855): 735–745.

JL 9.100–102 (10–4–56)

883.   LIVINGSTONE, David. *Missionary travels and researches in South Africa: including a sketch of sixteen years' residence in the interior of Africa, and a journey from the cape of Good Hope to Loanda on the west coast; thence across the continent, down the river Zambesi, to the eastern ocean. . . .* New York: Harper & brothers, 1858.
CL
IB 10; CPB2 (*c.* 1858)

884.   LOCKE, John. *An essay concerning the human understanding.*
TL, TX

Edition unknown; many available. T's library catalogue lists a "Philad. 1 v." edition, which I have been unable to locate. Locke's essay was required reading at Harvard, so the likelihood is that T purchased his copy there.

885.   LODGE, Thomas. *Glaucus and Silla. With other lyrical and pastoral poems.* Chiswick: from the press of C. Whittingham, 1819.
HL 1–5–42 (by Charles Stearns Wheeler)
LN; ME

886.   "The London and North-Western Railway." *Quarterly Review* 84 (1848–49): 1–65.

PJ 3 (*c.* 1849)

Unsigned review of Arthur Smith, *The Bubble of the Age; or, the Fallacies of Railway Investments, Railway Accounts, and Railway Dividends* (London: Sherwood, Gilbert, and Piper, 1848), the *Rules and Regulations* of the London and North Western Railway Company (1848), and *Herepath's Railway and Commercial Journal* (1848).

887.   LONG, George. *An atlas of classical geography. Constructed by William Hughes, and edited by George Long. With a sketch of classical geography and other additions, by the American editor. Containing 52 maps and plans on 26 plates, with an index of places.* Philadelphia: Blanchard and Lee, 1856.
TL

888.   LONG, Stephen H. *Voyages in a six-oared skiff to the Falls of Saint Anthony in 1817. . . .* Philadelphia: H. B. Ashmead, 1860.

TMJ

889.   LONGFELLOW, Henry Wadsworth. *Evangeline.*

CC, 182n

Edition unknown; mention is casual.

890.   LONGFELLOW, Henry Wadsworth. *Outre-mer; a pilgrimage beyond the sea.* 2 vols. New-York: Harper, 1835.

F1b (*c.* 1835)

891.   LONGFELLOW, Henry Wadsworth. "Seaweed." *Graham's Monthly Magazine* 27 (1845): 12.

CC, 53–54; PJ 2.127 (after 3–11–45)

892.   LOSKIEL, George Henry. *History of the mission of the United Brethren among the Indians in North America. . . . Tr. from the German by Christian Ignatius Latrobe.* London: The Brethren's society for the furtherance of the gospel, 1794.
HL 12–10–55
JL 8.34 (11–27–55); IB 9; IB 10; FB

893.   LOUDON, John Claudius. *Arboretum et Fruticetum Britannicum; or, The trees and shrubs of Britain, native and foreign,*

hardy and half-hardy, pictorially and botanically delineated,
and scientifically and popularly described. . . . 2d ed. 8 vols.
London: the author, 1844.
TL
CC, 81, 108; EX, 291–293, 310, 312; COR, 488 (8–17–57); JL
9.496–497 (7–30–57); 10.185 (11–15–57); 11.41–44 (7–
14–58); 12.18 (3–6–59); IB 10; FB

894.   LOUDON, John Claudius. *An encyclopedia of agriculture. . . .*
        5th ed. London: Longman, Brown, Green, and Longmans,
        1844.

        JL 8.387 (6–26–56)

895.   LOUDON, John Claudius. *Encyclopedia of plants, comprising*
        the description, specific character, culture, history, applica-
        tion in the arts and every other desirable particular respecting
        all the plants indigenous, or cultivated in, or introduced to
        Britain. . . . Ed. by J. C. Loudon. . . . London: Longman,
        Brown, Green & Longmans, 1855.
        TL; SNH 11–5–51, 2–21–52
        JL 3.220–221 (1–23–52), 229 (1–26–52), 250–252 (1–30–
        52); 4.112 (6–18–52), 394 (10–21–52); 12.18 (3–6–59); FB

        T's earlier references are to an 1841 edition.

896.   LOVELACE, Richard. In Anderson, Robert. *The Works of the*
        British Poets (q.v.).
        PJ 1.479 (10–22–43)
        "To Lucasta on Going to the Wars," "To Althea from
        Prison," "To His Dear Brother Colonel F.L.," "The Ant,"
        "The Snail," "On Mrs. Elizabeth Filmer," "Ode"
        LN

897.   LOVELL, Robert. *Sive enchiridion botanicum. Or, a compleat*
        herball. . . . 2d ed. Oxford: W.H. for Ric. Davis, 1665.
        TL

898.   LOWELL, Dr. Charles. "Notices—Communicated by Rev.
        Lowell." *Collections of the Massachusetts Historical Society,*
        4th ser., vol. 1 (1852): 90.

        CC 157; FB

899.   LUCRETIUS. *De rerum naturae.*

        JL 8.312 (4–26–56)

        Source and edition unknown.

900. LUDEWIG, Hermann Ernst. *The literature of American local history: a bibliographic essay, by Hermann E. Ludewig. . . .* New York: Printed for the author by R. Craighead, 1846.
TL

901. LYDGATE, John. In Chalmers (q.v.), vol. 1.
"The Story of Thebes"
PJ 1.399 (3–31–42)
"A Poem Against Idleness, and the History of Sardanapolus" (not in Chalmers)
WE, 57

902. LYDELL, Charles. *Principles of geology.* 5th ed. 4 vols. London: John Murray, 1837.
EL
PJ 1.187 (10–11–40), 195 (11–5–40)

903. LYELL, Charles. *A second visit to the United States of North America.* 2 vols. New York: Harper & brothers, 1849.
CL
JL 2.364 (7–31–51); IB 10

904. LYON, George Francis. *The private journal of Captain G. C. Lyon, of H.M.S. Hecla, during the recent voyage of discovery under Captain Parry.* Boston: Wels and Lilly, 1824.
TL

905. LYTTON, Edward George Earle Bulwer-Lytton, 1st baron Lytton. *Athens, its rise and fall; with views of the literature, philosophy, and social life of the Athenian people.* 2 vols. New York: Harper, 1837.
TL

906. LYTTON, Edward George Earle Bulwer-Lytton, 1st baron Lytton. *England and the English.* New York: J. & J. Harper, 1833.

F2a (*c.* 1836)

907. McCLINTOCK, Sir Francis Leopold. *The voyage of the Fox in the Arctic seas. A narrative of the discovery of the fate of Sir John Franklin and his companions. By Captain McClintock.* Boston: Ticknor and Fields, 1860.
CL
CPB2; IB 12 (*c.* 1860)

908. [McCULLOCH, John Ramsay]. *McCulloch's universal gazetteer. A dictionary, geographical, statistical, and historical. . . .* 2 vols. New York: Harper & bros., 1845–46.

EX, 49n

909.   McCulloh, James Haines. *Researches on America; being an attempt to settle some points relative to the aborigines of America, &c.* 2d ed. Baltimore: J. Robinson, 1817.
        TL; HL 1—19—54
        IB 8

910.   MacDonnel, D. E. *A dictionary of select and popular quotations, which are in daily use; taken from the Latin, French, Greek, Spanish, and Italian languages; translated into English. . . . 1st Amer. from 5th London edition. . . .* Philadelphia: A. Finley, 1810.
        TL

911.   Macgillivray, William. *Descriptions of the rapacious birds of Great Britain.* Edinburgh: Maclachlan & Stewart, 1836.
        TL
        JL 7.299 (4—9—55); FB

912.   MacGregor, John. *Commercial statistics. A digest of the productive resources, commercial legislation, customs, tariffs . . . of all nations. . . .* Vol. 5. London: C. Knight & co., 1850.

        CN (*c.* 1851)

913.   McKenney, Thomas L. *Memoirs, official and personal; with sketches of travels among the Northern and Southern Indians; embracing a war of excursion, and descriptions of scenes along the Western borders.* 2 vols. in 1. New York: Paine and Burgess, 1846.
        TL

        Given to T by Ellery Channing in 1857; originally the property of Margaret Fuller.

914.   McKenney, Thomas L. *Sketches of a tour to the lakes, of the character and customs of the Chippeway Indians, and of the incidents connected with the treaty of Fond du Lac. Also a vocabulary of the Algic, or Chippeway language. . . .* Baltimore: F. Lucas, Jr., 1827.
        HL 9—25—33
        IB 8 (*c.* 1853)

915.   Mackenzie, Sir Alexander. *Voyages from Montreal, on the river St. Lawrence, through the continent of North America, to the frozen and Pacific Oceans; in the years 1789 and 1793. With a preliminary account of the rise, progress, and present state of the fur trade of that country. With original notes by Bougainville and Volney. . . . Illustrated with maps. . . .* 2 vols. London: Printed for T. Cadell, jun. and W. Davies [etc.]; Edinburgh: W. Creech, 1802.
        HL 2—28—59
        EX, 100—101; IB 12; CPB2

916.   MCLELLAN, Henry B., Jr. *Journal of a residence in Scotland, and a tour through England, France, Germany, Switzerland, and Italy, with a memoir of the author, and extracts from his religious papers. Compiled from the manuscripts of the late Henry B. McLellan. By I. McLellan, jr.* Boston: Allen and Ticknor, 1834.
       TL

917.   MACPHERSON, James. *The genuine remains of Ossian, literally translated; with a preliminary dissertation.* By Patrick MacGregor. London: Smith, Elder & co., 1841.

       WE, 344–348; WA, 132; RP, 171; PJ 1.484–493 (11–7 to 11–21–43); CPB1

918.   MACTAGGART, John. *Three years in Canada: an account of the actual state of the country in 1826–1827–1828. Comprehending its resources, productions, improvements, and capabilities; and including sketches of the state of society, advice to emigrants, &c. . . .* London: H. Colburn, 1829.

       EX, 94; JL 2.225 (6–3–51); IB 4; CN

919.   MACY, Obed. *History of Nantucket; being a compendious account of the first settlement of the island by the English, together with the rise and progress of the whale fishery; and other historical facts relative to said island and its inhabitants.* Boston: Hilliard, Gray, 1835.

       JL 7.97 (12–29–54); IB 8

920.   MACY, Zaccheus. "A Short Journal of the First Settlement of the Island of Nantucket, with Some of the Most Remarkable Things that Have Happened Since, to the Present Time." *Collections of the Massachusetts Historical Society*, 1st ser., vol. 3 (1794): 155–160.

       IB 8 (*c.* 1854)

921.   MAGAPOLENSIS, Johannes, Jr. "A Short Sketch of the Mohawk Indians in New Netherland." *Collections of the New York Historical Society*, 2d ser., vol. 3, pt. 1 (1857): 137–160.
       HL 1–13–58
       IB 11

922.   *Magazine of horticulture, botany and . . . rural affairs.* Vols. 1–34, 1835–68. Boston: Hovey.

       JL 6.250 (5–9–54)

       T's Journal reference is to "Hovey's Magazine" for 1842 or 1843, in which he saw a list of plants.

923.   *Magazine of zoology and botany*. Conducted by Sir W. Jardine, bart., P. J. Selby, esq. and Dr. Johnston. . . . Edinburgh: W. H. Lizars; London: S. Highley, 1837, 1838 (vols. 1, 2).

FB (*c.* 1855)

T extracted miscellaneous natural history data from reviews and notices in vols. 1 and 2.

924.   *Mahābhārata. The Bhagavad-gītā; or, The sacred lay: a colloquy between Krishna and Arjuna on divine matters. An episode from the Mahābhārata. . . . A new edition of the Sanscrit text . . . by J. Cockburn Thomson*. Hertford: S. Austin, 1855.
TL

See next entry for references.

925.   *Mahābhārata. Bhăgvăt-gēētā, or Dialogues of Krēĕshnă and Ărjŏŏn (tr. Charles Wilkins)*. London: [n.p.], 1785.
HL 10–9–54
WE, 96–142 passim; PJ 2.253–261 passim (after 6–20–46); JL 4.153 (6–26–52)

926.   *Mahābhārata. Harivansa, ou Histoire de la famille de Hari, ouvrage formant un appendice du Mahabharata, et traduit sur l'original sanscrit par M. A. Langlois. . . . 2 vols*. Paris: Printed for the Oriental translation fund of Great Britain and Ireland; London: Sold by Parbury, Allen and co., 1834–35.
HL 9–11–49
WA, 85–87, 282; TR, 135–144 ("The Transmigrations of the Seven Brahmans"); CPBI

927.   *Mahābhārata. Nala and Damayanti and other poems. Translated from the Sanscrit into English by Rev. Henry Hart Milman, with mythological and critical notes*. Oxford: D. A. Talboys, 1835.
TL

928.   MAINE. Report of the State Geologist. Jackson, Charles T. *Second annual report on the geology of the public lands belonging to the two states of Maine and Massachusetts*. Boston: Dutton and Wentworth, state printers, 1838.
TL
MW, passim; PJ 2.276 (Fall 1846)

929.   MAINE. Report of the State Geologist. Jackson, Charles T. *Third report on the geology of Maine*. Augusta: Smith & Robinson, 1839.
TL

930.   MAINE, Jasper [attrib.]. In Chalmers (q.v.), vol. 6.
"To the Memory of the Incomparable Paire of Authors, Beaumont and Fletcher"
WE, 68

931.   MALCOLM, Sir John. See "Review of Sir John Malcolm's *The Life of Robert Lord Clive.*"

932.   MALLET, Paul Henri. *Northern antiquities; or, an historical account of the manners, customs, religion, and laws, maritime expeditions and discoveries, language and literature of the ancient Scandinavians . . . tr. from the French of M. Mallet by Bishop Percy. New edition, revised throughout, and considerably enlarged; with a translation of the prose edda from the original old Norse text; and notes critical and explanatory, by I. A. Blackwell, esq., to which is added, an abstract of the Eyrbyggja Saga, by Sir Walter Scott.* London: Henry G. Bohn, York Street, Covent Garden, 1847.
EL
FB; IB 9 (*c.* 1855)

933.   MANTELL, Gideon-Algernon. *Petrifications and their teachings; or, A hand-book to the gallery of organic remains of the British Museum.* London: H. G. Bohn, 1851.
CL
MW, 114; FB; IB 9 (*c.* 1855)

934.   MANU. *Institutes of Hindu law; or, the ordinances of Menu, according to the gloss of Culluca. Comprising the Indian system of duties, religious and civil. Verbally translated from the original, with a preface, by Sir William Jones. A new edition, collated with the Sanscrit text, by Graves Chamney Haughton.* . . . 2 vols. London: Rivingtons and Cochran, 1825.
TL
WE, 135, 148, 152, 153; PJ 1.280 (3–10–41), 313 (6–7–41), 324 (9–28–41), 407–426 passim (1842); ME

935.   "Maple Sugar." *New York Weekly Tribune,* April 24, 1857.

JL 9.340–341 (4–25–57)

936.   MARCET, Mrs. Jane (Haldimand). *Conversations on chemistry; in which the elements of that science are familiarly explained and illustrated by experiments, and sixteen copperplate engravings. To which are now added, explanations of the text . . . by Dr. J. L. Comstock.* . . . *8th American from the 6th London ed., rev., corr., and enl.* . . . Hartford: O. D. Cooke, 1824.
TL

937.   MARCY, Randolph Barnes. See United States. War Department (no. 1373).

938.   MARKHAM, G. In *England's Helicon* (q.v.).
       "Purest Plot of Earthly Mold."
       CPBI (*c.* 1841)

939.   MARLOWE, Christopher. *The works of Christopher Marlowe.*
       3 vols. London: W. Pickering, [etc., etc.], 1826.

       "Hero and Leander"
       WE, 201, 336, 337; PJ 1.477 (after 10–15–43), 490 (11–20–
       43); 2.80, 83, 95 (1842–44), 115 (after 8–1–44)

       Also a generalized reference to *Dr. Faustus* and *Dido Queen
       of Carthage* at PJ 1.457.

940.   MARMONTEL, Jean François. *Moral tales, by M. Marmontel.
       Translated from the French. 1st American edition.* 2 vols.
       New York: R. M'Dermut and D. D. Arden, 1813.
       HL 9–18–33 (vol. 1)

941.   MARQUETTE, Jacques. "Relation of the Voyages, Discoveries,
       and Death of Father James Marquette, and the Subsequent
       Voyages of Father Claudius Alloney. . . ." In French, B. F.,
       Historical Collections of Louisiana . . . (q.v.), vol. 4: 1–66.
       HL 12–7–58
       IB 11

942.   MARSHALL, John. *A history of the colonies planted by the
       English on the continent of North America, from their settle-
       ment, to the commencement of that war which terminated in
       their independence.* Philadelphia: A. Small, 1824.
       HL 6–10–34

943.   MARSTON, J. W. "Locke's Metaphysics Illustrated by Owens'
       Socialism." *Monthly Magazine* (London), 3d ser., vol. 4 (Aug.
       and Sept. 1840): 209–218, 313–316.

       LN (*c.* 1841)

944.   MARSTON, J. W. "Present Aspects of Poetry." *Monthly Maga-
       zine* (London), 3d ser., vol. 3 (June 1840): 646–653.

       LN (*c.* 1841)

945.   MARTINEAU, Harriet. *How to observe. Morals and manners.*
       Philadelphia: Lea Blanchard, 1847.
       TL

946.   MARTINEAU, Harriet, and Henry George ATKINSON. *Letters
       on the laws of Man's nature and development.* London:
       Chapman, 1851.

       JL 2.468 (9–7–51)

Conjectural; Journal reference is to "Miss Martineau's last book."

947.   MARVELL, Andrew. *The works of Andrew Marvell Esq.* 2 vols. in 1. London: E. Curll, 1726.

"A Dialogue Between the Soul and Body"
CC, 10; CPBI
"The Garden"
PJ 1.4 (10–37)
"Tom May's Death"
RP, 139; CPBI
"An Horatian Ode on Cromwell's Return"
RP, 152; EX, 308
"Upon Appleton House," "Music's Empire," "The Character of Holland," "On Milton's *Paradise Lost*"
CPBI

Edition listed was owned by HL; T's actual source unknown.

948.   MASSACHUSETTS. *Transactions of the Agricultural Society of Massachusetts* (1847).
TL

T listed this volume in his library catalogue, but I have been unable to identify it further.

949.   MASSACHUSETTS. GENERAL COURT. *Documents relating to the northeastern boundary of the state of Maine.* Boston: Dutton and Wentworth, Printers to the state, 1828.
TL

950.   MASSACHUSETTS. GENERAL COURT. *Report of the joint special committee upon the subject of the flowage of meadows on Concord & Sudbury Rivers, Jan. 28, 1860.* Boston: White, 1860.
TL

951.   MASSACHUSETTS. GENERAL COURT. *Report of the joint special committee, appointed to inquire into the means of preserving Cape Cod harbor.* . . . Boston: [n.p.] 1852.

CC, 163–164

The authors of an earlier report, in 1825, reprinted in this 1852 report, from which T quotes, were Zabdiel Sampson and Nymphas Marston.

952.   MASSACHUSETTS. GEOLOGICAL SURVEY. Hitchcock, Edward. *Final report on the geology of Massachusetts.* . . . 2 vols. Northampton: J. H. Butler, 1841.

CC, 16, 104, 150, 154

953.   MASSACHUSETTS. GEOLOGICAL SURVEY. Hitchcock, Edward.
        Report on the geology, mineralogy, botany, and zoology of
        Massachusetts. Made and published by order of the govern-
        ment of that state. . . . Amherst: Press of J. S. and C. Adams,
        1833.
        TL
        JL 14.44 (8–9–60)

954.   MASSACHUSETTS. ZOOLOGICAL AND BOTANICAL SURVEY. See
        Storer, David H., and W.B.O. Peabody.

955.   MASSILLON, Jean Baptiste. *Sermons.* Boston: Waite, Pierce &
        Co., [n.d.].
        TL

        Conjectural edition.

956.   MATAL, Jean. *America, sive novis orbis, Tabulis Aeneis Se-*
        cundum Rationes Geographicas Delineatus . . . Tabularum
        Darsa . . . Historicum rerum veste ornata sunt, describuntque
        in uniuscuiusq. Tabulae dorso, Provinciae . . . fines termi-
        nique . . . Coloniae Agrippinae: Excudebat Stephanus Hen-
        merden Typographus, Anno 1600.

        CN (*c.* 1850)

957.   MATHER, Cotton. In Barber, *Historical Collections* (q.v.).
        JL 8.163–165 (2–3–56)

        T quotes a letter by Mather describing the great snow of
        1716.

958.   MATHER, Cotton. *Magnalia Christi Americana: or, the eccle-*
        siastical history of New England, from its first planting in the
        year 1620, unto the year of Our Lord, 1698. In seven books.
        By the reverend and learned Cotton Mather. . . . *1st American*
        ed., from the London edition of 1702. (Vols. 1, 2). Hartford:
        Published by Silas Andrus. Roberts & Burr, Printers, 1820.
        HL 8–15–59
        CC 178; IB 12

959.   MATHER, Increase. *A brief history of the war with the Indians*
        in New-England. . . . Boston: John Foster, 1676.

        IB 12 (*c.* 1859)

960.   MAURY, Alfred. "Le Monde Alpestre et les Hautes Regions du
        Globe." *Revue des Deux Mondes* 27 (May 1860): 121–147.

        CPB2 (*c.* 1860)

961.   MAURY, Lieutenant M. F. "Address before the Geographical
       and Nautical Society." New York *Daily Times*, Feb. 16,
       1854.

       FB (*c.* 1854)

962.   MAURY, Lieutenant M. F. *The physical geography of the sea.
       By M. F. Maury, LL.D., Lieut. U.S. Navy. Second edition, en-
       larged and improved.* New York: Harper & Brothers, Pub-
       lishers . . . , 1855.
       CL
       FB (*c.* 1856)

963.   MAXIMILIAN, Alexander Philip, prinz von Wied-Neuwied. See
       Wied-Neuwied, Maximilian Alexander Philip, prinz von.

964.   MAYER, Brantz. *Tah-gah-jute; or, Logan and Captain Mi-
       chael Cresap; a discourse by Brantz Mayer; delivered in Balti-
       more, before the Maryland Historical Society . . . 9 May,
       1851.* Baltimore: Maryland Historical Society, 1851.

       IB 8 (*c.* 1854)

965.   MAYHEW, Henry. *London labour and the London poor.* 3
       vols. London: Newbold, 1851.

       JL 5.197–198 (5–28–53)

966.   MELVILLE, Herman. *Typee: a peep at Polynesian life. During
       a four months' residence in a valley of the Marquesas . . . rev.
       ed., with a sequel.* New York: Wiley and Putnam, 1846.
       EL
       PJ 2.315, 317 (Fall 1846)

967.   MENCIUS. See Pauthier, J.-P.-G.

968.   MENZEL, Wolfgang. *German literature. Tr. from the German
       of Wolfgang Menzel. By C. C. Felton.* . . . 3 vols. Boston: Hil-
       liard, Gray, and company, 1840.

       HM 13201 (12–5–40)

       Vols. 7–9 of George Ripley, ed., *Specimens of Foreign Stand-
       ard Literature* (q.v.). T's extracts quote Lorenz Oken and
       Gotthilf Heinrich von Schubert.

969.   MEREDITH, Louisa Anne (Twamley). *The romance of nature;
       or, the flower-seasons illustrated. By Louisa Anne Twamley.
       The plates engraved after the original drawings from nature
       by the author.* . . . London: C. Tilt, 1836.

       HM 13201 (1–16–41)

970.   METASTASIO, Pietro. *Dramas and other poems, of the Abbé*
        Pietro Metastasio. Tr. from the Italian by John Hoole. . . .
        3 vols. London: Printed for Otridge and son [etc.], 1800.
        HL 10–14–34, 4–28–36 (vol. 1)

971.   METELLUS SEQUANUS. See Matal, Jean.

972.   MEYER, Georg Friedrich Wilhelm.

        JL 3.316 (2–20–52) quotes a Meyer on lichens, but I have
        been unable to identify the reference further. Georg Friedrich
        Wilhelm Meyer is the probable source, since he was a promi-
        nent German writer on lichens, though little of his work was
        available in English at this time.

973.   MICHAUX, François André. *The North American sylva, or A*
        description of the forest trees of the United States, Canada,
        and Nova Scotia . . . to which is added a description of the
        most useful of the European forest trees. . . . *Tr. from the*
        French by F. Andrew Michaux. . . . 3 vols. Paris: Printed by
        C. D'Hautel, 1819.
        HL 4–30–51
        WA 251; EX, 220, 301; MW, 43–44, 269, 299; JL 2.142 (1–
        51), 195–201 (5–18–51); 11.385 (1–2–59); IB 2; IB 4; CPB2

        See also Nuttall, Thomas (no. 1036).

974.   MICHAUX, François André. *Voyage à l'ouest des monts Allé-*
        ghanys dans les états de l'Ohio, du Kentucky et du Tennessee,
        et retour à Charleston par les hautes-Carolines; contenant des
        détails sur l'état actuel de l'agriculture et les productions na-
        turelles de ces contrées. . . . *Avec une carte trèssoignée des*
        états du centre, de l'ouest et du sud des États-Unis. Paris:
        Dentu, 1808.
        HL 6–2–51
        EX, 221; JL 2.230–232 (6–8–51); 5.399 (8–24–53); 9.137
        (11–2–56), 397, 414 (6–12–57)

975.   MICKLE, William Julius. "Inquiry into the Religious Tenets
        and Philosophy of the Bramins." In Chalmers (q.v.), vol. 21.

        PJ 1.337 (11–29–41)

976.   MIDDLESEX SOCIETY OF HUSBANDMEN AND MANUFACTUR-
        ERS. *Transactions for 1851.* [n.p.], 1852.

        JL 3.327 (3–1–52)

977.   MILL, James. *The history of British India. By James Mill, esq.*
        . . . with notes and continuation by Horace Hayman Wilson.
        . . . 9 vols. London: J. Madden, 1848.
        TL

978.　MILLER, Hugh. *An autobiography, my schools and school-masters, or, The story of my education.* Boston: Gould and Lincoln, 1854.

IB 10 (*c.* 1857)

979.　MILLER, Hugh. *The foot-prints of the Creator: or, the Astero-lepis of Stromness. . . . From the 3d London ed. With a mem-oir of the author, by Louis Agassiz.* Boston: Gould and Lincoln, 1850.

JL 3.31 (9–28–51)

980.　MILLER, Hugh. *The old red sandstone; or, New walks in an old field. Illustrated with numerous engravings from the fourth London edition.* Boston: Gould and Lincoln, 1852.
CL
JL 3.30–31 (9–28–51)

981.　MILLER, Hugh. *The testimony of the rocks; or, Geology in its bearing on the two theologies, natural and revealed . . . with memoirs of the death and character of the author. . . .* Boston: Gould and Lincoln, 1857.

EX, 290; IB 10; FB (*c.* 1857)

982.　MILLER, Samuel. "A Discourse, Designed to Commemorate the Discovery of New York by Henry Hudson." *Collections of the New York Historical Society,* 1st ser., vol. 1 (1811): 17–45.

CC, 183–184

983.　MILLS, Charles. *History of the crusades, for the recovery and possession of the Holy Land.* 3d ed. 3 vols. London: [n.p.], 1822.
HL 5–28–34 (vol. 1)

984.　MILNER, Thomas, A.M. *The gallery of nature; or, Wonders of the earth and the heavens . . . condensed and revised by Caleb Wright. . . .* Boston: C. Wright, [1855].
CL
FB (*c.* 1857)

985.　MILTON, John. *Paradise lost, a poem, in twelve books.* Phila-delphia: Published by Johnson & Warner, . . . 1808.
TL
EEM, 79–83, 94; WE, 177; MW, 60–61, 64, 70; WA, 121, 263, 288; CC, 60; RP, 13, 14; PJ 1.12 (11–16–37), 17 (12–12–37), 18 (12–15–37), 19 (12–16–37), 171 (8–13–40), 225 (12–20–41), 238 (1–30–41); 2.7 (1842–44), 178 (8–23–45)

986. MILTON, John. *The poetical works of John Milton. . . . With
      principal notes of various commentators. To which are added
      illustrations, with some account of the life of Milton. By the
      Rev. Henry John Todd. . . .* 6 vols. London: Printed for
      J. Johnson [etc.] by Bye and Low, 1801.
      HL 10–27–36 (vols. 1, 5, 6), 2–6–37 (vol. 5)
      "Lycidas"
      WE, 253; WA, 173; CC, 110; EX, 220, 276; JL 7.28 (9–8–54);
      ME; F2a
      "Comus"
      PJ 1, 19 (12–12–37); ME; F2a
      "Il Penseroso"
      WE, 59; EEM, 74–78; ME
      "L'Allegro"
      EEM, 74–78; EX, 179; PJ 1.456 (4–27–43); ME
      "On the Morning of Christ's Nativity"
      PJ 2.265 (after 7–24–46)
      "On Shakespeare"
      WE, 177
      "To Sir Henry Vane the Younger"
      EEM, 37
      "Christmas Hymn," *Paradise Regained, Samson Agonistes*
      F2a

987. MILTON, John. *The prose works of John Milton; with a life of
      the author, interspersed with translations and critical re-
      marks, by Charles Symmons. . . .* 7 vols. London: J. Johnson
      [etc.], 1806.
      HL 12–5–36, 2–9–37 (vol. 2)

988. MILTON, John. *A selection from the English prose works of
      John Milton.* 2 vols. Boston: Bowles & Dearborn, 1826.
      TL

989. MILTON, John. *The works of John Milton, historical, politi-
      cal, and miscellaneous. Now more correctly printed from the
      originals, than in any former edition, and many passages re-
      stored, which have been hitherto omitted. To which is pre-
      fixed, an account of his life and writings.* 2 vols. London:
      Printed for A. Millar, 1753.
      HL 4–27–37

      Conjectural edition; see Cameron, "Books Thoreau Bor-
      rowed."

990. MINOT, Laurence. In Anderson, Robert, *The Works of the
      British Poets* (q.v.).
      "Lithes and I Sall Tell You Tyll the Bataile of Halidon Hyll,"
      "How Edward the King Come in Braband and Toke Homage
      of All the Land"
      LN (*c.* 1843)

991.   "Mirabeau. An Anecdote of his Private Life." *Harper's Magazine* 1 (Oct. 1850): 648–651.

WA, 322; JL 2.333 (7–21–51)

Reprinted from *Chambers' Edinburgh Journal*.

992.   MIRICK, Benjamin L. *The history of Haverhill, Massachusetts. By B. L. Mirick.* . . . Haverhill: A. W. Thayer, 1832.
TL
WE, 303; JL 3.282–285 (2–6 & 7–52)

993.   MONCEAU, Henri Louis Duhamel. See Duhamel du Monceau, Henri Louis.

994.   MONTANUS, Arnoldus. See Ogilby, John.

995.   MONTGOMERY, Alexander. In Sibbald, *Chronicle of Scottish Poetry* (q.v.), vol. 4.
"Hey Now the Day Daws"
WE, 117

996.   MONTGOMERY, James.

"The Dial"
WE, 319; LN
"What Is Prayer"
LN

Edition unknown. T's source for "The Dial" was probably a commonplace book of RWE's. "What Is Prayer" was widely reprinted.

997.   MONTRESOR, Col. See Arnold, Benedict.

998.   MOODIE, Susannah (Strickland). *Life in the clearings versus the bush.* New York: DeWitt & Davenport, 1854 [?].

IB 10 (*c.* 1856)

999.   MOODIE, Susannah (Strickland). *Roughing it in the bush; or, Life in Canada.* London: R. Bentley, 1852.

IB 8 (*c.* 1853)

1000.   MOORE, Thomas. "A Canadian Boat Song."

MW, 38–39; EX, 98

Source unknown; widely available.

1001.   MORELL, Thomas. See Ainsworth, Robert.

1002.   MORGAN, John Minter. *Colloquies on religion . . . and religious education. Being a supplement to "Hampden in the Nineteenth Century."* London: E. Moxon, 1837.

HM 13201 (1–16–41)

1003.   MORGAN, John Minter. *Hampden in the nineteenth century; or, Colloquies on the errors and improvement of society.* . . . 2 vols. London: E. Moxon, 1834.
AL
HM 13201 (1–12–40)

1004.   MORGAN, Lewis H. *League of the Ho-de-no-san-nee, or Iroquois.* New York: M. H. Newman & co. [etc., etc.], 1851.
EL
IB 8

1005.   MORLEY, Henry. *Pallissy the potter. The life of Bernard Pallissy of Saintes.* 2 vols. Boston: Ticknor, Reed, and Fields, 1853.

CPB2 (*c.* 1859)

1006.   MORRELL, Abby Jane. *Narrative of a voyage to the Ethiopic and south Atlantic Ocean, Indian Ocean, Chinese Sea, north and south Pacific Ocean, in the years 1829, 1830, 1831.* New York: J. & J. Harper, 1833.
HL 11–11–34

Conjectural; see following entry.

1007.   MORRELL, Benjamin. *A narrative of four voyages to the South sea, north and south Pacific ocean, Chinese sea, Ethiopic and southern Atlantic ocean, Indian and Antarctic ocean. From the year 1822 to 1831.* . . . New York: J. & J. Harper, 1832.
HL 11–11–34

Conjectural; as Christie notes (*Thoreau as World Traveler*, p. 326), the work T withdrew may have been Abby Jane Morrell, *Narrative of a Voyage to the Ethiopic and South Atlantic Ocean* . . . (New York: J. & J. Harper, 1833).

1008.   MORRISON, William. "Who Discovered Itasca Lake?" *Collections of the Minnesota Historical Society* 1 (1856): 417–419.

TMJ

1009.   MORSE, Jedidiah. *The American Gazetteer, exhibiting, in alphabetical order, a much more full and accurate account, than has been given, of the states, provinces, counties, cities, towns . . . on the American continent, also of the West-Indian*

*islands.... Collected and comp.... by, and under the direc-
tion of, Jedidiah Morse.... Illustrated with seven ... maps.
...* Printed in Boston: At the Presses of S. Hall, Thomas and
Andrews, and sold by E. Larkin, and other booksellers in Bos-
ton, by Gaine & Ten Eyck, and S. Campbell, New York [etc.,
etc.], 1797.
TL
MW, 66; CC, passim; JL 14.43 (8–9–60)

1010.   MORSE, Jedidiah. *Geography made easy: being an abridgement of the American universal geography.... 11th ed., cor.
...* Boston: Thomas & Andrews; J. T. Buckingham, printer,
1807.
TL

1011.   MORTON, Nathaniel. *New-England's Memorial.... 5th ed.
Containing besides the original work, and the supplement annexed to the 2d ed., large additions in marginal notes, and an
appendix; with a ... copy of an ancient map.* Boston: Printed
by Crocker and Brewster, 1826.

PJ 1.306 (4–30–41); 2.22 (1842–44), 191 (after 12–23–45)

1012.   MORTON, Samuel George. *Crania Americana; or, a comparative view of the skulls of various aboriginal nations of North
and South America. To which is prefixed an essay on the varieties of the human species. Illustrated by seventy-eight plates
and a colored map.* Philadelphia: J. Dobson, Chestnut Street;
London: Simkin, Marshall &c., 1839.
SNH 6–13–52
JL 4.146–147 (6–25–52), 205 (7–9–52), 226, 228 (7–14–
52); IB 6; FB

1013.   MORTON, Thomas. *New English Canaan or New Canaan.
Containing an abstract of New England, composed in three
bookes....* Amsterdam: J. F. Stam, 1637.
HL 3–2–57
CC, 67, 187; JL 9.288 (3–5–57); IB 10; FB

1014.   MOSCHUS. See *Greek pastoral poets.*

1015.   [MOURT, George]. "A Relation or Journal of a Plantation Settled at Plymouth in New England, and Proceedings thereof.
...." *Collections of the Massachusetts Historical Society,* 1st
ser., vol. 8 (1802): 203–239.

WA, 143; CC, 29n, 197–198, 199–200, 201; PJ 3 (Fall 1849);
IB 2

This is the narrative of the founding of the Plymouth colony,
by several hands, commonly known as "Mourt's Relation."

1016.   MOWATT, Anna. See Ritchie, Anna Cora (Ogden) Mowatt.

1017.   MOYSANT, François. *Bibliothèque portative des meilleurs écrivains François.* . . . Boston: [n.p.], 1810.
        TL

1018.   MUDIE, Robert. *The feathered tribes of the British islands.* 2 vols. London: Bohn, 1834.

        CC, 55–56, 89; CPB2

1019.   MURRAY, Hugh. *Historical and descriptive account of British India, from the most remote period to the present time. By Hugh Murray* . . . *[et al.] with a map and engravings.* New York: J. & J. Harper, 1832.

        WE, 151–152; PJ 1.177 (8–28–40), 409, 413 (1842); ME

1020.   MURRAY, Lindley. *English grammar, adapted to the different classes of learners. With an appendix containing rules and observations for assisting the more advanced students to write.* . . . *4th Hallowell, from the New York Stereotype edition.* Hallowell [Me.]: Published by Goodale, Galzier & Co., and C. Spaulding. Goodale, Galzier & co. printers, 1823.
        TL

1021.   MYRTLE, Minnie. See Johnson, Anna C.

1022.   NEGRĒS, Alexandros. *The orations of Aeschines and Demosthenes On the Crown. With modern Greek prologmena and English notes.* . . . Boston: Hilliard, Gray, Little, and Wilkins, 1829.
        TX

1023.   NEILL, Rev. E. D. "Dakota Land and Dakota Life." *Collections of the Minnesota Historical Society* 1 (1856): 254–292.

        TMJ

1024.   NEPOS, Cornelius. *Vitae excellentium imperatorum: cum versione Anglica* . . . *Or, Lives of the excellent commanders; with an English translation* . . . *by John Clark.* 10th ed. London: Printed for C. Hitch and L. Hawes, and W. Johnston, 1765.
        HL 6–26–37

1025.   NEUMAN, Henry, and G.M.A. BARETTI. *Dictionary of the Spanish and English languages.* . . . . 2 vols. Boston: Hilliard, Gray, Little & Wilkins, 1831.
        TL

1026.   *A new English–German and German–English dictionary.*
        Philadelphia: G. W. Mentz and Sohn, 1835.
        TL

1027.   NEW HAMPSHIRE HISTORICAL SOCIETY. *Collections of the*
        New Hampshire Historical Society. 3 vols. Concord, N.H.:
        Moore, 1824–32.
        TL
        EX, 4; CN

1028.   NEW YORK (State) MUSEUM, Albany. *Third annual report of*
        the regents of the university on the condition of the state cabi-
        net of natural history. Albany: Weed, Parson, & co., 1850.
        TL

1029.   *New York Tribune.*

        T was a regular subscriber to the weekly edition of Greeley's
        Tribune from about the beginning of 1852 on (see JL 3.208).
        There was also a daily edition, of course, and a semiweekly
        edition, both of which T also refers to. Quotations and clip-
        pings from all three are scattered throughout the Journal and
        Indian books.

1030.   NEWMAN, Edward. *A history of British ferns.* London: J. Van
        Voorst, 1840.
        HL 10–6–59
        CPB2

1031.   NIEBUHR, Barthold Georg. *The history of Rome. . . . Trans-*
        lated by Julius Charles Hare and Connop Thirwall. First
        American from the London edition. Philadelphia: Thomas
        Wardle, 1835.

        EX, 290

1032.   NIEBUHR, Barthold Georg. *The life and letters of Barthold*
        Georg Niebuhr. With essays on his character and influence,
        by the chevalier Bonsen, and Professors Brandis and Lorbell.
        New York: Harper & brothers, 1852.
        CL
        CPB2 (*c.* 1858)

1033.   *North American Review.* 248 vols. Boston, 1815–1940.
        HL 10–13–36 (vol. 9), IN after 12–8–36 (vols. 35, 41) & 11–
        36 (nos. 92–93)

1034.   NOTT. Josiah Clark, and George R. GLIDDON. *Types of man-*
        kind: or, Ethnological researches, based upon the ancient
        monuments, paintings, sculptures, and crania of races . . . il-

lustrated by selections from the inedited papers of Samuel George Morton. . . . Philadelphia: Lippincott, Grambo & co., 1857.

IB 12; CPB2 (*c.* 1860)

1035. NUTTALL, Thomas. *A manual of the ornithology of the United States and of Canada.* 4 vols. Cambridge: Hilliard and Brown; Boston: Hilliard, Gray, 1832–34.

EX, 111; JL 5.214 (6–1–53); 7.288 (4–6–55); 8.307–308 (4–24–56)

1036. NUTTALL, Thomas. *The North American sylva; or, A description of the forest trees of the United States, Canada, and Nova Scotia. . . .* 3 vols. Philadelphia: Robert P. Smith, 1853.
SNH 5–9–57
JL 6.265 (5–15–54); FB; IB 8

Continuation of Michaux's *North American Sylva* (no. 973).

1037. NUTTALL, Thomas. *An introduction to systematic and physiological botany. . . .* Cambridge, [Mass.]: Hilliard and Brown . . . , 1827.
TX

1038. OAKES, William. *Scenery of the White Mountains.* Boston: Crosby, Nichols and Co., 1848.

JL 11.19 (7–8–58), 23 (7–8–58), 37 (7–12–58)

1039. O'CALLAGHAN, E. B. *The documentary history of the state of New York; arranged under the direction of the Hon. Christopher Morgan, Secretary of State.* 4 vols. Albany: Weed, Parsons & co., public printers, 1850–51.
EL
IB 6; IB 8; FB; CN (1852–54)

T later (1858) received a copy of this work from H. S. Randall; the IB entries consist of numerous extracts of early correspondence from missionaries, military men, and others with early contact among the Indians of New York.

1040. OCCOM, Sampson. "An Account of the Montauk Indians, on Long Island." *Collections of the Massachusetts Historical Society,* 1st ser., vol. 10 (1809): 106–111.

IB 2 (*c.* 1849)

1041. OCKLEY, Simon. *The history of the saracens. . . . Giving an account of their most remarkable battles, sieges, &c . . . illus-*

*trating the religion, rites, customs, and manner of living of
that warlike people. . . .* 2 vols. 2d ed. London: Printed for
Knaplock [Vol. 2 for Knaplock or B. Lintot], 1708–18.
BA 9–23–40 (by RWE)
WE, 155, 380; EX, 174; PJ 1.186 (10–6–40), 210 (12–27–40),
416 (1842)

1042.   OEGGER, G. *The true Messiah; or, The Old and New Testa-
ments, examined according to the principles of the language
of nature.* Boston: Pub. by E. P. Peabody, 1842.
EL
PJ 1.364–365 (2–20–42)

1043.   OEHLENSCHLAGER, Adam Gottlob. "To Columbus Dying."
Tr. W. H. Furness (and Lucy Osgood). In *The Gift* for 1845.
Philadelphia: Carey and Hart, 1845, pp. 62–63.

CC, 11

1044.   OGILBY, John. *America: being the latest, and most accurate
description of the New world; containing the original of the
inhabitants, and the remarkable voyages thither.* London:
Printed by the author, 1671.

CC, 66, 179; EX, 91; JL 2.102 (11–17–50); 6.136 (2–21–54);
FB

1045.   OLMSTED, Frederick Law. *A journey through Texas; or, A
saddle-trip on the southwestern frontier: with a statistical appendix.* New York: Dix, Edwards & co., 1857.

IB 10; FB (*c.* 1856)

1046.   "One Hundred and Twelve Years Old." *New York Tribune,*
Aug. 19, 1857, p. 7.

JL 10.16 (8–28–57)

1047.   ORPHEUS. *Orphei Argonautica, Hymni, et De lapidibus, curante Andrea Christiano Eschenbachio . . . sum ejusdem ad
Argonautica notis & emendationibus. Accedunt Henrici Ste-
phani in omnia & Josephi Scaligeri in Hymnos notae.* Trajecti
ad Rhenum, apud Guilielmum vande Water, 1689.
TL

1048.   ORTELII, Abraham. *Theatrum orbis terrarum; opus nunc ter-
tio ab ipso auctore recognitum, multisque locis castigatum, &
quam plurimus novis tabulis atque commentariis auctum.*
Colophon: Antverpiae, Auctoris aere & cora impressum, ab-
solutumque apud Christophorum Plantinum, 1584.
HL 11–18–50
CC, 240; CN

1049.   OSBORN, Lieut. Sherard. *Stray leaves from an Arctic journal; or, Eighteen months in the polar regions, in search of Sir John Franklin's expedition, in the years 1850–51.* London: Longman, Brown, Green, and Longman's 1852.

JL 4.320 (8–27–52); IB 6; FB

1050.   OSSIAN. See Macpherson, James.

1051.   OSWALD, John. *An etymological dictionary of the English language. . . . Revised and improved. . . .* Philadelphia: E. C. Biddle, 1844.
TL

1052.   OTHEMAN, Edward. *Memoir and writings of Mrs. Hannah Maynard Pickard. . . .* Boston: D. H. Ela, 1845.
TL

Autograph of Sophia Thoreau.

1053.   OVID. *Publii Ovidii Nasonis metamorphosen libri xv, ad usem serenissimi delphini.* Philadelphia: Long & DeSilver, 1823.
TL
WE, 4, 110, 216; WA, 6, 314–316; PJ 2.366–369 (Winter 1846–47); JL 2.144–145 (between 1–10 and 2–9–51)

1054.   OWEN, David Dale. *Report of a geological survey of Wisconsin, Iowa, and Minnesota; and . . . Nebraska territory.* Philadelphia: Lippincott, Grambo & co., 1852.

IB 10; FB (*c.* 1856)

1055.   OWEN, Richard. *Palaeontology or a systematic summary of extinct animals and their geological relations.* Edinburgh: A. and C. Black, 1860.
BA 4–16–60 (by RWE)
IB 12

1056.   PAGE, Thomas. See "An American Survey of the Basin of the La Plata."

1057.   PALEY, William. *The principles of moral and political philosophy.* 2 vols. London: R. Faulder, 1806.
TL
RP, 67–68

Conjectural; many editions that fit T's description ("2 vols. London") available.

1058.   PALEY, William. *The works of William Paley. . . .* New ed. Philadelphia: J. J. Woodward, 1836.
TL

1059. PALFREY, John Gorham. *A discourse pronounced at Barnstable on the third of September, 1839.* . . . Boston: F. Andrews, 1840.

    CC, 172

1060. PALLADIUS. In *Scriptores rei rusticae* (q.v.)
    AL
    EX, 294, 308

1061. *Paradise of dainty devices.* See *England's Helicon.*

1062. PARK, Edwards Amasa, and Bela Bates EDWARDS, eds. *Selections from German literature.* Andover [Mass.]; New York: Gould, Newman and Saxton, 1839.

    COR, 48 (9–21–41)

    T recommended this volume to Isaiah Williams; his own acquaintance with it is not clear.

1063. PARK, Thomas, ed. *Helconia. Comprising a selection of English poetry of the Elizabethan age.* . . . 3 vols. London: Longman, Hurst, Rees, Orme, and Brown . . . , 1815.
    HL 12–7–41
    LN; CPB I

1064. PARKER, Nathan Howe. *The Minnesota handbook, for 1856–7.* . . . Boston: J. P. Jewett and company [etc., etc.], 1857.

    TMJ

1065. PARKMAN, Rev. Ebenezer. "An Account of Westborough (Mass.) by Rev. Ebenezer Parkman, January 28, 1767." *Collections of the Massachusetts Historical Society*, 1st ser., vol. 10 (1809): 84–86.

    PJ 3 (Fall 1849); IB 3 (*c.* 1849)

1066. PARKMAN, Francis. *History of the conspiracy of Pontiac.* . . . Boston: C. C. Little and J. Brown [etc., etc.], 1851.
    CL
    IB 8 (*c.* 1853)

1067. PARROT, Friedrich von. *Journey to Ararat.* . . . Tr. by W. D. Cooley. New York: Harper & brothers, 1846.

    JL 3.27 (9–27–51); 10.452–453 (6–2–58); FB

1068. PARRY, Sir William Edward. *Three voyages for the discovery of a northwest passage from the Atlantic to the Pacific.* . . . 2 vols. New York: Harper's Family Library, 1841.
    CL

EX, 177; PJ 1.494 (after 1–7–44); 2.89 (1842–44); JL 9.232 (1–26–57)

1069.   PATENT OFFICE Reports. See United States. Patent Office.

1070.   PATMORE, Coventry. *The angel in the house. . . .* 2 vols. London: J. W. Parker & son, 1854–56.
        EL
        COR, 422 (3–13–56)

1071.   PAUTHIER, Jean-Pierre-Guillaume. *Confucius et Mencius ou les quatre livres de philosophie moral et politique de la Chine.* Paris: Charpentier, 1841.

        WE, 132–133, 136, 264, 281–282; WA, 11, 88, 95, 134, 172, 218, 219, 315; RP, 78; EX, 236; COR, 446–447; JL 2.192 (5–6–51); CPB1

1072.   PEABODY, Elizabeth. *Aesthetic papers.* Boston: E. P. Peabody, 1849.
        TL

        Contains first printing of "Resistance to Civil Government."

1073.   PEABODY, Elizabeth. *Record of a school.* Boston: Russell, Shattuck & Co., 1836.
        TL
        COR, 53 (9–8–41)

1074.   PEABODY, W.B.O. See Storer, David H.

1075.   PEARSON, John. "Account of the Dimensions of American Trees." *Memoirs of the Philadelphia Society for the Promotion of Agriculture* 1 (1808): 176–182.

        CPB2 (*c.* 1860)

1076.   PEELE, George. In Anderson, Robert, *The Works of the British Poets* (q.v.).
        The Arraignment of Paris, Edward the First, The Old Wives Tale, David and Bethsabe, The Battle of Alcazar, "The Beginning, Accidents, and End of the Fall of Troy," "Polyhymnia," "The Honor of the Garter," "The Anglorum Feriae, England's Holidays"
        LN (*c.* 1843)

1077.   PEIRCE, Benjamin. *A history of Harvard university. . . .* Cambridge: Brown, Shattuck, and company, 1833.
        HL 6–16–35, 9–5–36

1078.   PELLICO, Sylvio. *My prisons, memoirs of Silvio Pellico. . . .* Cambridge [Mass.]: C. Folsom, 1836.

CL
RP, 84; COR, 78 (1–24–43)

1079.   PENHALLOW, Samuel. *The history of the wars of New-Eng-land, with the eastern Indians. . . .* Boston: Printed by T. Fleet [etc., etc.], 1726.
HL 4–26–59
CC, 185–187; IB 12

1080.   PERCY, Thomas, ed. *Reliques of ancient English poetry. . . .* 3 vols. London: J. Dodsley, 1765
EL, IN 3–13–37 (vol. 2), after 6–25–37 (vol. 3)
"My Mind to Me a Kingdom Is"
ME
"Essay on the Ancient Minstrels in England"
WE, 376
"Gentle River, Gentle River"
WE, 176; LN
"The Beggar's Daughter of Bednall-Green"
WE, 208; LN
"The Fairy Queen"
WE, 277
"The Dragon of Wantley"
PJ 2.303 (Fall 1846)
"The Ancient Ballad of Chevy Chase," "Sir Cauline," "Sir Patrick Spence," "Edom O'Gordon," "The Aged Lover Renounceth Love," "King Cophetua and the Beggar-Maid," "Death's Final Conquest, by James Shirley," "The Rising in the North," "The Patient Countess, by W. Warner," "The Farewell to Love, from Beaumont and Fletcher," "Ulysses and the Syren, by S. Daniel," "Winifreda," "Alcanzor and Zayda," "The Not-browne Mayd," "Sir Aldingar," "On Thomas Lord Cromwell," "Gentle Herdsman, Tell to Me," "K. Edward and the Tanner of Tamworth," "As Ye Came from the Holy Land," "Hardy-knute," "Victorious Men of Earth, by James Shirley," "Argentile and Curan," "You Meaner Beauties, by Sir H. Wotton," "Loyalty Confined, by Sir Roger L'Estrange," "The Braes of Yarrow," "Little Musgrave and Lady Barnard," "The Knight and Shepherd's Daughter," "Fair Margaret and Sweet William," "To Lucasta, on Going to the Wars," "The Birth of St. George," "Love Will Find Out the Way," "Unfading Beauty, by Tho. Carew," "Robin Goodfellow"
LN (c. 1841)

T also owned an undated one-volume edition of Percy.

1081.   PERLEY, Moses Henry. *Reports on the sea and river fisheries of New Brunswick.* Fredericton: J. Simpson, [Government] printer, 1852.

CC, 196

1082. PERRAULT, Julien. In *Jesuit Relations* (q.v.) for 1635.
       IB 8 (*c.* 1854)

1083. PERRY, Matthew Galbraith. *Narrative of the expedition of an*
       American squadron to the China seas and Japan . . . in 1852,
       1853 and 1854. 3 vols. Washington: A.O.P. Nicholson, 1856.
       TL

1084. PERSIUS FLACCUS, Aulus. In Juvenal, *D. Junii Juvenalis et*
       A. Persii Flacci satirae (q.v.).
       EEM, 122–127; WE, 307–312; ME

1085. PETER OF LANGTOFT. *Peter Langtoft's chronicle, as illustrated*
       and improv'd by Robert of Branne, from the death of Cadwa-
       laden to the end of K. Edward the First's reign. Transcrib'd
       and now first published, from a ms. in the Inner Temple Li-
       brary by Thomas Hearne. 2 vols. Oxford: Printed at the The-
       atre, 1725.
       HL 2–24–35

1086. PETERS, DeWitt Clinton. *The life and adventures of Kit Car-*
       son, the Nestor of the Rocky Mountains. . . . New York:
       W.R.C. Clark & co., 1858.

       IB 12 (*c.* 1859)

1087. PETERS, Samuel. *A general history of Connecticut.* London,
       1781; New Haven: Republ. by D. Clark and Co., Baldwin
       and Threadway, 1829.

       JL 9.75 (9–10–56)

1088. PFEIFFER, Ida. *A lady's voyage round the world. Trans. . . .*
       by Mrs. Percy Sinnett. New York: Harper & brothers, 1852.

       WA, 22–23, 112; JL 3.194–195 (1–15–52), 200 (1–17–52),
       205 (1–18–52); CPB2; FB

1089. PHELPS, Mrs. A. Hart Lincoln. *Familiar lectures on botany,*
       practical, elementary, and physiological. . . . 5th ed., rev. and
       enl. . . . New York: F. J. Huntington, 1837.

       FB (*c.* 1854)

1090. *Phelps and Squires travellers guide through the United States.*
       New York: [n.p.], 1838.
       TL

1091. *The phenix: a collection of old and rare fragments: viz. the*
       Morals of Confucius, the Chinese philosopher; the oracles of
       Zoroaster, the founder of the Persian magi; Sachnoiatho's

*History of the creation; the voyages of Hanno . . . ; King
Hiempsals History of the African settlements . . . ; and the
choice sayings of Publius Syrus. . . .* New York: W. Gowan,
1835.
AL
WE, 43–44, 127, 128, 226, 271, 391; ME

1092.   PHILLIPS, Henry. *The History of cultivated vegetables. . . .* 2
vols. London: H. Colburn and co., 1822.
AL
IB 12; CPB2 (*c.* 1859)

1093.   [PHILLIPS, Sir Richard]. *The universal preceptor.* Greenfield,
Mass.: A. Phelps, 1831.
TL

1094.   PICKERING, Charles. *The races of man; and their geographical
distribution.* London: H. G. Bohn, 1851.
EL
JL 5.392 (8–23–53), 410–411 (9–1–53); FB; IB 8

1095.   PICKERING, John. *A Greek and English lexicon, adapted to
the authors read in the colleges and schools of the United
States and to other Greek classics.* 2d ed. . . . Boston: Hilliard, Gray, Little and Wilkins, 1829.
TL

1096.   PICKETT, Albert James. *History of Alabama, and incidentally
of Georgia and Mississippi. . . .* Charleston [S.C.]: Walker
and James, 1851.

IB 8 (*c.* 1854)

1097.   PIERPONT, John. *Airs of Palestine, and other poems.* Boston:
J. Munroe and company, 1840.
TL

1098.   PIERPONT, John. *The American first class book.* Boston:
C. Bowen, 1836.
TL

1099.   PIERPONT, John. *Introduction to the national reader.* Boston:
Richardson & Lord, 1828.
TL

1100.   PIKE, Zebulon Montgomery. *An account of expeditions to the
sources of the Mississippi . . . during 1805, 1806, and 1807.
. . .* Philadelphia: C. & A. Conrad, 1810.
TL
IB 6; IB 8 (*c.* 1854); TMJ

1101.   PIKE, Zebulon Montgomery. "Pike's Explorations in Minnesota, 1805–06." *Collections of the Minnesota Historical Society* 1 (1856): 65–96.

TMJ

1102.   PINDAR. *Pindari Olympia, Pythia, Nemea, Isthmia, Caeterorum Octo Lyricorum carmina, Alcaei Sapphus, Stesichori, Ibyci, Anacreontis, Bacchylidas, Simonidis, Alcamanis, Nonnulla etiam aliorum.* . . . [Genevae]: Apud Henricum Stephanum, 1586.
TL

T's copy of Pindar has not been located. Harding, in *Thoreau's Library*, cites a different conjectural edition.

1103.   PINDAR. *Werke, Urschrift, Uebersetzung in den pindarischen Versmaassen und Erlauterungun von Friedrich Thiersh.* 2 vols. Leipzig: G. Fleischer, 1820.

TR, 11–133; WE, 189, 244

1104.   PLINY. . . . *Historiae mundi libri XXXVII.* . . . 3 vols. [Genevae]: Apud Jacobum Storer, 1593.
TL

1105.   PLINY. *The natural history of Pliny.* Trans. *John Bostock and H. T. Riley.* 6 vols. London: H. G. Bohn, 1855–57.

EX, 292, 299; CC, 170; HU; JL 13.16–17 (12–8–59), 104 (1–23–60)

1106.   PLUTARCH. *Lives. Tr. from the original Greek, with notes critical and a life of Plutarch by John Langhorne and William Langhorne, New ed., with corrections and additions.* . . . 8 vols. New York: Samuel Campbell, 1822.
EL
PJ 1.98 (12–39), 409–410 (1842); 2.164 (after 7–16–45)

T also owned a one-volume abridgment of the *Lives*, perhaps that edited and translated by John Langhorne (New York: W. C. Boradaile, 1832).

1107.   PLUTARCH. *Morals: Translated from the Greek by several hands. 5th ed., rev. and cor.* 5 vols. London: W. Taylor, 1718.
EL
WE, 16, 175; RP, 8, 10; PJ 1.93, 97–98 (12–39); ME

1108.   *Poetical Tracts.*

See Cameron, "Books Thoreau Borrowed," s.v.

1109.   POPE, Alexander. *Poetical works.* 5 vols. Baltimore: Neals,
        Wills, & Cole, 1814.
        TL
        "Essay on Man"
        EEM, 27
        "Essay on Criticism"
        PJ 1.30 (3–1–38)

1110.   POPE, John. See United States Army. Corps of Topographical
        Engineers.

1111.   POPE, John. See United States. War Department. *Reports of
        Exploration.*

1112.   PORPHYRIUS. *Select works of Porphyry; containing his four
        books* On abstinence from animal foods; *his treatise* On the
        Homeric cave of the nymphs; *and his Auxiliaries to the per-
        ception of intelligible natures. Tr. from the Greek by Thomas
        Taylor. With an appendix, explaining the allegory of the
        wanderings of Ulysses. . . .* London: T. Rodd, 1823.

        HM 13201 (4–16–41)

1113.   POST, Christian Frederic. See Thompson, Charles.

1114.   POST, Christian Frederick. *The journal of Christian Frederick
        Post, in his journey from Philadelphia to the Ohio. . . .* Lon-
        don: [n.p.], 1759.
        HL 12–10–55
        IB 9

1115.   POTTER, Chandler Eastman. "Appendix to 'Language of the
        Abnaquies,' by C. E. Potter of N.H." *Collections of the Maine
        Historical Society* 4 (1856): 187–193.

        CC, 156; MW, 320–325

1116.   POTTER, Chandler Eastman. *The history of Manchester . . .
        including ancient Amoskeag, or the middle Merrimack valley.
        . . .* Manchester, N.H.: C. E. Potter, 1856.

        JL 9.68 (9–8–56); IB 10

1117.   POTTER, Elisha R., Jr. "The Early History of Narragansett."
        Collections of the Rhode Island Historical Society 3 (1835):
        1–135.

        JL 6.67–68 (1–13–54)

        T attributes the information quoted, on the derivation of the
        name "Rhode Island," to H. R. Schoolcraft, who is not, how-
        ever, mentioned by Potter.

1118.   PRATT, Enoch. *A comprehensive history, ecclesiastical and civil, of Eastham, Wellfleet and Orleans, county off Barnstable, Mass., from 1644 to 1844.* . . . Yarmouth: W. S. Fisher and co., 1844.
HL 11–5–49
CC, 28–29, 33–36, 41, 65; JL 9.437 (6–17–57)

Also T's source for Heman Doane's poem addressed to a pear tree in CC, 34.

1119.   PRESTON, H. C. See Jaeger, Benedict.

1120.   PRICE, Sir Uvedale. *Essays on the picturesque, as compared with the sublime and beautiful; and on the use of studying pictures, for the purpose of improving real landscape.* 3 vols. London: Printed for J. Mawman, 1810.
HL 1–19–54
JL 6.103 (2–6–54)

1121.   PRIME, Samuel I. *Travels in Europe and the East.* . . . New York: Harper & brothers, 1855.

IB 12 (c. 1861)

1122.   PRINCE, Thomas. *A chronological history of New-England in the form of annals.* . . . 2 vols. Boston: Kneeland & Green for S. Gerrish, 1736, 1755.

CC, 182; IB 2 (c. 1849)

1123.   PRING, Martin. In Purchas, Samuel, *Purchas his Pilgrimes* (q.v.).
CC, 180–181, 194; IB 9

1124.   *The prose Edda.* See Sturluson, Snorri (no. 1304).

1125.   PULTENEY, Richard. *A general view of the writings of Linnaeus.* . . . *2d ed.* . . . *by William George Maton.* . . . *To which is annexed the diary of Linnaeus.* . . . London: J. Mawmon, 1805.
HL 11–5–51
FB

1126.   PULTENEY, William. "Address to the Commons."
F2a (c. 1837)

Source unknown; T's extracts from the speech describe Oliver Cromwell's diplomacy.

1127.   *Purāṇas. Bhāgavatpurāṇa. Le Bhâgavat purâṇa; ou, Histoire poétique de Křĭchṇa.* . . . 3 vols. Paris: Imprimerie royale, 1840–47.
TL

1128.   *Purāṇas. Vishṇupurāṇa. The Vishñu puráña, a system of Hindu mythology and tradition*. . . . London: J. Murray, 1840.
TL, HL 1–28–5, 10–25–54
WE, 284; WA, 270; CPB 1

1129.   PURCHAS, Samuel. *Purchas his Pilgrimes*. . . . 4 vols. London: Printed by W. Stansby for H. Fetherstone, 1625.
HL 3–16–52 (not withdrawn)
CC 190–192 passim; JL 3.352 (3–16–52); IB 9; IB 10

1130.   PURSH, Frederick. *Flora Americae Septentrionalis; or . . . description of the plants of North America*. . . . London: Printed for White, Cochrane, and co., 1814.

JL 8.437 (7–31–56); 11.43 (7–14–58); IB 10; FB; TMJ

1131.   *Putnam's Monthly Magazine* 2 (Dec. 1853).
TL

This issue contained the second half of Melville's "Bartleby, the Scrivener," but one speculates that T owned this issue for an article entitled "Night-Birds of North America."

1132.   QUARLES, Francis. *Divine Fancies*. . . . London: M. F[lesher], 1638.

"On Faith"
WE, 338
"To My Booke"
WE, 328; PJ 2.357 (after 12–2–46)

1133.   QUARLES, Francis. *Divine Poems*. . . . London: G. Sawbridge, 1706.

A Feast for Worms
WE, 66, 97
Job Militant
WE, 98

See also COR, 139 (9–14–43); T's edition not known.

1134.   QUARLES, Francis. *Emblems, divine and moral*. Chiswick: Printed by C. and C. Whittington, 1825.
TL
V, 2
EX, 313–314
II, 2
PJ 1.448 (4–11–43); 2.65 (1842–44); LN
I, 8
WE, 68; LN
II, 9
WE, 97; LN

II, 13
WE, 223; LN
II, 15
WE, 36; LN
III, 13
WE, 353; LN
IV, 7
WE, 15; LN
IV, 11
WE, 381; LN
I, 9, 11, 14; III, "The Entertainment," 1, 5, 15; IV, 2, 10, 12, 13; V, 4
LN

Hieroglyphikes
XIV
WE, 335; LN
IV, XIII
LN

At the time of his extracts in LN, T's source for Quarles's *Emblems* and *Hieroglyphics* was probably a volume or volumes now unknown in the New York Society Library. See COR, 139, 144, for his general references to reading Quarles while living on Staten Island in 1843.

1135. QUARLES, Francis. *The shepheards oracles: delivered in certain eglogues.* . . . London: J. Marriot, 1646.
TL
WA, 165; PJ 1.461–462 (9–1–43)

As T notes in this Journal entry, he read the *Shepheards Oracles* at the New York Society Library, but the edition is not known.

1136. QUENS, Jean de. In *Jesuit Relations* (q.v.) for 1655–56.
HL 1–26–57
IB 10

1137. RACINE, Jean. *Oeuvres de Racine.* . . . *Nouvelle édition.* 2 vols. Paris: [n.p.], 1741.
HL 1–20–35

1138. RAFFLES, Sir Thomas Stamford. *The history of Java.* . . . 2 vols. London: Black, Parbury and Allen [etc.], 1817.

CPB1; FB (*c.* 1851)

1139. RAFN, Carl Christian. *Antiquités américaines d'après les monuments historiques des Islandais et des anciens Scandinaves.* . . . Copenhagen: . . . imprimerie de J. H. Schultz, 1845.
HL 11–5–49
CC, 109, 147–148, 151, 195–196

The edition of Rafn T used may have been in an unidentified volume entitled "Six Tracts" that he withdrew from Harvard. See Cameron, "Books Thoreau Borrowed."

1140.   RAGENEAU, Paul. In *Jesuit Relations* (q.v.) for 1647–48, 1648–49, 1649–50, 1650–51, 1651–52, 1652–53. IB 10 (*c.* 1857)

1141.   [RALEIGH] RALEGH, Sir Walter. *The works of Sir Walter Ralegh, Kt. now first collected: to which are prefixed the lives of the author by Oldys and Birch.* 8 vols. Oxford: The University Press, 1829.
HL 12–10–41 (vol. 8)
Oldys's "Life"
PJ 1.174–176 (8–19 to 21–40), 359–378 passim (1–42 to 3–42)
"A Discourse of War," "Cabinet Counsel"
LN
"The Nymph's Reply to the Shepherd," "Another of the Same Nature [as the 'Nymph's Reply'] Made Since," "Upon Gascoigne's Poem Called 'The Steel-Glass,' " "The Shepherd's Praise of His Sacred Diana," "The Silent Lover," "The Lover's Absence Kills Me, Her Presence Kills Me," "His Love Admits No Rival," "His Pilgrimage," "On the Snuff of a Candle," "Sir W.R. the Night Before He Died," "False Love and True Love," "Elegy on Sidney"
LN
"A Description of the Country's Recreations," "Dispraise of Love and Love's Follies," "Phillidas' Love-Call to Her Coridon, and His Replying," "De Morte," "A Nymph's Disdain of Love," "Hymn"
CPB 1
"The Soul's Errand"
RP, 140
The History of the World
WE, 324; RP 46

See also T's essay on Raleigh in EEM, 178–218.

1142.   RAMMOHUN ROY, raja. *Translation of several principal books, passages and texts of the Veds, and of some controversial works on Brahmunical theology.* 2d ed. London: Parbury, Allen & co., 1832.
HL 4–26–50
WA, 217, 219; CPB 1

1143.   RAMSEY, Alexander. "Our Field of Historical Research." *Collections of the Minnesota Historical Society* 1 (1856): 43–52.

TMJ

1144.   RAMUSIO, Giovanni Battista. *Delle navigationi et viaggi. . . .* 3 vols. Venice, 1565–1613.

HL 2–28–59 (not withdrawn)
CC, 188, 190; CN; IB 4; IB 10

1145.   RANKING, John. *Historical researches on the conquest of
Peru, Mexico, Bogota, Natchez, and Talomeco, in the thir-
teenth century, by the Mongols, accompanied with elephants.*
. . . London: Longman, Rees, Orme, Brown, and Green,
1827.
HL 1–13–35

1146.   RASLES, Sebastien. *A dictionary of the Abnaki language in
North America. Published from the original manuscript of
the author, with an introductory memoir and notes, by John
Pickering.* In *Memoirs of the American Academy of Arts and
Sciences,* new ser., vol. 1 (1833): 375–574.

MW, 139, 322, 323; JL 10.290 (3–4–58)

1147.   REDPATH, James. *Echoes of Harper's Ferry.* Boston: Thayer
and Eldridge, 1860.
TL

Contains T's "A Plea for Captain John Brown" (RP, 111–
138).

1148.   REDPATH, James. *The public life of John Brown. With an au-
tobiography of his childhood and youth.* Boston: Thayer and
Eldridge, 1860.
TL

1149.   REES, Abraham. *The cyclopaedia; or Universal dictionary of
arts, sciences, and literature.* . . . 41 vols. Philadelphia: S. F.
Bradford [etc., etc.], 1810–24.
CL
JL 3.7–9 (9–21–51); 4.374–375 (9–30–52); 8.278 (4–12–
56); 10.5 (8–8–57); 11.263 (10–30–58)

1150.   REID, Mayne. *The boy hunters, or Adventures in search of a
white buffalo.* . . . Boston: Ticknor, Reed, and Fields, 1853.

IB 10; FB (*c.* 1857)

1151.   REID, Mayne. *The desert home; or The adventures of a lost
family in the wilderness.* . . . Boston: Ticknor, Reed, and
Fields, 1853.

IB 10; FB (*c.* 1856)

1152.   REID. Mayne. *The forest exiles; or, The perils of a Peruvian
family amid the wilds of the Amazon.* . . . Boston: Ticknor &
Fields, 1855.

IB 10; FB (*c.* 1856)

1153.   REID, Mayne. *The hunters' feast; or, Conversations around the camp-fire. . . .* New York: DeWitt & Davenport, 1856.
SL
IB 10; FB (*c.* 1856)

1154.   REID, Mayne. *The young voyageurs; or, The boy hunters in the north. . . .* Boston: Ticknor, Reed, and Fields, 1854.

JL 6.158 (3–9–54); IB 8; FB

1155.   REID, Mayne. *The young yagers; or A narrative of hunting adventures in Southern Africa.* Boston: Ticknor & Fields, 1858.

IB 10; FB (*c.* 1858)

1156.   RÉMUSAT, Jean Pierre Abel. See *Ju-kiao-li*

1157.   RENNIE, James *The faculties of birds.* London: Charles Knight, 1835.

PJ 2.76 (1842–44)

1158.   RENNIE, James. *Insect architecture.* London: C. Knight, 1830.
TL

1159.   RENNIE, James. *Insect miscellanies.* 2 vols. London: C. Knight, 1831.
TL

JL 9.347 (4–28–57)

1160.   RENNIE, James. *Insect transformations.* London: C. Knight, 1830.
TL
JL 10.182 (11–15–57); 11.169 (9–19–58); 12.183 (5–6–59)

1161.   "Report of a Committee of the Board of Correspondents of the Scots Society for Propagating Christian knowledge, who visited the Oneida and Mohekunah Indians in 1796." *Collections of the Massachusetts Historical Society,* 1st ser., vol. 5 (1798; rpt. 1835): 12–32.

IB 2 (*c.* 1849)

1162.   "Review of Edward Baines's *A History of the Cotton Manufacture in Great Britain.*" *North American Review* 52 (Jan. 1841): 31–56.

PJ 1.242 (1–31–41)

1163.   "Review of Paul Émile Botta's *Travels in Arabia* [*Relation d'un Voyage dans l' Yémen, entrepris en 1837, pour le Mu-*

séum d'Histoire Naturelle de Paris]." *Athenaeum*, Jan. 1, 1842: 3–5.

PJ 1.386 (3–23–42); WE 105, 126

1164.   "Review of Sir James Clark Ross's *A Voyage of Discovery and Research in the Southern and Antarctic Regions, During the Years 1839–1843.*" *North British Review* 8 (Nov. 1847): 177–214.

WE, 365–366

1165.   "Review of Sir John Malcolm's *The Life of Robert Lord Clive.*" *Edinburgh Review* 70 (Jan. 1840): 295–362.

PJ 1.173 (8–17–40)

1166.   "Review of William Scrope's *The Art of Deer-Stalking.*" *Edinburgh Review* 71 (April 1840): 98–120.

PJ 1.176 (8–21–40)

1167.   REYNOLDS, Jeremiah N. *Voyage of the United States frigate Potomac . . . during the circumnavigation of the globe, in the years 1831, 1832, 1833, and 1834. . . .* New York: Harper & brothers, 1834.
         IN between 12–8–36 and 3–13–37

1168.   REYNOLDS, Joseph. *Peter Gott, the Cape Ann fisherman.* Boston: J. P. Jewett & company, 1856.
         TL

1169.   RIBERO Y USTARIZ, Mariano Eduardo de. *Peruvian antiquities.* New York: A. S. Barnes, 1855.
         TL

         This is a conjectural entry. Harding lists this volume in T's library, on the basis of T's citation of "Peruvian Antiquities" in his library catalogue. T may have owned the second volume of United States Navy, *Naval Astronomical Expedition to the Southern Hemisphere* (q.v.), which treated Indian remains in Peru and Chile, and which T took notes on in IB 10 under the heading "Indian antiquities brought from Chile and Peru."

1170.   RICH, Obadiah. *Bibliotheca Americana Nova: A catalogue of books relating to America, in various languages, including voyages to the Pacific and around the world, and collections of voyages and travels printed since the year 1700. . . .* 2 vols. London: Rich and Sons, 1846.

CN

1171. RICHARDSON, Sir John. *Arctic searching expedition . . . in search of . . . Sir John Franklin. . . .* 2 vols. New York: Harper & brothers, 1852.
TL
EX, 48; JL 3.358–372 passim (3–23 to 3–31–52); 4.82 (6–5–52); IB 6; CN; FB; TMJ

1172. RICHARDSON, Sir John. *Fauna boreali-americana; or The zoology of the northern parts of British America. . . .* 4 vols. London: J. Murray [etc.], 1829–37.
HL 3–21–52
JL 14.231 (11–10–60); IB 6; FB

1173. RICKETSON, Daniel. *History of New Bedford, Bristol County, Mass.* New Bedford: The Author, 1858.
TL
IB 10 (c. 1858)

1174. RILEY, James. *An authentic narrative of the loss of the American brig Commerce . . . revised . . . by the author, in January, 1828.* Hartford, Conn.: Judd, Loomis & co., 1836.
CL
CC, 158; COR, 319 (1–21–54)

1175. RIPLEY, George, ed. *Specimens of foreign standard literature.* 9 vols. Boston: Hilliard, Gray, and Company, 1838–40.

HM 13201 (12–5–40); LN

See also Menzel, Wolfgang.

1176. RITCHIE, Anna Cora (Ogden) Mowatt. *Autobiography of an actress; or, Eight years on the stage.* Boston: Ticknor, Reed, and Fields, 1853.
CL
JL 7.43 (9–15–54)

1177. RITSON, Joseph, comp. *Ancient English metrical romances.* 3 vols. London: W. Bulmer, for G. & W. Nicol, 1802.
HL 12–6–41

1178. RITSON, Joseph, comp. *Robin Hood: A collection of all the ancient poems, songs, and ballads.* 2 vols. London: T. Egerton and J. Johnson, 1795.
HL 5–25–37
WE, 36, 117, 132, 167, 170; EX, 150, 207; PJ 1.346 (12–23–41); 2.377 (after 4–8–47); LN; ME

1179. RITTER, Heinrich. *The history of ancient philosophy. . . .* Tr. . . . Alexander J. W. Morrison. 4 vols. Oxford: D. A. Talboys, 1838–46.

WE, 107; LN

1180.   ROBERTS, Mary. *A popular history of the Mollusca.* . . . London: Reeve & Benham, 1851.
TL

1181.   ROBERVAL, Sieur de. See *Voyages de découverte au Canada.*

1182.   "Robin's Food." *New York Tribune,* April 2, 1859, p. 3.

CPB2

1183.   ROGERS, Nathaniel, ed. *Herald of Freedom* (newspaper).

WE, 85, 248, 300; RP, 49–57

1184.   ROGERS, Robert. *Reminiscences of the French war.* . . . *To which is added an account of the life and military services of Maj. Gen. John Stark.* . . . Concord, N.H.: L. Roby, 1831.

WE, 253

See also Johnson, *Thoreau's Complex Weave,* pp. 151–153, for T's use of this volume in an early draft of WE.

1185.   ROGERS, Samuel. *Recollections of the table-talk of Samuel Rogers. To which is added porsoniana.* New York: D. Appleton & company, 1856.
BA 12–18–60 (by RWE)
JL 14.311 (1–14–61); IB 12

1186.   ROGET, Peter Mark. *Thesaurus of English words and phrases.* London: Longman, Brown, Green & Longmans, 1852.
TL

1187.   ROGGEVEEN, Arent. *The first part of the Burning Fen. discovering the whole West Indies.* . . . Amsterdam: Peter Goos [etc.], 1675.

CC, 178; CN

1188.   ROLLIN, Charles. *The ancient history of the Egyptians, Carthaginians, Assyrians, Babylonians, Medes & Persians, Macedonians, and Grecians.* 4 vols. New York: Long, 1837.
TL, HL 10–21–34 (vol. 1), 9–3–35 (vol. 1), 10–29–35 (vol. 3), 11–5–35 (vols. 4–8)
PJ 1.466 (9–24–43)

The edition T borrowed from Harvard was an eight-volume Boston 1807 edition.

1189.   ROSIER, James. "A True Relation of the Most Prosperous Voyage Made this Present Year, 1605, by Captain George

Waymouth, in the Discovery of the Land of Virginia. . . ."
Collections of the Massachusetts Historical Society, ser. 3,
vol. 8 (1843): 124–157.

IB 2 (*c.* 1849)

1190.   ROSS, Alexander. *Mystagogus poeticus, or The muses inter-*
preter. . . . London: Thomas Whitaker, 1648.

WE, 58; PJ 2.184–186 (12–45)

1191.   ROUQUETTE, Adrien Emmanuel. *Les savanes, poésies améri-*
caines. Nouvelle-Orléans: A. Moret, 1841.
TL

1192.   ROUQUETTE, Adrien Emmanuel. *La thébaïde en Amérique, ou*
Apologie de la vie solitaire et contemplative. . . . Nouvell Or-
léans: Imprimerie Méridier, 1852.
TL

1193.   ROUQUETTE, Adrien Emmanuel. *Wild flowers, sacred poetry*
by the Abbé Rouquette. . . . New Orleans: T. O'Donnell
[etc.], 1848.
TL

1194.   ROWBOTHAM, John. *Practical grammar of the French lan-*
guage. . . . Boston: Hilliard, Gray, and company, 1832.
TL

1195.   ROYDEN, Matthew. In Chalmers (q.v.), vol. 3.
"An Elegie, or Friends Passion, for His Astrophill."
WE, 267

1196.   RUSKIN, John. *The elements of drawing. In three letters to be-*
ginners. . . . 2d ed. London: Smith, Elder, and co., 1857.
CL
JL 10.209–210 (11–27–57); CPB2

1197.   RUSKIN, John. *Modern painters, by a graduate of Oxford.* . . .
5 vols. New York: Wiley & Halstead, 1856.
CL
COR, 497 (11–16–57); JL 10.69 (10–6–57), 147 (10–29–57);
IB 10

1198.   RUSKIN, John. *Seven lamps of architecture.* New York:
J. Wiley, 1849.
CL
COR, 497 (11–16–57)

1199.   RUSSELL, Michael. *Life of Oliver Cromwell.* New York: J. &
J. Harper, 1833.
TL

1200.   SABINE, Lorenzo. *Report on the principal fisheries of the American seas.* Washington: Robert Armstrong, printer, 1853.

CC, 156–157; FB

1201.   SADĀNANDA Yogīndra. *A lecture on the Vedánta, embracing the text of the Vedánta-sára, by Jr. R. Ballantyne.* Allahabad: Printed for the use of the Benares College, by order of Govt., N.W.P., 1850.
TL

1202.   SADDHARMAPUṆḌARĪKA. *Le lotus de la bonne loi, traduit du sanscrit, accompagné d'un commentaire et de vingt et un mémoires relatifs au buddhisme, par m. E. Burnouf.* Paris: Imprimerie nationale, 1852.
TL

1203.   SA'DĪ. *The gûlistân; or, Rose Garden.* . . . Tr. Francis Gladwin. London: W. Bulmer, 1808.
EL
WE, 69, 78–79, 129–130, 304–305, 388; WA, 79; LN

1204.   SAGARD, Gabriel. *Le grand voyage du pays des Hurons, situé en L'Amerique.* . . . Paris: Chez D. Moreau, 1632.
HL 12–25–54
IB 9; FB

1205.   SAGARD, Gabriel. *Histoire dv Canada et voyages qve les freres mineurs recollects y ont faicts pour la conversion des infidelles.* . . . Paris: C. Sonnius, 1636.
HL 1–16–55; 2–15–58
JL 7.126 (1–20–55), 143 (1–25–55); IB 9; FB

1206.   ST. HILAIRE, Geoffroy. See "Life and Doctrine of Geoffroy St. Hilaire."

1207.   ST. JOHN, Bayle. *Adventures in the Libyan desert and the oasis of Jupiter Ammon.* New York: G. P. Putnam; [etc., etc.], 1850.

CPB2 (*c.* 1860)

1208.   SAINT PIERRE, Jacques Henri Bernardin de. *Studies of nature.* . . . *Tr. by Henry Hunter.* . . . 5 vols. London: Printed for C. Dilly, 1796.

CPB2: IB 12 (*c.* 1860)

1209.   SALLUST. *De Catalinae conjuractione, belloque jugurthino, historiae.* 4th ed. Boston: Hilliard, Gray and Co., 1833.
         TX

         Required for admission to Harvard.

1210.   SAMPSON, Zabdiel, and Nymphas MARSTON. "Commissioners' Report on Cape Cod Harbor."

         CC, 163–164

1211.   SANFORD, Henry S. *The different systems of penal codes in Europe; also, a report on the administrative changes in France, since the revolution of 1848.* Washington: B. Tucker, Senate printer, 1854.
         TL

1212.   SAY, Jean Baptiste. *A treatise on political economy. . . . Tr. by C. R. Prinsey. . . . 6th American edition. . . .* Philadelphia: Grigg & Elliot, 1834.
         TL, TX

1213.   SAY, Samuel. *Poems on several occasions: and two critical essays; viz, the first on the harmony, variety, and power of numbers . . . the second, on the numbers of Paradise Lost.* London: [n.p.], 1745.
         HL 3–30–37.
         CPB1; F6d

1214.   SCAPULA, Johan. *Lexicon greco-latinum, e probatis auctoribus locupletatum. . . .* London: impensis Joshua Kirtong & Samuel Thomson, 1652.
         HL 6–9–35

1215.   SCHILLER, Johann C. F. von. *Geschichte des dreissigjährigen Kriegs. . . .* 2 vols. Leipzig: F. C. Vogel, 1823.
         TL

1216.   SCHILLER, Johann C. F. von. *Maria Stuart. . . .* Stuttgart und Tübingen: Cotta, 1825.
         TL

1217.   SCHLEGEL, Friedrich von. *Lectures on the history of literature, ancient and modern. . . .* 2 vols. Philadelphia: T. Dobson and Son, 1818.
         HL 9–5–36 (vol. 1), 10–3–36 (vol. 2)

1218.   SCHOOLCRAFT, Henry Rowe. *Historical and statistical information respecting the history, condition, and prospects of the Indian tribes of the United States. . . .* 6 vols. Philadelphia: Lippincott, Grambo, 1851–57.

SNH 7–26–52 (vol. 1), 11–28–52 (vol. 3), 1–13–58 (vol. 5),
HL 12–7–54 (vol. 4)
EX, 90; CN; IB 6; IB 7; IB 8; IB 11

1219.   SCHOOLCRAFT, Henry Rowe. *Narrative of an expedition through the upper Mississippi to Lake Itasca . . . in 1832.* New York: Harper, 1834.

IB 6 (c. 1852)

1220.   SCHOOLCRAFT, Henry Rowe. *Oneota, or the red race of America.* New York: Wiley & Putnam, 1845.
TL
IB 4 (c. 1851)

1221.   SCOTT, Sir Walter. *Complete Works.* 7 vols. New York: Conner & Cooke, 1833–34.

"Lady of the Lake"
PJ 1.73 (5–21–39)
"Thomas the Rhymer"
WE, 137; PJ 1.469 (9–28–43)

1222.   SCOTT, Sir Walter. *Letters on demonology and witchcraft. Addressed to J. G. Lockhart, esq.* New York: J. & J. Harper (Harper's Family Library), 1830.
IN 3–30–37

1223.   SCOTT, Sir Walter. *Marmion; a tale of Flodden field.* Baltimore: Published by Joseph Cushing, 1812.
TL

1224.   SCOTT, William. *Lessons in elocution. . . .* Boston: Lincoln & Edmands, 1820.
TL

1225.   *Scriptores rei rusticae, Rei rusticae auctores latine veteres, M. Cato, M. Varro, L. Columella, Palládius. . . .* [Heidelbergae]: ex Hier. Commelini typographio, 1595.
AL (8–11–51)

For references see individual authors.

1226.   SCROPE, William. See "Review of William Scrope's *The Art of Deer-Stalking.*"

1227.   SELDEN, John. In Young, Alexander, *Library of the Old English Prose Writers* (q.v.).
PJ 2.211 (Fall 1845)

1228.   SENECA. *Medea, tragedy of Seneca. Ed. by Charles Beck.* . . .
Cambridge and Boston: J. Munroe & co., 1834.
TL

1229.   SEWEL, William. *The history of the rise, increase, and prog-
ress of the Christian people called Quakers.* . . . *3d ed., corr.*
Burlington, N.J.: Printed and sold by I. Collins, 1774.
TL

1230.   SHAKESPEARE II [pseud.]. *Shakespeare's romances. Collected
and arranged by Shakespeare II.* . . . 2 vols. London: Sherwood, Gilbert, and Piper, 1825.
IN 11–24–36

1231.   SHAKESPEARE, William. *The dramatic works.* . . . 2 vols.
Hartford, Conn.: Andrus & Judd, 1833.
TL
Antony and Cleopatra
RP, 12
As You Like It
WE, 68, 248, 341; CC, 186
Hamlet
WE, 63; RP 66
Julius Caesar
WE, 41, 124, 287; EEM, 70, 72; WA, 67; PJ 2.15 (1842–44)
King John
RP, 66
King Lear
WE, 282
Macbeth
EX, 119; PJ 1.151 (7–7–40)
The Merchant of Venice
PJ 1.462 (9–1–43)
A Midsummer Night's Dream
EEM, 74
Richard III
EX, 125; PJ 1.216 (1–2–41)
The Tempest
CC, 266
Twelfth Night
PJ 1.446 (1–3–43)
"Venus and Adonis"
PJ 1.458 (6–19–43)
"Sonnet 33"
WE, 189–190

T also withdrew three volumes of a fifteen-volume London
1793 edition from HL on 4–21–35.

1232.   SHATTUCK, Lemuel. *A history of the town of Concord.* Boston: Russell, Odiorne & Stacy, 1835.

TL

WE, 5, 51, 121, 212; EX, 115; PJ 2.103–104 (after 8–1–44);
JL 5.240–241 (6–10–53), 242 (6–11–53); 6.77 (1–27–54);
9.255–256 (2–15–57), 264 (2–16–57)

1233.   SHEA, John G. "History of the Discovery of the Mississippi
        River." In French, B. F., *Historical Collections of Louisiana*
        (q.v.), pt. 4 (1853): vii–xxxix.

        IB 11 (c. 1858)

1234.   SHEA, John G. "The Jogues Papers." *Collections of the New
        York Historical Society*, ser. 2, vol. 3, pt. 1 (1857): 163–229.
        HL 1–13–58
        IB 11

1235.   SHELLEY, Mary Wollstonecraft. *Lives of the most eminent
        French writers.* . . . 2 vols. Philadelphia: Lea and Blanchard,
        1840.

        HM 13201 (1841)

1236.   SHELLEY, Percy Bysshe. "Prometheus Unbound."

        MW, 235; LN (C. 1848)

        Edition and source unknown.

1237.   SHELLEY, Percy Bysshe. See Coleridge, Samuel T.

1238.   SHEPARD, Thomas. *The clear sun-shine of the gospel breaking
        forth upon the Indians in New England.* . . . London: Printed
        by R. Cates for J. Bellamy, 1648.
        HL 3–13–54
        IB 8

1239.   [SHEPPARD, Elizabeth Sara]. *Counterparts, or, The cross of
        love. By the author of "Charles Auchester."* Boston: Mayhew
        and Baker, 1859.
        CL
        JL 11.451 (2–20–59)

1240.   SHIRLEY, James.

        "Contention of Ajax and Ulysses"
        RP, 139
        "Death's Final Conquest," "Victorious Men of Earth"
        LN (c. 1841)

1241.   SIBBALD, James. *Chronicle of Scottish poetry; from the 13th
        century to the union of the crowns.* . . . 4 vols. Edinburgh:

Printed for J. Sibbald, by C. Stewart & co. [etc., etc.], 1802.
HL 6–26–37 (vol. 2), 12–10–41 (vols. 1–4)
WE, 89–90, 117; ME; LN

1242.   SIDNEY, Sir Philip. *The works of the honourable Sir Philip
Sidney, Kt., in prose and verse.* 14th ed. 3 vols. London:
W. Innys, 1724–25.
HL 12–10–41
PJ 1.434–435 (after 7–18–42)
"Arcadia," fragments from "Sonnets"
LN
"Defense of Poesy"
ME (8–19–37)

1243.   SIGOURNEY, Lydia Howard (Huntley). *Traits of the aborigines of America. A poem.* Cambridge: Hilliard and Metcalf,
1822.
HL 5–7–34

Conjectural; see Cameron, "Books Thoreau Borrowed."

1244.   SILLIMAN, Benjamin. *Remarks made on a short tour between
Hartford and Quebec, in the autumn of 1819. . . . 2d ed. . . .*
New-Haven: S. Converse, 1824.
HL 2–10–51
EX, 79, 98; CN

1245.   SIMONIDES. See *Greek Anthology.*

1246.   SIMPKINS, Rev. John. "A Topographical Description of
Brewster in the County of Barnstable." *Collections of the
Massachusetts Historical Society,* 1st ser., vol 10 (1809): 72–
79.

CC, 22–23

1247.   SITGREAVES, Lorenzo. See United States. Army. Corps of Topographical Engineers (no. 1361).

1248.   "The Skunk Skin Traffic." *New York Tribune,* April 1, 1859,
p. 7.

JL 12.122 (4–8–59)

1249.   SLEEMAN, Sir William Henry. *Rambles and recollections of an
Indian official.* 2 vols. London: J. Hatchard and son, 1844.

JL 4.209 (7–9–52); 14.334 (1861); FB

1250.   SMELLIE, William. *The philosophy of natural history. . . .
With an introduction and various additions and alterations,*

intended to adapt it to the present state of knowledge. By John Ware, M.D. Boston: Hilliard, Gray, and company, 1836.
TL, TX

1251.   SMET, Pierre Jean de. *Oregon missions and travels over the Rocky mountains, in 1845–46. . . .* New-York: E. Dunigan, 1847.

IB 3 (c. 1849)

1252.   SMITH, Edmund. *The Araucanians, or Notes of a tour among the Indian tribes of southern Chile.* New York: Harper's, 1855.

IB 10 (c. 1856)

1253.   SMITH, Sir James Edward. *An introduction to physiological and systematical botany. . . . 1st American, from the 2d English ed.; with notes, by Jacob Bigelow, M.D.* Philadelphia: Published by Anthony Finley, and Bradford and Read, Boston, 1814.
HL 5–18–37

1254.   SMITH, John. "A Description of New England." *Collections of the Massachusetts Historical Society,* 3d ser., vol. 6 (1837): 95–140.

MW, 153; CC, 178, 180, 201, 209; PJ 3 (Fall 1849); IB 8

1255.   SMITH, John. *The generall historie of Virginia, New-England, and the Summer Isles . . . from . . . 1584 to . . . 1626. . . .* London: Printed by I.D. and I.H. for E. Blackmore, 1632.
HL 2–9–53
WE, 89; MW, 90–92; CC, 142–143, 178, 209; JL 4.494 (2–23–53); 5.21 (3–15–53); 7.267 (3–23–55); IB 8

1256.   SMITHSONIAN INSTITUTION. *Annual Report of the board of regents.* Washington: Smithsonian Institution, 1851, 1852, 1854, 1855, 1856.
TL

1257.   SMYTH, Charles Piazzi. *Teneriffe, an astronomer's experiment: or, Specialties of a residence above the clouds.* London: L. Reeve, 1858.

JL 11.48–49n (7–15–58)

1258.   SMYTH, William. *Elementary algebra. . . .* Portland, Maine: Sanborn & Carter, 1851.
TL

1259.   SOPHOCLES. *The Antigone of Sophocles in Greek and English, with introduction and notes by John William Donaldson.* London: John W. Parker, 1848.
HL 9–4–55

See next entry for an earlier reference to *Antigone*.

1260.   SOPHOCLES. *Sophoclis tragoediae.* . . . Lipsiae: Typis et sumtibus F.C.G. Vogelii, 1831.
TL
Oedipus at Colonos
JL 9.372–373 (5–19–57)
Antigone
WE, 134, 135

1261.   "South American Scraps: La Plata." *Household Words. A Weekly Journal,* conducted by Charles Dickens, vol. 3, no. 68 (1851): 378–381.

FB (*c.* 1853)

1262.   SOUTHEY, Robert. *The poetical works of Robert Southey.* . . . *Ten volumes in one.* New York: D. Appleton, 1839.
TL

1263.   SOWERBY, George Brettingham. *Popular British conchology. A familiar history of the molluscs inhabiting the British Isles.* London: L. Reeve, 1854.
TL
CPB2 (*c.* 1855)

1264.   SOWERBY, Henry. *Popular mineralogy; comprising a familiar account of minerals and their uses.* London: Reeve & Bentham, 1850.
TL

1265.   SOWERBY, John E. *The ferns of Great Britain.* . . . London: J. E. Sowerby, 1885.
TL

Conjectural; see Harding, *Thoreau's Library,* s.v.

1266.   SPARKS, Jared, ed. *Library of American biography.* 10 vols. Boston: Hilliard, Gray; London: Kennett, 1836–39.
IN 9–12–36 (vol. 5)

1267.   *The Spectator; with notes and a general index. From the London stereotype edition.* . . . . 2 vols. in 1. Philadelphia: Published by L. Johnson, 1832.
TL
PJ 1.171 (8–13–40)

Autograph of J. Thoreau.

1268.   SPENSE, William. See Kirby, William.

1269.   SPENSER, Edmund. In Chalmers (q.v.), vol. 3.
        The Fairie Queens
        WE, 203, 208, 297, 334; WA, 142; PJ 1.460 (8–25–43), 461
        (9–1–43); LN
        "The Ruins of Rome"
        WE, 249; LN
        "The Ruins of Time"
        WE, 249
        "The Shepherd's Calendar," "Epithalamion"
        LN
        "Perigot and Cuddie's Roundelay"
        ME

1270.   *Spiritual Science.*

        As Harding points out (*Thoreau's Library*, p. 89), T's library
        catalogue lists a volume by this title that has not been identi-
        fied.

1271.   SPRAGUE, Charles J. Untitled contribution to *Proceedings of
        the Boston Natural History Society* 6 (1856–59): 396.

        JL 11.338 (11–20–58)

1272.   SPRENGEL, Kurt Polycarp. See Candolle, Augustin Pyramus
        de.

1273.   SPRINGER, John S. *Forest life and forest trees: comprising
        winter camp life . . . of Maine and New Brunswick.* New
        York: Harper & brothers, 1851.

        MW, 20n, 43–44n, 68–69n, 245, 321; FB

1274.   SQUIER, E. G. *Aboriginal monuments of the state of New
        York. . . .* Washington: Smithsonian Institution, 1850.
        (Smithsonian contributions to knowledge, vol. 2.)

        IB 8 (*c.* 1852)

1275.   SQUIER, E. G. "The Antiquities of Western New-York." *New
        York Tribune,* Jan. 3, 1849, p. 1.

        IB 3 (1849)

1276.   SQUIER, E. G. *The serpent symbol, and the worship of the re-
        ciprocal principles of nature in America.* New York: G. P.
        Putnam, 1851.
        AL
        IB 4, (*c.* 1851)

1277.   SQUIER, E. G. *Waikna; or, Adventures on the Mosquito shore. By Samuel A. Bard [pseud.] with sixty illustrations.* New York: Harper & brothers, 1855.

      IB 10; FB (*c.* 1857)

1278.   SQUIER, E. G., and E. H. DAVIS. *Ancient monuments of the Mississippi Valley.* New York: Bartlett & Welford [etc., etc.], 1848.

      IB 3 (*c.* 1849)

1279.   STÄEL-HOLSTEIN, Anna Louise Germaine. *Germany. Tr. from the French.* . . . 3 vols. in 2. New York: Eastburn, Kirk, 1814.
      EL
      PJ 1.32 (3–4–38)

      T's reference does not indicate that he was reading or had read Madame de Stäel's book, but it does demonstrate enough familiarity with its reputation, at least, to warrant inclusion here.

1280.   STALLO, John Bernhard. *General principles of the philosophy of nature . . . embracing the philosophical systems of Schelling and Hegel, and Oken's system of nature.* Boston: Wm. Crosby and H. P. Nichols, 1848.
      AL
      LN (*c.* 1848)

1281.   STANLEY, Edward. *A familiar history of birds; their nature, habits and instincts.* London: John W. Parker, 1851.

      FB (*c.* 1855)

1282.   STANLEY, Thomas. *The history of philosophy.* . . . London: Printed for W. Battersby [etc.], 1701.
      AL
      WE, 128

1283.   STANSBURY, Howard. See United States. Army. Corps of Topographical Engineers (no. 1359).

1284.   STARK, Robert MacKenzie. *A popular history of British mosses.* . . . London: L. Reeve, 1854.
      TL

1285.   STEBBING, Henry. *Lives of the Italian poets.* 3 vols. London: E. Bull, 1832.
      IN 9–12–36, 10–24–36

1286.   STEELE, Richard. See *The Spectator.*

1287.   STEPHENS, John Lloyd. *Incidents of travel in Egypt, Arabia Petrae, and the Holy Land.* 4th ed. 2 vols. New York: Harper & brothers, 1838.
CL
PJ 1.186–187 (10–11–40)

1288.   STERNE, Laurence. *The beauties of Sterne.* Boston: Andrews and Cummings [etc., etc.], 1807.
TL

1289.   STERNE, Laurence. *A sentimental journey through France and Italy.* London: C. Cooke [179–?].
TL

1290.   STEVENS, John, ed. *A new collection of voyages and travels . . . in all parts of the world. None of them ever before printed in English. . . .* London: J. Knapton [etc.], 1708–10.
HL 12–22–56
IB 10

1291.   STEWART, Dugald. *Elements of the philosophy of the human mind.* 2 vols. Cambridge: James Munroe and company, 1833.
TL, TX

1292.   STIMSON, Jeremy. "A Topographical Description of Hopkinton, in the County of Middlesex." *Collections of the Massachusetts Historical Society*, 1st ser., vol. 4 (1795; rpt. 1835): 15–19.

PJ 3 (Fall 1849)

1293.   STORER, David H., and W.B.O. PEABODY. *Report on the fishes, reptiles, and birds of Massachusetts. . . .* Boston: Dutton and Wentworth, state printers, 1839.
TL
EX, 103–129; WE, 88; CC, 115, 145; PJ 2.106 (after 8–1–44); JL 2.259 (6–14–51), 358 (7–29–51); 6.34 (12–20–53); 7.136 (1–24–55), 208 (2–22–55); 8.394 (6–27–56); 9.110 (10–11–56); 10.382 (4–23–58); 11.167 (9–18–58); 12.153 (4–21–59); 13.420–422 (7–25–60)

1294.   STORER, H. R. Untitled contribution to *Proceedings of the Boston Society of Natural History*, 5 (1854–56): 93.

JL 10.355 (4–5–58)

1295.   STORER, Thomas. "Wolseius Triumphans." In Park, Thomas, *Helconia* (q.v.).

WA, 268

1296. STORY, Joseph. *Commentaries on the constitution of the United States.* . . . Boston: Hilliard, Gray, and company [etc.], 1833.
TL

1297. STÖVER, Dietrich Johann Heinrich. *The life of Sir Charles Linnaeus . . . to which is added a biographical sketch of the life of his son.* . . . *Trans. Joseph Trapp.* London: B. and J. White, 1794.
HL 11–5–51
JL 3.117–118 (11–15–51), 120–122 (11–16–51), 181 (1–8–52); FB

1298. STRABO. *Strabonis Rerum geographicarum libri XVII.* . . . Amstelaedami: apud Joannem Wolters, 1707.

WE, 132; CC, 216; COR, 611 (4–10–61); JL 14.338 (5–8–60)

T's quotation from Strabo in CC was taken from Pliny's *Natural History* (q.v.).

1299. STRACHEY, William. "The Second Book of the First Decade of the Historie of Travaile into Virginia Brittania . . . 1607." *Collections of the Massachusetts Historical Society,* 4th ser., vol. 1 (1852): 219–247.

IB 9 (*c.* 1855)

1300. STRICKLAND, C. P. See Traill, Catherine Parr.

1301. STRICKLAND, Hugh E. "On the True Method of Discovering the Natural System in Zoology and Botany." *The Annals and Magazine of Natural History, including Zoology, Botany, and Geology* 6 (Nov. 1840): 184–194.

PJ 1.220 (1–11–41)

1302. STRICKLAND, Hugh E. See "The Dodo and Its Kindred."

1303. STURLUSON, Snorri. *The Heimskringla; or, Chronicle of the kings of Norway, Trans. Samuel Laing.* 3 vols. London: Longmans, Brown, Green and Longmans, 1844.
EL
EX, 82; JL 3.82 (10–26–51), 191–193 (1–15–52), 203 (1–17–52), 304–305 (2–15–52), 309–311 (2–18–52), 314–316 (2–20–52); 4.410 (11–4–52); IB 5; IB 7; FB; CPB2

1304. STURLUSON, Snorri. *The prose Edda.* In Mallet, Paul Henri, *Northern Antiquities* (q.v.).

EX, 291

1305.   "Subterranean Switzerland." *Littel's Living Age* 64 (Jan. 1860): 165–171.

IB 12 (*c.* 1860)

Anonymous article reprinted from *All the Year Round.*

1306.   SULLY, Maximilien de Béthune, duc de. *Memoirs of Maximilian de Bethune, Duke of Sully, prime minister of Henry the Great. . . . To which is annexed, The trial of Henry the Great.* 5 vols. Edinburgh: Printed by A. Donaldson, 1770.
IN between 12–8–36 and 3–13–37

1307.   SUMNER, Charles. *The barbarism of slavery. . . .* Washington: T. Hyatt, 1860.
TL

1308.   SUMNER, Charles. *Position and duties of the merchant; address before the Mercantile Lib. Assoc. . . . Nov. 13, 1854.* Boston: Ticknor and Fields, 1855.
TL

1309.   SUMNER, Charles. *Usurpation of the Senate. Two speeches of Hon. Charles Sumner, on the imprisonment of Thaddeus Hyatt. . . .* Washington: Buell & Blanchard, 1860.
TL

1310.   SURAULT, François Marie Joseph. *An easy grammar of the French language, for young beginners.* Boston: Richardson, Lord and Holbrook, 1831.
TL

1311.   SWAN, James G. *The northwest coast; or, Three years' residence in Washington territory.* New York: Harper & brothers, 1857.

CC, 213; IB 10 (*c.* 1857)

1312.   SWEDENBORG, Emanuel.

In a letter to B. B. Wiley in 1856 (COR, 446–447), T says that he is acquainted with Swedenborg "to a slight extent," but he does not mention any of Swedenborg's works by name. RWE had an extensive collection of Swedenborg titles in his library.

1313.   SWIFT, Jonathan. *Gulliver's Travels.*

There are allusive references to Brobdignag and Lilliput in PJ 1.22, 118, but no direct evidence that T had read *Gulliver's Travels.*

1314.   SYLVESTER, Joshua. "Probability of the Celestial Orbs Being
        Inhabited."

        CPBI (*c.* 1841)

1315.   TACITUS. C. *Cornelii Taciti opera ex recensione Io. Augusti
        Ernesti.* . . . 3 vols. Boston: Wells et Lilly, 1817.
        EL
        De Vita Ivli Agricolae
        RP, 142
        De Germania
        EX, 290

1316.   TALBOT, Edward Allen. *Five years' residence in the Canadas;
        including a tour through part of the United States of America,
        in the year 1823.* 2 vols. London: Longman, Hurst, Rees,
        Orme, Brown, and Green, 1824.
        HL 2–16–52
        FB

1317.   TANNER, Henry S. *New Hampshire and Vermont* (map). Phil-
        adelphia: Swift & Wilson, 1833.
        TL

1318.   TANNER, John. *A narrative of the captivity and adventures of
        John Tanner . . . during thirty years residence among the In-
        dians.* . . . New York: G. & C. & H. Carvill, 1830.
        HL 5–9–54
        JL 6.373–374 (6–21–54); 9.299 (3–20–57); FB; IB 8

1319.   TASSO, Torquato. *La Gerusalemme liberata.* Firenze: Presso
        L. Ciardetti, 1823.
        TL; IN between 12–8–36 and 3–13–37

        The edition T borrowed from IN was a two-volume London
        1770 translation by John Hoole.

1320.   TATLER. London, 1723 (vol. 2).
        TL

1321.   TAYLOR, Bayard. *Cyclopaedia of modern travel.* . . . Cincin-
        nati: Moore, Wilstach, Keys & co., 1856.

        IB 10 (*c.* 1857)

1322.   TAYLOR, Bayard. *Eldorado; or, Adventures in the path of em-
        pire.* New York: G. P. Putnam's, 1850.
        CL
        IB 8; IB 9 (*c.* 1855)

1323.   TEGNÉR, Esaias. *Frithiof's saga, or The legend of Frithiof. Tr. from the Swedish.* London: A. H. Baily and co., 1835.

HM 13201 (6–3–41)

1324.   TENNYSON, Alfred, Lord. *In memoriam.* Boston: Ticknor, Reed, & Fields, 1850.
TL

1325.   TENNYSON, Alfred, Lord. *Poems.* 2 vols. Boston: William D. Ticknor, 1842.
EL
PJ 1.436 (before 8–23–42)
"The Lady of Shalott"
WE, 179
"Locksley Hall"
WE, 124, 156

1326.   THATCHER, Benjamin B. *Indian traits; being sketches of the manners, customs, and character of the North American natives.* 2 vols. New York: [n.p.], 1844.
CL
IB 2 (*c.* 1849)

1327.   THATCHER, James T. *History of the town of Plymouth, from its first settlement in 1620, to the present time. . . .* Boston: Marsh, Capen & Lyon, 1835.
HL 9–4–55 (not withdrawn)
CC, 33; JL 2.365 (7–31–51); CN

1328.   THEOCRITES. See *The Greek Pastoral Poets.*

1329.   THEOPHRASTUS. *The characters of Theophrastus; Tr. from the Greek, and illustrated by physiognomical sketches. . . . By Francis Howell.* London: Josiah Taylor, 1824.

PJ 1.193 (11–2–40)

1330.   THEOPHRASTUS. *Theophrasti Eresi quae supersunt opera et excerpta librorum. . . .* 5 vols. Lipsiae: Sumtibus F.C.G. Vogelii, 1818–21.
HL 12–16–59
JL 13.133 (2–8–60), 240 (4–2–60)

1331.   THOMPSON, Charles. *An inquiry into the causes of the alienation of the Delaware and Shawanese Indians from the British interests . . . with the remarkable Journal of Christian Frederic Post. . . .* London: Printed for J. Wilkie, 1759.
HL 12–10–55
IB 9

1332. THOMPSON, Zadoch. *History of Vermont, natural, civil, and statistical.* . . . Burlington, Vt.: Pub. for the author, by C. Goodrich, 1842.
SNH 12–10–58
JL 8.366–367 (6–5–56); 9.63 (9–6–56), 73 (9–9–56); IB 11; CPB2

1333. THOMSON, James. In Chalmers (q.v.), vol. 12.
The Seasons
EEM, 76; EX, 170, 182, 183, 249; PJ 2.85–86 (1842–44)

1334. THOMSON, Thomas. *Travels in Sweden during the autumn of 1812.* London: Robert Baldwin, 1813.

EX, 141; PJ 1.26 (1–21–38)

1335. TIBULLUS. *Elegies.* . . .

I. 10
WA, 172

As Harding notes (*Variorum "Walden,"* p. 295), T's source for these lines was probably Evelyn's *Silva.*

1336. TIENHOVEN, Cornelius Van. "Information Relative to Taking Up Land in New Netherland." In O'Callaghan, E. B., *The Documentary History of . . . New York* (q.v.).

WA, 39; FB (*c.* 1854)

1337. TOCQUEVILLE, Alexis Charles Henry . . . de. *Democracy in America.* . . . *Tr. by Henry Reeve.* 4 vols. London: Saunders and Otley, 1835–40.

HM 13201 (4–15–41)

1338. TONTI, Henri de [attrib.]. *Relation de la Louisiane et du Mississipi.* In Bernard, Jean Frédéric, *Recueil de voyages* (q.v.).
HL 12–7–58
IB 11

1339. TOOKE, John Horne. *The diversions of Purley.* 2 vols. Philadelphia: Printed by Wm. Duane, 1806–7.

EEM, 91–92 (3–17–37)

1340. TOPSELL, Edward. *The historie of foure-footed beasts and serpents.* . . . London: Printed by W. Iaggard, 1607.
HL 2–6–60
WE, 364; EX, 318, 319; PJ 2.76 (1842–44); JL 13.149–153 (2–17–60), 159 (2–23–60), 167–168 (2–28–60); IB 12

As T notes in the Journal, this was a translation of an earlier work by Conrad Gesner.

1341. TORREY, John. *Flora of the state of New-York, comprising full descriptions of all the indigenous and naturalized plants hitherto discovered in the state.* . . . 2 vols. Albany: Carroll and Cook, 1843.
SNH 6–13–59 (vol. 2)
JL 12.252–253 (7–22–59)

1342. TOURNEUR, Cyril. *The Revenger's Tragedie.*

RP, 68

T's source for the lines from *The Revenger's Tragedie* he quotes in "Resistance to Civil Government" was probably Charles Lamb's *Specimens of English Dramatic Poets* (q.v.).

1343. TOUSSENEL, Alphonse. *L'esprit des bêtes; zoologie passionelle. Mammifères de France.* Paris: Librarie Phalanstérienne, 1855.

FB (*c.* 1853)

Although T's entry in the FB was clearly made in 1853, he does cite the 1855 edition. Perhaps this ascription was made at a later date; RWE owned an American edition dated 1852.

1344. TRAILL, Catherine Parr (Strickland). *The backwoods of Canada; being letters from the wife of an emigrant officer, illustrative of the domestic economy of British America.* London: C. Knight, 1836.
HL 2–15–58
IB 11

1345. *Treasury of knowledge and library of reference.* 5th ed. 2 vols. New York: Conner & Cooke, 1833–34.
HL 10–7–34

1346. TRENCH, Richard Chenevix. *On the study of words.* . . . *From the 2d London ed., rev. and enlarged.* New York: Redfield, 1852.

JL 4.466–467 (1–15–53), 482 (1–27–53); FB; IB 8

1347. TSCHUDI, Johann Jakob von. *Travels in Peru during the years 1838–1842.* . . . New York: Wiley & Putnam, 1847.
TL

1348. TUCKER, Abraham. *The light of nature pursued.* . . . 7 vols. London: Printed for R. Foulder [etc.], 1805.
HL 9–17–35

1349.   TUCKERMAN, Edward. *An enumeration of North American Lichenes . . . to which is prefixed an essay on the natural systems of Oken, Fries and Endlicher.* Cambridge, Mass.: J. Owen, 1845.
SNH 2–2–52
JL 3.281 (2–5–52), 286–287 (2–7–52); 4.112 (6–18–52); 6.158 (3–9–54); FB

1350.   TUCKERMAN, Edward. *A synopsis of the Lichenes of New England, the other northern states, and British America. . . .* Cambridge, Mass.: G. Nichols, 1848.
SNH 2–2–52

1351.   TUCKERMAN, Henry Theodore. *The Italian sketchbook. 2nd ed., enlarged.* Boston: Light & Stearns, 1837.
IN 3–13–37

1352.   TUFTS, Cotton. "Of the Word 'Schooner': A Communication from Cotton Tufts, Esq." *Collections of the Massachusetts Historical Society,* 1st ser., vol. 9 (1804): 234–235.

CC, 156–157

1353.   TURNER, Sharon. *History of the Anglo-Saxons.* 2 vols. London: Longman, Hurst, Rees, & Orme, 1807.
BA 12–14–37 (by RWE); HL 11–29–41
WE, 156; RP, 195; PJ 1.19–24 (12–37), 417 (1842); ME

1354.   TUSSER, Thomas. *Five hundred points of good husbandry.*

WE, 112; LN

T's source, according to LN, was a commonplace book of RWE's.

1355.   TYNDALL, John. *Glaciers of the Alps. . . .* Boston: Ticknor, Reed, and Fields, 1861.
EL
CPB2 (c. 1861)

1356.   TYTLER, Patrick Fraser. *Elements of general history; ancient & modern with a continuation terminating at the demise of George 3rd, by Edward Nares.* Concord, N.H.: Hill, 1824.
TL

1357.   TYTLER, Patrick Fraser. *Historical view of the progress of discovery on the more northern coasts of America, from the earliest period to the present time. . . .* New York: Harper & brothers, 1855.
TL

1358.   TYTLER, Patrick Fraser. *Life of Sir Walter Raleigh . . . including a view of the most important transactions in the reigns of Elizabeth and James I . . . with a vindication of his character from the attacks of Hume etc.* Edinburgh: Oliver & Boyd, 1833.
BA 10–7–42 (by RWE)
PJ 1.443–444 (after 10–15–42)

1359.   UNITED STATES. ARMY. Corps of Topograpical Engineers. *Exploration and survey of the great salt lake of Utah, including a reconnaissance of a new route through the Rocky Mountains.* Washington: R. Armstrong, public printer, 1853.

IB 8 (*c.* 1854)

Author was Howard Stansbury.

1360.   UNITED STATES. ARMY. Corps of Topographical Engineers. *Notes of a military reconnaissance, from Fort Leavenworth, in Missouri, to San Diego, in California. . . . Made in 1846–47 with the advanced guard of the "Army of the West." . . . By W. H. Emory.* Washington: Wendell and Van Benthuysen, 1848.

IB 10 (*c.* 1857)

1361.   UNITED STATES. ARMY. Corps of Topographical Engineers. *Report of an expedition down the Zuni and Colorado rivers by Captain L. Sitgreaves. . . .* Washington: R. Armstrong, public printer, 1853.
TL
COR, 353 (12–5–54); FB; IB 8

1362.   UNITED STATES. CENSUS OFFICE. 7th census, 1850. *Statistical view of the United States . . . being a compendium of the seventh census. . . . By J.D.B. DeBow. . . .* Washington: A.O.P. Nicholson, public printer, 1854.
TL

1363.   UNITED STATES. COAST AND GEODETIC SURVEY. *Report of the Coast Survey. Superintendent A. D. Bache.* Washington, 1850–58.
TL

These were annual reports; T also owned the volume *Sketches* accompanying the coast survey for 1851.

1364.   UNITED STATES. CONGRESS. 32d Congress. Senate. *Report on the trade and commerce of the British North American colonies and upon the trade of the great lakes and rivers, by Israel D. Andrews.* Washington, 1852.
TL

1365.   UNITED STATES. CONGRESS. 33d Congress. 1st Session. Sen-
        ate. *Report of the select committee of the Senate of the United
        States on the sickness and mortality on board emigrant ships.*
        Washington, 1854.
        TL

1366.   UNITED STATES. CONGRESS. 36th Congress. 1st Session. Sen-
        ate. *Report of the select committee of the Senate . . . on the
        late invasion and seizures of public property at Harper's
        Ferry.* Report No. 278. Washington, 1860.
        TL

1367.   UNITED STATES. DEPARTMENT OF THE INTERIOR. *Report of
        the United States and Mexican boundary survey. Made under
        the direction of the secretary of the Interior, by William H.
        Emory, Major First Cavalry, and the United States Commis-
        sioner.* 2 vols. Washington: C. Wendell, printer, 1857.

        JL 11.456 (2–25–59); IB 12 (vol. 1)

1368.   UNITED STATES. GENERAL LAND OFFICE. *Report on the geol-
        ogy and topography of . . . the Lake Superior land district, by
        John Wells Foster and J. D. Whitney.* 2 vols. Washington:
        Printed for the House of Representatives, 1850–51.
        TL

1369.   UNITED STATES. NAUTICAL ALMANAC OFFICE. *American
        ephemeris and nautical almanac.* Washington, 1855–.
        TL

1370.   UNITED STATES. NAVY. *Naval astronomical expedition to the
        southern hemisphere, during the years 1849–'50–'51–'52. . . .*
        2 vols. Washington: A.O.P. Nicholson, 1855.
        EL
        IB 10; FB (*c.* 1858)

        The portions of this report in which T was most interested
        were accounts of the natural resources of Chile by J. M. Gil-
        liss and of South American Indian remains by Thomas Ew-
        bank.

1371.   UNITED STATES. PATENT OFFICE. *Annual report of the com-
        missioner of patents.* Washington, 1851, 1853–59.
        TL
        JL 5.406 (8–31–53); 10.438 (5–20–58); 13.210–212 (3–22–
        60)

        Prior to 1862, when the Department of Agriculture was es-
        tablished, the reports on agriculture, to which T refers, were
        prepared and published by the Patent Office.

1372. UNITED STATES. TOPOGRAPHICAL BUREAU. *Report upon the military and hydrographical chart of the extremity of Cape Cod . . . projected from surveys executed during . . . the years 1833, 1834, and 1835, under the direction of James D. Graham.* . . . Washington, 1838.

CC, 118, 177–178

1373. UNITED STATES. WAR DEPARTMENT. *Exploration of Red river of Louisiana in the year 1852, by Randolph B. Marcy.* . . . Washington: A.O.P. Nicholson, printer, 1854.
TL
IB 8; FB (*c.* 1854)

1374. UNITED STATES. WAR DEPARTMENT. *Reports of explorations and surveys, to ascertain the most practicable and economical route for a railroad from the Mississippi river to the Pacific ocean, made under the direction of the secretary of war, in 1853–[6].* . . . 12 vols. in 13 pts. Washington: A.O.P. Nicholson, printer, 1855–60.
EL
IB 10; FB; CPB2 (*c.* 1856); TMJ

1375. *United States Magazine and Democratic Review.*
TL

Issues for May and December 1844 and October 1845 have been identified as belonging to T.

1376. Upanishads. See Asiatic Society of Bengal.

1377. UPHAM, Charles Wentworth: *Lectures on witchcraft, comprising a history of the delusion in Salem, in 1692.* 2d ed. Boston: Carter and Hendee, 1832.

F2a (*c.* 1836)

1378. UPHAM, Charles Wentworth. *Life, explorations and public services of John Charles Fremont.* Boston: Ticknor & Fields, 1856.
TL

1379. VAN DER DONCK, Adriaen. "Description of the New Netherlands. Tr. from the original Dutch by Hon. Jeremiah Johnson." *Collections of the New York Historical Society,* 2d ser., vol. 1 (1841): 125–242.
HL 8–11–51
WA, 39; JL 3.34 (9–28–51); IB 5; FB

1380. VARRO. In *Scriptores rei rusticae* (q.v.).
WE, 358; WA, 166; PJ 2.269–270 (after 7–24–46); JL 6.74–75

(1–19–54), 81–83 (1–27 & 29–54), 89 (1–31–54), 92–94
(2–3–54), 97 (2–5–54), 107–108 (2–8–54), 111 (2–9–54)

1381.   VASARI, Giorgio. *Lives of the most eminent painters, sculptors, and architects. . . .* 5 vols. London: H. G. Bohn, 1850–52.
EL
JL 3.464–465 (4–24–52)

1382.   VAUGHAN, Henry. "The Waif."

LN (*c.* 1844)

1383.   *Vedas. Rgveda. Rig-Veda-Sanhitá. . . . Translated from the original Sanskrit by H. H. Wilson.* 2 vols. London: Wm. H. Allen and Co., 1854.
TL
CC, 96; JL 8.134–135 (1–24–56)

T's source for the CC quotation was a London 1850 edition also translated by Wilson.

1384.   *Vedas. Samaveda. Sama Veda. Translation of the Sanhita of the Sama Veda. By the Rev. J. Stevenson, D.O.* London: Printed for the Oriental Translation Fund of Great Britain and Ireland, 1842.
HL 4–26–50
CPBI

1385.   VERPLANCK, Gulian C. *Discourse and addresses on subjects of American history, arts, and literature.* New-York: J. & J. Harper, 1833.
TL

1386.   VERRAZANO, Giovanni da. "The Voyages of John de Verazzano Along the Coast of North America from Carolina to Newfoundland, A.D. 1524." *Collections of the New York Historical Society,* 2d ser., vol. 1 (1841): 37–69.
HL 8–11–51
CC, 184, 187; IB 5

1387.   VERY, Jones. *Essays and poems.* Boston: C. C. Little & J. Brown, 1839.
EL
"In Him We Live, and Move, and Have Our Being,"
"Enoch," "Love," "Day," "Night"
ME (*c.* 1838)

T's source for these extracts was *The Western Messenger;* a magazine sympathetic to Transcendentalism published in Cincinnati; he also refers to Very in PJ 1.459 (8–25–43).

1388.   VIMONT, Barthélemy. In *Jesuit Relations* (q.v.), for 1640–45.
        HL 11–28–53
        JL 6.42, 45–46 (1–1–54), 50 (1–6–54); IB 8; IB 10

1389.   VINCENT, William. *The voyage of Nearchus from the Indus to the Euphrates, collected from the original journal preserved by Arrian, and illustrated by authorities ancient and modern.* . . . London: T. Cadell, jun. and W. Davies, 1797.
        EL
        CC, 169; FB; IB 10

1390.   VIRGIL. *Opera . . . ad usum serenissimi delphini. Juxta editionem novissiman Londiniensem.* . . . Philadelphia: M. Carey & Son, 1817.
        TL
        Aeneid
        WE, 131, 380; RP, 3; EX, 138; CC, 71, 73; PJ 1.110 (2–15–40), 165 (7 & 8–40)
        Eclogues
        WE, 90, 169, 391; EX, 144; PJ 1.13 (11–18–37), 14 (11–20–37); 2.4 (1842–44); 3 (Fall 1849)
        Georgics
        WE, 246; EX, 138, 139; PJ 1.212–213 (12–30–40), 215 (1–1–41); JL 13.26–27 (12–13–59)

1391.   VIRGIL. *P. Vergilius Maronis opera.* . . . Londini: Sumtibus Rodwell et Martin [etc.], 1822.
        TL

        For T's references to Virgil, see preceding entry.

1392.   VIRGIL. *The works of Virgil translated into English verse, by John Dryden.* 2 vols. Philadelphia: printed for John Conrad, 1814.
        TL

1393.   VIṢNUSARMA. See *Hitopadésa.*

1394.   VISVANATHA Nyayapancanana Bhattacharya Tarkalanara. *Bháshá Parichcheda, and its commentary, the Siddhánta Muktá Vali, an exposition of the Nyáya philosophy.* . . . Calcutta: Encyclopaedia Press, 1851.
        TL

1395.   VOLNEY, Constantine François Chasseboeuf, comte de. *Travels through Syria and Egypt, in the years 1783–1785.* . . . *Trans. from the French.* 2 vols. in 1. Dublin: White, 1793.

        PJ 1.251 (2–6–41); LN; HM 13201 (1–31–41)

1396.   VOLTAIRE, François Marie Arouet de. *Histoire de Charles XII.* . . . New York: Collins & Co., 1831.
        TL

        Autograph of Helen Thoreau.

1397.   VOLTAIRE, François Marie Arouet de. *Histoire de l'empire de Russie.* . . . 2 vols. Paris: Didot, 1815.
        TL

1398.   *Voyages de découverte au Canada, entre les années 1534 et 1542, par Jacques Cartier, le sieur de Roberval, Jean Alphonse de Xanctoigne, &c.* . . . *Réimprimés sur d'anciennes relations, et publiés sous la direction de la Société littéraire et historique de Québec.* Quebec: Imprimé chez W. Cowan et fils, 1843.
        HL 10–28–50
        EX, 38–39, 90–91, 96–99; CC, 186–188; CN; IB 4

        Vol. 4 of the *Transactions of the Literary and Historical Society of Quebec.*

1399.   VRANGEL, Ferdinand. *Narrative of an expedition to the polar sea, in the years 1820, 1821, 1822, and 1823.* New York: Harper and brothers, 1842.

        FB; IB 10 (*c.* 1857)

1400.   WADDINGTON, George, and Barnard HANBURY. *Journal of a visit to some parts of Ethiopia.* . . . London: J. Murray, 1822.
        HL 9–30–34

1401.   WAFER, Lionel. *A new voyage and description of the isthmus of America, giving an account of the author's abode there.* . . . London: Printed for J. Knapton, 1699.
        HL 2–28–59
        CPB2; IB 12

1402.   WALKER, John. *A critical pronouncing dictionary and expositor of the English language . . . to which are prefixed Principles of English pronunciation.* . . . New York: Collins & Hannay, 1823.
        TL

1403.   WALLER, Edmund. In Chalmers (q.v.), vol. 6.
        "Upon the Death of My Lady Rich," "A Panegyric to My Lord Protector . . ."
        F2a (*c.* 1836)

1404.   WALTON, Izaak. *The compleat angler; or, The contemplative man's recreation.* . . .

EEM, 33

Source and edition unknown.

1405.   WARBURTON, Eliot Bartholomew George. *The crescent and the cross; or, romance and realities of eastern travel*. 2 vols. in 1. New York: Wiley & Putnam, 1845.

PJ 2.168 (8–6–45)

1406.   WARBURTON, George. *Hochelaga; or, England in the new world*. . . . 2 vols. in 1. New York: Wiley & Putnam, 1846.

EX, 10, 30, 64, 82; JL 2.398 (8–18–51); CN; IB 4

1407.   WARD, Rev. William. *A view of the history, literature, and religion, of the Hindoos*. . . . Hartford, Conn.: H. Huntington, jr., 1824.

CPB2 (*c.* 1855)

1408.   WARE, Henry. *On the formation of the Christian character.* . . . Boston: Gray and Bowen, 1831.
TL

1409.   WARNER, William. In Percy, *Reliques of Ancient English Poetry* (q.v.).
"The Patient Countess," "Argentile and Curan"
LN (*c.* 1841)

1410.   WARREN, John Esaias. *Para; or, Scenes and adventures on the banks of the Amazon*. New York: G. P. Putnam, 1851.
SL
FB (*c.* 1851)

1411.   WARTON, Thomas. *The history of English poetry from the close of the eleventh to the commencement of the eighteenth century*. . . . Ed. Richard Price. 4 vols. London: T. Tegg, 1824.
HL 11–30–41
LN

1412.   WEBSTER, Daniel. *The private correspondence of Daniel Webster*. Ed. Fletcher Webster. 2 vols. Boston: Little, Brown, and company, 1857.
CL
CC, 98; IB 10; FB (*c.* 1857)

1413.   WEBSTER, Noah. *An American dictionary of the English language*. . . . Springfield, Mass.: G. & C. Merriam, 1848.
TL
JL 7.171 (2–4–55); 11.386 (1–2–59); IB 9

1414. WEST, John. *The substance of a journal during a residence at the Red River colony, British North America . . . in the years 1820, 1821, 1822, 1823.* London: L. B. Seeley and Son, 1824.
HL 10–6–59
IB 12

1415. WHATELY, Richard. *Elements of logic. . . .* Boston: J. Munroe & co., 1834.
TL, TX

1416. WHATELY, Richard. *Elements of rhetoric. . . .* Cambridge: Brown, Shattuck and company, 1832.
TL, TX
EEM, 83

1417. WHIPPLE, A. W. See United States. War Department. *Reports of Explorations and Surveys.*

1418. WHITE, Gilbert. *The natural history of Selborne; with observations on various parts of nature; and the naturalist's calendar. . . . With additions and supplementary notes by Sir William Jardine. . . . Ed. . . . Edward Jesse.* London: H. G. Bohn, 1851.
TL
JL 5.46 (3–23–53), 65 (3–26–53), 83 (4–2–53); 7.449 (8–5–55); 12.156–157 (4–23–59); FB

1419. WHITE, Joseph Blanco. *The life of the Rev. Joseph Blanco White, written by himself; with portions of his correspondence.* 3 vols. London: J. Chapman, 1845.

"Sonnet on Night and Death"
LN (*c.* 1847)

1420. WHITEHEAD, Charles Edward. *Wild sports in the South; or, The camp-fires of the Everglades. . . .* New York: Derby & Jackson, 1860.

CPB2 (*c.* 1860)

1421. WHITMAN, Rev. Levi. "A Letter from Rev. Levi Whitman Containing an Account of . . . Wellfleet and . . . Cape-Cod Harbours." *Collections of the Massachusetts Historical Society*, 1st ser., vol. 4 (1795; rpt. 1835): 41–43.

CC, 97, 135, 177

1422. WHITMAN, Rev. Levi. "A Topographical Description of Wellfleet. . . ." *Collections of the Massachusetts Historical Society*, 1st ser., vol. 3 (1794; rpt. 1810): 117–126.

CC, 82–83, 97, 100, 124, 126, 161, 176; PJ 3 (Fall 1849); IB 2

1423.   WHITMAN, Walt. *Leaves of grass*. Brooklyn: [n.p.], 1855.
         TL

         For T's references see following entry.

1424.   WHITMAN, Walt. *Leaves of grass*. 2d ed. Brooklyn: [n.p.],
         1856.
         TL
         COR, 441 (11–19–56), 444–445 (12–7–56); JL 9.149 (12–2–
         56)

1425.   WHITNEY, J. D. See United States. General Land Office.

1426.   WHITNEY, Peter. "An Account of a Singular Apple-Tree. . . ."
         Memoirs of the American Academy of Arts and Sciences 1
         (Boston, 1785): 386–387.

         EX, 312

1427.   WHITTLESEY, Charles. "Descriptions of Ancient Works in
         Ohio, 1850." In *Smithsonian contributions to knowledge*,
         vol. 3. Washington: Smithsonian Institution, 1851.
         SNH 12–29–52
         IB 8

1428.   "Who Is Brown, the Leader?" *New York Herald*, Oct. 19,
         1859, p. 10; Oct. 21, 1859, p. 1.

         RP, 124

1429.   WIED-NEUWIED, Maximilian Alexander Philip, prinz von.
         *Travels in the interior of North America. . . . Tr. from the
         German by H. Evans Lloyd. . . .* London: Ackermann and
         co., 1843.

         IB 4 (*c*. 1851)

1430.   WILKES, Charles. *Voyage round the world; embracing the
         principal events of the narrative of the United States Explor-
         ing Expedition. . . .* New York: G. P. Putnam, 1851.

         WA, 321

         T's allusion is not definitive, but Christie, *Thoreau as World
         Traveler*, considers Wilkes one of T's principal sources of in-
         formation about the South Seas and Antarctic.

1431.   WILKINSON, James John Garth. *The human body and its con-
         nection with man, illustrated by the principal organs*. Phila-
         delphia: Lippincott & Grambo, 1851.
         EL
         JL 2.451 (9–3–51), 462–463 (9–4–51); FB

1432.   WILKINSON, John Gardner. *A popular account of the ancient Egyptians. Rev. and abridged from his larger work.* . . . 2 vols. London: J. Murray, 1854.
EL
FB; IB 8 (*c.* 1854)

1433.   WILLEY, Benjamin Glazier. *Incidents in White mountain history.* . . . Boston: N. Noyes, 1856.
TL
JL 11.15 (7–7–58), 20 (7–8–58), 27 (7–8–58), 44 (7–14–58), 59 (7–19–58); 14.85 (9–13–60)

1434.   WILLIAMS, Roger. "A Key into the Language of America. . . ." *Collections of the Massachusetts Historical Society*, 1st ser., vol. 3 (1794; rpt. 1810): 203–239.

TR, 148; IB 2 (*c.* 1849)

1435.   WILLIAMS, Wellington. *Appleton's railroad and steamboat companion.* . . . New York: D. Appleton, 1848.
TL

1436.   WILLIAMSON, William D. *The history of the state of Maine; from* . . . *1620 to* . . . *1820.* . . . Hallowell, Me.: Glazier, Masters & co., 1832.

CC, 182, 191; MW, 320–325; PJ 2.276 (after 9–10–46); CN; IB 10

1437.   WILLIS, Nathaniel Parker. *Inklings of adventure.* . . . 2 vols. New York: Saunders and Otley, 1836.
IN 11–28–36

1438.   WILLIS, William. "The Language of the Abnaquies, or Eastern Indians." *Collections of the Maine Historical Society*, vol. 4 (1856): 95–117.

MW, 320–325

1439.   WILSON, Alexander. *American ornithology, or, The natural history of the birds of the United States.* . . . 9 vols. Philadelphia: Bradford and Inskeep, 1808–14.
HL 9–28–35 (vol. 5)

For T's references to Wilson see following entry.

1440.   WILSON, Alexander. *Wilson's American ornithology, with notes by Jardine* . . . *by T. M. Brewer.* New York: H. S. Samuels, 1852.
TL
CC, 103; JL 6.33–34 (12–29–53); 7.288–289 (4–6–55); 8.387 (6–25–56); 10.449 (5–30–58)

1441.   WILSON, Horace Hayman. *Select specimens of the theatre of the Hindus.* 2 vols. London: Parbury, Allen & Co., 1835.
TL
JL 8.134 (1–23–56)

1442.   WILSON, J. Leighton. *Western Africa: its history, condition, and prospects.* New York: Harper & brothers, 1856.
SL
IB 10 (*c.* 1856)

1443.   WILSON, John. *Lights and shadows of Scottish life.* Edinburgh: W. Blackwood, 1822.

CC, 40

1444.   WILSON, Walter. *Memoirs of the life and times of Daniel De Foe: containing a review of his writings, and his opinions. . . .* 3 vols. London: Hurst, Chance, and co., 1830.
HL 4–30–34 (vol. 1)

1445.   WINCKELMANN, Johann Joachim. *The history of ancient art. Tr. from the German by G. Henry Lodge, with the life of Winckelmann, by the editor.* 2 vols. Boston: Little, Brown, 1856.
EL
JL 9.244–245 (2–7–57); IB 10

1446.   WINES, Enoch Cobb. *Two years and a half in the navy: or, Journal of a cruise in the Mediterranean and Levant . . . in the years 1829, 1830, and 1831.* 2 vols. Philadelphia: Carey & Lea, 1832.
HL 11–11–34 (vol. 1)

1447.   WINSLOW, C. F. Untitled contribution to *Proceedings of the Boston Society of Natural History* 6 (1856–59): 414.

IB 12 (*c.* 1860)

1448.   WINSLOW, Edward. "Good News from New England: or, A True Relation of Things Very Remarkable." *Collections of the Massachusetts Historical Society,* 1st ser., vol. 8 (1801): 239–276.

CC, 29; JL 7.478 (10–2–55)

1449.   WINSLOW, Edward. "Mr. Winslow's Account of the Natives of New-England, annexed to his Narrative of the Plantations, A.D. 1624." In Belknap, Jeremy, *American Biography* (q.v.).

IB 2 (*c.* 1849)

1450.   WINTERTON, Ralph. *Fragments quadam accedunt etiam observationes Radulphi Wintertoni in Hesiodum. . . .* Cantabrigiae: ex officina Joan. Hayes . . . , 1677.
TL

1451.   WINTHROP, John. *A journal of the transactions and occurrences in the settlement of the Massachusetts and the other New-England colonies, from the year 1630 to 1644.* Hartford, Conn.: Elisha Babcock, 1790.
TL
WE, 82; CC, 186; PJ 1.476 (10–15–43)

1452.   "Wiskonsan—Trial of J. R. Vineyard: Correspondence of the New-York Tribune." *New York Tribune*, Nov. 4, 1843, p. 4.

PJ 1.481–482 (11–4–43)

1453.   WOLFE, Charles. "Burial of Sir John Moore at Corunna."

RP, 66

An extremely popular and widely available poem; T's source unknown.

1454.   WOLFF, Rev. Joseph. *Narrative of a mission to Bokhara in the years 1843–1845, to ascertain the fate of Col. Stoddard and Capt. Conolly. . . .* New York: Harper & brothers, 1845.

WE, 60, 127; PJ 3 (*c.* 1848)

1455.   WOOD, Alphonso. *A class-book of botany, designed for colleges, academies, and other seminaries.* 23d ed., rev. and enl. Boston: [n.p.], 1851.

FB (*c.* 1854)

1456.   WOOD, John George. *Illustrated natural history . . . with 450 original designs by William Harvey.* New York: Harper, 1854.

IB 9; FB (*c.* 1855)

1457.   WOOD, William. *New England's prospect. Being a true, lively, and experimental description of . . . New England.* 3d ed., London, printed 1639. Boston, New England: reprinted, Thomas and John Fleet, 1764.
HL 2–25–54
CC, 66–67; JL 7.109–110 (1–9–55), 132–137 (1–24–55); 9.264 (2–16–57); FB; IB 8; IB 9

1458.   WORCESTER, Joseph Emerson. *Elements of geography, ancient and modern; with an atlas. A new ed.* Boston: Hilliard, Gray, & co., 1832.
TX

Required for admission to Harvard.

1459.   WORDSWORTH, Christopher. *Memoirs of William Wordsworth, poet-laureate, D.C.L.* London: E. Moxon, 1851.
CL
FB (*c.* 1851)

1460.   WORDSWORTH, William. *Complete poetical works.* Philadelphia: Kay, 1837.
TL
"Resolution and Independence"
PJ 1.127 (6–14–40)
"Ode: Intimations of Immortality"
PJ 1.242 (1–30–41)
"My Heart Leaps Up When I Behold"
PJ 1.373 (3–14–42)
"Peter Bell"
EX, 144
"The World Is Too Much With Us"
MW, 181
"Goody Blake and Harry Gill"
WA, 251

1461.   WORDSWORTH, William. *The prelude, or growth of a poet's mind.* London: E. Moxon, 1850.
TL

1462.   WOTTON, Sir Henry. *Reliquiae Wottonianae.* . . . London: B. Tooke and T. Sawbridge, 1685.

"The Character of a Happy Life"
CPB1; LN (*c.* 1841)

1463.   WRANGELL, Ferdinand. See Vrangel, Ferdinand.

1464.   WRIGHT, Thomas. *Dictionary of obsolete and provincial English.* . . . London: H. G. Bohn, 1857.
TL

1465.   WYATT, Sir Thomas. "The Lover Complaineth of the Unkindness of His Love."
CPB1 (*c.* 1841)

1466.   WYTFLIET, Cornelius. *Descriptionis Ptolemaicae augmentum.* . . . Lovanii [Belgium]: Tipjis Iohannis Bogardi, 1597.
HL 11–18–50 (not withdrawn)
CN

1467.   WYTFLIET, Cornelius. *Histoire universelle des Indes Occiden-*
        tales. . . . Douay: F. Fabri, 1607.

        CC, 188; CN (*c.* 1850)

1468.   XENOPHON. *Minor works: viz., memoirs of Socrates; The*
        banquet; Hiero, on the condition of royalty; and Economics,
        or the science of good husbandry. Translated from the Greek,
        by several hands. London: J. Walker, 1813.
        EL
        PJ 1.129 (6–16–40)

1469.   XENOPHON. *Xenophontis de cyri institutione libri octo.* Ed.
        Thomas Hutchinson. Philadelphia: Watts, 1806.
        TL

1470.   *Yarmouth* [*Mass.*] *Register.*

        In JL 9.445 (6–20–57) T describes reading in this newspaper
        a notice of a forthcoming history of Cape Cod.

1471.   YARRELL, William. *A history of British birds.* 3 vols. London:
        J. Van Voorst, 1843.

        JL 7.288–290 (4–6–55)

1472.   YARRELL, William. *A history of British fishes.* London: Van
        Voorst, 1836.

        JL 2.358 (7–29–51)

1473.   YOUNG, Alexander. *Chronicles of the first planters of the col-*
        ony of Massachusetts Bay from 1623 to 1636. . . . Boston:
        C. C. Little and J. Brown, 1846.
        HL 11–18–50 (not withdrawn)
        CC, 29, 178; IB 4

1474.   [YOUNG, Alexander, ed.]. *Library of the old English prose*
        writers. 9 vols. Cambridge: Hilliard and Brown, 1831–34.
        IN 6–14–37 (vol. 2)
        PJ 1.60 (12–15–38)

        T's reference is to John Selden's *Table Talk.*

1475.   YOUNG, Edward. *The poetical works of Edward Young.* . . . 2
        vols. London: W. Pickering, 1834.

        Night Thoughts
        FIb (*c.* 1836)

1476.   ZIMMERMAN, Johann Georg. *Solitude.* Albany: Barber &
        Southwick, 1796.
        TL

1477. ZOROASTER. "Oracles of Zoroaster." In *The Phenix* (q.v.).
WE, 43–44, 127, 128, 226, 391

1478. ZOUCHE, Robert Curzon, baron. *A visit to the monasteries of the Levant*. New York: George P. Putnam, 1849.
TL

Index of Short Titles

297

Bibliography

Works Cited

The following citations expand references to primary and secondary sources in the comments on entries in the Bibliographical Catalogue.

BURNS, John R. "Thoreau's Use of the Bible." Ph.D. diss., University of Notre Dame, 1966.

CAMERON, Kenneth Walter. "Books Thoreau Borrowed from Harvard College Library." In *Emerson the Essayist*, 2.191–208. 2 vols. Raleigh, N.C.: The Thistle Press, 1945.

—— "Emerson, Thoreau, and the Society of Natural History." *American Literature* 24 (March 1952): 21–30.

—— "Thoreau Discovers Emerson: A College Reading Record." *Bulletin of the New York Public Library* 57, no. 7 (June 1953): 319–334.

—— "Ungathered Thoreau Reading Lists." In *The Transcendentalists and Minerva*, 2.359–388. 3 vols. Hartford: Transcendental Books, 1958.

CHRISTIE, John Aldrich. *Thoreau as World Traveler*. New York: Columbia University Press with the American Geographic Society, 1965.

HARDING, Walter. *Thoreau's Library*. Charlottesville: University Press of Virginia, 1957.

—— ed. *The Variorum "Walden" and the Variorum "Civil Disobedience."* New York: Twayne, 1962; rpt. New York: Washington Square Press, 1968.

JOHNSON, Linck C. *Thoreau's Complex Weave: The Writing of "A Week on the Concord and Merrimack Rivers" with the Text of the First Draft.* Charlottesville: University Press of Virginia, 1986.

RUSK, Ralph L., ed. *The Letters of Ralph Waldo Emerson*. 6 vols. New York: Columbia University Press, 1939.

Other Primary Sources

The following works have also provided significant information about various sources of Thoreau's reading. For specialized studies of the influence of

individual works, the reader should consult the bibliographies in Walter
Harding and Michael Meyer, eds., *The New Thoreau Handbook* (New York:
New York University Press, 1980), pp. 111–120, and Joel Myerson, ed., *The
Transcendentalists: A Review of Research and Criticism* (New York: The
Modern Language Association of America, 1984), pp. 385–503.

ALCOTT, Amos Bronson. Typescript catalogue of Alcott's library, Houghton Library, Harvard University.

BRENNAN, William. "An Index to Quotations in Thoreau's *A Week on the
Concord and Merrimack Rivers*." In *Studies in the American Renaissance:
1980*, ed. Joel Myerson, pp. 259–290. Boston: G. K. Hall, 1980.

CADY, Lyman B. "Thoreau's Quotations from the Confucian Books in *Walden*." *American Literature* 33 (March 1961): 20–32.

CAMERON, Kenneth Walter. "Books Thoreau Read Concerning Concord."
In *Transcendental Climate*, 3.1012–1021. 3 vols. Hartford: Transcendental Books, 1963.

—— "Chronology of Thoreau's Harvard Years." *Emerson Society Quarterly*
no. 15 (2 Qtr. 1959): 13–18.

—— "Emerson, Thoreau, and the Society of Natural History." *American Literature* 24 (March 1952): 21–30.

—— "Thoreau's Canadian Notebook." In *Transcendental Climate*, 1.244–
309, 2.310–411.

—— *Thoreau's Fact Book in the . . . Harvard College Library*. 2 vols. Hartford: Transcendental Books, 1966.

—— *Thoreau's Literary Notebook in the Library of Congress*. Hartford:
Transcendental Books, 1964.

—— "Thoreau's Notes on Harvard Reading." In *The Transcendentalists and
Minerva*, 1.130–358. 3 vols. Hartford: Transcendental Books, 1958.

—— *Transcendental Apprenticeship: Notes on Young Henry Thoreau's
Reading*. Hartford: Transcendental Books, 1976.

—— *Transcendental Reading Patterns*. Hartford: Transcendental Books,
1970.

—— *Young Thoreau and the Classics*. Hartford: Transcendental Books,
1975.

"Catalogue of Books Belonging to the Concord Town Library, 1855." Concord: Printed by Benjamin Tolman, 1855.

"Catalogue of Books in Stacy's Circulating Library." Concord: Benjamin
Tolman, Printer, 1860.

CHRISTY, Arthur F. *The Orient in American Transcendentalism*. New
York: Columbia University Press, 1932.

FRENCH, Allen T., Morris Longstreth, and David B. Little. *A History of the
Concord Free Public Library*. Concord: Concord Press Corp., 1973.

HARDING, Walter. *Emerson's Library*. Charlottesville: University Press of
Virginia, 1967.

HARDING, Walter. "A New Checklist of Books in Thoreau's Library." *Studies in the American Renaissance: 1983*, ed. Joel Myerson, pp. 151–186. Boston: G. K. Hall, 1983.

HOELTJE, Hubert H. "Thoreau and the Concord Academy." *New England Quarterly* 21 (March 1948): 103–109.

SEYBOLD, Ethel. *Thoreau: The Quest and the Classics*. New Haven: Yale University Press, 1951.

VAN ANGLEN, Kevin P. "Quotations in Henry Thoreau's *Excursions*." Typescript, Thoreau Textual Center, University of California–Santa Barbara.

—— "The Sources for Thoreau's Greek Translations." *Studies in the American Renaissance: 1980*, ed. Joel Myerson, pp. 291–299. Boston: G. K. Hall, 1980.

WHALING, Anne. "Studies in Thoreau's Reading of English Poetry and Prose, 1340–1660." Ph.D. diss., Yale University, 1946.

WILLSON, Lawrence. "The Influence of Early North American History and Legend on the Writing of Henry David Thoreau." Ph.D. diss., Yale University, 1949.

—— "Thoreau's Canadian Notebook." *Huntington Library Quarterly* 22 (May 1959): 179–200.

Index